THE HISTORY AND THEORY OF INTERNATIONAL LAW

The Right of Sovereignty

THE HISTORY AND THEORY OF INTERNATIONAL LAW

General Editors

In the past few decades the understanding of the relationship between nations has undergone a radical transformation. The role of the traditional nation-state is diminishing, along with many of the traditional vocabularies which were once used to describe what has been called, ever since Jeremy Bentham coined the phrase in 1780, 'international law'. The older boundaries between states are growing ever more fluid, new conceptions and new languages have emerged which are slowly coming to replace the image of a world of sovereign independent nation states which has dominated the study of international relations since the early nineteenth century. This redefinition of the international arena demands a new understanding of classical and contemporary questions in international and legal theory. It is the editors' conviction that the best way to achieve this is by bridging the traditional divide between international legal theory, intellectual history, and legal and political history. The aim of the series, therefore, is to provide a forum for historical studies, from classical antiquity to the twenty-first century, that are theoretically informed and for philosophical work that is historically conscious, in the hope that a new vision of the rapidly evolving international world, its past and its possible future, may emerge.

PREVIOUSLY PUBLISHED IN THIS SERIES

Crafting the International Order:
Practitioners and Practices of International Law since c.1800
Edited by Marcus M. Payk and Kim Christian Priemel

The Justification of War and International Order:
From Past to Present
Edited by Lothar Brock and Hendrik Simon

Remaking Central Europe:
The League of Nations and the Former Habsburg Lands
Edited by Peter Becker and Natasha Wheatley

The Right of Sovereignty

Jean Bodin on the Sovereign State and the Law of Nations

DANIEL LEE

Cover image: *Le vray pourtraict de l'assemblée des Estats tenuz en la ville de Bloys au moys de Decembre, l'an mil cinq cens soixante & seiz*. Anonymous woodcut, published by Robert Le Mangnier, 1577.

Bodin attended this assembly of the Estates-General in Blois as deputy of the Third Estate for Vermandois. He is seated with other deputies of the Third Estate in the lower right portion of the illustration.

OXFORD
UNIVERSITY PRESS

OXFORD
UNIVERSITY PRESS

Great Clarendon Street, Oxford, OX2 6DP,
United Kingdom

Oxford University Press is a department of the University of Oxford.
It furthers the University's objective of excellence in research, scholarship,
and education by publishing worldwide. Oxford is a registered trade mark of
Oxford University Press in the UK and in certain other countries

First Edition published in 2021

Published in the United States of America by Oxford University Press
198 Madison Avenue, New York, NY 10016, United States of America

British Library Cataloguing in Publication Data

Data available

Library of Congress Control Number: 2021937955

ISBN 978–0–19–875553–1

DOI: 10.1093/oso/9780198755531.001.0001

사랑하는 나의 딸을 위하여

For Elizabeth

Series Editor's Preface

The humanist legal scholar, historian, and philosopher Jean Bodin (c. 1530–1596) is widely interpreted as the inventor of an 'absolutist' conception of sovereignty. Sovereignty, on this conventional interpretation, consists in an unlimited power to command, a power that is itself not subject to any other human will. It is immediately obvious that much hinges on how we are to understand this power: is it a descriptive notion, or is it normative? Is power, that is, understood here as the brute ability to coerce, or is it something that emanates from a properly constituted legal authority? Does this power, in other words, create obligations on the part of the subjects it addresses, or does it merely force, and physically constrain, those subject to it?

Arguing against the conventional interpretation of sovereignty, Professor Lee, in this groundbreaking new monograph, shows that current jurisprudential debates about the nature of law and sovereignty have fallen prey to a kind of amnesia. Having all but forgotten Bodin, they seek to reenact arguments that had been waged long before Jeremy Bentham (1748–1832) and John Austin (1790–1859) sought to formulate a descriptive theory of law. In these current debates, Bodin, if mentioned at all, is usually seen as a predecessor of Austin's positivist, descriptive theory of law and sovereignty, as a proponent of what the legal philosopher H.L.A. Hart (1907–1992) derisively called the 'gunman theory' of law.

As Lee explains, however, Bodin insisted on treating sovereignty [*summum imperium*] 'fundamentally as a normative concept of right, not one of force,' because Bodin, along with his Roman sources, believed that one can have sovereignty only over those 'over whom one already has a *right*, and is thus entitled, to command': hence the title of the present book. As Lee shows, Bodin in fact reaches back to much earlier attempts by Cicero (106–43 B.C.E.) and Augustine (354–430) to state clearly the relationship between robber bands (the gunman) and legitimate sovereignty, aligning himself with some strands of that tradition and the idea that lawmaking as the key expression of sovereignty formally constrains what sovereignty is and what it can do.

Previous interpreters have gone astray because they thought that Bodin, by insisting on the sovereign authority of the state being 'freed from the laws,' *legibus soluta*, was expressing a legal positivism that anticipated Austin's descriptive 'gunman theory' of law. But nothing could be more misleading, Lee points out: while Bodin's sovereign is indeed essentially a lawmaker and therefore free to unmake and remake legislation [*leges*], this sovereign remains a normative authority, bound by the higher-order norms [*ius*] of the law of nature and the law of nations. The sovereign is necessarily *legibus solutus* qua legislator, but cannot possibly be *iuribus solutus* qua authority. Sovereignty can express itself by arbitrary will or by law, but it is conditioned by its very purpose – protection and the guarantee of contractual relations among subjects – to express itself through law.

This meant that sovereigns, according to Bodin, were in fact constrained by contractual obligations, which were not part of statute [*lex*], Bodin thought, but of higher-order law [*ius*]. Since the guarantee of contracts among subjects was an essential function of the sovereign, the sovereign is bound, almost as a matter of conceptual necessity, to keep contracts the sovereign is itself a party to. Contractual obligations, then, are for Bodin insulated from sovereign power, and here Lee discovers an anticipation of Hans Kelsen's (1881–1973) important international legal theory. In this and other ways, sovereignty as conceived by Bodin is shown by Lee to betray an internal normativity that reaches from matters domestic deeply into the international realm, which is as a consequence seen as shot through with both prudential and moral norms.

What makes the present monograph so appealing and indeed urgent is not just these important interpretive issues, but rather the fact that this is a book that is about sovereignty first and foremost. Professor Lee uses a historically sensitive interpretation of Bodin as an instrument to achieve a concept of sovereignty that can effortlessly hold its own in current debates and is indeed often brought in dialogue with current ideas in jurisprudence and international law. Perhaps paradoxically, it is especially the idea of sovereignty as a power carrying burdens of responsibility and fiduciary duties – an idea only recently defended by legal theorists such as Eyal Benvenisti and others – that Lee's Bodin makes very plausible. Sovereigns are duty-bound to protect their citizens and sometimes others. The sovereign is, Bodin argued, 'obliged to maintain his subjects in the security of their persons, properties, and families by force of arms and by laws'. These duties cannot be legislated away, for they are conceptually connected with the right of sovereignty. Thus burdened, the right of sovereignty may, Daniel Lee argues convincingly, serve again as the cornerstone for an international legal order.

Benjamin Straumann
New York
May 2021

Preface and Acknowledgements

I first encountered the name, Jean Bodin, in my senior year in college as an undergraduate at Columbia, when one Professor Julian H. Franklin offered a course on the theme of sovereignty. I never took that course, one of my greatest regrets. Julian was retiring, and I was graduating, in New York City mere weeks before the horrors of 9/11. But I remembered the name of Bodin. Little did I know then how central Bodin's political theory would become, not only for my own scholarship and professional life, but for how I would come to interpret and understand the many crises now defining political modernity.

As it happened, my first academic appointment was in the Society of Fellows at Columbia, which made possible a fortuitous reunion with Julian. By then, I had carefully studied all of Julian's major works, and I remember fondly the advice and encouragement I received from him in numerous seminars, lunches, and coffees we shared together. Even though we ultimately arrived at very different interpretations of Bodin's theory of sovereignty and the purposes of sovereignty in modern politics, I realize I never would have dedicated so many years to studying Bodin in the first place, were it not for Julian's groundbreaking work on Bodin's political thought. I need to begin, therefore, by acknowledging the enormous debt I owe him. Anybody who has studied Bodin in the English-speaking world is a beneficiary of Julian Franklin's academic legacy.

This study is the first book-length treatment of Jean Bodin's political and legal thought in English to be published in nearly a half-century, since the original publication of Franklin's *Jean Bodin and the Rise of Absolutist Theory* in 1973. Although I hope this book will be deemed a worthy successor to Franklin's work, my own approach questions – and ultimately rejects – the starting premise of Franklin's own work, which was that Bodin was an adherent of political 'absolutism'. Franklin, convinced of Bodin's absolutism and supposed opposition to constitutionalism, cannot help but interpret Bodinian sovereignty through the lens of early modern absolutist politics, as the obvious response to the civil unrest and religious violence unfolding in France in the 1570s.

But this assumption of absolutism (a category invented two centuries after Bodin's death) fundamentally misrepresents Bodin's purposes. As I'll argue in the chapters to follow, Bodin wasn't an absolutist, and his goal wasn't to promote an ideology of absolutism. Rather, it was to elucidate what he regarded as the quintessential quality of statehood, a point of vital importance both for the constitutional theory of state and public international law.

Modern scholars, suspicious of Bodin's alleged absolutism, have tried to keep a safe critical distance from Bodin's political theory. Like Franklin, generations of scholars in the English-speaking world have treated Bodin at arm's length, more as a historical pre-Enlightenment curiosity illustrating how *not* to think about sovereignty, rather than as someone whose ideas are worthy of serious academic engagement by specialists in law and across the social sciences. As a result, the most active scholarship on Bodin is now largely segregated from the mainstream of research in law and the social sciences, as a narrow antiquarian specialty of French intellectual and legal history.

This is unfortunate. Bodin was, and remains still, the preeminent theorist of state sovereignty in modern political and legal thought. Not only did Bodin anticipate and address many of the contemporary interpretive problems concerning sovereignty, some of which have now been addressed by the International Court of Justice, he is one of the principal sources of doctrines that have indelibly shaped modern public international law concerning sovereign immunity, the validity of international obligations and sovereign debts, and the indivisibility and imprescriptibility of sovereignty. So long as sovereignty continues to define the state-centric character of modern politics, Bodin will remain indispensable to lawyers, policymakers, and academic political theorists.

I do not regard this study as anything close to my final word on Bodin. Rather, I hope it will serve as an academic conversation starter and will inspire and provoke a new body of theoretical and interpretive scholarship on Bodin. There is a lot about Bodin's thought that I haven't been able to explore adequately in this book, and I know I will have more to say in the future. Hopefully, with this book, I'll have more interlocutors with whom I can share and continue this conversation about the merits of sovereignty and whether humanity is ready for a world beyond sovereignty.

I want to begin by thanking Benjamin Straumann and Anthony Pagden for suggesting that I write this book for a series on the intellectual history and theory of international law. I hesitated at first, because I didn't really think of Bodin as a theorist of international law and worried that I wouldn't have much to say about the international dimension of Bodinian sovereignty. Bodin is not usually considered one of the canonical founders of modern international law, in the same way that, say, Suarez, Grotius, and Pufendorf are. But I now feel that is an opinion that should be substantially revised, so long as sovereignty remains one of the constitutive elements defining the modern international system. What I've discovered in retracing many of Bodin's sources and reconstructing his arguments concerning the *ius gentium* is that internationality is baked into his concept of sovereignty. And I don't think I could have come to a fuller appreciation of this point without the initial encouragement I received from Benjamin and Anthony.

I also want to express my warmest thanks to Richard Tuck and Johann Sommerville who very graciously agreed to serve as commentators for a book manuscript workshop in 2017. Their extensive comments on an early version of the manuscript were instrumental in fundamentally reshaping the structure and content of the text, and I'm deeply grateful to them, as well as to the Berkeley Institute of International Studies, the Kadish Center for Morality, Law, and Public Affairs at the Berkeley School of Law, and the Robson Kernan Fund in Political Science for making that workshop possible.

Many colleagues have generously taken the time to read and comment on drafts of chapters, participate in correspondence on various substantive points in this book, or provide drafts of their own writing to me (especially during the COVID-19 pandemic). To them and to many others, I offer my heartfelt thanks and goodwill: Cliff Ando, Ed Andrew, Julian Arato, Ryan Balot, David Bates, Eric Beerbohm, Chuck Beitz, Mark Bevir, Ann Blair, Wendy Brown, Daniela Cammack, Simone Chambers, Samuel Chan, Josh Cohen, Marie Dominique Couzinet, Wim Decock, Helge Dedek, Charlie Donahue, David Dyzenhaus, Dan Edelstein, Robin Effron, Stefan Eich, Yannis Evrigenis, Bryan Garsten, the late Ralph Giesey, Ryan Greenwood, David Grewal, Kinch Hoekstra, Martti Koskenniemi, Chris Kutz, Jacob Levy, David Lieberman, Howell Lloyd, Martin Loughlin, Ken Pennington, Philip Pettit, Diego Pirillo, Diego Quaglioni, Jon Robinson, Michael Rosen, Quentin Skinner, Sarah Song, Pete Stacey, Simon Stern, Mario Turchetti, and Melissa Williams.

I also wish to thank the many excellent research assistants who have supported the work of this project over the past several years: Jason Brown, Shterna Friedman, Sibbyl Nickerson, and Rosie Wagner. I could not have completed this book without their vital contributions. Thank you to all of you.

I also want to take this opportunity to recognize the many outstanding students at Berkeley and Toronto, who, over the years, enrolled and participated in my seminar and lecture courses on sovereignty. I was able to explore many of the ideas that eventually made their way into this book in those settings. I received some of the most valuable feedback in these settings, and so, I give thanks to my students who made possible some of the most rewarding intellectual experiences I've had in my academic career. Needless to say, I'll take sole responsibility for whatever errors that may remain.

The chapters included in this volume have been presented at various academic conferences and colloquia in recent years, and I am grateful to my hosts and audiences for allowing me to present this material and for their valuable feedback and support: The American Political Science Association, the Conference for the Study of Political Thought, the University of Toronto (Faculty of Law, 'Sovereignty Lab'), the Bay Area Forum for Law and Philosophy, Tufts University, UCLA, Stanford University, Harvard University, Yale University, the Medieval Studies Colloquium at Berkeley, and Brooklyn Law School. I was particularly grateful to have had the opportunity to participate in the international conference on Jean Bodin organized at Oxford in 2014 and want to thank the organizers for inviting me.

This volume includes some previously published material: 'Jean Bodin', in *Great Christian Jurists in French History*, ed. Olivier Descamps and Rafael Domingo Osle (Cambridge: Cambridge University Press, 2019); 'Unmaking Law: Jean Bodin on Law, Equity, and Legal Change', *History of Political Thought* 39 (2018): 269–96; 'Citizenship, Subjection, and the Civil Law: Jean Bodin on Roman Citizenship and the Theory of Consensual Subjection', in *Citizenship and Empire in Europe, 200–1900: The Antonine Constitution after 1800 Years*, ed. Clifford Ando (Stuttgart: Franz Steiner Verlag, 2016). All the work in this volume, however, is original and appearing in print for the first time.

Most of the Roman and canon law authorities, commentaries, and *consilia* cited in this study, as well as Bodin's 1586 Latin *De Republica*, are taken from holdings in the Bancroft Library, the Robbins Collection at Berkeley, in addition to my personal copies of the 1591 *De Republica* and the 1569/74 Venice edition (Editio Postrema) of the *Digest*, *Code*, and *Volumen Parvum.* I am especially grateful to Jennifer Nelson for her expert guidance in navigating through the holdings of the Robbins Collection for this project and especially for tracking down some obscure canonistic sources on the web once the coronavirus shutdowns cut off my regular access to the Robbins. Additionally, I wish to thank Stephen Ferguson of the Rare Books and Special Collections at Princeton University Library who kindly prepared a digital reproduction of Bodin's *Iuris Universi Distributio* for my use.

Oxford University Press has been everything I hoped for in an academic publisher, and I am proud to continue partnering with them as an OUP author. I'm particularly grateful to the extraordinary editorial staff at the Press, Merel Alstein, Jamie Berezin, and Jack McNichol, who have always been supportive of my work and who have given me the time, especially during the coronavirus pandemic, to work on this manuscript.

This book appears at a critical moment in Bodin studies, with the appearance of several major new studies on Bodin such as Howell Lloyd's biography of Bodin, Mario Turchetti's critical edition of the French *République* and the Latin *De Republica*, and Sara Miglietti's critical edition of the *Methodus*. Regretfully, I was unable to study Sophie Nicholls' new study on Bodin and the Catholic League which was released just as I began production of this book. My hope is that *The Right of Sovereignty* will contribute to this growing body of new scholarship on Bodin's legal and political thought and restore Bodin to a place of prominence in the canon and in ongoing academic debates on sovereignty.

Finally, I want to express my heartfelt thanks to Rebecca, and to our children, Caleb and Elizabeth. Writing a book – let alone writing a book during a global pandemic – can be a terribly lonely, isolating experience, requiring an abundance of fortitude and patience. I have been blessed to have the steadfast support of a loving family who has helped me practise those virtues every day while writing this book.

Daniel Lee
Berkeley, California
March 2021

Table of Contents

Table of Abbreviations

Works by Bodin

De Republica	Jean Bodin, *De Republica Libri VI* (Paris: Jacques Du Puys, 1586).
Distributio	Jean Bodin, *Iuris Universi Distributio* (Paris: Jacques Du Puys, 1578).
Methodus	Jean Bodin, *Methodus ad Facilem Historiarum Cognitionem* (Paris: Apud Martinum Iuvenem, 1572).
République	Jean Bodin, *Les Six Livres de la République* (Paris: Jacques Du Puys, 1583).

Other Works

Aristotle	Aristotle, *The Complete Works of Aristotle*, 2 vols., ed. Jonathan Barnes (Princeton: Princeton University Press, 1985).
Colloquium	Jean Bodin, *The Colloquium of the Seven about Secrets of the Sublime*, trans. Marion Leathers Kuntz (University Park: Pennsylvania State Press, 1975).
De Legibus	Cicero, *De Legibus*, Loeb Classical Library 213, trans. Clinton Walker Keyes (Cambridge: Harvard University Press, 1928).
De Off.	Cicero, *De Officiis*, Loeb Classical Library 30, trans. Walter Miller (Cambridge: Harvard University Press, 1975).
De Re Publica	Cicero, *De Re Publica*, Loeb Classical Library 213, trans. Clinton Walker Keyes (Cambridge: Harvard University Press, 1928).
Ethics	Aristotle, *Nicomachean Ethics*, Loeb Classical Library 73, trans. Harris Rackham (Cambridge: Harvard University Press, 1926).
Exposé	Jean Bodin, *Exposé du Droit Universel*, ed. Lucien Jerphagnon, Simone Goyard-Fabre, René-Marie Rampelberg (Paris: Presses Universitaires de France, 1985).
Franklin	Jean Bodin, *On Sovereignty*, ed. and trans. Julian H. Franklin (Cambridge: Cambridge University Press, 1992).
Gaius	*Institutes of Gaius*, ed. Francis de Zulueta (Oxford: Clarendon Press, 1953).
Grotius	Hugo Grotius, *De Iure Belli ac Pacis Libri Tres*, Editio Nova (Amsterdam: Iohannes Blaeu, 1646).
Inst. [English]	*Institutes of Justinian*, ed. J.B. Moyle (Oxford: Oxford University Press, 1913).
Knolles	Jean Bodin, *The Six Bookes of a Commonweale*, trans. Richard Knolles (London: Impensis G. Bishop, 1606).
Miglietti	Jean Bodin, *Methodus ad Facilem Historiarum Cognitionem*, ed. Sara Miglietti (Pisa: Edizioni della Normale, 2013).
Plato	Plato, *Complete Works*, ed. John M. Cooper and D.S. Hutchinson (Indianapolis: Hackett, 1997).

Politics	Aristotle, *Politics*, Loeb Classical Library 264, trans. Harris Rackham (Cambridge: Harvard University Press, 1932).
Polybius	Polybius, *Histories*, Loeb Classical Library 138, trans. W.R. Paton (Cambridge: Harvard University Press, 1923).
Popular Sovereignty	Daniel Lee, *Popular Sovereignty in Early Modern Constitutional Thought* (Oxford: Oxford University Press, 2016).
Pufendorf	Samuel Pufendorf, *De Iure Naturae et Gentium Libri Octo* (Amsterdam: Apud Joannem Wolters, 1698).
Republic	Plato, *Republic*, Loeb Classical Library in 2 vols., ed. and trans. Chris Emlyn-Jones and William Preddy (Cambridge: Harvard University Press, 2013).
Stato	Jean Bodin, *I Sei Libri dello Stato di Jean Bodin*, ed. Margherita Isnardi Parente and Diego Quaglioni, 3 vols. (Turin: Unione Tipografico-Editrice Torinese, 1964).
Turchetti	Jean Bodin, *Les Six Livres de la République: De Republica Libri Six*, bilingual edition of Book I, ed. Mario Turchetti (Paris: Classiques Garnier, 2013).

Roman Law

I have generally consulted two editions, a French and an Italian, of the *Corpus Iuris Civilis*: The Lyon 1558/1560 and the Venice (*Editio Postrema*) of 1569/1574, both of which would have been accessible to Bodin.

D.	*Pandectarum Iuris Civilis* (Lyon: Apud Hugonem à Porta [Hugues de la Porte], 1560). *Pandectarum, seu Digestorum Iuris Civilis*, Editio Postrema (Venice: Apud Nicolaum Bevilaqua, 1569). *Digestum Vetus* [D.1.1.1–24.2.11]. *Infortiatum* [D.24.3.1–38.17.10]. *Digestum Novum* [D.39.1.1–50.17.211].
C.	*Codicis Iustiniani* (Lyon: Apud Hugonem à Porta, 1560). *Codicis Dn.Iustiniani*, Editio Postrema (Venice: Apud Nicolaum Bevilaqua, 1574) [C.1.1.1–9.51.13]. *Volumen* (Lyon: Apud Hugonem à Porta, 1558) [C.10.1.1–12.64.1].
Inst.	*Volumen* (Lyon: Apud Hugonem à Porta, 1558). *Institutiones Divi Caesaris Iustiniani*, Editio Postrema (Venice: Apud Nicolaum Bevilaqua, 1569).
Nov.	*Volumen* (Lyon: Apud Hugonem à Porta, 1558). *Novellae Constitutiones Divi Caesaris Iustiniani, Quae Authentica Vulgo Appellant*, Editio Postrema (Venice: Apud Nicolaum Bevilaqua, 1569).

Canon Law

Decretum	Gratian, Decretum Gratiani: Emendatum et notationibus illustratum una cum glossis, Gregorii XIII Pont. Max. iussu editum (Rome: In Aedibus Populi Romani, 1582).
X.	Gregory IX, Decretales [sive Liber Extra] D. Gregorii Papae IX (Rome: In Aedibus Populi Romani, 1582).
VI.	Boniface VIII, Liber Sextus Decretalium (Rome: In Aedibus Populi Romani, 1582).

Feudal Law

L.F.	*Volumen* (Lyon: Apud Hugonem à Porta, 1558). *Feudorum Libri Duo*, Editio Postrema (Venice: Apud Nicolaum Bevilaqua, 1574).

A Note on Texts

I have generally used the 1583 *République* (the standard version used in scholarship on Bodin) and the 1586 Latin *De Republica* for citations to Bodin. I have also consulted Kenneth McRae's edition of the 1606 English translation of Richard Knolles, *The Six Bookes of a Commonweale*. Readers should note that there are a number of substantial differences between the French and Latin texts, a point of ongoing interpretive difficulty in textual scholarship on Bodin's *République*. While the French text was written in the vernacular to reach a wide readership in France, especially the nobility, during the Wars of Religion, the Latin text was intended for a learned international readership acquainted with the use of legal authorities. Probably the most notable difference is the addition of a new chapter in the Latin *De Republica* III, *De ordinibus civium*, on the various ranks and orders of citizenship.[1] But there are numerous stylistic and substantive differences between the French and Latin texts, necessitating comparison of the corresponding texts.[2] In some cases, I have provided both the French and Latin texts to allow for comparison.

For the *Methodus*, I cite the 1572 edition. And, for the *Distributio*, I have relied chiefly on the original tabular presentation published in 1578, rather than the prose version published in 1580.[3] Bodin was a systematic and visual thinker and visualized conceptual relations throughout his work. The value of the tabular *Distributio* lies in its visual representation of how Bodin imagined the organizational structure and relation of legal concepts.

Bodin was professionally trained as a lawyer, and he provided copious citations to numerous legal authorities of Roman and canon law, collectively the 'common law' [*ius commune*] of Western legal science, both as in-text and marginal citations. He provided those citations using the extended form of abbreviated titles and incipits, instead of the modern numerical system standardized by Gibbon, Mommsen, and Krueger (for Roman law). While, to the untrained eye, and even for someone proficient in Latin, these citations may appear to be random strings

1 Howell Lloyd, *Jean Bodin, 'This Pre-eminent Man of France': An Intellectual Biography* (Oxford: Oxford University Press, 2017) 129 argues, following evidence in a study by Diego Quaglioni, that Bodin essentially plagiarized the work of the jurist, André Tiraqueau, *Commentarii de Nobilitate et Iure Primigeniorum* (Basel: Hieronymus Froben and Nicolaus Episcopius, 1561) and consequently 'perpetrated multiple errors, confusing the opinions of different jurists, distorting biblical quotations, even inventing new laws'. Cp. Diego Quaglioni, 'Una fonte del Bodin: André Tiraqueau, giureconsulto: appunti su *De Republica*, III.8', in *La République di Jean Bodin: Actes du Colloque de Pérouse, 14–15 Novembre 1980* (Florence: Olschki, 1981), *Il Pensiero Politico* 14: 113–27.

2 Lloyd, *Jean Bodin* 119–20 usefully summarizes the principal differences between the two editions.

3 Jean Bodin, *Juris Universi Distributio* (Cologne: Ioannes Gymnicus, 1580). A dialogue version was published by Jan Kocin, *Nova Distributio Iuris Universi* (Prague: George Nigrinus, 1581).

of text, these were, in effect, shortcuts revealing an interlacing of seemingly unconnected legal doctrines. For convenience, I have modernized these citations and present them in their standard numerical form.

Bodin also routinely and casually cited the medieval legal literature of commentaries and consilia using the sigla, or scribal abbreviations, for civilians and canonists, such as 'Bart' for Bartolus of Sassoferrato, 'Ant.But' for Antonio da Butrio, 'Innocet' for Sinibaldo Fieschi [Innocent IV], 'Panor' for Nicolas de Tudeschi [Panormitanus], 'Alex' for Alessandro Tartagni de Imola [Imolensis], 'Felin' for Felino Sandeo [Felinus Sandeus].[4] Where possible, I have tried to decipher these sigla and provide the full name and text of the cited authority.[5]

Many, though certainly not all, modern studies of Bodin's texts of political theory and law overlook these citations. But they are vital for understanding Bodin's theory as a whole, as they provide valuable materials and insights into Bodin's style of legal reasoning (by way of analogy to private law) as well as clues to retracing sources he may have accessed.[6]

I completed this book during the coronavirus pandemic and the terrifying California wildfires of 2020. The resulting lockdowns cut off access to primary sources in rare book collections that I would have needed. Out of necessity, I have relied on digital sources, some available on the internet, others generously supplied directly by colleagues and libraries around the world. While I have tried my best to proofread and verify all the sources I have cited, it is likely that there still may be errors which will require a further round of corrections and updating. I would ask readers who encounter such errors, first, for their understanding of the limitations imposed by these exceptional circumstances, and, second, to notify me or the publishers of such errors so that the text can be revised accordingly.

[4] Ralph Giesey, 'Medieval Jurisprudence in Bodin's Concept of Sovereignty', in *Verhandlungen der Internationalen Bodin Tagung in München*, ed. Horst Denzer (München: Beck, 1973) 174 indicates that Bodin's three most frequently cited sources, by far, were Bartolus, Baldus, and Alexander Tartagnus Imolensis. Howell Lloyd, at *Jean Bodin* 128 suggests that Bodin may have been 'relying upon collections or compendia of juristic materials rather than consulting the authors in question directly and *in extenso*'. Cp. Michel Reulos, 'Les Sources juridiques de Bodin: Textes, auteurs, pratique', in *Jean Bodin: Verhandlungen der Internationalen Bodin Tagung in München*, ed. H. Denzer (München: C.H. Beck, 1973). Such practice, however, would not have been out of the ordinary for lawyers pleading before courts or, like Bodin, preparing consilia.

[5] William Hamilton Bryson's *Dictionary of Sigla and Abbreviations to and in Law Books before 1607*, 2nd printing with corrections (Buffalo: William S. Hein & Co., Inc., 1996) has been an invaluable resource. An accessible introduction to the medieval system of civil and canon law citations can be found in Appendix I ('The Romano-Canonical Citation System') of James Brundage, *Medieval Canon Law* (London: Longman, 1995) 190–205.

[6] On this point, it is interesting that Bodin claims to have consulted the *Pandectes de Florence*, or *Littera Florentina*, regarded to be the authoritative surviving manuscript of Justinian's Roman law texts. *De Republica* 68 [1.7]. Cp. *Stato* 1: 323, n.13, suggests an alternate source in Guillaume Budé, *Annotationes Reliquae in Pandectas* (Paris: Michel de Vascosan, Robert Estienne & Jean de Roigny, 1542) 86.

Introduction

The modern legacy of sovereignty is one of profound ambiguity. It is, on the one hand, celebrated in the post-colonial era as the legal expression of a country's right of self-determination and the prize of political independence. Yet, sovereignty is also, on the other hand, condemned as an obstacle to the protection of other, arguably more urgent, values such as human rights, environmental and global justice, and the realization of a perpetual peace among nations. Given this ambiguity, commentators have suggested that maybe the world might be better off *without* sovereignty. The French philosopher, Jacques Maritain, once even proposed that we ought to 'eliminate sovereignty both as a word and as a concept' from the lexicon of modern political science and strive instead to imagine a politics without sovereignty.[1]

That fear of sovereignty is understandable. Maritain's vision of a sovereignty-free politics characteristically expressed the collective trauma of a generation that had witnessed the destructive consequences of an international order constructed upon antiquated 'Westphalian' notions of territorial state sovereignty. For witnesses of World War II and the Cold War, sovereignty became inextricably tied to the consequences of totalizing state power and its brutally dehumanizing technological efficiency in the atomic age.

That generational experience had fundamentally shaped the academic agenda of twentieth-century scholarship in jurisprudence and political science, which sought, in part, to tame, and even eliminate, sovereignty. Sovereignty scepticism was the driving force for writers in diverse intellectual traditions and fields, such as Giorgio Agamben, Hannah Arendt, Karl Barth, Ernst Cassirer, Robert Dahl, Jacques Derrida, Michel Foucault, Carl Friedrich, Hans Kelsen, and Harold Laski who sought a sovereignty-free (or at least sovereignty-tamed) law and politics. Some commentators had even boldly predicted the withering away of state sovereignty, eventually to be replaced by a pluralistic and interdependent system of international law and global governance.[2] One still encounters the occasional

[1] Jacques Maritain, 'The Concept of Sovereignty', *American Political Science Review* 44 (1950): 343. Cp. Hans Kelsen, *Das Problem der Souveränität und die Theorie des Völkerrechts* (Tübingen: Mohr, 1920) 320; Léon Duguit, *Law in the Modern State*, ed. Frida Laski and Harold Laski (London: Allen & Unwin, 1921).

[2] A prominent modern example is Francis Fukuyama, *The End of History and the Last Man* (New York: Free Press, 1992). Michael Hardt and Antonio Negri point to a similar conclusion in *Empire* (Cambridge: Harvard University Press, 2001). See also Neil MacCormick, 'Beyond the Sovereign State', *Modern Law Review* 56 (1993): 1–18.

The Right of Sovereignty. Daniel Lee, Oxford University Press. © Daniel Lee 2021.
DOI: 10.1093/oso/9780198755531.003.0001

dismissive remark that sovereignty is but a 'mistake' in practical or political reasoning, even a 'delusion' of political modernity that holds our political reasoning 'captive'.[3]

The reality, of course, is that we still inhabit a world where politics and law are experienced and practised through the framework of sovereign states, as much as some would prefer to wish them away. Indeed, the notion of sovereignty is still routinely invoked and exploited in contemporary politics to justify the permissibility of all sorts of actions attached to profound international consequences.

Consider some recent examples of these purported assertions of sovereignty. Sovereignty has been invoked by defenders of 'Brexit' – the political process of the United Kingdom's departure from the European Union under the provisions of Article 50 of the Lisbon Treaty – as a lawful assertion of 'British sovereignty' determined through referendum.[4] The President of the United States described America's abrupt withdrawal from the Paris Climate Accord in 2017 as 'a reassertion of America's sovereignty'.[5] The aspiration for sovereignty has also driven countless independence and secessionist movements, most recently the Catalan independence movement whose president, Carles Puigdemont, described the purpose of secession not 'in terms of nationalism, but of sovereignty'.[6] The environmental politics of climate change, too, has also generated fierce defences of state sovereignty, as the Brazilian President, Jair Bolsonaro, did, when responding to international critics of Amazon deforestation, in reasserting Brazilian sovereignty over a global interest in protecting the Amazon rain forests.[7] To be sure, public statements of these kinds are intended for public consumption to meet short-term political calculations. What they amply indicate, however, is the continuing rhetorical power of sovereignty and how deeply engrained the idea of sovereignty is.

But this is more than just about political rhetoric. Nothing can make this point more vividly today than the stark differences in national outcomes in responses to the COVID-19 global pandemic beginning in 2020, with some states relying on a strategy of vigorous testing and contact-tracing and others relying on strict

[3] Louis Henkin, 'That "S" Word: Sovereignty, and Globalization and Human Rights, et Cetera', *Fordham Law Review* 68 (1999): 2; 'The sovereignty of states in international relations is essentially a mistake'. Joan Cocks, *On Sovereignty and Other Political Delusions* (London: Bloomsbury, 2014); Jonathan Havercroft, *Captives of Sovereignty* (Cambridge: Cambridge University Press, 2011). Most recent in this literature is Don Herzog, *Sovereignty, RIP* (New Haven: Yale University Press, 2020).

[4] Noah Carl, James Dennison, and Geoffrey Evans, 'European But Not European Enough: An Explanation for Brexit', *European Union Politics* 20 (2019): 297.

[5] Administration of Donald Trump, 'Remarks Announcing United States Withdrawal from the United Nations Framework Convention on Climate Change Paris Agreement', Daily Comp. Pres. Docs., 2017 DCPD No.: DCPD201700373 (1 June 2017) 5.

[6] https://www.spiegel.de/international/europe/former-catalan-president-puigdemont-i-don-t-like-being-in-exile-a-1222545.html

[7] For the history and broader context of how sovereignty enters into Brazilian Amazon politics, see Ane Marie Todd, 'Environmental Sovereignty Discourse of the Brazilian Amazon: National Politics and the Globalization of Indigenous Resistance', *Journal of Communication Inquiry* 27 (2003): 354–70.

nationwide quarantines and border closures. Sovereignty as a fundamental principle of global politics, it seems safe to say, doesn't seem to be going anywhere.

Yet, despite its currency even in contemporary politics, sovereignty has become now possibly the most misunderstood and abused concept of modern political thought.[8] Martin Loughlin has lucidly diagnosed the difficulty:

> The concept [of sovereignty] is much misunderstood today, mainly because of a failure to acknowledge its intrinsic political and legal dimensions. Political scientists fail to recognize its juristic character, and confuse sovereignty with governmental power, while legal theorists strive to promote the autonomy of law and seek either to abandon the concept altogether or to convert it into an entirely metaphorical notion, the sovereignty of law.[9]

However, this perennial complaint that sovereignty is 'misunderstood' is nothing new and can potentially be traced back centuries.[10] Why has sovereignty escaped uniform definition and agreement?

One of the principal motivations for this study is rooted in my academic instinct as a scholar of political thought to embrace and engage, rather than to eschew, interpretive disagreements and to treat them as vehicles to explore the wider interpretive possibilities of a concept like sovereignty. In studying sovereignty, we want, not only to know what sovereignty is, but to apprehend a vision of what sovereignty might have been, and what it could be. That will surely require us to do more than taking the safe road of preemptively avoiding or disabling interpretive uncertainties. It requires us, instead, to venture down a more daring path, by cultivating and practising what the American political theorist, Sheldon Wolin, once regarded as the most vital function of political science – the imaginative capacity for creative political vision.[11]

Two Concepts of Sovereignty

What, then, is sovereignty? Etymology, I think, can help us find a way to approach this question. Consider the standard etymology which traces the linguistic origins

[8] This is the basic theme of a number of recent titles whose purpose is ultimately corrective in our understanding of sovereignty, such as Dieter Grimm, *Sovereignty: The Origin and Future of a Political and Legal Concept*, trans. Belinda Cooper (New York: Columbia University Press, 2015); Stewart Patrick, *The Sovereignty Wars: Reconciling America with the World* (Washington: Brookings, 2019).

[9] Martin Loughlin, 'Why Sovereignty?' in *Sovereignty and the Law*, ed. Peter Rawlings, *et al.* (Oxford: Oxford University Press, 2013) 35.

[10] Bodin's own treatment of sovereignty in *République* 122, 211; *De Republica* 78, 147 [1.8, 1.10] opens with a complaint that lawyers, philosophers, and historians all failed to understand and define sovereignty properly and, as a result, misunderstood its essential qualities.

[11] Sheldon Wolin, *Politics and Vision: Continuity and Innovation in Western Political Thought* (Princeton: Princeton University Press, 2004).

of 'sovereignty' to the French cognate, *souveraineté*, a nominalization of the adjective *souverain*.[12] One of its simple meanings is 'supreme', which in turn is said to be traceable to the Latin preposition, *super*, meaning 'above' or 'beyond'. It signalled not so much a concept of omnipotence, but rather a concept of supremacy.

The term's original application wasn't precisely limited to law and politics. It was, in fact, used widely in theology, to describe the mystical qualities of God's divinity and supremacy over Creation.[13] But as an attribute of independent states – and, in particular, the authority structure within those states – it was not clear what made one *souverain* or 'supreme' over others.

One way to answer this puzzle is to interpret sovereignty strictly in terms of *force* – more specifically, the coercive force capable of being asserted or threatened over the population of some geographical space, thereby inducing that territorially-bound subject population to behave in compliance with the desires of the enforcing regime. It is, on this account, just this brute fact of coercive force – 'hard power', as Joseph Nye once called it – and its potential to sustain social order that truly makes one 'sovereign' over others.[14] This is, of course, an old idea, constitutive of modern *Realpolitik* whose intellectual inspirations can be traced to Thucydides, Machiavelli, and Hobbes. And it is an idea that remains vital in the modern social sciences, especially in 'neo-realist' political science, which treats 'sovereignty' fundamentally as a concept of a 'hard' coercive power.

The advantage of conceptualizing sovereignty in terms of coercive force is that it avoids the messy task of having to reduce sovereignty to internal *beliefs* and *norms* on the part of those subject to a coercive power. On this theory, what makes one sovereign over me has *nothing* to do with my acceptance (or non-acceptance) of that sovereign. It makes no difference whether or not I believe in and accept the ruling power as legitimately sovereign. Even if I don't accept the reigning regime as legitimate, my externally observable, and even measurable, submissive behaviour is all that's necessary to show who's in charge and, thus, in a position of sovereignty.

Behaviour, not belief, is what counts. And since compliant behaviour can be externally observed and measured, practitioners of social science have favoured

[12] In my reading, I believe what Bodin was attempting to express by the term, *souveraineté*, was what might best be translated into modern English as the quality of 'high-ness'. The term signified the abstraction of this quality of supremacy, typically found in monarchs. But, given that his goal was a general theory of all states, it was not intended to be an exclusively monarchical notion of supremacy. Hence the quality of supremacy could, in Bodin's theory, also be detected in kingless republics as well, even in democracies. I have developed this argument at length in *Popular Sovereignty*, Chapters 5 and 6.

[13] J.L. Mackie, 'Evil and Omnipotence', *Mind* 64, No. 254 (1955): 200–12 is an attempt in modern philosophical theology to compare divine omnipotence to sovereignty. Perhaps the classic study exploring these themes of divinity and sovereignty is Ernst Kantorowicz, *The King's Two Bodies: A Study in Medieval Political Theology* (Princeton: Princeton University Press, 1957).

[14] Joseph Nye, *Soft Power: The Means to Success in World Politics* (New York: Public Affairs, 2009). Political scientists sometimes think of sovereignty in terms of the 'state capacity' to deliver social goods. We might, in a Hobbesian way, think of social order as the ultimate social good, the precondition for all other social goods that can be enjoyed in the company of others.

treating sovereignty primarily in terms of this state capacity to assert force that is effective in inducing compliant behaviour.

This approach works well in many cases, where states do in fact enjoy and control the 'state apparatus' for autonomous governance and enforcement of policy within a bounded territory. But it also raises difficult cases, such as states without sovereignty (such as 'weak' or 'fragile' states or developing states with low capacity), non-state actors *with* sovereignty (such as corporations, paramilitary or terrorist groups, etc.), and cases of 'pooled', 'fragmented', 'layered', or 'shared' sovereignty. One surprising result is the disaggregation of sovereignty from classical theories of statehood, such that even powerful non-state actors can be candidates for sovereignty, so long as such actors have the effective coercive capacity to induce compliance and submission.[15]

Lawyers were among the first to point out the shortcomings of conceptualizing sovereignty in terms of coercive force. The English legal philosopher, H.L.A. Hart, once famously caricatured this theory of sovereignty as nothing more than the sovereignty of the 'gunman' whose capacity to inflict bodily harm and, thus, control the behaviour of others was what made him sovereign. The caricature, though perhaps an over-simplification, remains useful for us because it invites us to consider what might be missing in a theory that reduces sovereignty to force. And what's missing is a notion of legitimacy or rightness, the shared belief that sovereignty isn't simply force, but a force grounded in *right*.[16]

The advantage of this alternative approach is that it avoids the reductive treatment of sovereignty strictly in terms of coercive force: One need not be a 'gunman writ large' in order to be a sovereign. On this theory, it isn't the force of arms that makes one sovereign (even disarmed sovereigns can still be sovereign). It is, rather, the *right* to hold those arms in the first place. And what upholds such a sovereign right ultimately is the shared collective belief that one is *entitled* to be in a position of preeminence over others.[17]

Unlike force which relies on a strict instrumental logic of consequences, right depends on a logic of appropriateness.[18] Needless to say, the two logics point to different reasons how and why one comes to be 'sovereign' over another. Whereas the logic of consequences relies strictly on a sovereign's capacity to use force to get its way with others, the second relies on collective beliefs and norms indicating why it

[15] It has also led some analysts to the misleading conclusion that we are now living in a period of a declining, eroding, or 'waning' state-centric sovereignty through globalization and the delegation and cooperative pooling of these sovereign functions to non-state actors. See, for example, David Lake, 'The New Sovereignty in International Relations', *International Studies Review* 5 (2003): 303–23.

[16] I thank David Dyzenhaus, however, for pointing out that, despite Hart's criticism of the Austinian gunman theory, his own theory of legal authority strategically manoeuvres around concepts of legitimacy and right: one can hold legal authority without resorting to coercion and also without legitimacy.

[17] It doesn't really matter what the content of the belief is. What matters is that *some* story, *some* narrative, *some* theory, is told to rationalize and legitimate *some* sovereign authority.

[18] James March and Johan Olsen, 'The Logic of Appropriateness', in *The Oxford Handbook of Political Science*, ed. Robert Goodin (Oxford: Oxford University Press, 2011).

is only right and proper that this one – and not that one – should be sovereign and worthy of obedience.

Taken together, then, sovereignty can be interpreted in one of these two ways – either as an empirical concept of force, or as a normative concept of right.[19] And while these two concepts of sovereignty can coincide and overlap, they aren't the same.

Given these two contrasting concepts of sovereignty, we might wonder then, what was the point of sovereignty? What was the anterior problem to which sovereignty was supposed to be the solution?

One standard answer was order. Sovereignty's purpose, it has been customarily argued, was to preserve social and political order, through the hard power of coercive force. This is the classic answer of *Realpolitik*, framing sovereignty in the cold logic of security and calculated self-interest. Viewed in this way, as an instrument of order, sovereignty was the antidote to what has been characterized as humanity's natural disorder. And without that force of sovereignty, all the advantages of an orderly – or what Thomas Hobbes called a 'commodious' – life would remain unattainable.[20]

Remarkably, so much of the modern historical and theoretical scholarship on sovereignty has absorbed this basic assumption and consequently presents a tidy narrative, according to which sovereignty was invented and introduced to the politics of early modern Europe as a calculated response to address the religious violence and radical politics associated with the Reformation.[21] Only the principle of sovereignty, understood as an abstract concept of order-preserving coercive force, could provide the proper security against the unpredictable dangers of weak states without the capacity to enforce order. This is, in short, the typical history narrated by theorists of international relations locating the origins of the modern 'Westphalian' state system.

[19] This distinction between 'force' and 'right' is one ultimately traceable to Cicero who distinguished between *vis* and *ius*. *Pro Sestio* in *Cicero Orations: Pro Sestio and In Vatinium*, trans. R. Gardner, Loeb Classical Library 309 (Cambridge: Harvard University Press, 1958) 160–61 [42.91–92]; *De Legibus* 3.42. The distinction is largely similar to Martti Koskenniemi's distinction between the 'legal' and 'pure fact' approaches to sovereignty attributed, respectively, to Hans Kelsen and Carl Schmitt in *From Apology to Utopia: The Structure of International Legal Argument* (Cambridge: Cambridge University Press, 2009) 228–33. The distinction remains a key feature of recent conceptual analyses of sovereignty, such as Stephen Krasner's distinction between 'authority' and 'control', *Sovereignty: Organized Hypocrisy* (Princeton: Princeton University Press, 1999) 10; Martin Loughlin's distinction between *potestas* and *potentia* in 'Why Sovereignty?' in *Sovereignty and the Law: Domestic, European and International Perspectives* (Oxford: Oxford University Press, 2013) 39; Evan Fox-Decent, *Sovereignty's Promise* (Oxford: Oxford University Press, 2011) 90–1.

I am not suggesting that these are the only two concepts of sovereignty, or that we ought to approach a conceptual analysis of sovereignty by way of bifurcation. All I am suggesting is the inadequacy of treating sovereignty solely in terms of the instrumental logic of consequences as effective force.

[20] Thomas Hobbes, *Leviathan*, ed. Richard Tuck (Cambridge: Cambridge University Press, 1996) 90.

[21] F.H. Hinsley, *Sovereignty* (Cambridge: Cambridge University Press, 1986); Krasner, *Sovereignty*; Daniel Philpott, *Revolutions in Sovereignty: How Ideas Shaped Modern International Relations* (Princeton: Princeton University Press, 2001); Grimm, *Sovereignty*.

This, of course, assumes that order was indeed the purported goal of sovereignty. But if it wasn't order, what else could it be?

Jean Bodin and the Right of Sovereignty

The principal focus of this book is the theory of sovereignty articulated by the sixteenth-century French jurist and philosopher, Jean Bodin (c.1530–1596). Described by one writer in the French Enlightenment as 'a most prolific genius of immense erudition', Bodin is a towering figure not only in the intellectual history of sovereignty, but in the history of political and legal thought, more generally.[22] Alberico Gentili, one of Bodin's earliest readers, included him among the 'most distinguished jurists of the land of France'.[23] And Pierre Bayle called him 'one of the most cunning men in France' [*l'un des plus habiles hommes qui fussent en France*].[24] He is, without doubt, the preeminent theorist of sovereignty whose agenda-setting writings on the topic directly influenced every major theorist of sovereignty who followed him, including Gentili, Grotius, Spinoza, Hobbes, Pufendorf, Leibniz, Rousseau, Gierke, Jellinek, Duguit, Schmitt, Heller, Laski, McIlwain, and Arendt among many others. He is still treated as the principal authority on sovereignty, cited (if perhaps not read) both by scholars as well as by courts.[25] Although Bodin most likely didn't coin the term, *souveraineté*,[26] as some have suggested, he offered what was perhaps the first systematic treatment of this mystical concept in the West, a task that was developed in several academic works on law, history, and politics: (1) an outline of general jurisprudence (the *Iuris Universi Distributio*, originally written around 1560, but first published in 1578); (2) a treatise on comparative historical methodology (the *Methodus ad Facilem Historiarum Cognitionem*, first published in 1566); and (3) Bodin's magnum opus, his general theory of state and

[22] Jean Charles de Lavie, *Abrégé de la République de Bodin* I (London: Chez Jean Nourse, 1755) Préface ii.

[23] Alberico Gentili, *De Iure Belli Libri Tres*, vol. 2, *The Translation of the Edition of 1612*, trans. John Rolfe (Oxford: Clarendon Press, 1933) 4 [1.1].

[24] Pierre Bayle, 'Jean Bodin', in *Dictionnaire historique et critique*, 5th ed. (Amsterdam, 1734) 2:33, reproduced in Pierre Mesnard, ed., *Oeuvres Philosophiques de Jean Bodin: Auteurs Modernes Tome V, 3* (Paris: Presses Universitaires de France, 1951) xxiii.

[25] Justice David Souter of the United States Supreme Court, for example, reveals a familiarity with Bodin and early modern political theory. He cites Bodin and Hobbes in his dissenting opinion to *Seminole Tribe of Florida v. Florida*, 517 U.S. 44 (1996): 151 n.44; 153–54, n.49. Souter cited Bodin again, in addition to Baldus, Eliot, and Hobbes, in his dissenting opinion to *Alden et al. v. Maine*, 527 U.S. 706 (1999): 797. International courts have also referred to Bodin, such as in the dissenting opinion of Judge Antônio Cançado Trindade in *Jurisdictional Immunities of the State* (Germany v. Italy: Greece intervening), Judgment, I.C.J. Reports 2012 (February 3), General List No. 143 at 240 [¶163].

[26] Grimm, *Sovereignty*, 13, citing, *inter alia*, Marcel David, *La souveraineté et les limites juridiques du pouvoir monarchique du IXe au XVe siècle* (Paris: Dalloz, 1954); Jürgen Dennert, *Ursprung und Begriff der Souveränität* (Stuttgart: Gustav Fischer, 1964); Helmut Quaritsch, *Souveränität: Entstehung und Entwicklung des Begriff in Frankreich und Deutschland vom 13. Jahrhundert bis 1806* (Frankfurt: Duncker & Humblot, 1986).

law (*Les Six Livres de la République*, first published in French in 1576 and translated into Latin as *De Republica Libri VI* in 1586).

Bodin was something of a Renaissance polymath.[27] Educated by the Carmelite Order in Paris and later trained in Toulouse to be a lawyer, Bodin's life work not only included canonical treatises in politics and jurisprudence, but also a translation and commentary of Oppian's *Κυνηγετικά* into Latin (*Oppiani de Venatione*, 1555), a practical guide on prosecuting witches (*De la Démonomanie des Sorciers*, 1581), a formal treatise on natural philosophy (*Universae Naturae Theatrum*, 1596), and a dialogue on natural religion (*Colloquium Heptaplomeres de Rerum Sublimium Arcanis Abditis*, first published in 1857). Much of Bodin's professional career, however, was in service to the French monarchy, and it was from the perspective of the monarchy that he witnessed the most violent decades of the French Wars of Religion which engulfed France in the 1560s and 1570s.

Given the immediate context of religious violence in which Bodin developed his political theory, it has long been assumed that Bodin introduced the concept of sovereignty as a practical instrument of statecraft in response to what the American sociologist Talcott Parsons would later describe as the problem of declining social order.[28] Seeing that Frenchmen were killing each other, and that France itself was falling apart in civil war, Bodin (it was thought) must have reasoned that only a powerful sovereign king with the proper tools of enforcement could preserve order in France. It is a tidy and attractive narrative that positions Bodin's theory as a precursor to later, perhaps more familiar, theories of Thomas Hobbes and John Austin who likewise conceptualized sovereignty as a device to enforce order through the strategic, one might say even ruthless, use of sanctions.

But as attractive as this narrative is, it overlooks the more basic point that Bodin arrived at the essentials of his theory of sovereignty years before the explosion of cataclysmic violence associated with the Massacre of St. Bartholomew in 1572.[29] To treat Bodin's writing on sovereignty merely as a convenient response to his immediate political context not only undervalues its originality, even brilliance, it also ignores the point that Bodin independently arrived at his concept of sovereignty as the result of his academic work in law and history.

The point of sovereignty, for Bodin, wasn't order, but something else. Indeed, order, simply by itself, wasn't valuable and even ancillary to sovereignty. And that is because anybody, with the appropriate tools, could enforce order – including even an unjust or illegal order.

[27] On this background, see Ann Blair, *The Theater of Nature: Jean Bodin and Renaissance Science* (Princeton: Princeton University Press, 1997) and Lloyd, *Jean Bodin*.

[28] Talcott Parsons, *The Structure of Social Action* (New York: McGraw-Hill, 1937). This is a central thesis of Julian Franklin, *Jean Bodin and the Rise of Absolutist Theory* (Cambridge: Cambridge University Press, 1973).

[29] This is an important point to keep in mind when evaluating Franklin's thesis that Bodin's thought evolved from an earlier, more moderate constitutionalist position in the *Methodus* before St. Bartholomew to a more absolutist position in the *République* after St. Bartholomew.

In explaining this point, Bodin often pointed to an illustration taken from Cicero as a sort of thought experiment – the violent force of lawless robbers, brigands, and pirates that roamed the highways and the high seas.[30] Suppose robbers and pirates used their illicit violence to capture and subdue innocent victims to comply with their captors' will.[31] One might describe the captured victim's fearful or desperate compliance to the force and will of their captors as a kind of order – even a kind of state. One might even go so far as to describe those terrorizing captors as 'sovereigns' over their captives.

But for Bodin, it would be a huge mistake to designate the sort of 'order' established by the naked force of robbers, brigands, pirates (and we may add Hart's gunmen) as equivalent to sovereign statehood – what Bodin called a *répubique* (or, in Latin, a *respublica*).[32] Suppose those robbers, brigands, and pirates were to be disarmed, so that their capacity to enforce order was suddenly to be suspended. Those formerly captive and subdued under their captors would have no reason to comply anymore. Indeed, they would be, Bodin argues, fully within their right to resist their erstwhile captors, precisely because they had no *obligation* to obey.

All of this analysis, of course, relies on imagining sovereignty as an empirical concept of force [*force*; *vis*] – which remains a dominant attitude in the social sciences. But what happens if we, instead, treat sovereignty as a normative concept of right [*droit*; *ius*], as it is in jurisprudence? Would we arrive at a different understanding of sovereignty's purpose than the one given to us by those who can only see sovereignty as a concept of force?

My answer in this book is yes. As I'll argue, Bodin conceptualized sovereignty strictly as a concept of a legal right [*droit*; *ius*] and not, as so many have assumed about Bodin, a concept of force [*vis*]. As William Farr Church once put it, 'he was throughout a theorist of right, not might. As such, he was poles apart from Hobbes'.[33] The purpose of sovereignty, moreover, wasn't so much to enforce order, as it has been so often suggested. Order was simply a nice by-product. Rather, the

[30] This is the first substantive point that Bodin makes in the *République*. Cicero, *On Duties*, Loeb Classical Library 30, trans. Walter Miller (Cambridge: Harvard University Press, 1913) 384–85 [*De Off.* 3.29.107]; Augustine, *City of God*, vol. 2, *Books 4–7*, Loeb Classical Library 412, trans. William Green (Cambridge: Harvard University Press, 1963) 16–17 [4.4].

[31] Such acts of illicit violence are categorized as *latrocinia* in the *Digest* of Roman law at D.49.15.24, to distinguish the violent outlawry of brigandage and piracy from lawful enemies [*hostes*] of Rome who, in war and *post bellum*, are entitled to legal rights, most notably, the right of postliminy.

[32] Bodin expands on this point by way of a legal analogy that Grotius would later use in *De Iure Belli ac Pacis* 1.3.4: that is the difference between legal marriage [*matrimonium iustum* and *iusta nuptia*] and mere concubinage. Only lawful marriage confers upon the husband the right of authority over the wife, essential to the family. Concubinage, by contrast, was mere coercive force and gave the male no right of authority over the female, nor did it establish the rights necessary for the family unit. Cp. *De Republica* 15 [1.3]: *Uxoris appellatione iustam ac legitimam intelligo, non concubinam.*

[33] Charles Howard McIlwain, 'Sovereignty Again', *Economica* 18 (1926): 253–56; William Farr Church, *Constitutional Thought in Sixteenth-Century France: A Study in the Evolution of Ideas* (Cambridge: Harvard University Press, 1941) 232. That should, moreover, not be surprising, given that Bodin was, by professional training, a lawyer.

ultimate purpose of Bodinian sovereignty was the unity of the state.[34] Sovereignty was the necessary element that bound together the many disparate parts of a state, so that they can become, in Bodin's words, one state [*une République*; *una respublica*]. Through sovereignty, the many become one.

What binds a state together as one unity, however, isn't force. Nor is it some mystical spirit of state. It is, instead, obligation.

This needs some explanation. Bodin, trained formally in the civil law, understood *obligatio* in the conventional way presented in Roman legal science, as a 'legal bond' [*vinculum iuris*] tying one party who is duty-bound to perform some act (the *obligor*) to another party who is correlatively entitled to benefit from that performance (the *obligee*).[35] The paradigmatic example is debt: the debtor is duty-bound to perform the duty of repayment [*solutio*], from which the creditor is entitled to benefit. What ultimately made obligation distinctive for Bodin was this interpersonal relational quality constituted by the mutuality of one's right and another's duty.[36] And he repurposed this notion of a bond tying duty-bound obligors to rights-holding obligees in explaining how sovereignty might forge a harmonic unity in the state.[37]

Bodin's key point is that sovereigns were obligees. Like creditors, sovereigns too were entitled to benefit from performances or services owed to them by their indebted subjects. But subjects weren't debtors, in any literal sense (unless of course they borrow from their sovereign on credit). They don't owe simply repayment of loans, as in the case of debtors. What they owe instead is *allegiance* – the duty of faithful obedience.[38]

What made the state one unity was common obligation. It wasn't just that subjects were tied [*ligati*; cp. *ob-ligati*] and duty-bound as obligors. The crucial point was that they were tied and duty-bound to one and the same sovereign authority, the one rightfully entitled to receive that allegiance. Only through this juridical frame of obligation (of obligors and obligees) is it really possible for us to see how Bodin saw sovereignty, not so much as a coercive tool for enforcing order in some geographically bounded space or territory, but rather as an imaginative tool

[34] On these contrasting interpretations, see the chapters by W.H. Greenleaf, 'Jean Bodin and the Idea of Order', Michel Villey, 'La justice harmonique selon Jean Bodin', and Michel Reulos, 'Les Sources juridiques de Bodin', in Horst Denzer, ed., *Jean Bodin: Verhandlungen der internationalen Bodin Tagung in München* (München: Beck, 1973) 23–39, 69–86, 416–22.

[35] The term, *vinculum iuris*, originates in the Roman law of obligations at Inst.1.13.pr.

[36] This juristic relationship positioning the obligor's duty as correlative to the obligee's right or entitlement has been typically called a Hohfeldian claim-right, after the analysis of Wesley Newcomb Hohfeld, 'Some Fundamental Legal Conceptions as Applied in Judicial Reasoning', *Yale Law Journal* 23 (1913): 30–32.

[37] The notion of 'harmony' is a recurring theme in Bodin's thought. His theory of justice identifies three forms of justice, patterned on the three Pythagorean ratios: arithmetic justice, geometric justice, and harmonic justice.

[38] Failure to perform that duty is, thus, framed as a legal wrong, even sacrilege, against the sovereign, *crimen laesae maiestatis*, outlined in the *lex Iulia de maiestate* D.48.4.1.

for visualizing the state as a structure of rights and duties, tethering subjects together to one common sovereign authority.

This 'right of sovereignty' (what Bodin variously called the *droit de souveraineté*, *ius maiestatis*, *ius summi imperii*) shall be the focus of this book. In what follows in this Introduction, I shall present a preview of the book's argument, a sort of 'overture' examining the principal thematic *leitmotifs* to be developed in the chapters to follow.

Preview of the Argument I: The Permissive Right of Sovereignty

The principal thesis that I shall be defending in this study is an interpretation of Jean Bodin's theory of sovereignty as a type of right: What Bodin calls 'sovereignty' – variously rendered in Bodin's writings as *summum imperium*, *souveraineté*, *maiestas*, ἄκρα ἐξουσία – mustn't be understood in terms of force, but in terms of right – and more specifically, as a special type of right sometimes called permissive right in the academic literature.[39]

What exactly is a 'permissive right'? The idea is an old one in legal thought: whatever act is not explicitly prohibited by law is not only permitted, but (even more) can be regarded a type of right.[40] Early statements of this principle can be found in classical and medieval sources, such as Justinian's *Digest* of Roman law and Gratian's *Decretum* of canon law.

As we shall see (Chapter 2), Bodin, who was formally trained as a lawyer and well-versed in these sources, made extensive use of this notion of a permissive

[39] It is, specifically, the permissive right of sovereigns to rule [*imperare*; *iubere*] subjects. On 'permissive rights' and permissibility, see Brian Tierney, *Liberty and Law: The Idea of Permissive Natural Law* (Washington: The Catholic University of America Press, 2014) and *The Idea of Natural Rights: Studies on Natural Rights, Natural Law, and Church Law, 1150–1625* (Atlanta: Scholars Press, 1997). Tierney has approached the notion of permissibility as a consequence of law (or the silence of law). I take a slightly different approach in emphasizing how permissibility of A's doing φ implies A's right to φ. In this respect, I follow the Stig Kanger-Lars Lindahl theory of right. Lars Lindahl, *Position and Change: A Study in Law and Logic* (Dordrecht: D. Reidel Publishing Company, 1977).

Note that, by treating sovereignty in terms of right, Bodin rejects outright any suggestion that sovereignty is effective coercive force. Indeed, force without right isn't even sovereignty at all. Bodin has another term for it – 'tyranny' – as we'll see in Chapter 5. In this respect, it will be useful to compare Bodin's argument of a right of sovereignty with the more critical approaches of Leslie Green, *The Authority of the State* (Oxford: Clarendon Press, 1990), A. John Simmons, *Moral Principles and Political Obligations* (Princeton: Princeton University Press, 1979), Joseph Raz, *The Authority of Law* (Oxford: Clarendon Press, 1979), M.B.E. Smith, 'Is There a Prima Facie Obligation to Obey the Law?' *Yale Law Journal* 82 (1973); Robert Paul Wolff, *In Defense of Anarchism* (New York: Harper and Row, 1970) who generally deny, or are sceptical of, any such 'right'.

[40] It is 'licit' [*licitum*] and expressed in legal sources by the term, *licet*, indicating that which is permitted. The notion of a 'licence' [*licentia*] is derived from this background idea of permissibility. It is a separate question whether such permissive right can be regarded a Hohfeldian 'claim-right', which imposes duties on others.

right in his theory.[41] One who is neither required by statute to do some act, φ, nor is prohibited by statute from doing φ, may well be said (owing to the absence of statute – or, as Hobbes would put it, by 'the silence of the laws') to have a permissive right [*droit*; *ius*] to φ.[42] And the crucial reason is this: whatever is permissible [*licet*] may well be said to be lawful [*iustum*] and, thus, done legally [*iure*]. Whatever is legal, moreover, is rightful.[43] Permissibility of one's φ-ing, in short, implies one's right to φ.

The one category of φ-ing that captured Bodin's attention was *imperium* – what might be anglicized (as Jeremy Bentham did) as 'imperation' – or, simply, command [*imperare*].[44] Bodin regarded such acts of command as instances of permissive rights. Suppose, for example, a senior military officer issues an order, commanding her troops to fire their weapons. Bodin interprets such an official command [*imperium*] as a 'right' [*ius*] of the commanding officer [*imperator*]. Of course, there might be several different, yet equally valid, ways to interpret the nature of this officer's right of command.[45]

Bodin, however, focused on the point that the officer's right was what Hohfeld called a 'liberty' or privilege-right: It is ultimately up to the officer to decide whether or not to issue such a command.[46] The officer can be said to have a right because she is under no duty *not* to command her subordinates. Being an officer, she is permitted to do what no one else, without a like permission, can, which is to command her subordinates. And because commanding, φ-ing, is permissible (in the sense that it is not prohibited of officers), it can be said that commanding is also lawful: It is right and proper that officers be able to command.

[41] Bodin, in fact, restated the commonplace in his early outline of general jurisprudence, the *Iuris Universi Distributio* 1578: fol. A, s.v.: *Sanctio*: *Sanctio seu iussum Principis aut summae in Republica potestatis, lex appellatur: quae aut universalis est, iubens aliquid, vetans, aut permittens*. One of Bodin's sources may have been D.1.3.7: *Legis virtus haec est imperare vetare permittere punire*.

[42] Leif Wenar 'The Nature of Rights', *Philosophy and Public Affairs* 33 (2005): 226–28 has usefully distinguished between 'singular privilege' (in von Wright's deontic logic: $\sim O(\varphi) \vee \sim O(\sim\varphi)$) and 'paired privilege' ($\sim O(\varphi) \wedge \sim O(\sim\varphi)$). The logician, Georges Kalinowski, in *La logique des norms* (Paris: Presses Universitaires de France, 1972) 113, previously termed this feature of standard deontic logic 'permission bilatérale'. Paired privileges confer upon the privilege-holder discretion of choice with respect to the act, φ. Hobbes hinted at this distinction indirectly in *Leviathan* when he suggests that the 'silence of the laws' signals not only 'permission', but an intentional 'praetermission'.

[43] It is a connection that ultimately is rooted in the double-meaning of *droit* (and the Latin *ius*) as both 'law' and 'right'.

[44] Jeremy Bentham, 'Source of a Law' [from Bentham Mss., UCL, Box 88b: 229–37] in *Bentham's Political Thought*, ed. Bhikhu Parekh (London: Croom Helm, 1973) 162.

[45] The officer's right might be described as a 'molecular right' constituted of several 'atomic' Hohfeldian incidents. It can be shown that the commanding officer enjoys at least three different incidents: a privilege-right, a claim-right, and a power-right. Wenar, 'Nature of Rights': 242 even illustrates how an officer's right is a higher-order power.

[46] What Wenar seems to be suggesting is the idea of 'indifference' in von Wright's deontic logic and, equivalently, *quod permissum est* in medieval deontic logic: G.H. von Wright, 'Deontic Logic', *Mind* 60 (1951): 3–4. The officer's situation, $\sim O(\varphi) \wedge \sim O(\sim\varphi)$, entails that the officer has a discretionary 'privilege-right' to (no-duty not to) φ.

The same analysis can be applied to the highest form of command, *summum imperium*, the supreme command of a sovereign over subjects. Acts of sovereignty are permissible, and thus, right, precisely because they are not explicitly prohibited (or otherwise regulated) by any law to which a sovereign authority is subject. And because sovereign acts are likewise 'legally' permissible, it follows that such acts should be treated as legal rights of the sovereign, in the same way that the *imperium* is the right of the commanding officer, the *imperator*.

But, at this point, one might object as follows: Can sovereigns actually be made 'subject' to any law or legal duty? After all, it has become something of a commonplace in the history of modern political thought to say that sovereigns, by definition, are subject to no law.[47] And even Bodin seems to say the same thing when he declares (using a familiar formulation derived from Roman law) that sovereigns are *legibus soluti* – which might roughly be translated as, 'free from legal obligations'.[48] Given that sovereigns are, as Bodin himself admits, *legibus soluti*, isn't everything, then, permissible to sovereigns? In other words, can anything be legally *impermissible* to sovereigns?

As it turns out, there *are* legal limits on what is permissible, even for sovereigns. Those legal limits, however, are not the product of ordinary positive legislation (*ius civile*): sovereigns cannot bind or limit themselves through their own laws. They are, instead, legal limits derived from natural law (*ius naturale*) and the law of nations (*ius gentium*), laws to which even sovereigns are always bound, and from which they cannot exempt themselves.[49]

What's striking in Bodin's legal theory is that the substance of natural law and the law of nations theoretically takes the same juridical structure as positive legislation.[50] Their function is not simply to counsel by good practical reasons, but

[47] Grotius, for example, in *De Iure Belli ac Pacis* 1.3.7 defines sovereigns as those 'not subject to the legal control of another [*alterius iuri*], so that they cannot be rendered void by the operation of another human will [*alterius voluntatis humanae arbitrio*]'. Grotius is likely thinking of D.49.15.7.1 which defines a 'free people' [*liber populus*] as one which is 'subject to the power of no other people' [*Liber autem populus est is qui nullius alterius populi potestati est subiectus*] (including the Roman people), and, thus, capable of diplomatic relations with Rome.

[48] The phrase is from the *Digest* at D.1.3.31: *Princeps legibus solutus est*. The legal history of this doctrine is explored in Brian Tierney, 'The Prince Is Not Bound by the Laws: Accursius and the Origins of the Modern State', *Comparative Studies in Society and History* 5 (1963): 378–400; Kenneth Pennington, *The Prince and the Law, 1200–1600* (Berkeley: University of California Press, 1993). Note that Ulpian's *legibus solutus* indicates only a Hohfeldian 'privilege-right', as an exemption from an otherwise generally binding duty. As we'll see in Chapter 2, it is not necessarily a Hohfeldian 'claim-right', a 'power-right', or an 'immunity-right'.

[49] The *Distributio* focuses on the classical juridical distinction between *ius naturale*, *ius gentium*, and *ius civile*, bundling the latter two together in the invented non-classical category of *ius humanum*. The *République/De Republica*, however, introduces the category of 'divine law' as a body of law, explicitly acknowledging that God is also a sovereign with the divine sovereign right of making and unmaking law – specifically, divine and natural law. On the *ius gentium*, see Jeremy Waldron, 'Foreign Law and the Modern *Ius Gentium*', *Harvard Law Review* 119 (2005): 132. See also Jeremy Waldron, *Partly Laws Common to All Mankind: Foreign Law in American Courts* (New Haven: Yale University Press, 2012).

[50] In this Introduction, I am using the conventional expression in Western legal science, *ius naturale* and *ius gentium*. Bodin's earlier work, in the *Distributio* and the *Methodus*, follows this convention. Notably, the *République* deliberately adopts the vocabulary of positive legislation to describe even

to *oblige* by precept the performance (or non-performance) of acts, φ, whether by requiring or prohibiting φ. And it is more than simply an obligation that binds, as canonists say, *in foro interno*. These are valid obligations, notwithstanding the question of their enforceability.[51]

Yet, what commentators on the *ius naturale* and the *ius gentium* have traditionally observed, since at least the High Middle Ages, is that the substance of these laws actually tend to take an open-ended permissive, rather than a preceptive, form. By identifying a minimum set of obligatory duties requiring or prohibiting φ, they also implicitly indicate what is legally non-obligatory and, thus, permissible.

Take, for example, self-defence, one of the first examples cited in Justinian's *Digest* (D.1.1.3). The use of violent force upon another is, as a general rule of natural law, ordinarily prohibited, but it is exceptionally permissible in special cases, such as defending one's self from 'force or injury'. But it is more than just a rule of natural law. Because it is permissible and licit (*licet*), it becomes a natural right.

Permissibility is even more important in the *ius gentium*, which may well be described, not so much as a code of legal duties, but as a catalogue of implied permissions available to all nations of humanity. Acquisition of private property, for example, has been described as originating as one such permission of the *ius gentium*.[52]

But the *ius gentium* has had a mixed legacy in the history of ideas, and that is because it is from this same body of law that wars – and the legal consequences of war – originally derived their legality, by way of permission. The Roman classical jurist, Hermogenian, famously declared – in a passage of the opening title of Justinian's *Digest* (D.1.1.5) instantly recognizable to every French lawyer of Bodin's lifetime – that it is 'from this law of nations' [*ex hoc iure*], that 'wars were introduced' [*bella introducta*] into the world.

But the *ius gentium* did more than simply recognize the legality of war [*bellum iustum*]. It also recognized the legality of the *consequences* of war. And the most important – and most illiberal – of these consequences was slavery, perhaps the most notorious legal permission of the *ius gentium*. For jurists of the *ius gentium*, what linked war and slavery together was the so-called 'right of conquest' [*droit de*

higher law, so that 'natural law' is rendered *loi naturelle/lex naturalis* and the common law of mankind is rendered *loi des gens/lex gentium*. That raises an interpretive puzzle for readers of Bodin: If natural law is *lex*, it must, by definition, be the product of positive legislation (since Bodin defines *lex* as the 'command of a sovereign'). The question is, who is the legislator? Bodin's later theological writings in the *Colloquium Heptaplomeres* on God as the *princeps naturae* – what might be translated as the 'sovereign over nature' – may help answer this important question.

[51] Bodin segregates the *validity* of an obligation from its *enforceability*. Even unenforceable obligations – what Pufendorf would later call 'imperfect obligations' – are nevertheless valid obligations. Remedies for performances still due can, thus, be sought through extrajudicial means.

[52] Grotius, *De Iure Belli ac Pacis* 2.2.5; cp. the title, *De adquirendo rerum dominio*, in the *Digest*, thus, distinguishes between *ius civile* and *ius gentium* methods of appropriating property such as D.41.1.5.7, 41.1.7.1, 41.1.9.3.

conquête; droit du plus fort]: whoever was victorious in war was legally entitled to enslave and become the master [*seigneur; dominus*] over the conquered party.[53] Indeed, conquest through war was, it was customarily thought, what legally transformed naturally free persons into slaves and, consequently, what introduced the master-slave relationship, *dominium* [cp. *seigneurie*; δεσποτεία], and the alleged legal right of mastery [*ius dominii; droit seigneurial*] – over slaves.[54]

Bodin was, as we'll see, thoroughly familiar with this derivation of slavery from the *ius gentium*, as a legal consequence of the permissive rights of war and conquest. But why stop at slavery? Couldn't other asymmetrical relations of power *also* be derived from the permissive rights of war and conquest?

Possibly the most consequential move in Bodin's line of reasoning was the thought that even sovereignty [*summum imperium*] – which, like slavery [*dominium*], can also be understood as an asymmetrical juridical relationship of command (between sovereign and subject) – was ultimately derived from war. And just as the *ius gentium* conferred a right of mastery [*ius dominii*] upon the *dominus* over his slave, so too did that same law (Bodin conjectured) confer, by permission, a right of sovereignty [*ius summi imperii*] upon the sovereign over its subject.

Needless to say, likening sovereignty to slavery is one of the oldest tropes in the history of political thought, originating with the master himself, Aristotle, who observed the family resemblance, but ultimately distinguished, between domestic δεσποτεία and proper political rulership.[55] Bodin's own treatment of slavery followed the Aristotelian tradition of analysis, juxtaposing slavery alongside sovereignty.[56] He did so to emphasize the point that sovereignty is fundamentally a 'relational concept'.[57]

[53] D.1.5.4, 1.5.5.1, 41.1.5.7, 41.1.7.pr. Bodin derived the term, *seigneur*, most likely from Louis Le Roy's translation of Aristotle's *Politics* which translated the Greek δεσπότης with the French *seigneur*, a term with overtones of feudal lordship. R. Koebner, 'Despot and Despotism: Vicissitudes of a Political Term', *Journal of the Warburg and Courtauld Institutes* 14 (1951): 275–302; Harold Ellis, *Boulainvilliers and the French Monarch: Aristocratic Politics in Early Eighteenth-Century France* (Ithaca: Cornell University Press, 1988) 36; Ingrid A.R. De Smet, 'Philosophy for Princes: Aristotle's *Politics* and Its Readers During the French Wars of Religion', *Journal of the Warburg and Courtauld Institutes* 76 (2013): 23–47. Richard Knolles, in his 1606 translation of Bodin into English, translated *seigneurie* and *dominium* into 'lordly' or 'masterlike' sovereignty.

Bodin uses the term, *le droit du plus fort*, in *République* 156, and it is the same term that Rousseau will use in the *Social Contract* I, 3. Dan Edelstein has suggested that Bodin may have been the first to use this phrase in 'Rousseau, Bodin, and the Medieval Corporatist Origins of Popular Sovereignty', *Political Theory* (January 2021): 18. doi:10.1177/0090591720985452.

[54] Bodin acknowledged the paterfamilial power of fathers as well. But unlike *dominium* and *imperium*, *patria potestas* was the only 'natural power'. *République* 29; *De Republica* 20 [1.4].

[55] *Politics* 1.7 (1255^b16–21); 3.6 (1279^a17–22).

[56] *République* 1.9 presents the different degrees of subjection, including feudal vassalage, clientage, as well as political subjection and slavery. *De Republica* 1.9 expands this list to nine degrees.

[57] I borrow the phrase, 'relational concept', from Martin Loughlin, *The Idea of Public Law* (Oxford: Oxford University Press, 2004) 83, 87. Sovereignty is sometimes spoken of as if it were a tangible commodity, something that can be held, alienated, prescribed, owned, possessed, ceded, stolen, and so on. Bodin himself treats sovereignty in this way at several key points, such as at *De Republica* 79 [1.8] and 148–49 [1.10]. But these are, I think, simply legal metaphors to help illustrate the point that the role and title of 'sovereign' is, like property, exclusive and transferable, not that sovereignty itself is a

Master	Sovereign
|	|
Slave	Subject

But they're not the *same* relational concept. Though slavery and sovereignty both were asymmetrical relations, the master-slave relationship of *dominium* was *sui generis* and inassimilable to the sovereign-subject relationship of *imperium*. Slaves weren't necessarily subjects. And masters weren't necessarily sovereigns. (*Similiter*: οἴκοι weren't necessarily πόλεις, even though both were types of κοινωνία).

In Bodin's political anthropology, however, there was a time when there was no such distinction to be made: Sovereign *imperium* just was despotic *dominium*. Indeed, as we'll see in Chapter 3, the first proper sovereign in Bodin's grand history of humanity was a *dominus*, a slaveholding warlord whose slaves were also his subjects. Only gradually, over many ages, did humans discover that sovereignty needn't also be slavery. One could be a subject to a sovereign without also being his slave. Such person could be, as Bodin would put it, a 'free subject' [*franc sujet*; *liber homo*].[58]

What ultimately made that transition possible, Bodin argued, was the invention of law [*loi*; *lex*] – positive legislation authored and enacted by humans, what jurists conventionally classified as *ius civile*. Once humans understood the ability to create, enforce, and manipulate a system of rules, how to create artificially, through the art of legislation [*legis actio*] and the equitable office of the judge [*officium iudicis*], the terms according to which their affairs could be impersonally and impartially governed, sovereignty no longer needed to take that despotic form of *dominium*, where the naked will [*volunté*; *arbitrium*] of the *seigneur* stood in for law.[59] An alternative form of *droit* sovereignty [*lege*], based on the rule of law, offered a vision not only of a world extirpated of despotic power but one capable of being shaped according to justice.

Bodin narrated the history of humanity as a liberation story, where humanity moved from a world of enslaved subjects ruled under despotic sovereignty [*souveraineté seigneuriale*] to one of free subjects ruled under lawful sovereignty [*droit*] and governed through magistrates exercising authority defined and limited by law.[60] Though pockets of lawless despotism still remained in Bodin's sixteenth century – Bodin frequently singled out the oriental despotisms of the Turks and

tangible commodity. I discuss this point in Chapter 2. It is important, however, that in imagining sovereignty as an interpersonal 'relational' concept that it is strictly an *in personam*, not an *in rem*, relation. That is because sovereigns are sovereign only over their subjects, not over all of humanity.

[58] *République* 68; *De Republica* 60 [1.6].

[59] *République* 393, 621; *De Republica* 272, 457–59 [3.3; 4.6] citing Pomponius' *Enchiridion* (D.1.1.2).

[60] Bodin identifies three types of monarchical rule: *seigneuriale, droit, tyrannie*. The first two are permissible under the common law of mankind. The third, however, is an impermissible act of force: It

the Muscovites – humanity had, by and large, become a world made up of nations governed not by seigneurial will, but by impersonal law.[61]

In this history, the invention of law marked a watershed moment: Law made possible the transformation of *seigneurie* into proper *souveraineté*. But what was so important about law? What actually was law, for Bodin?

Preview of the Argument II: Bodin's Concept of Law

Bodin famously defined law [*loi*; *lex*] as a form of command [*iussum*; *imperium*] – specifically as 'the command of a sovereign' over subjects.[62] Most commentators (disproportionately Anglo-American) have anachronistically concluded from this statement that Bodin must have subscribed to some crude version of what legal theorists now generally call 'the command theory of law' – a now-largely discredited theory most often associated with Jeremy Bentham and John Austin and famously caricatured by H.L.A. Hart as nothing more than the 'law' of the gunman or the highwayman willing to use deadly force to get his way.

What these commentators don't seem to realize is that, in all likelihood, Bodin would have probably disavowed a strict Austinian legal positivism. And that is because, as we'll see, Bodin insisted on treating 'command' [*imperium*; *iussum*] – and, therefore, law – fundamentally as a normative concept of right, not one of force (or 'sanction'). To wit: one can 'command' [*imperare*] only those over whom one already has a *right*, and is thus entitled, to command [*ius imperii*].[63] But without that anterior right to command others, commands ring hollow as empty, inconsequential, if bossy, utterances.[64] That is why, to return to our previous example, the commanding officer can command her subordinates, but not civilians. It is why

is the regime of the lawless pirate or brigand, which commands no allegiance. This French vocabulary is taken from Louis Le Roy's translation of Aristotle, *Les Politiques d'Aristote* (Paris: Michel de Vascosan, 1576).

Note that, though it is a liberation story of humanity from *seigneurial* sovereignty to *droit* sovereignty, it is not necessarily a 'republican' story of non-domination. Humanity may have eliminated *dominium* from sovereignty, but it hasn't eliminated 'domination'.

[61] There was, however, nothing inevitable or guaranteed about the 'free' world we happened to live in. Colonization of the New World, which Bodin interpreted as lawful acts of conquest under the *ius gentium* that legally could activate new titles of seigneurial sovereignty, threatened to reintroduce a New World of enslaved peoples.

[62] The command theory of law appears first in the *Distributio* fol. A, s.v.: *Sanctio seu iussum*. It is restated in the *Methodus* 234 ('134'), 261 and *République* 216, *De Republica* 150 [1.10]. I thank Mario Turchetti for locating the corresponding text in the *Methodus*.

[63] As we'll see in Chapter 2, this 'right of command' [*ius imperii*] is one of the permissive rights under the *ius gentium* just as the 'right of mastery' [*ius dominii*] over conquered slaves is similarly framed as a permissive right under the *ius gentium* on war.

[64] Austin actually seems to have understood, but failed to follow up, on this point. The reason why commands are binding is because the commander, whether sovereign or otherwise, already occupies that post.

creditors can 'command' their debtors to repay their loans, they can't 'command' random passersby on the street to pay them. Likewise, that is why sovereigns can command their subjects, by way of legislation, to do (or not do) φ, but can't command foreigners likewise to do the same.[65]

One could, of course, try to *force* others into compliance – say, by pointing a gun or otherwise threatening harm. Such use of coercive force might even be effective in subduing others through terror. Staring into the barrel of the Smith & Wesson pointed at you is, no doubt, a powerful motivator to comply with the gunman's wishes. And that is what the gunman tries to achieve by demanding of the victim, 'Your money or your life'.

But Bodin's point is that such uses of force, directed by one without any right to do so on another, aren't properly commands, let alone laws. (Nor are such acts, properly speaking, acts of war, since war is technically a formal juridical condition, licit under the *ius gentium*.) Instead, these illicit acts of force are what Bodin (channelling Cicero) called *latrocinia*, the sort of illicit force associated with the 'common enemies of mankind' [*communes hostes omnium*] – pirates, brigands, and robbers.[66] (As we'll see in Chapter 5, Bodin has one more item to add to that list: tyrants.) And just as the illicit force of pirates, brigands, and robbers may be resisted by contrary force, so too may the illicit force of tyrants likewise be met by the deadly contrary force of those victimized by a tyrant's force and fraud.

Force may well motivate compliance in a self-interested instrumental logic of consequences. But Bodin interprets command from a different angle, from the non-consequential normative logic of appropriateness. What ultimately gives a command its 'force', then, *isn't* the fear of the sanctions I'd suffer as a consequence of non-compliance.[67] It is, instead, obligation, whatever the sanction (or even, strikingly, the lack of sanction).[68] This is the crucial point in the juridical structure of Bodin's thought. Any genuine command, Bodin conjectures, presupposes some prior obligation. Even before sovereigns can direct specific commands toward

[65] For Bodin, all of humanity is bound under the law of nature and the law of nations, so on basic matters of morality, the sovereign needn't legislate. Natural duties are always binding whether or not sovereigns legislate.

[66] Cicero, *De Off.* 3.107. Hart's gunman and Hobbes' highwayman serve the same purpose that the pirate and the brigand served in Cicero's theory of natural law. On the significance of piracy, see Daniel Heller-Roazen, *The Enemy of All: Piracy and the Law of Nations* (New York: Zone Books, 2009).

[67] Such fear is certainly a powerful motivating force that drives behaviour. But Bodin isn't concerned about what motivates behaviour, even behaviour that aligns with someone else's wishes.

[68] One implication of this argument is that one can be bound even to weak – or, as Austin once put it, 'feeble' sovereigns. John Austin, *Province of Jurisprudence Determined*, ed. Wilfrid Rumble (Cambridge: Cambridge University Press, 1995) 168. This is an important point of contrast from the approach of modern political science where 'weak' or 'fragile' states – states whose capacity to assert effective coercive force over the population of a territory – are seen as having lost their sovereignty, on account of their declining 'state capacity'. Bodin, for his part, didn't see it that way: Loss of capacity, by itself, doesn't necessarily entail loss of sovereignty, for reasons we'll see in Chapter 2. Bodin develops his reasoning from a famous gloss on the *Digest* at D.1.1.5 which deals with *actiones* (legal remedies), which identifies in theory a class of legal obligations which are not enforceable through ordinarily legal remedies. One can, thus, be bound by an obligation, even if the obligation isn't actionable.

their subjects, there must first be some prior understanding of the respective roles that sovereigns and subjects are expected to perform, as well as the rights and duties assigned to each role. As Bodin explains, these roles of sovereign and subject can be usefully described in terms of 'obligation', positioning the sovereign's *right* to command subjects as correlating with the subject's *duty* to obey the sovereign's commands.

In the English-speaking world, we are accustomed to treating 'obligation' as a synonym for duty. But, as Peter Birks has once suggested, that is only one half of the concept, for obligation is as much a concept of right as it is a concept of duty.[69] As we saw earlier, Justinian famously defined *obligatio*, in his *Institutes* of Roman law, as *vinculum iuris* – a 'legal bond' (or, literally, 'chain'), tying duty-bound 'obligors' (those who owe some performance) to right-holding 'obligees' (those who are *owed* the obligor's performance, as a Hohfeldian claim-right). 'Obligation' was, thus, always to be understood in relational terms of obligor and obligee.

The paradigmatic example of such obligatory relationship was debt. By custom, civil lawyers were accustomed to picturing debtors as being 'tied' – even 'chained' [*ligati*], as debtors typically were in early Roman law until the *lex Poetilia* – to their creditors precisely because they were required by that debt to perform the duty of repayment [*solutio*].[70] Only once that debt had been repaid (or otherwise forgiven or transferred) can the debt be dissolved and the debtor 'released' [*solutus*] from the bond.

The same pattern, Bodin thought, could be observed in legislation: Subjects, like debtors, were obligors. They were also 'tied' [*ob-ligati*] to their sovereigns, because they were required to perform the 'duty' of obeying the sovereign's command – in a word, law. Remarkably, non-performance of that duty was thought to 'wrong' the sovereign, in the same way that debtor's default on a loan wronged the creditor. Of course, creditors and sovereigns each had their own remedies for enforcing duties owed and correcting the offence. And correspondingly, rationally self-interested debtors and subjects may be sufficiently motivated, though perhaps grudgingly, to perform their duties in response to such enforcement.

But observe that, for Bodin, *enforceability* of an obligation was handled separately from its *validity*. Obligations may still be valid, even if they can't be fully enforced through ordinary legal means – that is, by a court.[71] And that is because,

[69] Peter Birks, *The Roman Law of Obligations*, ed. Eric Descheemaeker (Oxford: Oxford University Press, 2014) 5.

[70] Max Radin, 'Secare Partis: The Early Roman Law of Execution against a Debtor', *American Journal of Philology* 43 (1922): 32–48.

[71] This is a doctrine of central importance to Bodin, as in *Distributio* fol. E, s.v.: *Legis actio duplex*, distinguishing between legal remedies that are *extraiudicialis* and those that are *forensis*. Bodin argues for a more capacious understanding of an *actio* than the one offered by Gaius and Justinian in the Roman law of actions (e.g. Inst. 4.6.pr). But at *Distributio* fol. B, s.v.: *Facta*, he joins the critique of his contemporary, François Connan, who in his unconventional *Commentariorum Iuris Civilis*, suggested that Gaius and Justinian both construed the word, *actio*, too narrowly to mean a *forensis actio*, litigated in court. The upshot, for Bodin, is that not all *actiones* are to be battled in the courtroom.

from Bodin's perspective, the subject's duty of obedience isn't a calculated response based on the logic of consequences; it is the outcome of a normative logic of appropriateness within legal science.

This analysis, needless to say, is fundamentally different from modern approaches. And, as we'll see, the consequences of this analysis for Bodin's legal and political theory will be profound. But before proceeding any further, it might be appropriate to address one potential objection. Recall the original reason why Bodin is so heavily focused on the concept of law: Bodin's thesis is that the introduction of law allowed for the transition from seigneurial sovereignty to a properly *droit* sovereignty, where subjects were no longer to be treated as the personal slaves of the sovereign.

Now, it might be objected here that Bodin's analysis of law as command doesn't really help distinguish slavery from sovereignty, since, it could be argued, that masters too, in a sense, 'command' [*imperare*; *iubere*] and 'give law' to their slaves. Supposing that masters *do* 'command' their enslaved subjects, what prevents us from categorizing such seigneurial commands of masters addressed to their enslaved subjects as 'law' as well?

As we can now see, it really depends on which concept of 'command' is operative in the stated objection. If we were to follow Austin and treat commands ultimately as the naked brute force of coercive sanction, then we might see how masters [*seigneurs*; *domini*] might plausibly be said to 'command' [*dominare*] their slaves in the same way that they can 'command' beasts of draught and burden – by the whip. To be clear, Bodin acknowledges that, by the *ius gentium*, masters may have acquired the right to be a master (thus, their use of force is legally permissible). But it is specifically a *ius dominii*, not a *ius imperii*.

That is, of course, not the concept of command at work in Bodin's own analysis of command. The officer, in our earlier example, has *imperium* as a right to command her subordinates. But she doesn't 'own' her subordinates, as a *dominus* might own and 'dominate' [*dominare*] live chattel. Since 'command' entails obligation, it follows that only those with legal personality – that is, those capable of being either a duty-bound obligor or a right-holding obligee – can even be commanded. But slaves, deprived of legal personality, fundamentally lacked that juridical capacity. Slaves, while they may have been human, weren't persons [*persona*] at all; they were things [*res*] – assets. Rightless and dutiless, slaves could never be party to an obligation. The stunning conclusion from all this is that slaves can't technically be 'commanded' [*imperantur*], for the same reason that, say, oxen can't be 'commanded': commands [*imperia*] are addressed only to persons capable of obligation, not to things (which slaves are: 'mancipable things' – *res mancipi*).[72]

[72] Bodin seems to anticipate Hobbes' distinction in *On the Citizen*, ed. Richard Tuck and Michael Silverthorne (Cambridge: Cambridge University Press, 1998) 103 [*De Cive* 8.2–3] between the slave under no obligation to the master [*ergastulus*] and the slave under obligation [*servus*].

But even though slaves can't technically be 'commanded', they can be 'owned'. And it is this concept of property ownership – *dominium* – that ultimately helps explain the difference between slavery and sovereignty. To wit: despotic *seigneurs* own their subjects, as their personal slaves. Lawful *souverains*, by contrast, command their subjects through law. The right of the *seigneur* does not correlate to any duty of the slave: slaves can't have any duties. Instead, it is an *in rem* right directed against the whole world.

The grand historical transition chronicled by Bodin from seigneurial sovereignty to lawful sovereignty, thus, reflected a corresponding transition (to riff on Henry Maine) from property to obligation, as the juridical model of sovereignty. To be clear, both types of sovereignty conferred, by permission of the *ius gentium*, active legal rights on sovereigns.[73] But they were fundamentally different classes of legal rights. Because seigneurial sovereigns asserted claim of ownership – *dominium* – over their enslaved subjects, their right of sovereignty was a right *in rem*. Lawful sovereigns, by contrast, saw their subjects, not as slaves, but as obligors, over whom they were entitled to assert *imperium*, an actionable right *in personam* over duty-bound subjects.[74]

Preview of the Argument III: Absolute Power

Bodin imagined law to function as a *binding-device*. And sovereigns were the chief engineers of those binding-devices.[75]

According to Bodin, sovereigns crafted law as an instrument to bind [*ligare*] and require subjects to perform specific acts, φ. Indeed, in a famous passage of the *République*, Bodin would even remark that the essence of sovereignty was just this right of legislation – to oblige others to φ, or $\sim\varphi$, through formal expressions of command [*imperium*]. All other sovereign rights, he noted, were ultimately reducible to, and derived from, this one.

He specified, however, that legislation wasn't just about making new laws. It also involved crucially the *unmaking* of old law – that is, its repeal, annulment, rescission. And that is why Bodin, almost without exception, defined legislation as both 'the sovereign power of making *and unmaking* of a law' [*iubendae ac tollendae legis summa potestas*].[76] The repeal and rescission of existing legislation – Cicero

[73] Unlike tyrants, who held no legal rights.

[74] For a succinct discussion of the *in rem/in personam* distinction, see Barry Nicholas, *Introduction to Roman Law* (Oxford: Clarendon Press, 1962) 99–103. Note that classical Roman law initially introduces the distinction *not* in connection with rights, but with 'actions', the sort of legal remedies that one can plead at the *in iure* stage of litigation, before the magistrate.

[75] Though, in practice, such legal engineering ultimately becomes, as Bodin will say, the 'duty of the judge' [*officium iudicis*]. It's worth remembering that sovereigns are fully entitled to (and arguably, for Bodin, expected to) delegate the responsible exercise of sovereignty, such as jurisdiction, to professionals – judges, military officers, diplomats, and politicians.

[76] *De Republica* 155 [1.10].

once classified it in four ways, *derogare, abrogare, subrogare, obrogare* – were to be counted as sovereign (or even judicial) acts of legislation – more precisely, what Hans Kelsen once called 'negative legislation'.[77]

Bodin observed that unmaking an existing law had the opposite effect of making or enacting a new law. If the effect of a law was to bind subjects under a duty to φ, the effect of repealing a law must do just the opposite: It must *unbind* and *release* [*solvit*; *absolvit*] subjects from that obligatory duty to φ, by negating and dissolving the bond.[78] For this reason, modern legal positivists, observing this asymmetry between making and unmaking law, have refused to treat rescission as genuinely affirmative legislative acts. John Austin is a case in point:

> Laws to repeal laws, and to release from existing duties must . . . be excepted from the proposition 'that laws are a species of commands.' In so far as they release from duties imposed by existing laws, they are not commands, but *revocations* of commands.[79]

Bodin's position, which anticipated Kelsen's notion of negative legislation, differed sharply from the Austinian doctrine. Sovereigns can make law and, thus, bind [*ligare*] subjects under a general legal duty (in the notation of modern deontic logic, O(φ)). Likewise, by that same right of sovereignty, sovereigns (or their authorized designees: courts) can *unmake* law and, in so doing, release [*solvere*] subjects from the legal duty, so that duty is effectively negated (in the notation of modern deontic logic, ~O(φ)). For Bodin, both were legislation, positive and negative: Releasing [*solvendi*] someone from duty was as much an effect of legislation as binding [*ligandi*] someone under duty.[80]

Bodin evidently placed the greatest importance on the sovereign power to release subjects from legal obligations by repealing legislation, and he anticipated what Hohfeld would recognize in his classic analysis of rights: A's ability to alter B's rights and duties is itself a right, a higher-order 'power-right' over B. This is true even in cases where an obligee, A, (instead of binding [*ligandi*] B under a newly created duty) releases [*solvit*] the obligor, B, from a prior duty. Austin simply saw such a situation as nothing more than the negation of a prior obligation. But Bodin, like Hohfeld, saw something else going on here. Even though the obligor is released

77 *De Republica* 87, 98, 154–5. Cicero, *De Re Publica*, trans. Clinton Walker Keyes, Loeb Classical Library 213 (Cambridge: Harvard University Press, 1928) 210 [3, §33]. Hans Kelsen, *General Theory of Law and State*, trans. Anders Wedberg (Cambridge: Harvard University Press, 1945) 268.

78 Suppose a sovereign at t_1 enacts a law that binds subjects to a duty, O(φ). Later, at t_2, the sovereign enacts another law – more specifically, a countermand – that rescinds the original law, effectively releasing subjects, so that they are now, ~O(φ). Austinian positivism denies that the latter is legislation because legislation, as commands, must bind. Any de-imperactive act that unbinds and releases another can't, therefore, really count as law.

79 Austin, *Province of Jurisprudence Determined* 32.

80 I discuss the theological significance of binding and unbinding, ultimately originating in the Gospel in Matthew 16:19 as a Scriptural source of Papal *plenitudo potestatis*, in Chapter 4.

from a specific duty, B may still be vulnerable or, in the archaic legal sense of the term, 'obnoxious' [cp. *obnoxium*: susceptible to injury or liability] to A's residual 'power-right' to alter again B's situation. A could always reintroduce an entirely new duty binding B.

Sovereigns too have this power to release through 'negative legislation' – whether by abrogating entirely, or otherwise partially derogating from, the obligatory force of an existing law. The immediate effect of such sovereign action would be the expansion of subjects' rights and, correspondingly, the diminution of subjects' duties. Again, Austin can't see such sovereign action as anything but the negation of a prior legislative command. Not so, however, for Hohfeld and, I'd argue, Bodin: the sovereigns' ability to create a new juridical situation for all subjects, whether through binding or releasing, reveals the sovereign's higher-order power.

Because the effect of this higher-order legislative power was to release [*absolvere*] subjects and, thus, change their relational position with respect to the sovereign, he not only called it a power, but specifically called it (or so I shall argue in Chapter 4), *puissance absolue*, *potestas absolvendi*, 'absolute power'. It was the sovereign's power to release a subject from obligation, not unlike the priestly power to absolve and release from the bond of sin. This 'absolute power' was the *sine qua non* of sovereignty. So important was absolute power that Bodin placed it in what is probably the most famous sentence in the entire *République*, his definition of sovereignty: *Souveraineté est la puissance absolue & perpetuelle d'une Republique*.[81]

Much has been written about the legacy of 'absolute power' in modern political theory. Lord Acton once famously quipped that absolute power corrupts absolutely. According to one standard interpretation, Bodin's invocation of 'absolute power' in his treatment of sovereignty should serve as sufficient evidence for us to conclude that his was a theory aligned ideologically with royal 'absolutism' (a term invented by liberal historians in the post-French Revolutionary period).[82] Most likely, Bodin acquired this reputation through the work of his most ardent early modern readers – Michel de la Serre, James VI and I, Pierre Grégoire, William Barclay, Alberico Gentili, Hugo Grotius, Peter Heylyn, Robert Filmer, Thomas Hobbes, and Jacques-Bénigne Bossuet – whose genuine absolutist commitments led them creatively to repurpose Bodin's theoretical writings for royalist polemical purposes and *not* for what Bodin had actually intended, a juridical *science du droit*.[83]

81 *République* 122 [1.8].

82 The most important defender of this absolutist interpretation of Bodin is Julian Franklin.

83 On Bodin's influence on early modern absolutists, see J.H.M. Salmon, *The French Religious Wars in English Political Thought* (Oxford: Clarendon Press, 1959); Johann Sommerville, 'English and European Political Ideas in the Early Seventeenth Century: Revisionism and the Case of Absolutism', *Journal of British Studies* 35 (1996): 168–94; J.H.M. Salmon, 'The Legacy of Jean Bodin: Absolutism, Populism or Constitutionalism?' *History of Political Thought* 17 (1996): 500–22; Glenn Burgess, *Absolute Monarchy and the Stuart Constitution* (New Haven: Yale University Press, 1996); Howell Lloyd, ed., *The Reception of Bodin* (Leiden: Brill, 2013); Ioannis Evrigenis, 'Sovereignty, Mercy, and Natural Law: King James VI/I and Jean Bodin', *History of European Ideas* 45 (2019): 1073–88.

Filmer, the royalist English author of *Patriarcha*, is a typical example of this absolutist interpretation of Bodin. Bodin is Filmer's most important modern authority cited in his exposition of the 'absolute power' of kings.[84] It is, on Filmer's view, total, unlimited, unaccountable power, belonging to one king. And indeed, this same language was later adopted by Filmer's fiercest critic, John Locke, who identified as unlawful the 'absolute, arbitrary, unlimited, and unlimitable power' of kings.[85]

This may be the legacy of absolute power. But it is a profound mischaracterization of the purpose of 'absolute power' in Bodin's theory. We know this, first of all, because Bodin himself tried to disavow such absolutism in his earliest critical responses to the first readers of the *République*.[86] He even seems to have anticipated this potentially absolutist interpretation of absolute power, by preemptively refuting the Decretalist theory crafted by canonists that the popes enjoy an unlimited and absolute power [*potentia absoluta*] – what medieval canonists referred to as the *plenitudo potestatis*: the canonists were, apparently, the real absolutists. As Bodin put it, absolute power was never meant to be interpreted as a complete and unconditional release from all laws, licensing complete lawlessness.[87] Absolute power isn't absolutist.

Yet, despite Bodin's own disavowal, the absolutist interpretation remains unchallenged as the standard view. There is a strange inconsistency about it. Few, if any, would regard Blackstone, the English defender of common law and liberty, an 'absolutist' despite his liberal use of the term, 'absolute power', in his *Commentaries*. Yet, he, unlike Bodin, has escaped (thanks largely to the work of 'Whig historians') the curse and stigma of being labelled an 'absolutist' on the wrong side of history.

What, then, was absolute power? A short passage in what remains probably the most-read chapter in Bodin's *République*, 'De la souveraineté', tries to answer this question: 'It is nothing but the power of overriding ordinary law [*deroger au droit ordinaire*; *ordinario iuri* [Bodin glosses this as *patriis legibus*] *derogare potest*]'.[88]

[84] Constance Smith, 'Filmer, and the Knolles Translation of Bodin', *Philosophical Quarterly* 13 (1963): 248–52.

[85] John Locke, *Two Treatises of Government*, ed. Peter Laslett (Cambridge: Cambridge University Press, 1988) 148 [I, §9].

[86] *République*, Epistola [sig. $B4_{vo}$]; [Jean Bodin], *Apologie de René Herpin pour La République de I. Bodin* (Paris: Jacques Du Puys, 1581) 4_{vo}, acknowledges that no obedience is due to tyrants.

[87] *République* 131; *De Republica* 84 [1.8].

[88] *République* 133; *De Republica* 86 [1.8]. Turchetti 470–3. Cp. *République* 156; *De Republica* 102 [1.8], writing against the canonistic doctrine that private property can be legally seized by the Pope, contrary to natural law, by invoking *absoluta potestas*, Bodin characterizes the illegality of the Decretalist opinion, treating it instead as seizure 'by force and by arms' [*par force, par armes*; *vi & armis*]. In the French, he describes the canonist view as *le droit du plus fort*, a phrase that will appear in Rousseau, *Social Contract* as the chapter heading of I, 3. Here, the French *République* specifies again that 'absolute power is nothing other than the power of derogating civil laws' [*le puissance absolue n'est autre chose que derogation aux loix civiles*]. Cp. *De Republica* 290 [3.4], where Bodin contrasts Innocent IV's view, in his *Commentaria in Decretalium* (on X.1.29.31), with the view of other jurists (Bodin singles out Baldus on X.1.3.17, and Accursius *Gloss. Ord.* and Cino da Pistoia [Cynus], *Lectura Super Codice* on C.1.22.6; D.1.4.1; X.1.2.7) that a 'sovereign prince can derogate from the law of nature' [*principem iuri naturae*

The term, 'absolute power', is itself distracting and even misleading conjuring up images of royal excess and lawlessness. But the concept behind the term is actually a fairly simple idea about what Bodin believes is necessary for any legal system to be independent and self-contained – in other words, 'sovereign'.[89]

Suppose a legal system is the sum-total of all first-order rules and commands requiring subjects to φ. Absolute power, then, is just the capacity to issue second-order commands – or, as I've suggested earlier, Hohfeldian 'powers' – altering those first-order commands (so that they take the form of nested commands). Its function is, in the original sense of the word, 'derogatory', in that they 'derogate' from the full force of the law. It empowers the sovereign to dismantle existing first-order commands, whether in part or whole, so as to chip away and nullify the obligatory force of law itself. Through the exercise of absolute power, then, sovereigns can lessen and impair the force and validity of an otherwise binding statute, and this can happen through the grant of privileges or pardons. Through that same absolute power sovereigns can also amend, and even repeal, legislation outright – as it is every sovereign's right so to do. In theory, a sovereign could even exercise absolute power to release a subject entirely from *all* positive legal obligations so that they may be, as Pompey and Augustus were said to be, *legibus omnibus in perpetuo solutus sit*.[90]

Probably the most important and counterintuitive point of all to emphasize is that absolute power was a legally *limited* power – limited specifically in its scope of applicability. Bodin specified that the absolute power of releasing subjects from legal duties applied only to duties arising from positive legislation, its *ius civile*. Asserting absolute power, sovereigns may unbind and release subjects from any and, potentially, even all positive legal duties. What sovereigns can never touch with their absolute power were the sacred and immutable juridical norms of the *ius divinum*, the *ius naturale*, and the *ius gentium*.[91] Even sovereigns, Bodin reminded

derogare posse]. Cp. X.3.8.4 of Innocent III which invokes the power of dispensation as part of the Papal plenitude of power.

89 Hans Kelsen, *General Theory of Norms*, trans. Michael Hartney (Oxford: Clarendon Press, 1991) 106–14.

90 *République* 131; *De Republica* 84–5 [1.8]. What Pompey (by the *lex Gabinia*) and Augustus (by the *lex de imperio*) enjoyed was *not* sovereignty, but rather, Hohfeldian privileges: they were released from all legal duties [*legibus omnibus soluti*], to which all other Romans remained bound. But though they enjoyed Hohfeldian privilege-rights, Pompey and Augustus did not have the other incidents that made up the full 'molecular' right of sovereignty: claim-rights and power-rights. That is, in a modern Hohfeldian analysis, the reason why Bodin thinks Pompey and Augustus can be said to be *legibus soluti* and yet not be sovereign. See *Popular Sovereignty* Ch. 1 on the historiography of the *lex de imperio Vespasiani* on Bodin's understanding of Roman constitutional history.

91 Bodin renders these legal categories as *lex divina*, *lex naturalis*, and *lex gentium*, to stress that even these categories of law are, in theory, positive legislation [*lex*: *iussum summae potestatis*] – just not *human* positive legislation, traceable to the command of any *human* legislator. Bodin's late writings on natural philosophy and theology develop this theme further.

his readers, were human, and, as humans, sovereigns too were bound by these higher laws and 'cannot exempt themselves by invoking absolute power'.[92]

Consider Bodin's analysis of contractual duties as an illustration of this last point (Chapter 2). As a general principle, all obligors are bound and required to perform their valid contractual duties, *not* because performance is a statutory legal duty required by a sovereign's positive legislation. Obligors are bound, instead, because performance is a natural legal duty permanently required by the *ius naturale* and the *ius gentium* of all humanity, including sovereigns. Indeed, even God, Bodin pointed out (citing Peter of Lombard) is bound by his contracts and promises. Sovereigns, even though they are *legibus soluti*, thus, cannot lawfully release [*solvere*] themselves, by an exercise of absolute power, from contractual obligations without having first secured the consent of other contractually bound parties, whether those parties may be a sovereign's own subjects, foreigners, or even another sovereign.[93]

What, then, was the point of absolute power? Why was it necessary for sovereigns to have not only the power to bind subjects through law, but also the power to release – or, in other words, to 'absolve'– subjects *from* law?

The answer, in short, is that the law itself was an imperfect device with which sovereigns can rule subjects. And like any device which is the product of human artifice, laws needed constant 'maintenance' performed by its sovereign engineer.

This is an old theme in the history of jurisprudence. In order for it to be effective as a tool for governing, the law itself must be susceptible to change and reform over time. Some non-trivial degree of elasticity or flexibility in the law will always be necessary, as a corrective remedy to the unforeseen, though inescapable shortcomings intrinsic to any legal system.[94] This would be true even for laws enacted with the best of legislative intentions and authored by the best of legislators – a Moses, a Lycurgus, a Solon, a Justinian. Laws which may make perfect sense today may turn out for future generations to be 'excessively obscure' [*nimis obscuré*] in meaning, or may simply be 'unfair' [*iniqua*] in its application to future contexts.[95]

Some of these observations are the result of Bodin's expertise in comparative legal history. Laws and customs which may once have performed a genuinely valuable social purpose in some bygone age become ossified artefacts. Having lost their utility, they instead become fetters. This is the situation, Bodin thinks,

[92] *De Republica* 100 [1.8].

[93] *De Republica* 87 [1.8], citing C.1.14.5, D.50.16.19, 2.14.58, 50.17.35. On contract in canon law, see Wim Decock, *Theologians and Contract Law: The Moral Transformation of the Ius Commune, c.1500–1650* (Leiden: Brill-Nijhoff, 2012). The specific Decretalist debates on contract and absolute power has been discussed in Pennington, *Prince and the Law* 155.

[94] What that degree should be, however, is open to debate: 'The magistrate [or judge] can bend the law and its interpretation, either to soften or to toughen it, provided that in bending it he takes good care not to break it'. Franklin 58; *République* 223; *De Republica* 155 [1.10], citing D.37.5.6, 48.19.11, 40.9.12, 48.18.1, 48.16.1, D.42.1.32, 1.1.7, D.37.1.1

[95] *Distributio* fol. F, s.v.: *Iudicis Officium*.

early modern states like France find themselves, weighed down by the burden of inherited and potentially harmful legal enactments, especially particularistic privileges, from which they cannot easily free themselves.[96]

It is the greatest mistake, however, to think that sovereigns can't do anything about it. If laws *can't* be changed at all, it means that the sovereigns aren't really sovereign at all. Instead of being masters of the law, sovereigns would instead be enslaved by their own laws. Observe the thrust of Bodin's objection. He's *not* saying that a sovereign confronted with an irrevocable law actually has lost the right of sovereignty. Instead, what he's saying is that a sovereign who resignedly confesses that there's nothing to be done about an allegedly irrevocable law fundamentally misunderstands the nature of sovereignty which, in essence, is about engineering laws by making, remaking, or even unmaking them.

This is why, for Bodin, tools used to 'entrench' positive legislation (for example, by attaching stipulations such as supermajority requirements immunizing legislation from amendment or repeal) can have no effect.[97] They try, unsuccessfully through law, to bind the sovereign's own lawmaking hands. But, as Bodin famously will declare, sovereigns cannot bind themselves with their own legislation, for the same reason that one cannot make a promise with oneself or owe a debt to oneself.[98]

It's not just for the sake of utility that sovereigns have the absolute power to change the law. The more important reason is justice – and specifically what Bodin calls 'harmonic justice'.[99] Laws are supposed to be instruments of justice. But left untouched, they can, over time, become sources of profound injustice, disrupting the natural harmony that a just social and political order requires. It is, thus, the duty of sovereigns – and, in practice, the equitable 'duty of judges' [*officium iudicis*] acting on the authority of their sovereign – to review and, if necessary, remould the law so that it better approximates what justice requires, to give to everyone what they are rightfully owed, their due [*ius suum*].

[96] Bodin defines 'privilege' in the same way that it is understood in the civil law and Cicero, *De Legibus* 3.44, as an exceptional *ius singulare*, creating an exemption from an otherwise binding legal duty (or conversely, a Hohfeldian liberty). *Distributio* fol. A, s.v.: *Lex*: *Singularis*: *Beneficium praeter legem*; *Privilegium contra legem*. *De Republica* 150 and 153 [1.10]: *Privilegium appello legem in unum aut paucos cives latam.*

[97] On Bodin's denial of perpetual or irrevocable legislation, see *République* 148, *De Republica* 96 [1.8], and my 'Unmaking Law: Jean Bodin on Law, Equity and Legal Change', *History of Political Thought* 39 (2018): 269–72.

[98] This is the 'maxim of civil law' referenced by Rousseau in *Social Contract* I, 7: D.45.1.108.1; cp. Diego Quaglioni, 'Les citoyens envers l'État: The Individual as a Citizen from Bodin's *République* to Rousseau's *Contract Social*', in *The Individual in Political Theory and Practice*, ed. Janet Coleman (Oxford: Clarendon Press, 1996); Edelstein, 'Rousseau, Bodin, and the Medieval Corporatist Origins': 5–6 suggests also D.4.8.51.

[99] *République* 1020 [6.6]: *La iustice harmonique* is based on harmonic proportions, rather than arithmetic or geometric proportions. Cp. the criticism of the mathematician, Johannes Kepler, on Bodin's theory of harmonic justice in his 'Political Treatise', included in *The Harmony of the World*, trans. E.J. Aiton, A.M. Duncan, J.V. Field (Philadelphia: American Philosophical Society, 1997).

Preview of the Argument IV: The Sovereign State

It is worth remembering in previewing all this that the main subject of Bodin's grand treatise on law and politics wasn't actually sovereignty, but rather, the state [*république*; *respublica*].[100] Bodin's *Six Livres de la République* was perhaps the first modern example of what German jurists would later call an *allgemeine Staatslehre* – a 'general theory of the state'. In this respect, modern German-speaking jurists who specialized in public law – Georg Jellinek, Johann Bluntschli, Hermann Heller, Carl Schmitt, and Hans Kelsen – rightly saw Bodin as a pioneer in this field.

Bodin's stated goal in the *République* was to define and identify the principal elements of statehood, the subject of Chapter 1 in this book. Sovereignty, as the opening text of the *République* intimates, was only one of those elements: The state was imagined to be a pluralistic association of associations, bound together under one common sovereign authority.[101] It's noteworthy that Bodin explicitly envisioned the state, *not* in territorial terms, but in associational and juridical terms.[102] Political science has adopted the Westphalian habit of imagining the sovereign state strictly in territorial terms, such that sovereignty is nothing but a sort of proprietary *in rem* claim over land.[103] But for Bodin, territory, while important for a state's well-being, was inessential to statehood. What a state shared in common *wasn't* shared territory, but shared obligation.[104] All subjects who made up a state were obligors duty-bound to one common obligee entitled to their service – their obedience. And, on Bodin's analysis, they remained obligors (that is, subjects)

[100] Nor was sovereignty the core of the *Distributio*, which purported to give a Ramist analysis of *ius* – 'law'. He mentions sovereignty only twice at fol. E, s.v.: *Legis actio*: *Forensis*: *Imperiosa*: *Imperium* and fol. F, s.v.: *Ex adiunctis iurisdictio*.

[101] *Methodus* 237 ('137'); *République* 1, 12–13; *De Republica* 1, 9–10 [1.1; 1.2].

[102] Lauren Benton, *A Search for Sovereignty: Law and Geography in European Empires, 1400–1900* (Cambridge: Cambridge University Press, 2009) 287–88. An alternative view, however, is found in Sara Miglietti, 'Sovereignty, Territory, and Population in Jean Bodin's *République*', *French Studies: A Quarterly Review* 72 (2018): 18.

[103] One recent example is Anna Stilz, *Territorial Sovereignty: A Philosophical Exploration* (Oxford: Oxford University Press, 2019).

[104] I've suggested elsewhere that it is instead 'shared subjection'. Daniel Lee, 'Citizenship, Subjection, and the Civil Law: Jean Bodin on Roman Citizenship and the Theory of Consensual Subjection', in *Citizenship and Empire in Europe, 200–1900: The Antonine Constitution after 1800 Years*, ed. Clifford Ando (Stuttgart: Franz Steiner Verlag, 2016).

I'm not suggesting that territory was unimportant to Bodin's political thought. He comments at length and was concerned about territorial integrity for good government. My claim is simply that territory was not an essential feature of Bodin's state, which was a type of association, not a type of land. For this reason, Bodin is able to sidestep the so-called 'particularity problem' in the normative theoretical literature on territory, such as A. John Simmons, 'On the Territorial Rights of States', *Philosophical Issues* 11 (2001): 303–14; Anna Stilz, 'Why Do States Have Territorial Rights?' *International Theory* 1 (2009): 187–88; Lea Ypi, 'A Permissive Theory of Territorial Rights', *European Journal of Philosophy* 22 (2014): 288–312. On territoriality in Bodin's thought, see Miglietti, 'Sovereignty, Territory, and Population'.

wherever they happened to be geographically located, so long as that obligation remained valid and active.[105]

Of course, humans can join together and associate in all sorts of different ways – families [οἶκοι], for example.[106] But families aren't states. Indeed, this was the very first point in Aristotle's *Politics*.[107] And Bodin largely followed the customary Aristotelian analysis isolating the exceptional character of the state as a *societas civilis*.[108] But, whereas Aristotle found the distinctive quality of the state in the equality of status among its members and the state's ethical purposes, Bodin's analysis instead focused singly on the question of authority, something that, Bodin thought, Aristotle utterly failed to do.[109]

To wit: what made the state distinctive was the 'sovereign' authority it rightfully and independently asserted over its members. Families are, in Bodin's mind, also ruled and held together by authority, but it is authority of a fundamentally different kind – domestic or paterfamilial authority.

Only sovereign [*summum*] authority – its form, whether monarchical, aristocratic, or democratic, was irrelevant – was exclusive to states: Without it, there can be no state. This is why complex pluralistic associations that, from afar, may have the superficial appearance and quality of statehood don't deserve the title of statehood. Nor, for that same reason, do they deserve the sovereign *rights* and appurtenances of statehood, such as the right of war or the right of embassy. Only sovereign states, and no other entities, are entitled to wage war and conclude peace. What this means is that even quasi-state entities or state-like entities that may have the appearance of statehood (think of minor principalities, city republics, leagues and federations, colonies, or the Church) nevertheless lack the sovereign right to engage in war or diplomacy. For such entities to use force would be no different, in Bodin's mind, from the lawless violence of the pirate or the brigand.

Lacking sovereignty, they lack absolute power. In practice, what that means is that non-state entities, while certainly they may exercise whatever limited and defined powers may have been lawfully conceded to them, they lack what only genuine states have: the creative power to reconstitute and refashion a realm and

[105] As we'll see in Chapter 3, Bodin clarifies this point in *République/De Republica* 1.6 on citizenship. In discussing a number of high-profile cases that made its way on appeal to the Parlement of Paris, Bodin clarified that the political obligation of an expatriate subject doesn't expire simply by passage of time. Exit, for Bodin as well as for many early modern jurists and theorists who commented on the topic of exile, wasn't simply geographical, but also juridical.

[106] Anna Becker, *Gendering the Renaissance Commonwealth* (Cambridge: Cambridge University Press, 2020), Chapter 3 focuses specifically on the family in Bodin's thought.

[107] Aristotle, *Politics* 1.1, 1252[a].

[108] *De Republica* 328 [3.7].

[109] Bodin recognizes that states should aim for the 'good life'. But even states that fail to achieve that noble goal are nevertheless still states. Ethical considerations are inessential to Bodin's political science as they were for Aristotle. It is also worth remembering that, despite Bodin's criticism of Aristotle, Aristotle did develop at least the outline of a theory of authority in *Politics* 3.6. Bodin at *République* 212–13; *De Republica* 148; Turchetti 677 [1.10] instead, looked to *Politics* 4.13 (1298[a]).

its destiny ultimately under *their* (and not someone else's) control.[110] This political ideal has been called various things in history – political liberty, independence, national self-determination, decolonization. Bodin called it sovereignty. But it is the state – the whole association of subjects and lesser associations that make up the state – that is the ultimate beneficiary and owner of that sovereignty. And since the site of Bodinian sovereignty is the state, or *respublica*, I will begin this book with a study of Bodin's theory of statehood in order to situate the function that sovereignty performed in his larger body of thought.

The Scope of This Study

Bodin provides the point of entry into this study of sovereignty. But in some ways, this is not really a book about Bodin. And so, I think it is appropriate in closing this Introduction to say some words not only what this book is about, but also what this book *isn't* about.

In this respect, the first thing to say is that this is not intended to be an intellectual history of Bodin and the early modern French context. There are already many excellent historical studies that do just this, and I make use of this literature where it is appropriate for my own aims.[111] I'd go even further and say that there are perhaps too many studies that approach Bodin strictly as an object of intellectual history, rather than as a source for legal and political theory.[112]

There's nothing wrong, of course, with treating Bodin as an object of historical scholarship. But it becomes problematic when it generates the artificial expectation that this can be the *only* way to study a figure like Bodin. The consequence of such an attitude is that historical scholarship privileges the narrowly reductive view that Bodin can *only* be properly understood as a product of his time – and in particular, the French Wars of Religion. It is a balkanizing view of scholarship I reject.

At the same time, I should clarify that this book isn't intended to be an unreserved defence of Bodin's theory of sovereignty against modern sovereignty-sceptics. While I have done my best to reconstruct the substance of the theory as accurately as I can for a modern academic readership, I have no personal interest in defending Bodin's theory where it is, in my considered judgment, indefensible on the merits. Where appropriate, I will state my objections.

[110] Bodin sometimes discusses this point in connection with colonial or provincial administration of Roman provinces. Provincial governors [*praesides provinciarum*] lawfully hold *imperium* and *iurisdictio* over their assigned provinces during their time in office. Provinces were largely autonomous and seem even to be sovereign states. But so long as they remained deferential to Roman 'greater-ness' [literally, *maiestas*], provinces were subordinate dependent entities, lacking the sovereign right to wage war.

[111] Lloyd, *Jean Bodin*; Marie-Dominique Couzinet, *Histoire et Methode a la Renaissance* (Paris: J. Vrin, 1996); Blair, *Theater of Nature*.

[112] This may in part be due to the desire to keep a respectable critical distance from Bodin's allegedly 'absolutist' views.

Setting the indefensible aside, however, I believe there is enormous intellectual value in studying Bodin's theory. One cannot help but admire what Paul Lawrence Rose once called the 'total vision' emerging from Bodin's system of thought, encompassing not only law and politics, but also his theology and natural philosophy.[113] It projects a vision of sovereign statehood that is, in fundamental ways, recognizably familiar. Bodin's own analysis and defence of sovereignty, then, can function as an instrument to assist us in diagnosing and possibly reforming what Istvan Hont once characterized as the 'permanent crisis' of a humanity divided into sovereign nation-states.[114] It is my belief, however, that such a task requires an honest assessment of the merits, the purposes, and the workings of sovereignty. And we have no better source to guide us in making that assessment than Bodin.

[113] Paul Lawrence Rose, *Bodin and the Great God of Nature: The Moral and Religious Universe of a Judaiser* (Geneva: Librairie Droz, 1980) 2.

[114] István Hont, 'The Permanent Crisis of a Divided Mankind: Nation-State and Nationalism in Historical Perspective', in *Jealousy of Trade: International Competition and the Nation-State in Historical Perspective* (Cambridge: Harvard University Press, 2010).

1
The State

Jean Bodin is instantly recognized in political science, international relations, and jurisprudence as the canonical authority on the modern concept of sovereignty. Yet, he has become, as some commentators have observed, an authority more often cited than read.[1] As a result, some basic interpretive questions surrounding the origin of the modern concept of sovereignty remain unanswered.

This chapter explores one fundamental question: Why did Bodin even bother to study sovereignty in the first place? One common explanation points to Bodin's own experience of living through the most turbulent years of the French Wars of Religion during the period of the Reformation. As a witness to the religious violence threatening social order and, potentially, the dissolution of the French polity itself, Bodin was said to have arrived at his concept of sovereignty as the answer to what the American sociologist, Talcott Parsons, would describe, in the twentieth century, as the modern problem of social order. In this respect, it has become common, particularly in Anglophone scholarship, to treat Bodin as a French precursor to the English political philosopher, Thomas Hobbes, who crafted his own theory of sovereignty in the midst of the political violence of the seventeenth-century English Civil War, as the solution to the problem of declining order so memorably portrayed in his depiction of the anarchical state of nature, the war of all against all [*bellum omnium contra omnes*].

There's no question, of course, that the political crisis of religious disunity, which threatened the vision of France as one harmonious kingdom united by 'one faith, one law, one king' [*une foi, une loi, un roi*], was a central motivation for Bodin's political theory. Indeed, the Preface to his most important work of political theory, *Les Six Livres de la République*, states directly that he wrote the work in part to address the 'raging storm' [*l'orage impétueux*] of religious violence endangering the French 'ship of state' [*vaisseau de nostre république*].[2]

But it would be profoundly misleading to treat Bodin's chief work of legal and political theory as nothing more than a mere *livre de circonstance*, or to view Bodinian sovereignty as a political concept relevant only to the religious politics of Valois France. As Bodin put it throughout his writings, he wasn't concerned with particulars [*singulorum*] or the affairs of any one particular state, even his native

[1] J.H. Burns, 'Sovereignty and Constitutional Law in Bodin', *Political Studies* 7 (1959): 174; Giesey, 'Medieval Jurisprudence' 167.

[2] Preface to the *République* sig. $a2_{vo}$; cp. Preface to the Latin *De Republica* sig. $a2_{vo}$.

The Right of Sovereignty. Daniel Lee, Oxford University Press. © Daniel Lee 2021.
DOI: 10.1093/oso/9780198755531.003.0002

France. He was only concerned with universals [*universorum*], the affairs common to all states.[3] And sovereignty was, in Bodin's system of thought, something universal to be found in all states, ancient and modern, not just in France. Sovereignty was the definitive quality of statehood; without it, no assemblage of persons can properly be called a 'state' – or, as he termed it, a *respublica*.

Bodin's principal motivation for studying sovereignty was, thus, academic, not chiefly political. In fact, it was related to an intellectual problem that had already preoccupied Bodin years before the traumatic events of St. Bartholomew in 1572. By training, Bodin was a lawyer, and he identified himself as a practitioner of the legal science. This legal science was, by convention, the science of Roman law, which, as Bodin put it, was merely 'the civil law of only one specific state' [*ius civilis singularis cuiusdam civitatis*].[4] What Bodin wanted was much more ambitious, a grand system of general jurisprudence universal to all states. He strove to undercover a *ius gentium* – a body of law common to all peoples, and not just of Rome or France. Given the grand scope of such a system of law for the whole of human society, it would, in his view, be *absurdum* 'to establish from Roman law the whole universal law' of humanity [*ex Romanis legibus … de universo iure statuere*].[5]

Bodin's distaste for this Roman law fetish turned him instead to sources beyond Rome – the Persians, the Greeks, the Egyptians, the Hebrews, and the Turks, among others – but with a specific purpose in mind. He wished to gather 'the laws of all states, or those of the most famous states' so that 'the wise may compare them … and forge the best type of state from among them [*optimum genus ex iis conflarent*]'.[6] History, not the staid science of Roman law, was to be the raw material for a general jurisprudence, and, for this reason, comparative historiography became essential to Bodin's general jurisprudence. As he put it, 'the best part of universal law [*ius universum*] was to be found in history'.[7] And that required, above all, studiously collecting and comparing the histories and legal customs of diverse states, recording their 'beginnings, growth, constitutional forms, revolutions, and downfalls' [*rerumpublicarum initia, incrementa, status, conversiones, exitus*].[8]

Though the principal unit of analysis in this effort was the state, it wasn't clear what counted as a state, as a point of historiography. So few classical sources, Bodin lamented, addressed this central theoretical problem to his satisfaction. The few that did try – most notably, Aristotle, Polybius, and Dionysius of Halicarnassus – failed, in his view, precisely because they neglected, so Bodin asserted, to treat the notion of sovereignty properly.[9] Bodin, thus, took up the challenge of supplying a

[3] *Methodus* sig. ∴3_{ro}.
[4] *Methodus* sig. ∴3_{ro}.
[5] *Methodus* sig. ∴3_{ro}. The *ius universum* mentioned here (and at the bottom of the same page: *iuris universi formam … in tabula*) is the subject of the *Distributio*, completed just before Bodin turned his attention to the *Methodus*.
[6] *Methodus* sig. ∴3_{vo}.
[7] *Methodus* [sig. $b3_{ro}$].
[8] *Methodus* 16.
[9] *République* 212–13; *De Republica* 148 [1.10].

theory of state that could apply across historical periods and guide the larger project of culling a general jurisprudence from the accumulated and distilled historical experiences of particular states in human history. And he did this for the first time in the *Methodus*.

But the concept of the state would become the principal object of investigation in the *République*, which would give Bodin the opportunity to craft his own general theory of state as an intellectual challenge in its own right, and not simply as a problem of historiography. And it was in the context of articulating this *Staatslehre* that Bodin saw the need for his comprehensive doctrine of sovereignty.

The aim of this chapter is to present an outline of the main elements of Bodin's theory of state, in order to place into context the unifying function of sovereignty. The chapter will open with a note on Bodin's choice of vocabulary in articulating his concept of state – the French *république* and its Latin equivalent, *respublica*. In Bodin's usage, *république* (and *respublica* in Latin) designated the state in its most generic sense, of all constitutional forms, including even monarchies. As we'll then see in the next section, this helped Bodin to distinguish genuine states from non-state entities that lacked some of the essential qualities of statehood. The chapter will then proceed to investigate those constituent elements of states, such as the family (what he called the *societas naturalis*) and collegial and corporate bodies (what he called *societas civilis*). Bodin's vision of the state emerges as a pluralistic, compound association made up of natural and civil associations. What holds this association together, however, is the obligatory bond of sovereignty. Indeed, sovereignty is what really distinguishes state from loose associations and alliances based on relations of friendship and mutual courtesy.

The Language of Statehood: The *Respublica*

Bodin defines the state in the very first sentence of his treatise devoted to that concept.[10] He writes:

> A state is a lawful government of many households and of that which is common to them, joined together with a sovereign power.[11]
> A state is a multitude of families and their common affairs governed by a sovereign power and reason.[12]

[10] Following a convention established by Margherita Isnardi Parente in translating *république* and *respublica* into the Italian *lo stato*, I translate this central term into English as 'state', especially to avoid the anti-royalist 'republican' connotations associated with *respublica*. Cp. Lloyd, *Jean Bodin* 111 supplies evidence suggesting that this was likely the translation that Bodin himself would have favoured.

[11] *République* 1 [1.1]: *République est un droit gouvernement de plusieurs mesnages, & de ce qui cur est commun, avec puissance souveraine.*

[12] *De Republica* 1 [1.1]: *Respublica est familiarum rerumque inter ipsas communium summa potestate ac ratione moderata multitudo.*

Perhaps the first – and in some ways, the most important – point to stress is Bodin's *vocabulary* of statehood.[13] Bodin, writing first in French and then later in Latin, chose to denominate this core concept of state by the terms *république* and *respublica*, terms which, in the sixteenth century, began to display all the classic signs of semantic instability and change.[14]

As Bodin very well knew, the Latin word, *respublica*, (along with its vernacular European cognates, such as the French *république* and the Italian *repubblica*) enjoyed a privileged place in Western political discourse, ever since Cicero supplied (and Machiavelli revived) the gold standard of republican political analysis. In his treatise expressly devoted to that topic, *De Re Publica*, Cicero defined the *respublica* as:

> The property of a people. But a people is not any collection of human beings brought together in any sort of way, but an assemblage of people in large numbers associated in an agreement with respect to justice and a partnership for the common good.[15]

In the sixteenth century, *respublica* functioned as (what political theorists often describe as) an 'essentially contested' term, and the contestation reflected the stark ideological cleavages driving conflicts emerging from Reformation politics.[16] For some, the term signalled exclusively a very specific form of constitution, exemplified above all by the classical example of the Roman Republic. On this view, what distinguished a republic – such as the Roman one – from all other states was, not so much its admixture of power, as Polybius and Cicero once maintained, nor the populist orientation of its politics, as some commentators attribute to Machiavelli's revival of Roman republican politics.[17] Rather, the key feature was its *kingless* constitution (hence, the typical contrast drawn in the republican literature between

[13] The focus on Bodin's peculiar use of language has become a theme in a range of recent studies by Stéphane Beaulac, 'The Social Power of Bodin's "Sovereignty" and International Law', *Melbourne Journal of International Law* 4 (2003): 1–28; Stéphane Beaulac, *The Power of Language in the Making of International Law: The Word Sovereignty in Bodin and Vattel and the Myth of Westphalia* (Leiden: Martinus Nijhoff, 2004); Daniel Lee, 'Sources of Sovereignty: Roman *Imperium* and *Dominium* in Civilian Theories of Sovereignty', *Politica Antica* 2 (2012): 79–94; Oisín Keohane, 'Bodin on Sovereignty: Taking Exception to Translation?' *Paragraph* 38 (2015): 245–60.

[14] The semantic instability of the term, *respublica*, has been documented in James Hankins, 'Exclusivist Republicanism and the Non-Monarchical Republic', *Political Theory* 38 (2010): 452–82.

[15] Cicero, *De Re Publica* 1.39: *Res populi, populus autem non omnis hominum coetus quoquo modo congregatus, sed coetus multitudinis iuris consensu et utilitatis communione sociatus.* The text was rediscovered in a nineteenth century palimpsest. In Bodin's age, it was known only indirectly through other sources that used Cicero – chiefly, Augustine and Lactantius. Cicero applied the term, *respublica*, to translate into Latin the Greek titles of the major works of political theory by Plato and Aristotle, on the *Politeia*.

[16] The classic article introducing the term was W.B. Gallie, 'Essentially Contested Concepts', *Proceedings of the Aristotelian Society* 56 (1956): 167–98. However, the contestation over *respublica* was not exclusively ideological, but more likely academic.

[17] John McCormick, *Machiavellian Democracy* (Cambridge: Cambridge University Press, 2011).

monarchies and republics). Lorenzo Valla summed up the republican doctrine when he declared, 'Wherever there is a king, there is no *respublica*' [*Ubi rex est, ibi res publica non est*].[18]

All republics, on this view, shared that one point in common. They, by definition, necessarily *excluded* kingly rule, in the belief that all monarchs were really 'masters' [δεσπότης; *domini*; *seigneurs*] whose arbitrary will deprived their people of liberty, by reducing subjects to a servile condition of slavery.[19] Since kingless republics exclude the source of slavery, it was thought that only republics could be genuinely free states. It was, therefore, a contradiction in terms to imagine a *respublica* ruled by a prince.

What must be stressed is that this doctrine of 'exclusivist republicanism' (as James Hankins has called it), insisting that republics may not be ruled by monarchs, was an early modern innovation and interpolation in the political theory of the *respublica*.[20] To illustrate by comparison, one only needs to look at the *Glossa Ordinaria* on Roman law, one of the central sources for medieval European legal science, to see that the medieval glossator of Roman law, Accursius, does precisely what the exclusivist republican theory disallows – he pairs the *respublica* together with the rule of a *princeps*. In one famous gloss on Justinian's *Code* (at C.2.54(53).4), he calls the *princeps* the *tutor reipublicae*, or 'legal guardian of the state in minority'.[21] The same princely *respublica* emerges in Leonardo Bruni's humanist translation of Aristotle's *Politics*, where 'kingly rule' [*regia potestas*] is identified as one type of *recta respublica*.[22] The sudden pace of semantic change in the meaning of *respublica* in the sixteenth and seventeenth centuries led the English republican, Algernon Sidney, writing in 1683, to observe how quickly the term, once non-ideological, became exclusively an anti-royalist term of art: 'If a Commonwealth signifies the common good … and which Bodin puts upon it when he … calls

[18] Lorenzo Valla, *On the Donation of Constantine*, I Tatti Renaissance Library, trans. G.W. Bowersock (Cambridge: Harvard University Press, 2008) 43 [§50] .

[19] This idea was the inspiration for the revival of classical republican political theory in the so-called 'neo-Roman' scholarship championed by Philip Pettit, *Republicanism: A Theory of Freedom and Government* (Oxford: Oxford University Press, 1997) and Quentin Skinner, *Liberty Before Liberalism* (Cambridge: Cambridge University Press, 1998).

[20] Hankins indicates that this 'exclusivist' view was popularized by Machiavelli, among authors in the Italian Renaissance, who distinguished between those states governed by 'a plurality of persons' as in a democracy or oligarchy and those states governed by *uno solo*. Hankins, 'Exclusivist Republicanism' 453.

[21] The gloss on C.2.54(53).4 is regarded as the cornerstone for what Walter Ullmann has called the 'minority thesis' – the civilian legal doctrine that the *princeps* is in the status of a legal guardian, or *tutor*, over the *respublica* which legally is comparable to an underage minor who, though a rightsholder, is incapable of exercising those rights. On the minority thesis, see Walter Ullmann, 'Juristic Obstacles to the Emergence of the Concept of the State in the Middle Ages', *Annali di Storia del Diritto* 12/13 (Milan: Guiffré, 1968/69): 43–65; William Freegard, *Roman Law and Resistance Right: A Study of Question Three of the Vindiciae Contra Tyrannos*, Ph.D. Dissertation (Iowa City: University of Iowa, 1971) 77–113; Joseph Canning, *The Political Thought of Baldus de Ubaldis* (Cambridge: Cambridge University Press, 1987) 193–95.

[22] Hankins, 'Exclusivist Republicanism' 465.

[France] a republic, no good man will be ashamed of it... It is strange how the word should so change its signification with us in the space of twenty years'.[23]

Needless to say, Bodin, who openly celebrated the comparative advantages of monarchy, was no republican, even though he claimed to offer a political theory of the *république*. He implicitly disavowed the exclusivist doctrine of republicanism, and we can see this plainly in his indifferent treatment of both democracies and monarchies as types of *république/respublica*. What seems reasonably clear is that, in Bodin's usage, the term, *république/respublica*, didn't signify a particular *type* of state – such as a 'free state' or 'popular state' or 'kingless state', as it did for, say, Cicero or Machiavelli. Instead, it was intended to designate the state, genericially *as such* – whatever its particular constitutional form or the quality of its politics. Bodin's *respublica* was equivalent, then, to what political theorists of later generations would designate instead by the term, *civitas*, as Grotius, Hobbes, and Pufendorf did.[24]

Bodin's *respublica* marked a theoretical concept of statehood in the most generic sense possible, a juridical and political category inclusive of all possible 'forms of state' (a phrase that Bodin rendered in Ciceronian Latin as *status reipublicae*), whether princely or popular, small or large, wealthy or impoverished, homogeneous or heterogeneous. Structured in this way, Bodinian statehood encompassed the smallest city-republics such as Ragusa and Geneva, as well as vast empires such as the Tartar empire, whose borders were 'defined by the course of the sun' [*solis cursus definiuntur*].[25] By broadening the scope of applicability in this way, Bodin even allowed his native France, ruled by its 'most Christian king', to be regarded as a type of *respublica* – a non-republican *république*.

Bodin's first priority, then, was to sanitize and depoliticize the language of statehood, even before there could be a theory of statehood. He wanted no part of the then-extant political debates on what constituted the *vera respublica* or the *optimus reipublicae status*. Instead, what he needed was a value-neutral category of statehood that could traverse not only the emerging ideological boundary lines separating republicans from royalists and democrats from oligarchs, but also the temporal boundary lines separating antiquity from modernity.

What is less clear is the reason *why* Bodin insisted on using such a polysemous, value-laden word like *respublica*, a word fraught with interpretive difficulty, to denote what he intended to be a generic and ostensibly value-neutral concept. Bodin could have followed the example of Machiavelli who, in attempting to isolate and

[23] Algernon Sidney quoted in Hankins, 'Exclusivist Republicanism' 474–75. Hankins locates this source in Jonathan Scott, *England's Troubles: Seventeenth Century English Political Instability in European Context* (Cambridge: Cambridge University Press, 2000) 76.

[24] Grotius, *De Iure Belli ac Pacis* 1.1.14, 1.3.7 (which is referencing D.49.15.7.1); Hobbes, *De Cive* 5.11; Pufendorf, *De Iure Naturae et Gentium* 7.2.13.

[25] *Methodus* 238; *République* 13; *De Republica* 10 [2.1]. Vattel will make essentially the same point in Emer de Vattel, *On the Law of Nations*, trans. Thomas Nugent, ed. Béla Kapossy and Richard Whatmore (Indianapolis: Liberty Fund, 2008) 75 [*Le droit des gens*, Preliminaries, §18].

conjecture upon a generic category of state, felt he had to assign a new unique term corresponding to that referent, *lo stato*.[26] And, as it turned out, Machiavelli's language of state has become our modern language of state in modern politics and jurisprudence (even if it's not necessarily *our* theory of state).[27]

But Bodin didn't do this. This was by deliberate calculation. Bodin wanted to take advantage of the inbuilt polysemous quality of the terms, *république* and *respublica*, in part to introduce what might be described as a programme of linguistic reform and restore a discipline and parsimony to the emerging modern science of law and state.

The broad nomenclature of statehood, introduced by Bodin, was designed to perform two crucial functions at once. On the one hand, it made possible a methodical and broadly comparative analysis of states in all their historically observable forms. This was the strategy of Bodin's treatise on historiography, the *Methodus ad Facilem Historiarum Cognitionem* (first published in 1566), which took as its primary concern the methodological problems associated with using historical texts as evidence used to construct a grand universal history of humanity (which was, in Bodin's day, a fashionable intellectual project in Renaissance historiography). How might it be possible, if at all, to compare the recorded historical experience of peoples separated by vast distances in time and place? An antiquarian purist perhaps might say there's simply nothing to compare.

Bodin's position, by contrast, opens the possibility for such comparative analysis, so long as we have the right conceptual tools to make a valid comparison. His most important suggestion in that work – a move that is often underappreciated – is his general view that the state, the *respublica* (and not, say, class or a heroic world-historic individual), must be regarded as the principal unit of analysis and the relevant agent of change in the writing of universal history.[28] But in privileging the state, Bodin was not designating a specific historical state (such as, say, the Roman Republic) or even a specific *form* of state (such as, say, monarchy), but rather an abstract concept of state, of which history provided countless instantiations. Valois France of the sixteenth century is, thus, as much a state as was Elizabethan England, Rome under Caesar's dictatorship, or Athens under Pericles' generalship. Even the Swiss cantons are properly to be classified as instances of Bodinian states. Despite differences specific to each historical case, including differences in the style

[26] Niccolo Machiavelli, *The Prince*, ed. Quentin Skinner and Russell Price (Cambridge: Cambridge University Press, 1988) 5: 'All the states, all the dominions that have held sway over men, have been either republics or principalities.' On Machiavelli's theory of state, see Peter Stacey, 'Free and Unfree States in Machiavelli's Political Thought', in *Freedom and the Construction of Europe*, vol. 1, *Religious Freedom and Civil Liberty*, ed. Quentin Skinner and Martin Van Gelderen (Cambridge: Cambridge University Press, 2013) 176–94, as well as the forthcoming study by Stacey on the theory of the state in Machiavelli.

[27] On the disjunction between the language and theory of state and the genealogy of this disjunction, see Quentin Skinner, 'A Genealogy of the Modern State', *Proceedings of the British Academy* 162 (2009) 325–70.

[28] *Methodus* 16.

of their politics, they're all states. The starting point, for Bodin, should be to identify what features all these states share in common.

States and Non-States

Bodin's nomenclature of statehood tacitly performed another function of perhaps even greater importance than the first. By indicating the essential elements constituting a proper state, Bodin's analysis also does, by implication, just the opposite. It implicitly indicated what *cannot* be a proper state and, hence, was undeserving of that title – one might even say, the dignity – of statehood.[29]

It must be remembered that Bodin was developing his theory of state in a pluralistic, ante-Westphalian world imagined as being composed of a heterogeneous collection of states and quasi-state entities. This pluralistic ante-Westphalian heterogeneity was vital to the framing of Bodin's project. Whereas the modern Westphalian world of public international law and politics was assumed, by axiom, to be a 'system of states' populated *only* by unitary states, of whatever constitutional form (republican or monarchical), the ante-Westphalian world knew no such axiom. Consequently, for someone like Bodin, the state was but one among many heterogeneous rivals or 'competitors' (as Hendrik Spruyt once memorably described it) in an ante-Westphalian world inhabited by the Church, feudalities, autonomous city-states, bishoprics, corporate bodies, all as political rivals competing for power.[30] The point can be visually illustrated by comparing a sixteenth-century map of Europe with one from the twenty-first century.[31]

Given this pluralistic heterogeneity of ante-Westphalian politics, it isn't unreasonable to ask what was historically judged to be the proper 'subject' of international law. An answer might be deduced by determining what sort of actors were entitled to exercise those actions understood to be uniquely constitutive of international relations – the right of embassy and the rights of war and reprisal.[32] If we know who can send and receive diplomats and who can engage in war, then we can reasonably conclude that the actor must be a subject of international law.[33]

[29] Bodin, thus, anticipates a critical distinction in Grotius' theory of state separating *coetus perfectus* from *coetus imperfectus*.

[30] Hendrik Spruyt, *The State and Its Competitors: An Analysis of Systems Change* (Princeton: Princeton University Press, 1994).

[31] This is the theme of Jordan Branch, *The Cartographic State: Maps, Territory, and the Origins of Sovereignty* (Cambridge: Cambridge University Press, 2013).

[32] These were central themes explored in the medieval law of war, including Bartolus' *Tractatus represaliarum* and John of Legnano's *Tractatus de bello, de represaliis et de duello*. On this legal literature, see Ryan Greenwood, *Law and War in Late Medieval Italy: The Jus Commune on War and Its Application in Florence, c.1150–1450*, Ph.D. Dissertation (Toronto: University of Toronto, 2011).

[33] These questions concerning the proper subject of international law have been explored in a number of recent studies: Philip Stern, *The Company-State: Corporate Sovereignty and the Early Modern Foundations of the British Empire in India* (Oxford: Oxford University Press, 2011); Ryan Greenwood,

But observe that being a *subject of international law* isn't the same as being a *state*, in this ante-Westphalian context.[34] This observation is what makes Bodin's theory of state all the more noteworthy. For the first time in the history of modern international law (and keep in mind that Bodin is developing his theory independently of Vitoria and the School of Salamanca, and before Gentili, Suarez, Grotius, Hobbes, Pufendorf, Vattel, and the English School theorists), Bodin synthesizes these two non-equivalent ideas together to articulate what will become a cardinal principle of international law, the dictum that the one and only subject of international law is the state, and the state alone. Commentators have long assumed that Bodin's theory of sovereignty was strictly intended to be, as Merio Scattola put it, an 'interior concept', and thus had very little to offer to modern international law.[35]

This is the first major idea articulated in Bodin's *République*, which attempts to distinguish between states and non-states. Because states are the only proper subjects of (what we – following Bentham – would call) 'international law', only they are entitled to enjoy certain legal advantages from which non-state entities are excluded. One such advantage is the legal right of postliminy, a valuable *post bellum* right of restitution or restoration of status central to the law governing Roman warfare.[36] The one condition of postliminy, however, is that it is valid only for lawful combatants, or *hostes*, engaged in a lawful war – what in classical law is called a *bellum iustum* (see Chapter 5).[37]

What, then, makes one a lawful combatant? Bodin answers by appeal to a principle drawn from the *Digest* of Roman law – an act of formal declaration:

'War and Sovereignty in Medieval Roman Law', *Law and History Review* 32 (2014): 31–63; Jens Bartelson, *War in International Thought* (Cambridge: Cambridge University Press, 2018).

[34] This point still holds in the post-Westphalian context as well. James Crawford, *Brownlie's Principles of Public International Law*, 8th ed. (Oxford: Oxford University Press, 2012) 116–26. A landmark exploration of non-state legal personalities in international law is discussed in Max Huber's opinion in the *Island of Palmas*, United States v. Netherlands, Award (The Hague, April 1928) *Reports of International Arbitrial Awards* 2:858–59.

[35] Merio Scattola, 'Jean Bodin on International Law', in *System, Order, and International Law*, ed. Stefan Kadelbach, Thomas Kleinlein, and David Roth-Isigkeit (Oxford: Oxford University Press, 2017) 81; cp. Ryan Martinez Mitchell, 'Jean Bodin's Law of Nations', *Political Theology* 21 (2020): 550–69.

[36] D.49.15.4; 49.15.5; 49.15.19.

[37] Grotius makes the same point, at *De Iure Belli ac Pacis* 1.3.4 and 3.3.1, in distinguishing between wars that are formal and *solemne ex iure gentium* and wars that are informal and *minus solemne*. Only the first can be called a *bellum iustum*, indicating a formal legal condition between sovereign states who have declared themselves to be *hostes*. Grotius tries to illustrate the contrast by way of analogy to Roman marriage law, distinguishing a formal *iustum matrimonium* (formal marriage ceremony) from mere *contubernium* (cohabitation of slaves), and Roman law of succession, distinguishing a formal *iustum testamentum* from a mere codicil. Grotius is making the same point that Bodin is making: *Testamentum & nuptiae solemnes peculiares quosdam ex iure civili effectus habeant*. Cp. *De Republica* 15 [1.3]: *Uxoris appellatione iustam ac legitimam intelligo, non concubinam*. On this theme, see Sharon Achinstein, 'Hugo Grotius and Marriage's Global Past: Conjugal Thinking in Early Modern Political Thought', *Journal of the History of Ideas* 81 (2020): 195–215.

> 'Enemies' [*hostes*] are those who declare war against us, or those against whom we publicly declare war: all others are 'brigands' or 'pirates'.[38]

This influential text in the history of international law, known simply by its incipit used in medieval Roman law as the *lex Hostes* [or *l.Hostes*], is Bodin's very first citation in the *République*. It explains that the juridical category of the lawful enemy 'combatant' is limited only to those who have formally entered into a state of war by lawful declaration, a procedure detailed in Roman law through the requirements of the so-called 'fetial rite' of the *rerum repetitio*.[39] As Bodin will later explain in the text of the *République* and elsewhere, states – and only states – have the exclusive right to declare war [*bellum indicere*] – and, by implication, the capacity to have war declared upon them (since war requires omnilateral declaration by all warring parties).[40] Above all, by restricting war exclusively to states in this manner, Bodin has likewise restricted the legal advantages of war, such as the right of postliminy, to states as well.

Non-states can, of course, engage in violence, but they can't, according to Bodin's analysis, engage in acts of war that entitle warring parties to legal advantages. The implication of this argument, then, is exclusionary. Those lacking the sovereign right of declaring war can't claim postliminy – or, for that matter, any other legal advantage to which states lawfully engaged in war as combatants are entitled to claim. In making this assertion, Bodin is likely thinking of those heterogeneous non-state and quasi-state entities making up the ante-Westphalian world. But the specific examples cited in the *lex Hostes* of non-state combatants suggest that Bodin had another specific category in mind to draw this distinction between state and non-state as clearly as possible.

In the *lex Hostes* of Roman law that Bodin cites, the contrast is drawn between genuine lawful combatants [*hostes*], on the one hand, and 'brigands and pirates' [*latrones aut praedones*], on the other.[41] No one doubts, of course, that piracy and brigandage involve the use of violent force. The question is whether the sort of organized violence involving brigandage and piracy can also legally be called 'war', in the same way that inter-state violence between legal *hostes* can be called war.

[38] There are two versions of this text in the *Digest*, at D.49.15.24 and 50.16.118. Bodin cites both versions at various places – *République* 2 [1.1]; 109 [1.7]; 278 [2.2]; *De Republica* 603 [5.6]. Cp. Grotius' treatment of this theme in *De Iure Belli ac Pacis* 3.3.1.

[39] David Bederman, *International Law in Antiquity* (Cambridge: Cambridge University Press, 2001) 231–33. Cp. *République* 760; *De Republica* 562–3 [5.5].

[40] *Distributio* fol. A, s.v.: *Ius Publicum*; *République* 224; *De Republica* 155 [1.10]. This particular right of declaring war should be interpreted as a Hohfeldian 'power'. Its purpose is to create a new juridical relation between states as *hostes*, as defined under the *lex Hostes*. See Hohfeld, 'Some Fundamental Legal Conceptions': 44.

[41] Chapter 5 will investigate an important extension of the latter category – tyrants. Like pirates and brigands, tyrants too have no legal standing. Their regime is simply based on an illicit force without right.

Bodin's answer is that it cannot, for a simple reason. As we'll see in Chapter 5, war is fundamentally a rule-governed *juridical* condition, defined ultimately by the *ius gentium* – the 'law common to all of mankind' – and activated only by those who, as subjects of that *ius*, have the legal capacity to 'declare war publicly' [*bellum indicere*] – namely, sovereign states.[42] Bodin's narrowly state-centric view of war, reducing war to a kind of legal transaction or legal process carried out between and by states, effectively eliminated whole categories of violence that was conventionally thought to be valid acts of war in medieval law, such as feuding or reprisals.[43] It also eliminated categorically from the narrowing conceptual space of war the violence of lawless 'gangs of robbers and pirates' [*latronum ac piratarum caetus*] intent, as Bodin put it, on 'seek[ing] the destruction of states and other civil associations' [*Rerum publicarum & civilis societatis eversionem moliuntur*].[44] Such illicit force without right, while potentially terrifying and effective in subduing others, doesn't make it war. It only makes it illegal 'brigandage' or 'piracy' [*latrocinium*], which falls far outside the categorical boundary of rule-governed warfare.

At first glance, this appears to be nothing more than an academic distinction without a difference. But lawyers will immediately see Bodin's point. Robbers and pirates – or, indeed, any non-state actor – can never enjoy the protections and advantages that benefit lawful combatants in a *bellum iustum* – like postliminy. Those advantages, however, are not limited only to postliminy. They include all the advantages that are bundled together in that package of rights called 'sovereignty'. While states are beneficiaries of those sovereign rights (and thus, imposing duties on others to respect those sovereign rights), robbers and pirates are, as it were, outside the boundaries of all law and legality and are, therefore, rightless outlaws.

The striking conclusion that emerges, then, from this application of the *lex Hostes* in just the opening paragraphs of the *République* is the fundamental point that authentic statehood, the juridical condition of being a genuine *respublica*, mustn't be conferred indiscriminately upon any entity capable of organized violence, like brigands or pirates. That is because naked violence, by itself, isn't what makes a state, but, rather, *droit* (and correspondingly in Latin, *ius*).

42 The term, *bellum indicere*, is taken from the 'fetial procedure' of warmaking in the Roman *ius fetiale* (or *ius feciale*, as Bodin sometimes writes). See Bederman, *International Law in Antiquity* 233, which cross-references Cicero, *De Officiis* 1.11.34–36. Bodin mentions the *ius fetiale* by name on *De Republica* 1, where he states explicitly that *latrones ac piratae ab omni iure faeciali* [i.e. *fetiali*] *procul summoventur*.

43 Bodin observes at *République* 248, *De Republica* 171–72 [1.10] how the privatizing of violence through letters of marque and the right of reprisal [*ius represaliorum* or *clarigatio*] risked further violence through the *temerité* of those abusing the *droit de represailles*.

44 *De Republica* 1. Bodin's use of the term *societas civilis*, a partnership made up of *cives*, generally follows Ciceronian usage, which treats it as a rough Latinization of Aristotle's κοινωνία πολιτική – the *polis*. It is not meant to signal 'civil society', as it is used in modern social thought, such as in Hegel or Marx. As I discuss later in this chapter, Bodin will specify that, *societas civilis*, encompassing associational bodies such as *collegia*, *corpora*, as well as states, is to be contrasted against the *societas naturalis* of the family.

This appeal to 'lawfulness' or 'rightness' (which is how one might translate the difficult terms, *droit* and *ius*, into English), indeed, is the principal reason why Bodin feels it is necessary to specify in his opening definition of the state that it is a structure of *droit gouvernement*, instead of a structure of brute *force* without right – like a gang of robbers.[45] But there's also an intellectual purpose in stressing this point at the outset; too many 'ignorant' and 'vain historians', he says, have made the critical mistake of attributing statehood to entities which, though capable of controlling and even 'monopolizing' organized violence, don't deserve that title and status.

Bodin is deliberately evoking the Augustinian (and ultimately Ciceronian) worry, articulated in the *De Civitate Dei*, that perhaps war-capable states, led ultimately by imperfect fallen humans, can never be legitimate, but nothing more than 'great robber bands' [*magna latrocinia*]: 'With justice taken away, what are states but large robber bands? And what are robber bands but small states?'[46] The difference for Bodin, as it was for Augustine and Cicero, was justice or 'rightness' – this elusive notion of *droit/ius*. Distinguishing between state and non-state, then, boils down ultimately to a question of justice.

Bodin viewed his world of the later sixteenth century, shaped by religious warfare, imperial conquest, and popular uprisings, as one co-populated by states and non-states alike. This analysis suggests that, for Bodin, many violent conflicts, conventionally thought to be wars, actually fail to meet the legal criterion of a genuine *bellum iustum*. Even 'civil wars' such as the Dutch Revolt or 'wars of religion' would not, on this analysis, technically be counted as wars because the combatants to such violent conflicts have no right of war in the first place.

Bodin's first argument to distinguish genuine states from non-states, thus, relied on a technical analysis of the state's monopoly over the legal right to engage in war and conclude peace, and specifically the *post bellum* rights of postliminy, exclusive to states as legal combatants. But the point could, in principle be generalized beyond the specific case of war and peace. Just as states are exclusively entitled to state-exclusive rights of postliminy, so too are states exclusively entitled to all other legal 'rights', inaccessible to non-states.

Bodin called these exclusive legal rights of states *the rights of sovereignty* [variously, *droits de la majesté, droits & marques de souveraineté, iura maiestatis, iura summi imperii*]. In his three principal works on law and politics, the *Distributio*, the

45 Bodin's juxtaposition of 'rightness' [*droit*; *ius*] and 'force' [*force*; *vis*] anticipates a distinction that will frame some of the major theoretical texts to follow in the Enlightenment, especially those of Locke and Rousseau. The Latin *De Republica*, however, drops the normative language of *ius*.

46 Augustine, *City of God* 2:16–17 [4.4]. *Remota itaque iustitia quid sunt regna nisi magna latricinia? Quia et latrocinia quid sunt nisi parua regna?* Otto Brunner describes this as 'one of the basic postulates of medieval political thought, the idea of justice, without which a state was inconceivable' in *Land and Lordship*, trans. Howard Kaminsky and James Van Horn Melton (Philadelphia: University of Pennsylvania Press, 1992) 6.

Methodus, and the *République*, he not only enumerates these sovereign rights[47] but he also declares the core principle, later to be influential for Arnisaeus and Hobbes, that these sovereign rights of states are to be regarded as whole, imprescriptible, inalienable, and indivisible.[48]

The attribution of such rights exclusively to states carries several important implications, three of which are worth mentioning here. The first is simply that the analysis of sovereign rights is, according to Bodin, the key to sharpening the distinction between states and non-states; if we know what the legal rights of sovereignty are, then we will also know whether a given entity is properly a state or not. For Bodin, then, the question of whether some community is a state ultimately becomes a juridical one involving rights, a point that will become especially important in later chapters of this study as we proceed to investigate the substance of his legal and political theory.

The second point is to say that Bodin relies on a fairly robust concept of rights, and it is theoretically possible to translate his analysis of rights into a modern Hohfeldian or Kanger-Lindahl framework.[49] He is, it is fair to say, a theorist of rights, and his theory of sovereignty, as I'll argue in the following chapters, resides in what Judith Jarvis Thomson has once called the 'realm of rights'.[50] But we have to be especially careful, because his is a concept of rights that belongs to a specifically Continental juridical tradition of rights. A distinctive feature of this tradition is that it presupposes a tight conceptual connection between 'right' and 'law', a relic of the Continental legal science of the *ius commune* on which it is based – the European legal system based principally on Roman and canon law.[51] Because of their connection, both of these notions of right and law were conventionally signified by the same word in modern European languages: *droit* in French, *diritto* in Italian, *Recht* in German, *derecho* in Spanish, just like *ius* in Latin.[52] Right wasn't

[47] *République* 212–13; *De Republica* 148 [1.10]. Cp. *Methodus* 261, 234–35 ('134', '135'); *Distributio* fol. A, s.v.: *Ius Humanum: Ius Gentium: Antecedens.*

[48] While the doctrine of indivisibility appears in Hobbes, *Leviathan* 127, Hobbes cites Bodin by name in connection with sovereign indivisibility in the *Elements of Law Natural and Politic*, ed. J.C.A. Gaskin (Oxford: Oxford University Press, 1994) 167. The list of *iura summi imperii* at *On the Citizen* 88 [*De Cive* 6.18] is interestingly identical to Bodin's list of sovereign rights in *Methodus* 261. Henning Arnisaeus, *De Jure Majestatis Libri Tres* (Frankfurt: Typis Andreae Eichorn, 1610) 209–11 [2.1.1]. Grotius notably rejects Bodin's indivisibility doctrine: Hugo Grotius, *Commentarius in Theses XI: An Early Treatise on Sovereignty, the Just War, and the Legitimacy of the Dutch Revolt*, ed. Peter Borschberg (Bern: Peter Lang, 1994) 127, 130 [*Theses IV*] and *De Iure Belli ac Pacis* 1.3.17, 2.14.1.2. In general, see Thomas Berns, 'Bodin: La Souveraineté Saisie Par Ses Marques', *Bibliotheque d'Humanisme et Renaissance* 62 (2000): 611–23, which suggests an Aristotelian source for Bodin's decomposition of sovereignty into its constitutive *marques* or *iura* in *Topics* 102ª18.

[49] Hohfeld, 'Fundamental Legal Conceptions'; Stig Kanger, 'Rättighetsbegreppet', in *Sju filosofiska studier tillägnade Anders Wedberg den 30 mars 1963* Philosophical Studies No 9 (Stockholm: Department of Philosophy, University of Stockholm, 1963); Lindahl, *Position and Change*.

[50] Judith Jarvis Thomson, *The Realm of Rights* (Cambridge: Harvard University Press, 1990) 3.

[51] On the background of the *ius commune*, see Manlio Bellomo, *The Common Legal Past of Europe, 1000–1800*, trans. Lydia Cochrane (Washington, D.C.: The Catholic University of America Press, 1995).

[52] This linguistic curiosity in Continental juridical discourse has contributed to some confusion in modern Anglophone treatments of the term, *ius naturale*. Some insist on translating it as 'natural right', while others prefer to translate it as 'natural law'. What participants in this academic discussion seem

something different from law. Rather, as Hans Kelsen once put it, 'the right *is* law—law in a subjective sense of the word in contradistinction to "law" in an objective sense, that is, a legal order or system of norms'.[53]

Needless to say, the linguistic connection isn't random. It signals the basic idea in Western jurisprudence that there can't be a right without an accompanying law. Rights are, as Bentham once put it, creatures of the law: no law, no right. Contrast this with common law systems based on English law, where it is theoretically possible to separate conceptually and linguistically the two terms, so that one can imagine, in theory, a set of rights unattached, or anterior, to law. Among Anglophone writers on the theory of rights and law, Thomas Hobbes exemplifies this peculiar way of thinking:

> Right and Law ... ought to be distinguished; because RIGHT, consistenth in liberty to do, or to forbeare; Whereas LAW, determineth, and bindeth to one of them: so that Law, and Right, differ as much, as Obligation, and Liberty.[54]

But this, the possibility of rights in a lawless (or 'natural') world, is precisely what Continental legal science disallows. What separates someone like Bodin from someone like Hobbes is the fundamental point that right [*ius*], in order for it to be actionable and more than just an empty word, requires and presupposes law [*ius*], of some kind.[55]

The third and final point to observe is this: If states can hold, claim, and assert rights as the law allows, they can, for that very reason, also hold obligations and be bound to perform certain duties. This is an insight of monumental importance, not only for Bodin's theory, but more generally, for the structure of classical international law which imagined states not only as bearers of rights, but also as bearers of duties.[56] States, though notionally are independent of legal obligations to each other and to their own subjects, nevertheless find themselves burdened under all

to misunderstand is that this is not a matter of interpretive choice. *Ius naturale* signals both a system of legal duties as well as rights: Rights and law come together as a package and entail each other. Tierney, *The Idea of Natural Rights* 32–3.

53 Hans Kelsen, *Pure Theory of Law*, trans. Max Knight (Berkeley: University of California Press, 1967) 125.

54 Hobbes, *Leviathan* 91. Hobbes tries to get around this difficulty by assigning the term, *lex*, to the English word, 'law'. But this isn't a satisfactory solution. Both words, *ius* and *lex*, meant 'law'. But there is a subtle difference between *ius* and *lex*, the latter being used only for positive legislation, such as popular legislation in classical Roman law (such as the *lex Hortensia*, the *lex Valeria*, the *lex Vocania*, and the *lex Iulia*).

55 In order to distinguish the two semantic functions of *ius*, modern jurists have sometimes distinguished between 'subjective *ius*' and 'objective *ius*' which will be discussed in Chapter 2. This distinction is sometimes designated as *droit subjectif/droit objectif*. See Helge Dedek, 'From Norms to Facts: The Realization of Rights in Common and Civil Private Law', *McGill Law Journal* 56.1 (2010): 77–114.

56 Luke Glanville, *Sovereignty and the Responsibility to Protect: A New History* (Chicago: University of Chicago Press, 2013); Fox-Decent, *Sovereignty's Promise*.

kinds of obligations. And that is precisely because sovereign rights presuppose an objective legal order in which those rights are made actionable. States, like natural persons, are embedded within this legal order, and it is from this background legal order that sovereign states derive, not only their rights, but also their obligations as sovereign entities.

The State as Compound Association

So far, we have considered the *summa divisio* of Bodin's thought, the distinction between states and non-states, as well as the significance of that division. Bodin made that distinction, by identifying those 'sovereign rights' constitutive of, and exclusive to, states, such as the right to declare war, *bellum indicere.* But we haven't yet considered directly the question what a Bodinian state [*respublica*] actually is, and why *they* should be bearers of sovereign rights. That is our next task.

Bodin formally defines the state for the first time in the *Methodus ad facilem historiarum cognitionem*, first published in 1566 and revised in 1572. The sixth, and by far the longest, chapter of that work – entitled, *De Statu Rerum Publicarum* (a Ciceronian phrase, which, following Bodin's own usage, I translate as 'On the form of states') – is a treatise-nested-within-a-treatise, functioning as a preview for ideas to be developed more fully in his principal treatise on political theory, the *République.*[57] It is in this important lengthy chapter that Bodin first defines the state, or *respublica*: 'The state is nothing other than a multitude of families [*familiarum*] or corporations [*collegiarum*] subjected under one and the same sovereign authority [*imperium*]'.[58]

Among the several points to observe in this definition is its remarkably broad scope. This was by design. Bodin sought to craft what we might characterize as a very 'thin' theory of state, stripped of as many particular details as possible without losing the very essence of statehood itself. Generality was his goal. It is, in this respect, noteworthy what Bodin conspicuously omits in his theory of state, elements such as territory, a shared language, and a common religion; these are not the sort of things that make one state. He did so for a specific purpose – in order to maximize the versatility and applicability of his theory across historical contexts, so as to enable the practising historian (for whom this work was intended) to compare states, whether ancient or modern, using a single analytical vocabulary and conception of statehood.

[57] This is not unlike the relationship between Hobbes' *De Cive* and *Leviathan*, a comparison suggested by Richard Tuck in *The Sleeping Sovereign: The Invention of Modern Democracy* (Cambridge: Cambridge University Press, 2016) 30–35. Tuck, in agreement with Miglietti's commentary on the *Methodus*, rejects the earlier interpretive consensus of Jean Moreau-Reibel, Myron Piper Gilmore, Julian Franklin, suggesting discontinuity between the *Methodus* and the *République*.

[58] *Methodus* 237 ('137').

Even more important was the explicitly associational character of Bodin's concept of state. To wit: the state, for Bodin, is in its essence an association – a *societas*, a κοινωνία, a *coetus* – and he freely uses the classical language of state as a *societas civilis* (Cicero's Latinization of the Aristotelian κοινωνία πολιτική) to reinforce its associational character.[59] It is vital to stress this basic and what otherwise would be a relatively uncontroversial point, in part because so many modern readers of Bodin have adopted the peculiarly post-Westphalian habit of treating sovereignty as a *cipher* for statehood, almost as if they were signifiers for the same thing, when in fact they are, at least for Bodin, two distinct concepts.[60] Such conceptual confusion is only exacerbated by retrospectively projecting a modern Hegelian analysis of state, which relies on an anachronistic and very un-Bodinian distinction between 'state' and 'civil society'. It must be remembered that, before Hegel's pioneering analysis of the category of 'civil society' [*bürgerliche Gesellschaft*], the Latin term, *societas civilis*, just was the state: a partnership [*societas*] of co-equal fellow citizen-partners [*socii*].[61]

One consequence of this failure to respect the Bodinian distinction between the state and its sovereignty is that modern scholarship has obscured a vital quality of Bodin's state – its fundamentally pluralistic, associational, and even heterogeneous character, as a collective whole made up of many different parts. This is worth stressing, considering that Bodin's political theory has typically been portrayed as the foil against which the so-called pluralistic theory of state has been defined.[62] But what we actually find instead is a political theory that belongs, or so I shall now argue, within this 'pluralistic' tradition of politics, and that is because Bodin's own theory of what constitutes a properly independent state emphasizes the heterogeneity and internal complexity of states. Indeed, Bodin's state turns out to be surprisingly hospitable to what has often been called the 'principle of subsidiarity'. And we see this, above all, in how Bodin defines the state in explicitly associational terms.

But if the Bodinian state is imagined to be a type of association, what were the constituent units that made up a proper Bodinian state? A comment in the Preface

[59] The *République* has the term *communauté* which notably differs from the term, *compagnie*, used in Louis Le Roy's rendering of the state [*cité*] as a *compagnie civil* in his translation of Aristotle, *Les Politiques d'Aristote* (Paris: Michel Vascosan, 1576) 3.

[60] At least one major recent study has denied altogether that Bodin had a sufficiently well-worked-out account of the political community, separate from sovereignty. Richard Tuck in *Sleeping Sovereign* 84–5 focuses on the Grotian distinction between the *subiectum commune* and the *subiectum proprium* of sovereignty which Grotius introduces at *De Iure Belli ac Pacis* 1.3.7, to contrast with Bodin who makes no such distinction between the 'common' and 'proper'. There is, however, a slippage between state and sovereignty on 64.

[61] As we'll see in a moment, the state [*respublica*], for Bodin, *just is* a kind of civil society [*societas civilis*], a claim that would make little sense on a classical Weberian analysis. On this theme of *societas* and the state, see Michael Oakeshott, *On Human Conduct* (Oxford: Clarendon Press, 1975).

[62] Recent studies in pluralism continue to presuppose Bodin's alleged hostility to a pluralist theory of state, such as Jacob Levy, *Rationalism, Pluralism, and Freedom* (Oxford: Oxford University Press, 2015); Victor Muniz-Fraticelli, *The Structure of Pluralism* (Oxford: Oxford University Press, 2014); David Runciman, *Pluralism and the Personality of the State* (Cambridge: Cambridge University Press, 1997).

to the French *République* concerning 'each member of the *république*' [*chacun member de la république*] suggests a heterogeneous body made up of families, corporations, colleges, estates, and communities [*familles ... corps & colleges, estats et communautez*].[63] States were *compound associations – associations of associations*.

Bodin's early analysis of the state in the *Methodus* indicates what he judged to be the main constituent elements of the state – *familia* and *collegia*. But the *République* reveals what is arguably his more mature, considered judgment that the state is, in its essence, an association or union made up families [*plusieurs mesnages; familiarum ... multitudo*]. Ultimately, the family is the principal building-block of the Bodinian state. And at the very minimum, every state must consist of at least three separate families, with each family consisting of at least five members.[64] Indeed, the family, as Bodin put it, is the 'natural association' from which the civil association of the state is derived.[65] And he admits straightaway that it is entirely possible to imagine a state 'without corporate bodies' [*sine collegiis & corporibus*], but it is impossible to imagine a state without the foundation of the family.[66]

Societas Naturalis: The Family

Two things need to be said, at the outset, about the family in Bodin's theory of state.[67] The first is that Bodin seems to recognize and endorse what is a foundational axiom of both ancient law and cultural anthropology: The family – and not the individual – is the basic social unit and the principal constituent building-block of the state, what Anna Becker has described as 'the fundamental entities on which society, politics, and culture pivoted'.[68] But in prioritizing the 'molecular' unit of the family, rather than the free and equal 'atomic' individual, his purpose was *not* so much to advance an illiberal hostility to the individual nor to a notion of

[63] *République*, Preface sig. a3$_{\text{ro.}}$ Cp. *République* 14 [1.2], where he defines the state as many parts and members united *en un corps parfaict de republique*.

[64] *République* 11–12; *De Republica* 9 [1.2]. Bodin's reasoning for why a state must consist of at least three families is assembled from a critical joint reading of D.22.5.12 (on *pluralis*), 50.16.85, and 50.16.196.pr. Arguing against the principle of D.22.5.12 which declares that two is minimally sufficient to make up a *pluralis*, Bodin cites instead D.50.16.85, which states that three persons are always minimally necessary to make a corporate body or association [*collegium*]. This principle is applied to the constitution of a state: Since families are the constitutive unit of states, there must be at least three families.

[65] *République* 474; *De Republica* 328 [3.7]. Cp. Bodin's reading of D.50.16.195.1, which outlines the principle that a *familia* is not just a reference to the property of the family estate or the family as a unit, but also the individual *persons* who are members of the family.

[66] *République* 474; *De Republica* 328 [3.7]; cp. 45 [1.6]: *Neque Respublica sine familiis, neque urbs sine moenibus et aedificiis stare magis possunt, quam solaria vel tecta sine parietibus ac fundamentis.* Becker observes the resemblance of this comment to Leonardo Bruni's commentary on Aristotle's *Oeconomica* which states that cities cannot exist without families. Becker, *Gendering the Renaissance Commonwealth* 114.

[67] On this theme in general, see Ginevra Conti Odorisio, *La famille et l'état dans la République de Jean Bodin* (Paris: L'Harmattan, 2007).

[68] Becker, *Gendering the Renaissance Commonwealth* 107–8.

an abstract individual right prior to ends.[69] Instead, he was developing a theory of state without prioritizing an assumption of methodological individualism.

The second point is, in my view, even more important. The family, though it is the constituent building-block of the Bodinian state, itself also resembles the state, in that both are associations united under a common authority.[70] Like the state, the family too is characterized by an undifferentiated 'rule over many subjects' [*un droit gouvernement de plusieurs subjects*; *imperium plurium subditorum*]. The subjection of many under the authority of one head of household or patriarch [*un chef de famille*; *paterfamilias*] just is what makes one family.[71]

What Bodin makes clear immediately is that his concept of family wasn't intended to be a narrow 'nuclear' or 'conjugal' conception, where family membership is defined essentially by biological or consanguine ties of shared ancestry or kinship. The 'subjects' of a Bodinian family certainly might include natural-born children.[72] But it also may include persons of all status or rank, such as 'slaves, freedmen, and freemen who voluntarily subject themselves to the head of the household'.[73] Ties of blood, whether with each other or with the *paterfamilias*, are thus unnecessary for membership in a family. What *is* necessary is common subjection under one paterfamilial authority.

All this is to reinforce Bodin's basic axiom about the family: *Anybody* can, in theory, become a member of *any* family.[74] One can, of course, be born into a family and naturally fall under the subjection of the *paterfamilias*.[75] Birth, however, isn't

69 It's unclear whether Bodin was even capable of imagining something like the 'unencumbered' individual self, *as such*, detached from and prior to the roles and status that define the place, the rank, and the function of persons in family and society.

70 *République* 11 [1.2]: *Tout ainsi donc que la famille bient condite, est la vraye image de la Republique, & la puissance domestique semble a la puissance souveraine: aussi est le droit gouvernement de la maison le vray modelle du gouvernement de la Republique.*

71 *République* 10 [1.2]. Bodin has two targets. One is Aristotle who treats domestic or 'oeconomical' management of the household [οἶκος] as fundamentally a different kind of activity from the skill of 'political' rule required in a proper state [πόλης]. Where Aristotle seems content to reduce management of the household to wealth accumulation [χρηματιστική], Bodin castigates both Aristotle and Xenophon (who authored a treatise on οἰκονομία) for thinking that *imperium* over a family is qualitatively different from *imperium* over a state.

The other target is Roman law. Bodin cites D.50.16.195.pr, but his analysis of paterfamilial authority in the succeeding chapters is deeply critical of the substance of Roman family law concerning the husband's domestic powers of *manus* over wives and the father's natural *potestas* over children, suggesting instead that the *ius gentium* (what he calls, equivalently, *populorum omnium leges* at *De Republica* 15) has abrogated the force of a once-valid and active Roman law. This is a striking example of a form of legal reasoning that will become critical to his argument later on, that a rule of *ius gentium* can override a rule of *ius civile* (in this case, of the XII Tables).

72 *République* 11; *De Republica* 9 [1.2].

73 *République* 11; *De Republica* 9 [1.2].

74 Here, then, is a preview of Bodin's theory of citizenship, which will be explored in greater detail in Chapter 3: anybody can, in theory, become a citizen of any state. And just as legal adoption and adrogation are available for individuals to subject themselves legally under the paterfamilial authority of a new family, the equivalent of naturalization is available for foreigners to subject themselves legally under a new sovereign authority and become citizens (or 'free subjects', as Bodin would put it) of a new state.

75 As Bodin specifies, in *République* 29; *De Republica* 20 [1.4], this is the only type of power that is natural. Becker, at *Gendering the Renaissance Commonwealth* 121–23, points out that Bodin's position

the only way whereby one falls, as the lawyers say, *in potestate patria*. The law allows for such a change of personal status [a *capitis diminutio*], sinking from a status of independence *sui iuris* to one of dependence *alieni iuris*, through legal devices, such as by adoption or 'adrogation', as if it were a free transaction effected by consent of willing parties through a process of 'cession' or 'mancipation'.[76]

Yet, for all the superficial similarities between families and states, it's clear that they're not the same. Bodin can at least agree with Aristotle's starting premise in the *Politics*: The state isn't simply a 'large family', and the family isn't a 'small state'.[77] What differentiated them concerned the nature of the authority over each. This will surely be a familiar strategy for anyone who has read Aristotle or Xenophon, who distinguish between the 'oeconomical' sort of ruling appropriate to the domestic management of the οἴκος (a domain of inequality) and the 'political' or 'civil' sort of ruling in turn appropriate to civic stewardship of the πόλις (a domain of civic equality).

Bodin's own argument, however, was framed (as it so often was) as a criticism of Aristotle.[78] It's misleading, Bodin thought, to characterize the paterfamilial function as being limited *only* to matters of accumulation. Aristotle's ahistorical presentation (Bodin thought) obscured how paterfamilial authority, once broad in scope in the earliest stages of human civilization, eroded over time – by positive legislation, by custom, by desuetude – and was transferred over to the public authority of states, so that what remained with the patriarchs of the Hellenic world at the time of Aristotle was limited to accumulation. It wasn't mere coincidence, Bodin added, that the ancient prerogatives and rights of paterfamilial authority overlapped with many of the prerogatives and rights typically thought to be associated only with public authorities of state.[79]

departs from the *opinio communis* of civilians who stress that paterfamilial *patria potestas* is exclusive to the *ius civile*, not common by the *ius gentium* or *ius naturale*. The Aristotelian scholar, Antonio Montecatini, singled out both Bodin and Connan on this point.

[76] Likewise, *potestas patria* can be formally dissolved, and the child set at liberty and become *sui iuris*, through the legal device of emancipation, modelled on both the sale and conveyance of property before witnesses [*mancipatio*] and the release of slaves through manumission. This symmetry of binding and releasing of children from the paterfamilial power is central. Bodin even comments on the thrice-sale feature of Roman emancipation in the XII Tables at *De Republica* 22 [1.4].Bodin's purpose in allowing for such a capacious concept of family was partly driven by his intellectual concerns to explain the diverse familial practices and forms of domestic life in history.

[77] Aristotle, *Politics* 1.1, 1252^{a}13, itself a challenge to Plato's frequent assertion that the relations among citizens of a πόλης can be reconstituted so that they come to resemble the relations among family members.

[78] To be fair to Aristotle, it should also be stressed that Bodin wasn't all that charitable to Aristotle either. This is a common problem in Bodin who conveniently reframes arguments or omits details, in such a way that better supports his own view.

[79] Bodin notes, for example, that heads of families, like sovereign princes, have quasi-legislative powers, empowered to issue family-specific codes of laws, a *droit particularier* or *ius familiare*, that can theoretically 'derogate' from an otherwise binding law or custom, *République* 17; *De Republica* 13 [1.2]. Bodin compares the *droit particulier* to exemption-creating privileges and immunities that release particular subjects from an otherwise binding legal obligation.

Most important of these rights was *patria potestas*, the paterfamilial power of life and death over children [*potestas vitae ac necis in liberos*] – the same sort of violent power that the Roman law *Digest* (D.2.1.3) described as the magistrate's public 'power of the sword', the *merum imperium in privatos*. Heads of households, Bodin reminds us, once held this absolute discretionary right to execute summarily members of his household under his authority, long before there were states and magistrates with *imperium*.

How, then, did we get from a world where patriarchs originally held the power of life and death over their families to a world where magistrates with *merum imperium* have monopolized that right to inflict lawfully deadly violence? The story that Bodin tells is a complicated account of legal change introduced by the overreaching 'ambition of magistrates' intent on centralizing and expanding the scope of their jurisdiction and, correspondingly, derogating from the original paterfamilial right of power.[80]

On this point, Roman history was paradigmatic for Bodin. At its founding, Rome was barely a state in any recognizable modern sense. It would be more accurate, Bodin thought, to treat it as a simple archaic association of families or clans [*gentes*], organized into larger tribal units [*curiae*].[81] In this context, the families and clans of early Rome were each thought to be jurisdictionally autonomous, each almost like imperfect mini-states, under the authority of the 'father' [*pater*; πατήρ] and patrons who were entrusted with the care and 'protection' [*patrocinium*; προστασία] of the plebeians assigned to them and making up a 'family'.[82] These fathers, Bodin observed, held jurisdictional rights, acting as judges over family members.

Yet, even though this domestic power of life and death, once within the purview of *patresfamilias*, would ultimately be confiscated by public authorities of state, Bodin saw this as a grave injustice that must be remedied, specifically by restoring and recognizing this paterfamilial right. And that is because, in his legal theory, the paterfamilial power of life and death over children was (and theoretically still is, in dormancy) a natural right. That is, it was a legal right which fathers held, not by positive legislation (*ex iure civile* or *ex iure Quiritium*), but as a permissive right of the natural law (*ex iure naturali*).[83]

80 *République* 36; *De Republica* 24 [1.4].

81 One of Romulus' first acts, as the legendary founding king of Rome, was reputed to be the division of the Roman populace into three main tribes, and the subdivision of those tribes into *curia* and *gentes*. Standard classical accounts are Livy *Ab Urbe Condita* 1.13.7 and Cicero, *De Re Publica* 2.14. Dionysius of Halicarnassus, *Roman Antiquities*, vol. 1, Loeb Classical Library 319, ed. Earnest Cary (Cambridge: Harvard University Press, 1937) 1:332 [2.7.3] compares the Roman divisions of *gens* to the Greek φυλή or τριττὺς and *curia* to the φράτρα or λόχος.

82 Bodin likely may have relied on the account of Dionysius of Halicarnassus, *Roman Antiquities* 1:334, 1:338 [2.8.1; 2.9.3].

83 *République* 32; *De Republica* 22 [1.4]. Bodin chose to render the terms, 'law of nations', 'law of nature', and 'divine law' by the unconventional form of *lex gentium*, *lex naturae*, and *lex divina* (rather than *ius gentium*, *ius naturale*, and *ius divinum*). In my discussion, I have chosen to follow the more conventional form, which Bodin also uses in his earlier writings. But, as I'll discuss in Chapter 4, Bodin

Contrast this paterfamilial power over children with the limited power of husbands over wives in marriage. Unlike children, wives (not in a manus marriage) were generally immune from their husband's power of life and death. The reason for this was that marriage (unlike fatherhood) was strictly a legal relationship defined (and, thus, limited) by positive legislation, not by the *ius naturale*.[84] No one is, by nature, a wife or husband. Husbands, thus, had no natural rights or powers over their wives, let alone a natural power of life and death. Whatever powers they *did* have was due to the positive legislation and generally accepted legal principles of the *ius gentium* that recognized the legal act of matrimony, such as a Roman *manus* marriage, and conferred defined legal rights upon husbands (unlike concubinage which conferred none). Some things they could do legally by this legal right of matrimony: Bodin cites Dionysius of Halicarnassus' account of the archaic law of Romulus which legally allowed four instances – and *only* these four instances – where a husband could legally kill his wife.[85] What they could *not* do was exercise the same sort of discretionary power of life and death that fathers exercised over children.

Needless to say, this ancient history of domestic violence probably isn't the most attractive or persuasive argument. But Bodin's purpose certainly wasn't to persuade his readers about the paterfamilial right; he was horrified by this aspect of Roman law. His goal, instead, was to make a more technical point about the *legality* of that supposed right.[86] By what law could *patria potestas* be considered a legal *right*?

The *patria potestas* was customarily regarded one of the quintessential features of Roman family law (and largely contributed to the modern reputation of Roman law as an illiberal law, as Étienne Pasquier judged the *patria potestas* to be in the *Recherches de la France*).[87] But it was always understood, by convention, to be an archaic practice exclusive to Romans, as the text of Justinian's *Institutes* tries to

subscribes to a voluntarist theory of legislation, where all binding law, including higher law, must ultimately be traceable to the command of some lawmaking sovereign will, whether human or divine. The implication is that Bodin allows for the theoretical possibility that natural law and divine law, as species of positive legislation, can be *unmade* by a divine legislator. Note, however, Bodin's comment, at *République* 19; *De Republica* 14 [1.3] which links *recta ratio* to *divina voluntas*, thereby skirting around the Euthyphro problem of divine command.

The *ius Quiritium* specifies more precisely the *ius civile* as it applies exclusively to Roman citizens (= *Quirites*).

84 Cp. *République* 15 [1.2]. *Distributio* fol. B, s.v.: *Negotium mercenarium*, where marriage (or rather, the marriage dowry) is treated as a kind of real contract [*nuptiarum contractus*], comparable to the contract of partnership [*societas*]. There, Bodin defines the legal marriage act as *viri et uxoris conventio ad mutuam vitae coniunctionem*.

85 *De Republica* 16 [1.3], citing Dionysius of Halicarnassus, identifies adultery, bearing a child, the counterfeiting of keys, and wine consumption. Turchetti 207, n.23 locates the likely source in *Roman Antiquities* 2.25. Bodin's utilitarian reasoning for divorce in 1.3 is striking.

86 Becker, *Gendering the Renaissance Commonwealth* 179: 'The conjugal relationship was central to understanding Bodin's notion of power, and especially the power of the sovereign.'

87 Donald Kelley, 'The Rise of Legal History in the Renaissance', *History and Theory* 9 (1970): 191–2.

make clear: 'The right of *patria potestas*, which we hold over children, is exclusive [*proprium*] to Roman citizens'.[88]

Bodin, willing to look beyond the conventional boundaries of Roman law, took issue with that assertion of Roman exclusivity, in part because it made the paterfamilial power of life and death a legal right created and defined strictly by positive legislation.[89] His argument reflected his stylistically eclectic use of ancient historical sources to make a more theoretical point.

It's simply not true, Bodin argues, that only *Roman* fathers exercised the power of life and death over members of their family. The practice, Bodin points out, was licit and common among many peoples of antiquity; he cited practices of the Persians, the Celts, the peoples of Upper Asia, and the West Indies.[90] We even have, Bodin points out, textual evidence, or testimonies, in sources that allegedly document the practice, such as in Caesar's *Bellum Gallicum* and, above all, in Scripture.[91]

All of this was to make a more general point that the right of *patria potestas* isn't simply a product of positive legislation. In Bodin's view, the effect of the XII Tables was entirely superfluous, seeing that the right was already fully valid and legal, by divine law [*iure divino*], natural law [*iure naturali*], and the common law of mankind [*iure gentium*]. Even if the Romans had never enacted the XII Tables, the right of *patria potestas* would still be valid and lawful.[92]

One critical consequence of this reasoning is that the right can't simply be abrogated by ordinary legislative (or even equitable praetorian) means; just as no positive legislation created the right of *patria potestas*, no contrary negative legislation, let alone an act of judicial review, can take it away.[93] Much less can the right be nullified by desuetude, which does nothing to alter the full force and validity of the right. The only way to change a natural right, Bodin thinks, is to amend or rescind

[88] Inst.1.9.2. The term, *proprium*, indicates that it is a *ius proprium* specific to the Roman *civitas* [hence, *ius civile* or, what is the same thing, the *ius Quiritium*], as opposed to a *ius commune* which is shared among all *gentes*. See also D.1.2.2.12; Gaius of D.1.1.9.

[89] Table IV of the XII Tables: 'To a father shall be given over a son the power of life and death'. There remains a more technical question whether Bodin regarded the praetorian law of the *ius honorarium* as having derogatory effect on the paterfamilial power *ex iure civili*.

[90] *De Republica* 22 [1.4], citing Aristotle. Cp. Becker, *Gendering the Renaissance Commonwealth* 123, argues that Bodin in this passage is 'invoking laws from ancient civilizations ... [and] thereby still referred to other civil laws, not to natural law.' I read this differently; Bodin is identifying a legal consensus among the laws of different nations on a common legal concept. This style of reasoning exemplifies Bodin's appeal to the *ius gentium*.

[91] Deuteronomy 21:18–21. However, this passage does not entirely support Bodin's point, since it is the men of the city, and not the father alone, who carries out the punishment of stoning the rebellious child to death.

[92] What positive legislation *could* do, however, was provide for legal remedies justiciable before a court to protect the natural right. That is the same argument for private property: Property is a natural right that is valid whether or not a legal system formally recognizes it. But a legal system can always create actionable legal remedies in order to protect that natural right.

[93] Because it is, in his view, a product of divine legislation, it can only be taken away by contrary divine legislation.

the natural law creating that right in the first place, something no human legislator can do.[94]

It is for these reasons that Bodin treated the paterfamilial power of *patria potestas* as particularly exceptional. Unlike the *imperium in subditos* of princes and magistrates or the *dominium in servos* of the master, paterfamilial power of *patria potestas*, Bodin argued, was the only legal power that can rightfully be said to be derived from nature [*a natura*].[95] Because of its 'natural' foundations in the paterfamilial power, the family – and only the family – can be said to be a 'natural associaton' [*communauté naturelle*; *societas naturalis*].

But at this stage of the analysis, some theorists have been tempted to take a further bold step. If the patriarch is empowered by nature with the power of life and death, like a sovereign, couldn't we say then that the family is actually a kind of state? This is the line of reasoning developed most fully and famously in *Patriarcha* by Sir Robert Filmer, the English defender of royal authority and scrupulous reader of Bodin, and it is also the argument that John Locke would later take as the main foil against which he would develop his own theory of limited government. It's also an argument that makes an appearance in Chapter VIII of Hobbes' *De Cive*, where Hobbes declares in aggressively anti-Aristotelian fashion that a *regnum* is nothing but a *familia magna*, just as a *familia* is nothing but a *regnum parvum*.[96] Both are two sides of the same coin, in that they both require *dominium*, whether that of a father (paternal *dominium*), a master (despotic *dominium*), or a sovereign (political *dominium*).

Bodin, for his part, resists the temptation to make this move. Families may be state-like, but they're not states, for two key reasons. The first concerns the pluralistic foundations of Bodin's theory of state: The state is, by definition, heterogeneous in its internal constitution. The diversity of elements making up a state is something to be found only in states, but never, it seems, in families. The thought here is that family members can't form subsidiary associations within families, in the same way that members of states can form, say, a *collegium*. Family life does not allow a division between *res communis* and *res propria*, between what is common and what is private, in the same way the public life of state requires.[97]

The other key difference concerns the nature of paterfamilial authority and sovereign authority. It is true that patriarchs are in a sense 'sovereign' over their

[94] Bodin supplies another argument in passing, suggesting that the *ius gentium* (what he variously characterizes as *populorum omnium leges* at *De Republica* 15) has abrogated the force of a once-valid Roman law. This is a stunning example of a point of legal theory that will become critical: the case of a higher law overriding positive legislation (specifically, the XII Tables).

[95] *République* 29; *De Republica* 20 [1.4]. Bodin reflects on the wide and narrow significations of the word, *potestas*, in this passage. He cites Seneca as his source, but he is also likely thinking of D.50.16.215.

[96] Hobbes, *De Cive* 8.1. See also Daniel Lee, 'Sovereignty and *Dominium*: The Foundations of Hobbesian Statehood', in *Hobbes's On the Citizen: A Critical Guide*, ed. Robin Douglass and Johan Olsthoorn (Cambridge: Cambridge University Press, 2020).

[97] Cp. the revealing comment *contra Platonem* of *De Republica* 11 [1.2]: *Nihil publicum esse potest, ubi nihil sit privatum.*

families. But those patriarchs are themselves subject to a superior. They are duty-bound and 'obliged [*obligée*; *cogatur*] to contribute something' to the state of which they are members, in the form of taxation, tolls, or extraordinary imposts.[98] Sovereigns, by contrast, are – by definition, as we'll see – 'free' [*soluti*] of such obligations: It is an essential quality of sovereignty to be exempt from having to perform legal obligations such as paying taxes, tolls, and imposts, as everyone else is required to. Free of all such legal obligations, sovereigns (as a famous medieval legal dictum put it) 'recognize no superior on earth in temporal affairs' [*rex in regno suo superiorem non recognoscat in temporalibus*].

Patriarchs, thus, carry an unusual dual identity in Bodin's system. Though they are like sovereigns with a *domesticum imperium* within the domain of their households [*familiarum principes*], once they step outside, they become ordinary subjects, like any other subject, 'who is duty-bound to another sovereign power' [*qui summae alterius potestati obligatur*].[99] Indeed, Bodin begins his treatment of citizenship (Chapter 3) with the patriarch, and he does so for a simple reason. Though patriarchs are entirely free and *sui iuris*, they are, from the point of view of sovereignty, subjects [*subditi*] like everyone else. Indeed, sovereignty produces an egalitarian, levelling effect, repositioning patriarchs, sovereigns over their families, so that they are forced to stand at the same level as any other subject – women, children, slaves, and the poor.

Societas Civilis: *Collegium*, *Corpus*, *Respublica*

Not all associations, of course, are families. While families are the most important constituent unit of the state, it wasn't the only unit. Bodin imagined a grand typology of associations, of which the family, or the 'natural association' [*communauté naturelle*; *societas naturalis*], was only meant to be one species.

The other species is what Bodin labelled the 'civil association' [*communauté civile*; *societas civilis*], a capacious category that was thought to include numerous sub-species – the *collège*/*collegium* and the *corp*/*corpus*, as well as the state [*république*; *respublica*].[100] Taken together, natural associations and civil

[98] *République* 16; *De Republica* 12 [1.2]; *République* 431; *De Republica* 300 [3.5]. The point is restated in a more systematic way at the start of 1.3, where Bodin introduces two sets of distinctions, between [1] *potestas publica* which, in turn, can be [1a] *legibus soluta* or [1b] *legibus imminuta* (*De Republica* 300 has *legibus obligatur*) and [2] *potestas privata*, one of which is the paterfamilial power limited in scope only to the family.

[99] *De Republica* 45–6 [1.6].

[100] It might be tempting for a modern reader to treat this category of *societas civilis*, as an early modern version of what the modern social sciences generally call 'civil society', typically defined (as in Hegel, Tocqueville, and Marx) in contradistinction to the state. But it is easy to see why this must be an anachronism, and this is because the state itself – the *respublica* – is also a *kind* of *societas civilis* [or *communauté civile*]. *République* 474; *De Republica* 328.

associations were the two major species included under the genus of 'association' [*communauté*; *societas*;].

Bodin properly treats civil association in a chapter of *République/De Republica* III.[101] It is clear that Bodin intends to treat the *collège/collegium* and the *corp/corpus* as connected, both indicating types of intermediary associations typically found within a state.

We might dispense, first, with a preliminary question: Why does he use two separate terms, *collegium* and *corpus*, to denote this category of civil association? The most likely answer can be found in how he defines and distinguishes between these two. *Collegium* (in the Latin text) is defined as a *legitimi trium pluriumve personarum eiusdem conditionis consociatio* [a *consociatio* of three or more persons of the same legal status].[102] By contrast, the *corpus* is defined as *plurium collegiorum coniunctio*.[103] This treatment of *collegia* and *corpora* together indicates that Bodin was likely following the naming convention and analysis of the title in the *Digest*, *De collegiis et corporibus* (D.47.22) dealing with corporate or collegial bodies in civil law. Bodin's definition of a *collegium* as an association of *legitimi* persons relies on the distinction in D.47.22.1–3 between those that are *illicita* and those that are properly *legitima*. Taken together, these *collegia* and *corpora* constitute the vast range of 'intermediate' civil associations making up what the modern social sciences typically call 'civil society' (and, thus, I will treat 'civil association' – *societas civilis* – as equivalent to Bodin's *collegia* and *corpora*). Membership of these associations is what accounts for the pluralistic and internally differentiated heterogeneous character of the Bodinian state.

It's equally important to stress that Bodin's study wasn't meant to be an abstract, ante-empirical, social theory of groups. His study of civil association reads more like a comparative sociology of associational life and reveals the sort of associations he had in mind. Among those were occupational 'colleges of merchants and of all tradesmen' [*opificum omnium et mercatorum collegia*], of philosophers such as 'among the Pythagoreans', 'of physicians, of scholarly men' [*aut medicorum, aut scholasticorum hominum*], 'of farmers' [*agricolarum*].[104] Bodin's analysis also reflects the shared devotional corporate life of later medieval Christendom expressed institutionally in the form of monasteries, cathedral chapters, and colleges

[101] He briefly touches upon the subject in *Methodus* VI. This aspect of Bodin's political theory has been explored in a number of studies: Vittor Ivo Comparato, 'Mediazione politica e teoria dello Stato: Note su Bodin e Hobbes', *Archivio Storico Italiano* 1 (1986): 17–33; Richard Bonney, 'Bodin and the Development of the French Monarchy', *Transactions of the Royal Historical Society* 40 (1990): 43–61; Luca Mannori, 'Per una preistoria della funzione amministrativa', *Quaderni Fiorentini per la storia del pensiero giuridico moderno* 19 (Milan: Giuffré, 1990): 323–504.

[102] *De Republica* 327 [3.7]. This is an application of the rule of D.50.16.85. Bodin's use of the term, *consociatio*, is remarkable, as it is the same term used by one of his first major critics, Johannes Althusius, in the *Politica Methodice Digesta*, the historical inspiration for Arend Lijphart's 'consociational democracy'. Arend Lijphart, 'Consociational Democracy', *World Politics* 21 (1969): 207–25.

[103] Cp. *De Republica* 330 [3.7].

[104] *République* 477; *De Republica* 330 [3.7].

which, as Bodin has observed, have expanded to an 'infinite number' [*in infinitum numerum excreuerunt*].[105]

Perhaps most noteworthy of all are the associations of public authorities, what he designated as *collegia* empowered with jurisdiction by concession, *summi principis beneficio et concessu*.[106] Bodin takes his example from Roman colleges of magistrates such as the college of tribunes, the college of praetors, and the college of quaestors, all acting on behalf of the Roman state. But he is also thinking of collegial courts, such as the French Parlements of his time, the Imperial *Reichskammergericht*, and the Roman Rota.[107]

Recognizing this proliferation of associational life, Bodin explicitly integrated the social reality of civil associations into his theory of state. This is a point worth underlining, for two related reasons. Bodin is typically seen as one of the chief antagonists of modern pluralism, an interpretive artefact of the principal theorists of pluralism – von Gierke, Maitland, Figgis, and Cole. And that interpretive position has been uncritically reproduced in the most recent scholarship on the theory of pluralism. But what Bodin's study of civil association suggests instead is precisely what pluralists advocate, the widespread dispersal of jurisdiction, decision-making, and social activity, especially in the early modern states with which he was familiar.

This leads then to the other point to underline, which is that civil associations in Bodin's theory performed, just as in the theory of modern pluralism, something like a moderating and stabilizing function for the whole state. Associational life is valuable specifically because it minimizes social conflict, creates civic 'harmony' (a notion of special significance in Bodin's moral and legal theory), and promotes solidarity – what we might, in contemporary academic language, characterize as 'social capital'.[108] This is an argument typically associated with later French social and political theorists – most notably, Montesquieu, Tocqueville, and Guizot in their writings on intermediate associations – but it isn't simply coincidence that Frenchmen, though separated by centuries from each other and motivated by different intellectual concerns, would arrive at a common and remarkably cohesive interpretive understanding of the social function of civil associations. The reason for this interpretive cohesion is because their first point of reference was the system of estates, orders, and ranks constituting the principal legal institutions of *ancien*

105 *De Republica* 330 [3.7].

106 *De Republica* 331–32 [3.7]. On Bodin's use of the term, *iurisdictio*, see *Popular Sovereignty* Ch. 3 *passim*. It originates from a technical debate in legal theory on the relationship of *imperium* and *iurisdictio* in Roman law, in connection with D.1.21.1, 2.1.1, and 2.1.3.

107 *De Republica* 161 [1.10]. Bodin dives into the details of collective decision-making in collegial courts at *De Republica* 292, citing Roman and French court procedure using the norm of majority rule.

108 Robert Putnam, *Making Democracy Work: Civic Traditions in Modern Italy* (Princeton: Princeton University Press, 1993). What Bodin seems to be imagining is something like a complex of network-relations, whereby *collegia* can form *corpora*, and from which both, in turn, can be transformed into a *universitas* or *consociatio*.

regime France.[109] Indeed, it was precisely this system that led Bodin to characterize the French monarchy as the archetype of what he will call a properly *droit monarchie*.[110]

But the French were not the only ones to discover and implement the practical advantages of associational life. The great ancient lawgivers, Numa, Solon, and Lycurgus, all established *confrairies, colleges & communautés* in Rome, Athens, and Sparta, as tools to promote civic unity and friendship among citizens.[111]

Why do associations produce this stabilizing effect? The simple answer is that civil associations are very good at manufacturing and cultivating bonds of civic friendship and amity [*amitié*; *amicitia*; cp. φιλία].[112] Through the sharing of a common life, strangers – and perhaps even enemies too – can become friends.[113] This is beneficial for any state. A state whose citizens are positioned as friends not only avoid civil conflict, they also promote the overall unity – or 'harmony', as Bodin prefers – of the state.[114] It is for this reason, then, that Bodin describes friendship as 'the sole foundation of all society' [*le seul fondement de toute societé*].[115] And since civil associations best promote amicable relations of friendship, Bodin ultimately advances a thesis of institutional design; lawgivers should favour building robust institutions that cultivate civic bonds of friendship.

This argument justifying civil associations in terms of amity and friendship may seem like an unusual and surprising turn in the direction of Bodin's argument. But the turn is explained partly by Bodin's oblique use of classical moral theories of 'civic friendship', a topic of special interest in Renaissance moral thought.[116] Indeed, in the sixteenth century, the ethics and virtue of friendship was a standard topic of Renaissance moral theory, discussed by Erasmus and Montaigne. Bodin makes no explicit reference to a particular classical source on this point, but the argument clearly owes much to the Greek principle, cited prominently by Plato in the *Republic*, that all things are to be held in common among friends [*amicorum esse omnia communia*].[117]

[109] Roland Mousnier, *The Institutions of France Under the Absolute Monarchy, 1598–1789*, 2 vols., trans. Arthur Goldhammer (Chicago: University of Chicago Press, 1984). Charles Loyseau, 'Cinq livres du droit du offices', in *Les oeuvres de Maistre Charles Loyseau* (Lyon, 1701).

[110] This is in contrast to a *monarchie seigneuriale* (exemplified by Ottoman rulership) or *tyrannie*.

[111] *République* 476; *De Republica* 329 [3.7]: *ex societatibus, corporibus & collegiis*.

[112] The Greek, φιλία, is one of several terms that can be translated as 'love'. But, as Plato explains in *Symposium* and *Lysis*, it isn't the only term that can mean 'love'.

[113] Friendship does not extend, however, to brigands and pirates, as Bodin explains at *République* 814; *De Republica* 604 [5.6]. Since they are outside the scope of the *ius gentium*, there can be no *amicitia*, *societas*, or *commercium cum piratis ac latronibus*.

[114] Or, *amitié-harmonie*, as Sara Miglietti calls it, 'Amitié, Harmonie et Paix Politique chez Aristote et Jean Bodin', *Astérion: Philosophie, Histoire des Idées, Pensée Politique* 7 (2010): ¶¶26–29.

[115] *République* 477 [3.7]; cp. *De Republica* 329–30 expresses the point slightly differently.

[116] See Sibyl Schwarzenbach, 'On Civic Friendship', *Ethics* 107 (1996): 97–128.

[117] Plato *Republic* IV, 423^{c}; *Phaedrus* 279^{c}; Aristotle, *Ethics* 8.9, 1159^{b}31; Cicero, *De Off.* 1.51. On the reception of this principle in early modern moral thought, see Kathy Eden, 'Between Friends All Is Common: The Erasmian Adage and Tradition', *Journal of the History of Ideas* 59 (1998): 405–19.

The political significance of the principle, however, is to be seen in how classical political theorists imagine the constitution of the state as an extension of friendship [φιλία], rather than as an expression of justice [δίκαιον]. Aristotle offers what is perhaps the canonical treatment of this extension in the *Nicomachean Ethics*, where he explains that:

> Friendship [φιλία] seems ... to hold states together, and lawgivers [seem] to care more for it than for justice [δίκαιον]; for unanimity seems to be something like friendship, and this they aim at most of all, and expel faction as their worst enemy; and when men are friends they have no need of justice.[118]

The contrast between friendship and justice might be explained in terms of what each does to the relations between persons. While friendship tends to bring people together, justice can tear them apart.[119] Better, then, to cultivate those humane, gentler virtues that strengthen civic bonds of friendship.

Bodin seems to have been moved by this argument. Which, Bodin asks, is a more reliable foundation for maintaining the state – friendship or justice? The advantage of justice (Bodin is thinking of the commutative justice delivered in the courts of kings and judges) is that it can end controversies and settle conflicts between citizens, thereby restoring the civil peace necessary for states. The disadvantage, however, is that the peace secured by the swift and terrible sword of justice is only a fragile peace. As Bodin writes, 'Justice may indeed resolve conflicts, but not hatred. Indeed, it may often turn friends into foes'.[120]

If the choice, then, is between cultivating friendship and cultivating justice, this is an easy call for Bodin: Friendship [*l'amitié*; *amicitia*] is 'far more necessary than justice itself for maintaining [the state]'.[121] Φιλία, as well as the gentler humane virtues necessary for friendliness, softens hearts hardened by the sword of justice. It, in fact, obviates the need for justice, as 'disputes [*controversiae*] are uprooted, and citizens are themselves reconciled to each other and to the state with the greatest tranquility and goodwill'.[122] And since civil associations (Bodin thinks) reliably

[118] *Ethics* 8.1, 1155^{a}22–6; 8.9–10, which Montaigne cites in 'Of Friendship', in *Essays*, trans. J.M. Cohen (New York: Penguin, 1958) 92. Cp. De Smet, 'Philosophy for Princes'.

[119] James Schall in the essay, 'Friendship and Political Philosophy', *Review of Metaphysics* 50 (1996): 126, nicely explains why justice is the 'most terrible of the virtues'. Justice 'requires us to render what is due to everyone no matter what his character or relationship to us is', whether close friend or total stranger. This alienating effect of an abstract justice is precisely what worried Bodin about states without a proper sense of harmony among its members, and one important reason why he introduces the category of 'harmonic justice' as a third alternative to the two principal theories of justice, commutative and distributive.

[120] *République* 477: *l'amitié est ... beaucoup plus requise entre les hommes que la justice: Car la iustice, qui iamais n'est ployable, retenant so droiture, fait bien souvent les amis ennemis*; *De Republica* 330 [3.7]: *Cum lites quidem iudiciorum exitu, non tamen odia finiantur.*

[121] *République* 477; *De Republica* 330 [3.7].

[122] *République* 477; *De Republica* 330 [3.7].

secure and cultivate civic friendship and amity, the state demands a robust associational life – what we might today call 'civil society' – in the Bodinian state.

As a strictly theoretical matter, no civil association is technically necessary for statehood. States can exist without them since states are, by Bodin's original definition, fundamentally unions of families. But given these practical advantages of associational life, Bodin must conclude that no state can last for long without civil associations. And that is because such associational life, Bodin thinks, cultivates these civic bonds of amity that can sustain states over time. In this way, civil associations serve a vital practical purpose for all states, so vital that Bodin indicates they may as well be necessary.

From Alliance of Friends to Statehood

Let us take stock. In Bodin's political theory, the state [*république*; *respublica*] is fundamentally an association [*communauté*; *societas*]. Specifically, it is a compound association made up of lesser associations. And these lesser associations, as we now see, are the 'natural association' [*societas naturalis*] of families and the 'civil association' [*societas civilis*] of collegial or corporate bodies.

How are all these lesser constituent associations tied together so that they jointly form one civic unity – *une république*? What is the 'bond' [*vinculum*] that ties [*ligat*] the plural elements of this political *societas* together as one state?

Consider now one possibility, the Aristotelian idea of civic friendship as the basis of statehood. Friendship, as Bodin has tried to argue, certainly confers instrumental advantages to the state. As Bodin put it, cultivating civic friendship among citizens makes the state much easier to govern, for reasons we have seen.

Is it, however, sufficient? Suppose families, *collegia*, and *corpora* join together and are united, *par amitié*. Could that resulting association of friends be a state?

Bodin explicitly recognized this as a theoretical possibility, but only to rule it out as a model for statehood: 'Friendship alone cannot make one and the same state' [*denique magnam amicitiae communionem, efficere non possunt ut una sit et eadem Respublica*].[123] So that his readers can see the difference clearly, Bodin draws the contrast clearly: A group of families that are merely 'joined through friendship' [*par amitié alliées*] make only one *corp* or *communauté*. By contrast, a group of families that are obliged and subjected to one sovereign authority [*alliés par puissance souveraine*] make one state.[124]

Though *amicitia* isn't enough for statehood, it *is* enough, however, to make alliances and leagues – an international 'society of states' (a theme I'll return to in the

[123] *Methodus* 249. Otherwise, states in friendly relations – Bodin's example was the bilateral international relation between France and Spain – might mistakenly be regarded as one state.
[124] *République* 474 [3.7].

Conclusion). Indeed, 'friendship' [*amicitia*], like the hostility of an 'enemy' [*hostis*], turns out to be, in Bodin's theory, one of the foundational concepts of international relations.

There's a theoretically urgent reason for this move: Bodin wants his readers to be alert to the tendency to mistakenly treat a league or alliance of independent states as if it were one united state. Leagues, Bodin insists, aren't states. The Swiss Confederation of thirteen cantons is Bodin's preferred case in point. By the middle of the sixteenth century, it became conventional to regard the Swiss Confederation emerging from the Swabian War as a *de facto* independent state. Swiss statehood was finally defended in what would become the definitive treatise on Swiss constitutional theory, the *De Republica Helvetiorum* by the theologian, Josias Simler: 'Certainly the many peoples and cities making up the Swiss [*Helvetiorum*] are not few; [the Confederation] is nevertheless one citizenry [*una civitas*] and one state [*una Respublica*]'.[125] Bodin's purpose, however, was to deny statehood – and therefore, sovereignty – to the Swiss; it isn't one state, but a league of thirteen independent states, tied together, not by sovereignty, but only by *amicitia*.[126] The same might be said for the many leagues in antiquity, such as the Amphictyonic, the Achaean, and the Aetolian Leagues.[127]

There's also a more academic, historiographical reason for Bodin's interest in this matter, a concern voiced in the *Methodus*. Historians, Bodin observes, were often confronted with the challenge of explaining how and when an alliance of independent states, originally allied loosely in friendship, ultimately became united as one state. Take again, for example, the Achaean League [*Achœorum societas*; *Ligue des Acheans*]. The history of the League is, as Bodin points out, deceptive, concealing its transformation from a simple defensive alliance of three independent cities to become one independent and united state.[128] Although the Achaean League did eventually, according to Bodin's analysis, become one state, it wasn't always a state, and the failure to see this difference has led to fundamental misunderstandings of the politics, especially the foreign policies, of the Achaeans.

The same point can be illustrated in the history of Rome, Bodin's most important illustration. It's easy to forget, Bodin points out, that Rome only gradually, and relatively late in its history, became one unitary state. At its founding, however, Rome was just one among many peoples and tribal communities, cohabiting the Italian

[125] Josias Simler, *De Republica Helvetiorum Libri Duo* (Zurich: Christopher Froschauer, 1576) fol. 1_{vo}. The contrasting analyses of Simler and Bodin on the Swiss case have been studied recently by Thomas Maissen, *Die Geburt der Republik: Staatsverständnis und Repräsentation in der frühneuzeitlichen Eidgenossenschaft* (Göttingen: Vandenhoeck & Ruprecht, 2006) 45–76.

[126] *République* 110, *De Republica* 71 [1.7]; *Methodus* 249–50.

[127] *République* 114, *De Republica* 75 [1.7]. We might also speculate, based on this Bodinian reasoning, that the United States under the Articles of Confederation wasn't one state, but thirteen independent and sovereign states joined together in 'a firm league of friendship' (Articles §3). The principal author of the Articles was John Dickinson, a lawyer who read law in Philadelphia and at the Middle Temple.

[128] *République* 115, *De Republica* 75 [1.7].

peninsula. From this assortment of Italic peoples and communities emerged first, *not* a state, but an international society of states.

Rome's early attempts at establishing 'foreign relations' with neighbouring communities [*socii*] chiefly involved forging ties of amity, hospitality, and comity, on equal terms. These international ties of friendship were formalized through treaties [*foedera*] that created an international society, of which Rome was but a partner and member-state. Because of the supposed equality between Rome and the neighbouring *socii* (or equivalently, *foederati*) these *foedera* were famously described by Livy as *foedera aequa*.[129] Imagining Rome as a unitary state concealed the internal differentiation among the various peoples and communities that made up Rome.

Rome's rapid rise as the dominant Mediterranean military power, however, shattered that myth of equality and incentivized Romans to reimagine how these amicable ties of friendship with the *socii* could be strategically exploited as an instrument of domination to fuel Rome's war machine. In this respect, relations of *amicitia* became something more than simply an international ethic of hospitality and comity: It became the basis for a strategic military alliance, *societas et amicitia* [cp. φιλία καὶ συμμαχία], whereby Rome, as the dominant partner, offered protection to its allied *socii* and *foederati* in exchange for a steady supply of manpower.[130] In this way, Rome's ambitious war policy of conquest and expansion reduced the standing of the *socii* to mere protectorates.

Bodin described this asymmetrical relationship between Rome and her allies explicitly as *clientela*, with Rome in the superior role of *patronus*. A new kind of foreign relation, thus, emerged during Rome's spectacular rise as the unquestioned military superpower of the Mediterranean world – not one of subjection, but of protection, with client-states as Rome's 'protectorates'.[131] What distinguished this

[129] Livy, *History of Rome*, vol. 4, *Books 8–10*, trans. B.O. Foster, Loeb Classical Library 191 (Cambridge: Harvard University Press, 1926) 4:12–13 [*Ab urbe condita* 8.4.2]; *History of Rome*, vol. 9, *Books* 31–34, ed. and trans. J.C. Yardley, Loeb Classical Library 295 (Cambridge: Harvard University Press 2017) 9:574–77 [*Ab urbe condita* 34.57.7–9]; *History of Rome*, vol. 11, *Books 38–40*, ed. and trans. J.C. Yardley, Loeb Classical Library 313 (Cambridge: Harvard University Press, 2018) 11:322–23 [*Ab urbe condita* 39.37.13]. The terms, *foederati* and *socii*, were used interchangeably and implied at least a formal notion of sovereign equality. Bodin identifies *aequum foedus* as one of two possible forms of international *amicitia* at *De Republica* 579 [5.6], the other being *foedus iniquum*.

[130] Bodin, at one point, describes an international political economy of protection, where the 'protection offered by the powerful' [*patrocinia potentiorum*] can be secured for a price – or, more literally, rent [*mercede conduci*] – as a quid pro quo [*trafiquer la protection à prix d'argent*]. *République* 785, *De Republica* 582 [5.6]. See Conclusion.

[131] This asymmetrical *amicitia* is what Bodin called *foedus iniquum*. It reappears in the major treatises of international law – e.g., Grotius, *De Iure Belli ac Pacis* 1.3.21, 2.15.6–7, Pufendorf, *De Iure Naturae et Gentium* 8.9.4; Pufendorf, *On the Duty of Man and Citizen*, ed. James Tully, trans. Michael Silverthorne (Cambridge: Cambridge University Press, 1991) 173 [*De Officio Hominis et Civis* 2.17.§3], and Vattel, *Law of Nations* 83 [*Droit des Gens* 1.1.5] as a type of treaty. Theodor Mommsen, *Römisches Staatsrecht*, vol. 3(1) (Leipzig: Verlag von S. Hirzel, 1887) 653–60 [3.1] notably contests the authenticity of this *foedus aequum/foedus iniquum* distinction. Thomas Poole, 'The Idea of the Federative', in *The Double-Facing Constitution*, ed. Jacco Bomhoff, David Dyzenhaus, and Thomas Poole (Cambridge: Cambridge University Press, 2020) 72 n.57, highlighted an interesting reply to Mommsen by Carl Schmitt in the *Nomos of the Earth*.

relation was the giving and receiving of a mutual faith, something that (Bodin asserts) was not to be found in vassalage; whereas a 'vassal pledges faith to his lord, but does not receive' faith in turn, a client, by contrast, 'pledges and receives faith [from the patron] in turn [*dat fidem accipitque vicissim*]'.[132]

Yet, despite the clear asymmetry of power between Rome and her allies, Rome didn't (at least not yet: prior to the first century B.C.E.) annex and Romanize their allied client states. The *socii* weren't subjects, but foreign partners – albeit junior partners – in an alliance. And precisely for this reason, Bodin argued, these *socii*, foreigners to Rome and lacking Roman citizenship, could not technically be regarded properly as a part of the Roman state.

Rome, thus, continued to operate according to the juridical fiction of a *foedus aequum*, establishing the international bond of friendship.[133] In principle, the *socii* were formally independent of Rome and could even be called 'independent peoples' [*liberi populi*], as the jurist Proculus suggests in a famously difficult passage in the *Digest*:

> A nation [*populus*] is independent [*liber*] when they are subject to no other power. Likewise, it remains independent when they are allied to another by treaty, when they establish diplomatic ties of friendship on equal terms [*aequo foedere*], or even when a treaty [i.e. *foedus inaequum*] includes the provision that an allied nation must courteously [*comiter conservaret*; cp. comity] preserve the sovereignty [*maiestas*; greater-ness] of another nation.[134]

Bodin cited this passage (and reportedly even consulted the *littera Florentina* to corroborate textual accuracy) to make the point that, even while the free *socii* were clients and protectorates of Rome, the *socii* nevertheless were always understood to have 'retained their sovereignty' [*maiestatem retinere suam*], with the condition that the *socii* recognize and respect the 'greater-ness' [*maiestatem*] of Rome.[135] They were, at the same time, equal and unequal.

All of this is background for Bodin's striking thesis about Roman statehood: What many historians hitherto thought of as 'Rome', for most of its history in the Republican period, wasn't even a unitary state at all. Rather, Rome was really

[132] *De Republica* 68 [1.7]. Bodin's source for the feudal law rule on the asymmetrical giving of faith is the L.F. 2.6, 2.55, 2.26.1. Isnardi Parente, *Stato* 1:321; Turchetti 401. Cp. *De Off.* 1.56.

[133] Linda Zollschan, *Rome and Judaea: International Law Relations, 162–100 BCE* (London: Routledge, 2017) 114 *et seq.*

[134] D.49.15.7.1: *Liber autem populus est is, qui nullius alterius populi potestati est subiectus: sive is foederatus est item, sive aequo foedere in amicitiam venit sive foedere comprehensum est, ut is populus alterius populi maiestatem comiter conservaret.* The phrase, *aequo foedere in amicitiam venit*, is an explicit gesture towards Livy, *History of Rome* 9:574–77 [*Ab urbe condita* 34.57.7–9].

[135] *De Republica* 68 [1.7]. On Rome's *maiestas* or 'greater-ness' in Roman foreign relations, see Clifford Ando, *Law, Language, and Empire in the Roman Tradition* (Philadelphia: University of Pennsylvania Press, 2011) 74, 103–6.

just a congeries of independent states bound together by treaties of international friendship and fellowship.

Of course, it didn't stay this way forever. The *socii* were ultimately subsumed under the *imperium* and became fully subject to the *maiestatem populi Romani*, becoming proper subjects of a united Roman state. The key moment in Bodin's analysis was the Roman Social War (91–88 B.C.E.), fought between Rome and the *socii* who, as foreigners, were deprived of the advantages of Roman citizenship and demanded citizenship [*civitas*]. The result of the war was the concessive legal grant of citizenship to the *socii* by way of two landmark statutes of the Late Republic, the *lex Iulia de civitate Latinis et sociis danda* and the *lex Plautia Papiria de civitate sociis danda*.

What changed? Simply stated, the *socii* were, prior to the Social War, foreigners to Rome. But after the Social War and passage of the citizenship legislation, the *socii* were fully Roman, no longer free and independent peoples, but now fully subject to the *maiestas Romani populi*. Protection was replaced with bona fide subjection. For Bodin, this was the moment when Romanization reached its maturity and was complete.

Conclusion

What allowed Rome, once a confederate league of independent *socii* joined by *foedera* in friendship, finally to become one unitary state? Bodin's answer, in a word, was 'subjection'. Once the peoples of Rome's *socii* sank from protection into the servile condition of Roman citizenship, by surrendering their own residual *maiestas*, could they finally be counted as genuine members of one independent and unitary Roman state.[136]

To whom were these *socii* subjecting themselves? Bodin is careful; it's not simply Rome, but more specifically, the 'Roman people'. By pledging their faith and allegiance to the *maiestatem populi Romani* did these hitherto 'free' peoples immediately bind themselves to obey Rome's sovereign authority.

A general point can be extracted from this archetypical analysis of the Roman Republican constitution. What made Rome (*post Bellum Sociale*) one state, rather than a league of many independent communities, was shared subjection to one common superior, one authority. For the Roman Republic, that superior happened to be the Roman people [*Populus Romanus*].[137]

[136] On the use of Roman citizenship as a tool of domination and forced subjection, see Clifford Ando, ed., *The Antonine Constitution after 1800 Years: Citizenship and Empire in Europe, 200–1900* (Stuttgart: Franz Steiner Verlag, 2016).

[137] Hence, the formulation, *in maiestatem populi Romani*, used in Roman treaties. R.A. Bauman, 'Maiestatem Populi Romani Comiter Conservanto', *Acta Juridica* 19 (1976): 19–36.

But this analysis could be applied to any independent state. What binds the many elements of a state – the *societas naturalis* and *naturalis civilis* – together as one state, instead of as just a league, *isn't* simply their mutual feelings of goodwill and *amicitia*. It is their shared subjection to one common superior authority – or, as Bodin puts it in the *Methodus* – to be *sub unum & idem imperium subiecta.*[138]

That 'vertical' relationship or bond between subjects and a common superior authority was, for Bodin, the indispensable element of statehood, what tied the state together, as one unity. It is this vertical relationship, tying sovereigns and subjects together, that Bodin will call 'sovereignty'.[139]

Sovereignty is, as Martin Loughlin has (rightly, I believe) argued, a 'relational concept', and so it was also for Bodin.[140] Sovereignty signals a special kind of obligatory relationship between sovereigns and subjects that are constitutive of all states. Note, however, that sovereignty is not the *only* relational concept. Indeed, a principal aim of Book I of Bodin's *République* was to compare sovereignty with (and distinguish it from) other kinds of relations that could be, and have been, mistaken for sovereignty. Bodin identifies three for comparison:

> VASSALAGE: the relation between lord and vassal
> PROTECTION: the relation between patron and client
> SLAVERY: the relation between master and slave.[141]

Like these others, sovereignty (the relation between sovereign and subject) is also a relational concept, but it is *sui generis*, irreducible to any of these other three.

What, then, sets sovereignty apart? That will be the principal question motivating the analysis of the remaining chapters.

[138] *Methodus* 237 ('137'). This is how he explains France's unity as one state, despite its many religious and social divisions.

[139] Modern international law, however, has raised some doubts concerning Bodin's basic principle that the essential criterion of statehood is sovereignty, such as: *Customs Regime between Germany and Austria*, Advisory Opinion, 1931 P.C.I.J. (ser. A/B) No. 41 (September 5): 77 [§§160–64]; *Lighthouses in Crete and Samos* (France v. Greece), Judgment, 1937 P.C.I.J. (ser. A/B) No. 62 (October 8): 127 [§121]; 136 [§166].

[140] Loughlin, *Idea of Public Law* 65, 87.

[141] There is a notable difference in the degrees of subjection in the French *République* 162–63 and the Latin *De Republica* 108–9. Whereas the French text identifies only six degrees (the sixth degree being *le subiect naturel*, indicating the sovereign-subject relation), the Latin text identifies nine degrees (the ninth degree being slavery).

2
The Right of Sovereignty

Bodin's greatest contribution to the theory of sovereignty was to offer a systematic interpretation of the concept as a special kind of legal right. His analysis would have far-reaching consequences for the modern understanding and application of sovereignty in modern jurisprudence and political science.[1] My goal in this chapter, and the next, is to unpack this Bodinian concept of a *droit de souveraineté*, the 'right of sovereignty'.[2]

Let me begin by revisiting the point on which I concluded the previous chapter: sovereignty, for Bodin, was understood to be a relational concept. Just as slavery [*dominium*] signified a relation between master and slave, and protection [*patrocinium*] signified a relation between patron and client, sovereignty too signified a relation – that between sovereign and subject.[3]

But this was a special kind of relation whose definitive quality was the obligatory bond tethering subjects to their sovereigns.[4] As Bodin put it, what makes someone a subject (and, thus, a member of a state) is nothing else but the fact that he is 'bound' [*obligatur*] to his sovereign, and not unlike the manner in which a debtor is said to be bound [*obligatur*] to his creditor.[5] Just as debtors are bound to perform their duty of repayment, which creditors are entitled to claim, so too are subjects bound to perform their duty of obedience, which sovereigns are likewise entitled to claim.[6]

The juridical model that Bodin evidently had in mind in conceptualizing sovereignty was the *obligatio* of Roman law. Justinian's *Institutes* (3.13.pr) famously defined *obligatio* as *vinculum iuris*, a legal chain or tether.

[1] Later attempts to enumerate the rights of sovereignty will follow Bodin as a standard authority on this topic – for example, Henning Arnisaeus, *De Jure Majestatis Libri Tres* (Frankfurt: Typis Andreae Eichorn, 1610) 209 [2.1.1]; Richard Zouch, *Elementa Jurisprudentiae* (Leiden: Elzevir, 1652) 101–4.

[2] It is important to clarify that 'the right of sovereignty', as I attribute to Bodin, is unrelated to what Joel Feinberg once called a 'sovereign right monopoly'. Joel Feinberg, 'The Nature and Value of Rights', *Journal of Value Inquiry* 4 (1970): 618.

[3] Benedetto Croce, *Politics and Morals*, trans. Salvatore J. Castiglione (New York: Philosophical Library, 1945) 17: 'In the relationship between ruler and ruled sovereignty belongs to neither but to the relationship itself'.

[4] Cp. D.44.7.3.pr.

[5] *De Republica* 46–47 [1.6]: *summae alterius potestati obligatur*. Cp. Inst. 3.14.3.

[6] The *ius suum* appears in the opening sentence of Justinian's *Institutes*: Inst. 1.1.pr (cp. D.1.1.10.pr, Ulpian): *Iustitia est constans et perpetua voluntas ius suum cuique tribens.* ('Justice is the constant and perpetual will of giving to each his due [*ius suum*: or 'what is rightfully owed']'.)

The Right of Sovereignty. Daniel Lee, Oxford University Press. © Daniel Lee 2021.
DOI: 10.1093/oso/9780198755531.003.0003

> An 'obligation' is a legal bond (or chain), with which we are bound by a necessity of performing some act according to the laws of our state.[7]

Bodin's principal thesis concerning sovereignty is that it is, like a debt, fundamentally an obligatory relation: it is a bond tethering obligors to obligees. It's important to begin with this point to narrow, at the outset, the field of interpretive possibilities and avoid mistaking Bodinian sovereignty for something it was not supposed to be.

In this regard, the first thing to say is that Bodinian sovereignty was not intended to be a concept of naked coercive power, as such – or, in other words, brute force, what Cicero once simply called, *vis*.[8] This is so for the simple reason that power (whether in its 'hard' or even 'soft' forms), while it may very well be effective, as Thucydides, Machiavelli, and Hobbes have taught in their *Realpolitik* of power, in shaping or even controlling the preferences, the beliefs, and the behaviour of others, may nevertheless be an illegitimate power – or, as Locke would put it, a 'force without right'.[9]

The recurring Ciceronian trope of robbers, brigands, and pirates, which Bodin invokes in the opening page of the *République*, vividly illustrates Bodin's point, by way of analogy.[10] A robber or a pirate may, by force or fraud (*vi aut clam* as Bodin states, borrowing language from the title, *Quod vi aut claim*, D.43.24), successfully subdue and force someone else to submit to his will, but that's all they do.[11] Robbers and pirates simply overpower and coerce their victims; they don't 'rule' or 'govern' them. Their force is a power to which robbers and pirates have no *right* to exercise in the first place. They lack what might be described as 'standing to demand' that others 'act in a particular way'.[12] And so, for this reason, they can claim no legal protection or recognition for their actions. Anybody using mere force, like pirates and brigands, were like *proscripti*, 'outlaws' condemned to live beyond the boundary of legality and right.[13]

[7] Inst. 3.13.pr (Moyle). *Obligatio est iuris vinculum, quo necessitate adstringimur alicuius solvendae rei, secundum nostrae civitatis iura.*

[8] On Cicero's distinction between 'force' [*vis*] and 'right' [*ius*], see *Pro Sestio* 42.91–92; *De Legibus* 3.42, and more generally on this point, Bruce Frier, *The Rise of the Roman Jurists* (Princeton: Princeton University Press, 1985) 118–19.

[9] John Locke, *Two Treatises of Government*, ed. Peter Laslett (Cambridge: Cambridge University Press, 1988) 281 [II, §19]. Cicero's influence on Locke concerning this point is palpable – e.g., at *Two Treatises* 272, 274, 279 [II, §§8, 11, 16].

[10] The modern anglophone legal theorist versed in Austin and Hart should take note that the Ciceronian/Augustinian trope of robbers, brigands, and pirates serves the same function as the 'gunman situation' in Hart, *Concept of Law* 6–7, which is Hart's caricature of John Austin's command theory of law.

[11] *De Republica* 149 [1.10].

[12] Margaret Gilbert, *Rights and Demands: A Foundational Inquiry* (Oxford: Oxford University Press, 2018) 57–8.

[13] Unlike lawful combatants [*hostes*] in a legally declared war [*bellum iustum*] whose rights of postliminy are protected under the *ius gentium*, robbers and pirates are protected under no law. They are, as Cicero famously put it in *De Off.* 3.29.107, 'the common enemy of all mankind' [*communis hostis omnium*] who may licitly be killed by anyone. In Roman law, outlaws were formally declared in a

What distinguishes sovereignty from the merely effective power of the robber or the pirate, in Bodin's formulation, was something lacking in the latter, 'right' – a term Bodin designated in the French and Latin texts, respectively, by *droit* and *ius*, and a concept implied by Bodin's juridical model of obligation. Whereas sovereigns are entitled to demand obedience from their subjects, robbers and pirates, by contrast, have no such right. What they do have is merely *force*. It therefore becomes theoretically possible in Bodin's mind to distinguish between those regimes which, like the regime of robbers and pirates (and of gunmen), exercise no more than an illegitimate power over a subdued population, from a proper sovereign authority exercising a sovereignty to which it is rightfully entitled. How exactly Bodin draws this critical distinction will be developed in the following chapters, but for now, I only want to underline the more basic point that Bodinian sovereignty is, in its essence, a juridical concept of right [*droit*; *ius*] entailing an obligatory relation, not one of force [*force*; *vis*]. I might restate the point in a more provocative way to highlight the distinctiveness of Bodin's thesis: without right [*droit*; *ius*], there can be no sovereignty – *even if* there is effective coercive power.[14]

The work of this chapter will involve an investigation of Bodin's theory of right, a necessary preliminary before we consider specifically the right of sovereignty. I will reconstruct that theory using the materials that would have been available to him – Roman law and, to a lesser extent, canon law.

The chapter begins by addressing the question how a lawyer like Bodin might have derived a theory of actionable rights from Roman law (generally regarded as illiberal in its hostility to the notion of rights). The answer, I'll argue, is to be found in the law of actions – remedies actionable in court. While classical lawyers may have operated on the assumption that there can be no right without a remedy [*actio*], Bodin belonged to a generation of lawyers willing to challenge that dogma and decouple rights from remedies, so that even unactionable rights could still be regarded as legally valid. I'll next consider why rights are designated in French by *droit* (and equivalently the Latin *ius*) in Bodin's legal vocabulary: all 'subjective' rights [*droits*; *iura*] in Bodin's theory are, in principle, correlative to duties defined ultimately by some 'objective' law [*droit*; *ius*].

Bodin, however, was a legal pluralist who acknowledged at least three different orders of law – natural law [*ius naturale*], the law of nations [*ius gentium*], and the civil law [*ius civile*]. While each category of law gave rise to obligations (and correspondingly, rights correlative to those obligations), not all of these obligations were

proscriptio, a published list of outlaws and exiles whom anybody was permitted to kill. Bodin identifies the *proscriptio* as a means of law enforcement in the *Distributio* fol. F, s.v.: *Iudicium: Poenale.*

[14] Charles Howard McIlwain elegantly makes this point in 'Sovereignty Again'. This is why, as we'll see, states whose sovereignty has been illegally seized by force or fraud lack a proper sovereignty while under the *de facto* regime of the usurper.

actionable in court. Some were, as the jurists say, 'naked' obligations, a point I'll illustrate in some detail by examining contractual obligations.

Bodin took an interest in these theoretical matters because, in his view, all sovereigns were, by definition, subject to natural law and the law of nations (even though they may be exempt from their own laws). While these 'higher' laws certainly burdened sovereigns under obligations – including the duty to perform contracts – it was from these same 'objective' laws that sovereigns derived their 'subjective' rights of sovereignty. These rights Bodin called *imperium*, and the remainder of the chapter will be devoted to showing how *imperium* – even *summum imperium*, or 'sovereign authority' – was a species of legal right.

From Remedies to Rights in Western Legal Science

What evidence do we have that Bodin even held a concept of a legal right, let alone a legal 'right of sovereignty'? Bodin, of course, did not write in English, nor was his system of thought compatible with a common-law (and typically liberal) juridical framework of rights. He wrote in Latin and French. He was formally trained in civil – that is, Roman – law, exposed to French legal practice in the Parlement of Paris, and evidently familiar with the essentials of canon law and the *Decretals*. These cultural and historical differences will make our task more difficult, but not – I think – impossible.

One place to begin is by taking notice of Bodin's professional background as a lawyer of the European *ius commune*.[15] Anyone who has studied classical Roman law and society, as Bodin did for years in Toulouse, one of the major centres of legal learning and scholarship in France, will surely come to some appreciation of the countless ways that people in ancient societies could be wronged, simply through the non-performance of legal duties in private transactions. Loans, for example, might not be repaid on time by an insolvent debtor. Purchased goods might not be delivered by an unscrupulous vendor. A pupil's estate might be embezzled by his untrustworthy tutor. Property held in trust might not be handled with proper care by a reckless depositary. And so on.

It is a foundational rule of justice that those who have been wronged – creditors wronged by debtors, buyers wronged by vendors, pupils wronged by tutors, depositors wronged by depositaries – must get their due – their *ius*, what is owed to them. This is exactly how the Roman jurisconsult, Ulpian, quoted in Justinian's *Digest* and in the opening sentence of Justinian's *Institutes*, defines 'justice': it is 'the constant and perpetual will of giving to each his due' [*ius suum*].[16] Wrongs must,

[15] The *ius commune* is a shorthand reference to the Continental legal science of Roman, canon, and feudal law. Bellomo, *Common Legal Past of Europe*.

[16] D.1.1.10.pr and Inst.1.1.1.

as a requirement of justice, be 'righted' or rectified (and, for this reason, justice is sometimes described as 'rectificatory').[17] It is in fact, as Bodin states in an explicitly Ciceronian tone, 'necessary for the preservation of human society among men to render to each his due,' as the law requires.[18] The problem is that such justice, howsoevermuch one believes oneself to be in the right, can be realized through extralegal, potentially destructive means and degenerate into endless cycles of blood feuds, vendettas, acts of vengeance, private wars – hardly the sort of means that can preserve the bonds of amity making up a *societas humani generis*.

What distinguishes the science of jurisprudence is the notion that justice need not, and must not, be sought out on the streets nor on the battlefield. It can and should be sought instead through legal means in an impartial court, a forum which can adequately provide the due process and, above all, the tools for getting one's due and 'righting' the wrongs one has suffered at the hands of others, without also introducing socially destructive consequences that can create even further injustices. This is why classical jurists have repeatedly stated that the fundamental 'duty of the judge' [*officium iudicis*] is 'the duty of declaring *ius*' [*officium ius dicentis*; cp. *iuris-dictio*].[19]

Sitting in the seat of judgment, judges 'right' wrongs by giving the injured party his due, his *ius*. And the principal means by which a court can give justice is the legal remedy, or *actio*, the court-enforced vehicle, whether in the form of monetary damages, or some other equitable form of relief, used to adjudicate and enforce a litigant's claim of right.[20] From the lawyer's point of view, there simply cannot be a right without a concomitant remedy: a right without a remedy is indeed no right at all.[21] This is why, for the classical jurist, finding the proper remedy to a plaintiff's claim of right is what really matters. It might even be said that the jurist's obsessive

[17] *Ethics* 5.2, 1131a1.

[18] *Distributio* fol. A, Dedicatio: *Cum enim ad tuendam hominum inter homines societatem, suum cuique tribuere necesse sit.*

[19] D.2.1.1; Inst.4.17. Cp. *République* 223; *De Republica* 155 [1.10]. Cp. *Distributio* fol. A, s.v.: *Ius sine sanctione*: *Aequitas*; fol. F, s.v.: *Iudicis Officium*; *Methodus* 263–64. Judges are charged with the duty to 'supplement or correct the laws' (cp. D.1.1.7.1: *vel supplendi vel corrigenda iuris civilis*) and 'moderate the severity or lenience of the laws' (D.48.19.13) as equity requires.

The term, *officium iudicis*, carries special significance in medieval canon law, where it indicated an equitable remedy actionable in the confessor's court of conscience [*in foro interno*] to enforce performance of 'naked agreements' [*pacta nuda*]. The *officium iudicis* was later replaced by a new remedy, *denunciatio evangelica*, by Innocent IV and Panormitanus on X.2.1.13 (cited by Bodin at *République* 134, 153, 190; *De Republica* 86, 100, 130), which, as a fundamental principle, made all agreements, whether 'naked' or 'clothed' [*vestimenta*], actionable. Cp. Baldus on X.1.35.1. Wim Decock, *Theologians and Contract Law: The Moral Transformation of the Ius Commune, 1500–1650* (Leiden: Brill, 2013) 92–3; 124–29.

[20] D.44.7.51: *Nihil aliud est actio quam ius quod sibi debeatur, iudicio persequendi*. Bodin defines *actio* as the *ipsius legis executio, vis, ac potestas*, which he juxtaposes against a 'mere act' [*facta nuda*]. Without justice, a sovereign's actions would be no different from the gangsterish outlawry of robbers and pirates.

[21] *Ubi ius ibi remedium*: Roman lawyers would likely take an additional step to say that, in civil law, the *only* thing that matters is the remedy to enforce performance or provide recompense for loss. This is why classical Roman law has been described as a legal system organized, not on the concept of legal rights, but legal remedies.

focus on identifying remedies (in contrast to the moral philosopher's focus on rights, the remedies notwithstanding) was exactly what separated the legal science of jurisprudence from the moral science of ethics.

This can explain why the Roman law which Bodin absorbed was a legal system fundamentally based on remedies – or, as the Roman jurisconsults put it, *actiones*. Rights are worthless without judicially enforceable remedies. Anybody who has studied Roman law even minimally can appreciate this point in the very design of Justinian's *Digest* which functions, in large part, as an extensive catalogue, not so much of vague, abstract rights, but of concrete, legally defined *actiones* available to litigants suing for their rights.[22] If you've been wronged, you'd naturally want to know your options and how to get your justice – that is, how to 'right' the legal wrong you've suffered. But to do that, you'd really need to know what *actio*, or remedy, is available for you to plead in court. Roman rights-talk, thus, quickly dissolves into lawyerly remedies-talk, and it was in this juridical language of remedies – or *actiones* – that jurists trained in the legal science of Roman law approached what Judith Jarvis Thomson once called 'the realm of rights'.

In the English-speaking world, one sometimes encounters the suggestion that Roman law was an illiberal legal system actively hostile to the notion of individual rights. Some commentators even suggest that 'subjective' or 'active' claim-rights, as products of modernity, were entirely unknown in Roman jurisprudence.[23] But we can now see how these are misguided and uninformed judgments, because they misunderstand the juridical and explicitly procedural form in which a legal right was expressed and enforced in a Roman court – by way of an *actio*. Inasmuch as Roman law was, as Gaius described it, a law of actions, it was, by implication, also a system of rights.[24]

[22] Randall Lesaffer usefully illustrates the principle by way of example with modern civil law systems, which recognize a general principle of liability for delicts, separate from remedies for such wrongs. See *The Code Napoleon; or, The French Civil Code* (London: William Benning, 1827) 378 [3.4.2, §1382]; *Civil Code of the Netherlands*, trans. Hans Warendorf, Richard Thomas, Ian Curry-Sumner. (Alphen aan den Rijn: Kluwer Law International, 2009) 677 [6.3.1; Article 6:162, §1], to contrast with the remedy-based approach of Roman law and specifically the *Lex Aquilia*, such as D.9.1.1, 9.2.2, and 9.2.27.5. See Lesaffer, *European Legal History: A Cultural and Political Perspective* (Cambridge: Cambridge University Press, 2009) 73–4.

[23] Richard Tuck, *Natural Rights Theories* (Cambridge: Cambridge University Press, 1979) 7–8, attributes this view chiefly to a number of studies by Michel Villey including, 'L'idée du droit subjectif et les systems juridiques romains', *Revue historique de droit*, Series 4v, 24–5 (1946): 201–28; 'Le *jus in re* du droit romain Classique au droit modern', *Publications de l'Institut de droit romain de l'université de Paris* 6 (1950): 187–225; 'Les origines de la notion du droit subjectif', in Michel Villey, *Leçons d'histoire de la philosophie du droit* (Paris: Dalloz, 1957); 'Le genèse du droit subjectif chez Guillaume d'Occam', *Archives de philosophie du droit* 9 (1964): 97–127; *La Formation de la Pensée Juridique Moderne* (Paris: Montchrestien, 1968).

[24] Cp. Inst.3.14(15); C.4.34; D.16.3; Cicero, *De Off.* 1.10. Thus, the creditor gets *ius suum* by pleading an *actio commodati* against the insolvent debtor. The buyer [*emptor*] get *ius suum* by pleading an *actio empti* against the vendor. The pupil gets *ius suum* by pleading an *actio tutelae* against his embezzling tutor. The depositor gets *ius suum* by pleading an *actio depositi directa* against the reckless depositary. The case of the pupil is noteworthy: while they have an *actio tutelae* available as a remedy, pupils, owing to their vulnerable status, also have an equitable remedy, or *auxilium*, available to them, known as the *restitutio in integrum*.

Bodin, of course, was thoroughly familiar with the systematic focus on remedies in the classical Roman law of Gaius and Justinian. Yet, he was never entirely satisfied by the narrowly procedural, or (as he put it) 'forensic' [*forensis*], way the Romans conceptualized rights exclusively in terms of justiciable remedies.[25] While Bodin seems to have accepted the basic principle, *ubi ius ibi remedium* (where there is to be a right, there must be a corresponding remedy), which captured the Roman juridical logic of rights (and wrongs), it wasn't clear why remedies enforcing one's rights can only be sought in court. What is a litigant, who has suffered some injury or otherwise is entitled to some benefit or service, to do if there were no actionable remedies recognized by a court? What if, indeed, there were no court with 'proper' jurisdiction?[26] Would that mean the litigant has no right at all, or that there is no liability? That is the unavoidable conclusion of classical jurisprudence which privileged remedies over rights (it is also the reason why there are so many *actiones* to learn and navigate in Roman law sources).

Without any available *actio* to sue, the litigant had no way to enforce legally his right against the party [*in personam*] who had injured him and seek relief. This presented no problem in classical law: There was no such thing as an unenforceable or unactionable right. A right was, by implication, an actionable right to pursue a legal remedy.[27]

But it *was* a problem for post-classical jurists, like Bodin, who willingly acknowledged, as a theoretical point, that substantive legal rights [*iura*] can, and should, be treated separately from the procedural legal remedies [*actiones*] used by courts to enforce those rights.[28] It was, thus, possible, even by medieval lawyers of the thirteenth century, to speak intelligibly of a valid substantive right [*ius*] – even a 'natural' right – without a concomitant civil remedy.

[25] *Distributio* fol. E, s.v.: *Legis Actio*. For Bodin, Gaius and Justinian 'improperly' reduced actions only to 'forensic actions' [*forensis*]. Classical law, Bodin thinks, overlooks a whole range of actions [*facta*] that are of a juridical nature, yet not so much matters of court procedure, let alone court-enforced remedies. Bodin cites D.50.16.175 and 50.16.218 showing the origin of *facta* from *facere*, 'to do' or 'to make'. Bodin's examples are legal acts like agreements, wills, delicts, obligations, discharges, acquisitions, and alienations: 'These are the things which give birth to forensic actions' (D.27.10.7). Bodin's line of thought here follows the innovative legal theory of his contemporary, François Connan.

[26] The term, *iurisdictio propria*, is a technical term in the Roman public law governing procedure in trials. See *Popular Sovereignty* Ch. 3, especially 90–108.

[27] For this reason, it has been suggested that, instead of right, it may be more accurate to describe the obligor's *ius suum* as a 'protected interest'. See Geoffrey Samuel, 'Le Droit Subjectif and English Law', *Cambridge Law Journal* 46 (1987): 264–86. On subjective right in classical Roman law, see Giovanni Pugliese, '*Res corporales, res incorporales* e il problema del diritto soggetivo', in *Studi in onore di Vincenzo Arangio-Ruiz*, vol. 3 (Naples: Jovene, 1953) 223–60; Max Kaser, 'Zum *Ius*-Begriff der Römer', in *Essays in Honour of Ben Beinart*, vol. 2, *Acta Juridica* (1977): 63–81; Charles Donahue, 'Ius in the Subjective Sense', in *A Ennio Cortese*, ed. Domenico Maffei, vol. 1 (Rome: Il Cigno, 2001): 506–35; Peter Garnsey, *Thinking about Property: From Antiquity to the Age of Revolution* (Cambridge: Cambridge University Press, 2007).

[28] Here is the genesis of the modern lawyerly distinction between substantive law and procedural law, a distinction that is largely nonexistent in classical law.

As the Roman lawyer H.F. Jolowicz once observed, this decoupling of rights from remedies represented one of the major achievements in the development of modern private law in the West: when right 'became the leading conception in private law, there could be no doubt that the differences between types of action ... were really differences of substantive right'. And so, because of this shift from concrete remedy to substantive right, 'modern codes of civil law therefore ha[d] no need for a special part on Actions', as classical Roman law required.[29] What lawyers needed, instead, was a theory of substantive legal rights, as such, separate from the actionable civil remedies used in procedure to enforce those rights.

Droit Objectif and *Droit Subjectif*

What we can tell with some confidence is that Bodin, like many of his contemporaries and predecessors of the *ius commune*, evidently embraced this decoupling of rights from remedies. Indeed, he wrote freely of substantive legal rights throughout his writings in both French and Latin such as the *droit d'aubain*, the *droit de taille*, the *droit de marque ou de represailles*, the *droit Royeaux*, the *ius bellum indicere*, the *ius provocationis*, the *ius magistratuum*.[30] He even applied this notion of rights to his analysis of sovereignty – *droit de souveraineté*, *ius summi imperii*, *ius maiestatis* – so that, as we'll see, even sovereignty was to be understood fundamentally as being constituted of various legal rights.

Following well-established convention, Bodin chose to speak of legal rights using the Latin term, *ius* (and, equivalently, the French term, *droit*). But there is a basic interpretive problem regarding these words, *droit* and *ius*, which merits closer attention. As any lawyer in the civil law tradition will know, *droit* and *ius* certainly can be used to convey what, in English, might be expressed as a 'legal right', such as in the notion of the *ius ad rem*, a species of property right. But these same words, *droit* and *ius*, also mean 'law', as in the opening title of Justinian's *Digest* which divides all law into 'natural law' [*droit naturel*; *ius naturale*], the 'law of nations' [*droit des gens*; *ius gentium*], and the 'civil law' [*droit civil*; *ius civile*].[31]

[29] H.F. Jolowicz, *Roman Foundations of Modern Law* (Oxford: Clarendon Press, 1957) 81. The Napoleonic French Civil Code, for example, does not contain a separate title specifically on the law of actions.

[30] Mogens Chrom Jacobsen, *Jean Bodin et le dilemme de la philosophie politique moderne* (Copenhagen: Museum Tusculanum Press, University of Copenhagen, 2000) 86 *et seq*.

[31] D.1.1.1, 1.1.6. Basic misunderstanding of the dual function of these words, *droit* and *ius* (and other cognates in Romance and Germanic languages such as *Recht*, *diritto*, *derecho*), in legal thought has led to countless mistranslations in modern English scholarship such as 'the right of war and peace' (for Grotius' *De iure belli ac pacis*), 'the right of nature and of nations' (for Pufendorf's *De iure naturae et gentium*), 'the right of nations' (for Vattel's *Le droits des gens*), and 'the philosophy of right' (for Hegel's *Philosophie des Rechts*). The modern Cambridge edition of Montesquieu's *Spirit of the Laws*, ed. Anne Cohler, Basia Miller, and Harold Stone (Cambridge: Cambridge University Press, 1989) 7 is a typical example, where *droit des gens* and *droit civil* are mistranslated as 'right of nations' and 'civil right'.

Bodin's decision to conceptualize rights in this legal language of *droits* and *iura* was not an arbitrary choice. As a lawyer, Bodin intuitively understood, and exploited, the dual linguistic function of these words, which sometimes meant 'law', sometimes 'right', and sometimes both 'law' and 'right'.[32] It can be difficult for a modern (and particularly, anglophone common-law) readership to track these subtle semantic shifts as well as the relation between these two seemingly unconnected meanings. Indeed, at least one theorist has famously proposed a linguistic reform, stipulating that *ius* (and, presumably, its modern vernacular cognates such as *droit*, *diritto*, and *derecho*) should be understood strictly as a Hohfeldian liberty-right, and not, in any way, as a law whose contrary effect is obligatory, thereby restricting such liberty.[33] Modern civil lawyers, recognizing the polysemous quality of *droit* (and *ius*), have tried to offer a heuristic scheme to clarify these two meanings, through the juridical distinction between *droit objectif* and *droit subjectif*. It is a distinction that has caused much misunderstanding and unnecessary metaphysical speculation, particularly in anglophone jurisprudence and philosophy.[34] But the basic idea of the distinction is fairly simple and worth incorporating into our study of Bodin's own theory of *droit*.

Consider, first, *droit objectif*. One way to interpret *droit* (or *ius*), as we've seen, is to think of it as a self-contained body of law or legal system, the sum-total of norms, indicating the proper rules of obligatory conduct, binding on members of a law-governed human society. Viewed in this way, *droit* is just a shorthand term indicating a vast collection of specific legal rules which, taken together, define the juridical relations between persons and the duties that are owed to each other.[35] *Droit objectif* tells us legally what is right, what is wrong, what is permissible, what is impermissible, and, above all, *when* one has been wronged.

In an ideal world of 'full compliance' (as political philosophers like to say), all obligatory duties defined in a system of *droit objectif* would be performed, and all legal rules obeyed. Of course, we don't live in such an ideal world. We live in a non-ideal world of, at best, 'partial compliance', which acknowledges the unjust reality that laws are regularly broken, and duties go unperformed.[36] Because we live in this

[32] This is, in fact, precisely the reason why he feels compelled to distinguish between *loi/lex* and *droit/ius*, in recognition of the ambiguity contained in the latter. *Loi/lex* are used specifically to denote a generally binding positive legislative command [*imperium*] of a sovereign authority, what Bentham will later call sovereign acts of 'imperation', resulting either in the creation or elimination of legal duties. Not all laws, however, are the result of sovereign legislative commands, and so, Bodin is careful only to use *loi/lex* in cases of positive legislation. See Chapter 4. Cp. François Connan, *Commentariorum Iuris Civilis Libri X* (Lyon: Apud Haeredes Iacobi Iunctae, 1566) 30–31 [1.8, §7].

[33] Hobbes, *Leviathan* 91.

[34] For one egregious example, see Holly Smith, 'Subjective Rightness', *Social Philosophy and Policy* 27 (2010): 64–110.

[35] It is sometimes suggested that a *droit objectif* refers to a notion of justice or 'rightness'. It certainly could, but it is not necessary.

[36] The 'full' and 'partial' compliance distinction originates in John Rawls, *A Theory of Justice*, rev. ed. (Cambridge: Belknap Press of Harvard University Press, 1999) 206–17 [§§38–39], 308–9 [§53]. The distinction has been foundational to the recent debate on whether political theory should strive to be

non-ideal world of injustice, it becomes necessary for the law and its institutions to do more than simply establish 'objective' norms and rules for us to live by. The law must provide the corrective tools and remedies to rectify (literally, to make 'right' again, as Aristotle understood 'rectificatory' justice) such wrongs and injuries suffered in this non-ideal world of ours. And in order to do that, it's necessary to empower all those who are 'subject' to an 'objective' legal system and bound to observe its rules with the *liberty* to act according to their own discretion in matters not explicitly prohibited (or, as Hobbes would later put it, in 'the silence of the laws'), as well as the legal *power* to act as the law allows to protect one's interests and to get what is 'due' to them.[37] These legal liberties and powers of 'subjects' of the law to act in favour of their interests represent the 'subjective' aspect of *droit* – the *droits subjectifs*.

Anybody who is subject to an 'objective' legal system can be entitled to hold and assert 'subjective' rights.[38] I am, for example, a legal subject of the 'objective' laws of California. Those laws are obligatory in that they impose legal duties on all those subject to it. The California Civil Code, to take a random example, defines the legal duties of depositaries in California to deliver deposits upon demand. In doing so, however, it also acknowledges the 'subjective' legal rights of the depositors, by that same 'objective' Civil Code, to sue for undelivered assets.[39]

But the point extends beyond ordinary private individuals like myself. Even sovereigns, whether in the form of a sovereign prince or a democratic sovereign people, can be 'subjects' of 'objective' law and, precisely for that reason, sovereigns can be entitled to hold and assert *droits subjectifs*, or 'subjective' rights, just as I can hold and assert 'subjective' rights under the 'objective' laws of California.[40] But to

an 'ideal' theory assuming full compliance with abstract principles of justice, or instead a realistic 'non-ideal' theory assuming only partial compliance.

[37] I describe these legal entitlements as 'liberty' and 'power' in a specifically Hohfeldian way, to make the more general point that negative permissive liberty and positive legal powers both can be regarded as 'subjective rights'. Hobbes' phrase, 'the silence of the law', appears in *Leviathan* 152.

[38] In fact, as we'll see in just a moment, Bodin is prepared to make a stronger claim: everybody is subject to an 'objective' legal system of universal scope, the 'objective' legal norms deriving from the *ius divinum*, the *ius naturale*, and the *ius gentium*.

[39] *The Civil Code of the State of California*, Vol. 1, 1st ed., annotated by Creed Haymond and John Burch (San Francisco: A.L. Bancroft & Company; Sumner Whitney & Co., 1874) 559–61 [Article II, §§1822–25].

[40] The possession of sovereign right *eo ipso* is what makes one a sovereign: no one is, by nature, a sovereign, just as no one is, by nature, a subject.

Bodin adhered to what has recently been called the thesis of 'constitutional indifferentism' concerning the constitutional form of sovereignty. In Bodin's view, sovereignty can take one of three possible forms – monarchy (if the right of sovereignty is vested in one person), aristocracy (if vested in a few, or a numerical minority), or democracy (if vested in the many, or a numerical majority, or the people at large). While Bodin recognized the practical differences between these three forms and even preferred monarchy over aristocracy and democracy, he nevertheless recognized all three as valid forms of sovereignty. I have discussed Bodin's indifferentism at length elsewhere, in *Popular Sovereignty* 226. For this discussion, I will assume that the legal subject capable of holding the legal rights of sovereignty can be (as Bodin often put it) either 'the people or the prince', *République* 122: *au people ou au Prince*; *De Republica* 79 [1.8]: *princeps populusve*.

what 'objective' law can a sovereign authority really be said to be 'subject'? After all, isn't freedom *from* the laws – or as the lawyers say, being *legibus solutus* (D.1.3.31) – the essential quality of sovereignty?

Before proceeding any further, three clarifications should be stressed about the *droit objectif/droit subjectif* distinction. The first is that this is only a heuristic, simply intended to assist in the understanding of the two distinct, though inseparable, features of all *droit* (or *ius*).[41] So much of the modern historical scholarship on rights, particularly in modern anglophone scholarship, has made the unfortunate mistake of treating *droit objectif* and *droit subjectif*, as if they were separate concepts, unattached to each other. And, as a result, commentators have participated in a longstanding academic debate on whether rights should more properly be regarded as 'objective' or as 'subjective,' as if it were a matter of interpretive choice. Legal historians, moreover, have recently given the debate a twist, by turning it into a question of chronology, basically asking how and when *droit objectif* became *droit subjectif*.[42]

What commentators in these debates fail to see is that these are not so much separate concepts, as they are two sides of the same coin. Hans Kelsen explained this dual feature:

> The right *is* law – law in a subjective sense of the word in contradistinction to 'law' in an objective sense, that is, a legal order or system of norms. [This is why] in German and French legal language, the same word, namely *Recht* and *droit*, is used to designate 'right' as well as 'law,' as a system of norms forming a legal order. Hence, in order to distinguish right and law, it is necessary to speak ... in French of *droit objectif* and *droit subjectif*.[43]

Thus, the whole interpretive debate on whether *droit* (or *ius* or *Recht*) should properly be 'objective' or 'subjective,' is fundamentally misguided and based on a faulty understanding of the *droit objectif/droit subjectif* distinction.[44] Indeed, because

[41] The terms, 'objective' and 'subjective', derive from baroque era German jurisprudence in the age of Leibniz, Achenwall, and Wolff. The origin of the distinction has been attributed to Joachim Georg Darjes' *Institutiones Iurisprudentiae Universalis* and David Nettelbladt's *Systema Elementare Universae Iurisprudentia Naturalis*. Thomas Mautner, 'How Rights Became Subjective', *Ratio Juris* 26 (2013): 116; Alejandro Guzmán, 'Historia de la Denominación del Derecho-Facultad Como Subjectivo', *Revista de Estudios Histórico-Jurídicos* 25 (2003): 407–43. I thank Helge Dedek for discussion of this point.

[42] Perhaps the *locus classicus* of this literature is Michel Villey, *Leçons d'Histoire de la Philosophie du Droit* (Paris: Dalloz, 1957).

[43] Kelsen, *Pure Theory of Law* 125.

[44] Benjamin Straumann, *Roman Law in the State of Nature* (Cambridge: Cambridge University Press, 2015) 163–65 makes the same point with respect to Grotius, arguing that the connection of subjective right to *actiones* was a legacy of the legal humanist, Donellus. Helmut Coing, 'Zur Geschichte des Begriffs "subjektives Recht"', in Coing, *Gesammelte Aufsätze zu Rechtsgeschichte, Rechtsphilosophie, und Zivilrecht, 1947–1975*, vol. 1 (Frankfurt am Main: Klostermann,1982) 251–54; Peter Haggenmacher, 'Droits subjectifs et systeme juridique chez Grotius', in *Politique, droit et théologie chez Bodin, Grotius et Hobbes*, ed. Luc Foisneau (Paris: Kimé, 1997).

they are inseparably tied together, it's not really up to us (nor to licentious translators, for that matter) as a matter of interpretive choice whether we ought to treat *droit* (or *ius*) more in an 'objective' sense or in a 'subjective' sense. As we'll see below, this objective/subjective duality will have profound consequences for Bodin's own theory of the *droit de souveraineté*, in that sovereignty, as a juridical construct, will also have both an objective and subjective dimension built into it.

The second point to make about the subjective/objective distinction concerns what we might characterize as the inescapably juridical character of rights. In short, rights [*droits subjectifs*] *entail* the law [*droit objectif*]. Put another way, without some anterior system of law (and specifically the *duties* imposed by such laws), there can be no correlative rights. And that is because law defines not only what is permissible (right) and impermissible (not right), it also empowers individuals to act legally in ways that would otherwise, were it not for the law, be impossible.

One consequence immediately follows: if all rights (in the sense of *droit subjectif*) entail some anterior law (in the sense of *droit objectif*), it follows that there can't be any 'natural' (or we might even say 'human') right that can exist *simpliciter* on its own in a legal vacuum of lawlessness, beyond any legal order. Every 'subjective' right must be traceable back to, and paired with, some 'objective' law or norm that gives the right its purpose.

This needn't make Bodin a strict legal-positivist with respect to rights. While some 'subjective' rights (such as the *ius suffragii*, the right to vote, or the *ius provocationis*, the right of appeal) certainly owe their validity and existence to some anterior positive legislation, not all rights-creating objective laws must be *positive* laws.

This leads to the third, and final, point of clarification that must be made concerning *droit objectif*. What actually counts as a proper *droit objectif*? In modern scholarship, the concept has often been associated with the academic literature on the theory of natural law, the *Naturrechtslehre*. As a result, commentators have often assumed, possibly unintentionally, that *droit objectif* must be a byword for natural law or the *ius naturale*.[45] Of course, it is certainly true that the *ius naturale* exemplified a *droit objectif*, as a system of legal rules, specifying what is right and wrong, permissible and impermissible.

But natural law wasn't the only *droit objectif*. Any legal system could be regarded *droit objectif*, even positive legislation. The *ius civile* of Roman law was the archetypical example of such positive legislation, insofar as it was a collection of legal rules specifying what is legally permissible and impermissible. The same could be said of the French customary laws, or *coutumes*, as well as the *ius gentium*. Even the laws of California might be regarded a system of *droit objectif*.

[45] Tierney, for example, approached his study of objective law in connection with the history of natural rights, thereby giving the impression that objective law was only concerned with matters of natural law and natural right.

It is grossly misleading, therefore, to think that there's only one type of *droit objectif.* Instead, jurists embraced a kind of legal pluralism when it came to the *droit objectif,* imagining multiple 'objective' legal orders coexisting with each other, like layers of legal rules, *iura* or *droits*, stacked one on top of, and intersecting with, each other.[46] This is the basic picture presented in the classical tripartite *divisio iuris* in Roman law which identified three coexisting legal orders, or *droits objectifs*:[47]

Droit objectif
Ius naturale
Ius gentium
Ius civile

Bodin accepted this basic axiom of legal pluralism. The whole universe, he explained, was governed according to multiple coexisting legal orders, objective

[46] One of the great academic disputes of modern legal theory concerns the question whether coexisting systems of objective legal rules can be reduced into one grand unified system of law. Hans Kelsen famously affirmed that theoretical possibility, a school of legal thought now known as 'monism', whereby legal norms of international law are treated as reducible to, and overlapping with, norms of civil law. W.B. Stern, 'Kelsen's Theory of International Law', *American Political Science Review* 30 (1936): 736–41; François Rigaux, 'Hans Kelsen on International Law', *European Journal of International Law* 9 (1998): 325–43.

[47] This is the classical tripartite division of law of Ulpian, Gaius, and Papinian into *ius naturale, ius gentium*, and *ius civile*, see D.1.1.1.3–4, 1.1.6, 1.1.7, 1.1.9. Taken together, the three traditional categories of law constitute what Bodin calls 'the whole law' [*ius universum*].

While Bodin's typology in the *Distributio* is inspired by Justinian's system, Bodin's is slightly more complex: The principal division of law, in *Distributio* fol. A, s.v.: *Eius* [i.e. *iuris*] *Divisio*, is between *ius naturale* and *ius humanum*. The latter is then subdivided into *ius gentium* and *ius civile*. One reason for this is to deemphasize the relative importance of the Roman *ius civile* whose alleged universality as a basis for legal science Bodin challenges in the *Distributio* and in the *Methodus*. The other is a methodological point: 'The well-known division of law distinguishes *ius naturale, ius gentium*, and *ius civile*. But a διχοτομεῖν is more convenient, and, as far as possible, one-to-one distinctions; thus, Aristotle and Plato divide justice into natural and legal, which is the division Paul followed [at D.1.1.11]'. Cp. D.1.1.1; 1.1.4–9; Inst.1.2.1–2. Bodin's sources for this point about dichotomy may likely have been Plato's *Statesman*, 302e and Aristotle, *Ethics* 5.2, 1134^{b}18. I thank Kinch Hoekstra for discussion of this point.

The division of law in the *République* is notably different in two ways. First, Bodin has added divine law to natural law and the common law of mankind. Second, he conspicuously uses the terms, *lex* and *loi*, to designate these categories of law. Natural law is *lex naturalis*; divine law is *lex divina*; the common law of mankind is *lex gentium omnium*. The literature on these themes is vast: Maurizio Bazzoli, 'Il diritto naturale nella *République* di Jean Bodin', *Critica Storica* 7 (1968): 586–93; Janine Chanteur, 'L'idee de loi naturelle dans le *République* de Jean Bodin', in *Verhandlungen der Internationalen Bodin Tagung in München*, ed. Horst Denzer (München: Beck, 1973); Albert Cremer, 'Le genèse du droit des gens modern et la conscience européenne: Francisco de Vitoria et Jean Bodin', in *La conscience européenne aux XVe et XVIe siecles: Actes du Colloque international organisé à l'ENSJF*, 30 September–3 October 1980 (Paris: École Normale Supérieure de Jeunes Filles, 1982); S. Mastellone, 'Bodin e la scienza politica dei gens de loi', *Diritto e potere nella Storia Europea* (Florence: Olschki, 1982); Jean Terrel, *Les théories du pacte social: Droit naturel, souveraineté et contrat de Bodin à Rousseau* (Paris: Editions du Seuil, 2001).

droits or *iura*. And it was his ambition, from an early stage, to explicate the logical structure of all these laws, what he sometimes referred to collectively as *ius universum*, the totality of all law.

One important consequence now follows from this pluralistic *divisio iuris universi*. If, as Bodin acknowledges, there are multiple categories of ('objective') law, it follows that there correspondingly must also be multiple categories of (subjective) right (since *droit objectif* entails *droit subjectif*, and vice-versa) and of obligation.[48] The Civil Code of California, to recycle an earlier example, is a system of 'objective' legal norms giving rise to legally defined civil-law obligations. But that same Civil Code also, by implication, gives rise to 'subjective' civil-law rights actionable by those legally entitled to sue and benefit from the performance of obligations due to them.

We could say the same thing about natural law. Like civil law, natural law too is a system of 'objective' legal norms giving rise to natural-law obligations. And like civil law, natural law also gives rise to 'subjective' natural-law rights. And so on for the common law of peoples – that is, the *ius gentium*. What results, then, is a multilayered system of subjective rights and obligations mirroring the multiplicity of objective legal orders:

[48] Bodin identified four basic types of obligations in the *Distributio* fol. D, s.v.: *Obligatio est quadruplex*:

(1) *obligatio naturalis*: *ex iure naturali*
(2) *obligatio naturalis et* [*iuris*] *gentium omnium*: *ex iure naturali et gentium*
(3) *obligatio ex iure gentium, non tamen naturalis*: *ex iure gentium* [on this point, Bodin cites D.1.5.4 and 12.6.60]
(4) *obligatio civilis*: *ex iure civili*

Bodin's contemporaries, however, approached the *divisio obligationum* somewhat differently. The French humanist jurist, Hugues Doneau [Donellus], cited this passage by Bodin in his own treatment of obligations in his influential treatise (a monument of French humanist legal scholarship), *Opera Omnia: Commentariorum de Iure Civili*, vol. 3 (Lucca: Typis Joannis Riccomini, 1763) col. 425 [12.2.2]. François Hotman, to take another example, in his popular textbook on civil law, the *Partitiones Iuris Civilis Elementariae* (Basel, 1571) 79, argued that the *divisio* was *tripartita*, such that obligations were either *naturales*, *civiles*, or *mixtae*.

Note that Bodin, in a decidedly un-humanist manner, acknowledges the vulgar medieval juridical distinction between the primary and secondary *ius gentium*, which explains how he arrives at four species of obligation from the classical tripartite division of law. This passage has been described as a typically 'synthétiste' discussion of the four species of obligation. Simone Goyard-Fabre, 'Commentaire Philosophique de L'Exposé du Droit Universel', in *Jean Bodin: Exposé du Droit Universel* (Paris: Presses Universitaires de France, 1985) 136. The Glossators, however, treated the *obligatio naturalis* and *obligatio iurisgentium* as interchangeable. *Gloss. Ord.* on D.1.1.5, s.v.: *Obligationes*: *Obligatio iuris gentium dicitur naturalis et e converso*.

There is an extensive literature on the Roman law of obligations available to a modern anglophone readership such as Barry Nicholas, *An Introduction to Roman Law* (Oxford: Clarendon Press, 1962) 99–103 or the more technical treatments by Birks, *Roman Law of Obligations* and Reinhard Zimmermann, *The Law of Obligations: Roman Foundations of the Civilian Tradition* (Oxford: Clarendon Press, 1990). A more recent treatment in English is to be found in Martin Hogg, *Obligations: Law and Language* (Cambridge: Cambridge University Press, 2003). The two major classical sources that readers should consult are Gaius and Justinian, who divide the types of obligations differently.

Droit objectif	*Droit subjectif*	*Obligatio*
Ius naturale	Rights *ex iure naturali*	*Obligatio naturalis*
Ius gentium	Rights *ex iure gentium*	*Obligatio iuris gentium*
Ius civile	Rights *ex iure civili*	*Obligatio civilis*

Of these three, however, only the rights and obligations emanating from the civil law, or *ius civile*, were traditionally thought to be enforceable by way of a civil remedy, or *actio*. In other words, you are entitled to sue for enforcing performance of obligations defined under civil law. But you cannot sue to enforce performance of obligations defined by the *ius naturale* or the *ius gentium*. And the reason for this was simple: as the glossator, Accursius, famously put it in the *Ordinary Gloss* to the *Digest*, *actiones sunt a iure civili* (legal remedies are derived only from positive legislation).[49] The *actio* used to assert subjective rights and to enforce performance of civil obligations, were wholly creatures of positive legislation, the *ius civile*. The implication was that *actiones* only applied to obligations of the *ius civile*, but not to obligations arising from the *ius naturale* and the *ius gentium*.

What about 'subjective' rights and obligations of the *ius gentium* and the *ius naturale*? Could they also be asserted or enforced by way of action? The view in classical Roman law was that, while they were valid sources of law and generally obligatory, they weren't actionable in the same way. No *obligatio naturalis* or *obligatio iuris gentium* could be enforced by a court (unless, as we'll soon see, they were additionally 'clothed' by a civil remedy or legal norm enacted specifically for that purpose of enforcement).[50] So, according to the Glossatorial position, even though there may, in principle, be rights and obligations *ex iure gentium* and *ex iure naturale* (such as the naked duty to perform one's promises, or *pollicitationes*), there are no remedies available for litigants (nor, for that matter, a court with proper jurisdiction) to plead so as to enforce performance of such higher-law duties.[51]

Droit objectif	*Droit subjectif*	*Obligatio*	Remedy
Ius naturale	Rights *ex iure naturali*	*Obligatio naturalis*	
Ius gentium	Rights *ex iure gentium*	*Obligatio iuris gentium*	
Ius civile	Rights *ex iure civili*	*Obligatio civilis*	*Actio*

[49] *Gloss. Ord.* on D.1.1.5, s.v.: *Obligationes*. Three texts of the *Digest* were essential in establishing this principle D.1.1.5, 1.1.7, 1.2.2.6.

[50] The metaphor of clothing as an actionable remedy for an obligation can be found in Placentinus, *In Codicis Summa* (Mainz, 1536) 44 [C.2.3]; Azo, *Azonis Summa, Locuples Iuris Civilis Thesaurus* (Basel: Per Ioannem Heruagium, 1563) col. 67 [C.2.3, §§15–17]; *Gloss. Ord.* and Bartolus on D.2.14.7.5; Baldus on X.1.6.16. In general, Decock, *Theologians and Contract Law* 111.

[51] On the *pollicitatio*, see D.50.12.1.1.

While you may have a valid natural duty to perform your promises, you can't, according to the Glossatorial doctrine, be sued for failing to perform a natural duty.[52]

Taken together, the *ius gentium* and the *ius naturale* presented an unusual situation, opening the possibility of subjective rights without corresponding actionable remedies, a notion simply unthinkable in classical law. Jurists in the modern civil law tradition – Donellus, Grotius, Selden, Pufendorf, Leibniz, Vattel, Stair, Pothier, and Austin – all recognized this notional category of a subjective right-without-remedy, which they simply called 'imperfect rights' (and correspondingly, 'imperfect obligations') – 'imperfect' [*imparfait*] because they were nonjusticiable and unenforceable by any ordinary court.[53] They were to be contrasted with 'perfect rights' and 'perfect obligations' [*parfait*; *perfectus*, a verbal participle from *perficere* = to execute, to complete], both of which were characterized by the availability of an actionable civil remedy.[54]

Writing just on the eve of the introduction of the perfect/imperfect distinction, Bodin never used that terminology (although he was well aware of the perfect/imperfect distinction in other areas of civil law).[55] He nevertheless understood

[52] Pennington, *Prince and the Law* 147–49 explains this remained the standard view of medieval civilians, until the middle of the thirteenth century.

[53] Donellus, *Commentariorum de Iure Civili* col. 425 [12.2.2], Grotius, *De Iure Belli ac Pacis* 1.1.4; John Selden, *Table Talk* (Chiswick: Whittingham, 1818) 205; Pufendorf, *De Iure Naturae et Gentium* 1.1.19, 1.7.7 and *Elementorum Jurisprudentiae Universalis Libri II* (Jena: Sumptibus Johannis Meyeri, Typis Johannis Wertheri, 1669) 119–20 [1.12.3]; Gottfried Wilhelm Leibniz, 'Codex Iuris Gentium' [Praefatio], in *Leibniz: Political Writings*, ed. Patrick Riley, 2nd ed. (Cambridge: Cambridge University Press, 1988) 172–73; Vattel, *Law of Nations* 74–75 [Preliminaries, §17]; James Dalrymple, Viscount of Stair, *Institutes of the Laws of Scotland* (Edinburgh: Andrew Anderson, 1681) 116–17 [Title 10, §§6, 9]; Robert Joseph Pothier, *A Treatise on the Law of Obligations*, Vol. 1, trans. William David Evans (London: A. Strahan, 1806) 1–2; Austin, *Province of Jurisprudence Determined* 32–3. Kant and Mill use the terms, 'perfect' and 'imperfect' obligations, but in a sense quite different from the jurists' usage. See, in general, George Rainbolt, 'Perfect and Imperfect Obligations', *Philosophical Studies* 98 (2000): 233; Joachim Hruschka, 'Supererogation and Meritorious Duties', *Jahrbuch für Recht und Ethik* 93 (1998): 93–110; Andrew Schroeder, 'Imperfect Duties, Group Obligations, and Beneficence', *Journal of Moral Philosophy* 11 (2014): 557–84. Grotius' treatment, at *De Iure Belli ac Pacis* 1.1.7 (beginning with the 1642 edition), references Cicero, *De Off.* 1.20 and suggests that the Grotian imperfect *aptitudo* is intended to align with Cicero's *beneficentia* or *liberalitas*, both of which are thought to be morally obligatory, but legally unenforceable. Grotius is sometimes credited with coining the distinction, but it is already in the humanist jurisprudence of the sixteenth century. Connan, for example, distinguishes between *transactio perfecta* and *transactio imperfecta* in *Commentariorum Iuris Civilis* (Paris: Jacques Kerver, 1553) fol. 355_{vo}.

[54] The perfect/imperfect distinction was used in a number of places in Roman private law such as in the law of gifts (distinguishing between perfect and imperfect gifts) and the law of sale (e.g. C.8.44[45].24: *perfecta venditio*; D.18.1.19: *emptio imperfecta*). Probably the most important source that would affect the modern distinction between perfect and imperfect rights, however, was the classical distinction between *lex perfecta* (which had a *sanctio*) and *lex imperfecta* (which did not have a *sanctio*, such as the *Lex Cincia* regulating gifts).

A fragment of Ulpian (*De Legibus et Moribus*, §§1–2) indicates the category of a *lex minus quam perfecta*, but a lacuna in the fragment leaves out what *lex imperfecta* is. Bodin's contemporary and erstwhile rival, Jacques Cujas, in *Observationes et Emendationes*, vol. 2 (Köln: Apud Ioanem Gymnicum, 1587) 113 [19, §30], has provided a substitute text: *Imperfecta lex est, veluti Cincia, quae supra certum modum donari prohibet*, an interpolation approved by von Savigny. See T.A.J. McGuinn, 'The Expressive Function of Law and the *Lex Imperfecta*', *Roman Legal Tradition* 11 (2015): 1–41.

[55] Although Bodin never used the perfect/imperfect distinction, he comes close to it with the notion of a *conventio perfecta* (a completed agreement) at *Distributio* fol. B, s.v.: *Conventio: Contractu firmata cui synallagma inest ex facto vel datione perfectionem accipit.* Bodin made extensive use of the principles

the basic logic of the distinction and anticipated the modern juristic problem of 'imperfect' subjective rights and obligations arising from the *ius naturale* and *ius gentium* in an early work on general jurisprudence, the *Iuris Universi Distributio*, originating from Bodin's time in law school at Toulouse.[56] There, Bodin criticized the excessively narrow way the classical law of Gaius and Justinian understood the term, *actio*, to mean strictly a 'forensic action' [*actio forensis*] litigated in court to enforce performance of an obligation.[57]

Bodin's worry was the same worry that led lawyers to decouple subjective rights from remedies. He wished to avoid the conclusion drawn from the Roman law of actions that genuine legal rights can only be those actionable through civil remedies enforced by a court. The validity of a substantive legal right, Bodin thought, needn't be dependent on whether it is tied to a civil remedy: one can, in principle, have a subjective right, even if one does not have a civil *actio* attached to that right. Strictly as a matter of legal theory, then, Bodin acknowledges that subjective rights can be extracted from obligations deriving from the *ius naturale* and the *ius gentium*. And it is from those 'objective' higher law norms that Bodin plans to extrapolate the 'subjective' rights of sovereignty.

Bodin on Contractual Obligations

There is no better place to see how Bodin extrapolates subjective *droit* from objective *droit* than in his treatment of contractual obligations.

To begin, let's return to the Glossatorial principle: *Actiones sunt a iure civili.* This originated as a gloss on D.1.1.5, one of the most famous passages in Justinian's *Digest*, which stated, in part, that contractual obligations are ultimately derived from the *ius gentium*: *Ex hoc iure gentium ... obligationes institutae.* The point of

of D.32.[1].23, C.6.23.3, C.4.48.1, and C.8.54[55].4: *République* 128, 149 153, 870; *De Republica* 82, 95, 97, 100, 721 [1.8; 6.5].

[56] Lloyd, *Jean Bodin* 55–6 suggests some examples in this Ramist humanist genre of universalizing 'systems' or 'outlines' of civil and canon law. Particularly noteworthy is the *Partitiones Iuris Utriusque* (Basel, 1571) of Johann Thomas Freigius which, like Bodin's *Distributio*, presented a Ramist organization of concepts in civil and canon law in tabular form. On the use of such Ramist tables and 'branching diagrams', see Ann Blair, *Too Much to Know: Managing Scholarly Information before the Modern Age* (New Haven, Connecticut: Yale University Press, 2010). Lloyd, *Jean Bodin* 23 explores Forcadel's influence.

[57] Following the academic fashion of the period, Bodin was emboldened to criticize Gaius' standard tripartite *divisio* of civil law into persons, things, and actions. As he put it, the Roman jurisconsults overlook all 'the things which give birth [*oriuntur*] to forensic actions' in the first place. *Distributio* fol. B, s.v.: *Facta.* Bodin's criticism appears to echo Connan's criticism of Cajo who, as Connan put it, seems to think the term, *actio*, means 'nothing other than just suing for one's right' [*persecutionem istam iuris sui*]. Connan, *Commentariorum Iuris Civilis Libri X* (Lyon: Apud Haeredes Iacobi Iunctae, 1566) 76 [2.1].

Accursius' gloss was to stress that, even though obligations may be derived from the *ius gentium* (and, thus, binding on all law-governed peoples), the actionable remedies used to enforce performance of legal obligations always derive from positive legislation, from the *ius civile*. So, while obligations defined in the *ius civile* may be actionable, obligations defined in the *ius naturale* and *ius gentium* were not. Without any civil remedy in the form of an *actio* to enforce performance in a court, these obligations (and the rights ensuing forth from them) were 'imperfect'.

That didn't mean, however, that there was no remedy *at all*. It just meant that a different sort of remedy was appropriate. Just as disputes involving a civil obligation can be resolved by a civil action litigated in court, so too could disputes arising from the *ius naturale* or the *ius gentium* likewise be resolved, though not by ordinary civil actions promulgated by the *ius civile*, but by a different species of remedy.

Bodin's insight was, thus, to argue for a much more capacious understanding of 'remedy' than was allowed by Gaius and Justinian in classical Roman law, one recognizing that not all *actiones* needed to be *forenses*, litigated in court as operations of the civil law.[58] While some claims, of course, could – and probably should – be satisfactorily answered by a civil or 'forensic action' [*actio forensis*] in an ordinary court – that is, an action formally 'deployed in court before a judge [*apud iudicem*]' for the purpose of obtaining some relief – there were, in theory, many other 'subjective' rights that, though lacking a civil 'forensic' remedy defined in civil law, were nevertheless legally valid and enforceable through equitable remedies of the *ius naturale* and the *ius gentium*.[59]

Classical Roman law asserted that only contractual obligations arising from the *ius civile* were actionable in court.[60] In Roman law, these were the so-called

[58] This distinction between *actio in rem* (concerning property) and *actio in personam* (concerning obligation) is foundational to the conceptual architecture of Roman law of actions. Bodin integrated this basic distinction into his legal theory, at two points. One is found, not surprisingly, in his outline of 'forensic' remedies [*legis actio forensis*] which divides remedies into those which are *realis*, those which are *personalis*, and a third hybrid category, those which are *mista*. *Distributio* fol. E, s.v.: *Ex materia, actio triplex*.

The other is his discussion of those legal acts [*facta cum iure coniuncta*] which can potentially give rise to the need for a forensic remedy. Again, like his discussion of remedies, he distinguishes between those acts which involve acquisition or alienation of some asset [*acquisitio rei iurisve alienatio*] from those acts which involve obligation and release [*obligatio et obligationis solutio*]. *Distributio* fol. D, s.v.: *Facta: Cum iure coniuncta quae*. It is especially noteworthy that Bodin thinks ownership and possession can extend not only over 'things' or 'assets' [*res*], but also over 'rights' [*ius*]. Thus a 'forensic' *actio in rem* can result in the acquisition 'of a thing or a right' [*rei iurisve*].

[59] *Distributio* fol. E, s.v.: *Legis Actio Duplex*; fol. B, s.v.: *Facta*. Bodin cites D.11.1.4, 1.1.11–12, Inst.1.1.4. *Apud iudicem* is the second phase of a Roman trial once a judge has been appointed, contest of issue has been determined, and jurisdiction has been delegated, after the initial *in iure* proceeding before a magistrate. Among the examples, in *Distributio* fol. E, s.v.: *Extraiudicialis*, of extrajudicial actions are *ritus sacrorum, legislatio, magistratuum creatio, forma comitiorum, actiones tabellionum seu stilus notariorum*, among others.

[60] But there are a number of notable exceptions such as the *condictio indebiti* (the action to recover assets which were not owed to others) which is described as a natural law remedy: D.12.6.15.

'nominate' contracts.[61] And connected to each of these contracts were specific civil remedies, or *actiones*, to enforce performance of duties arising from those contracts – and *only* from those contracts. So, for example, contracts of buying and selling [*emptio-venditio*] were enforced by the *actio venditi* (for the seller, the *vendor*) and the *actio empti* (for the buyer, the *emptor*). Contracts of partnership [*societas*] were enforced by the *actio pro socio* (by one partner, or *socius*, against another). Contracts of deposit [*depositum*] were enforced by the *actio depositi directa* (for the depositer against the depositary) and the *actio depositi contraria* (for the depositary against the depositer). And so on.

However, not all agreements [*pacta*; *conventiones*; Bodin sometimes says *pacta conventa*], needless to say, counted legally as enforceable contracts.[62] While the *ius civile* provided actionable remedies to parties engaged in many types of formal legal agreements, it nevertheless left unprotected or (to use a metaphor used in medieval contract law) 'unclothed' all sorts of informal or formless agreements – that is, agreements lacking in the formal, even ritualistic, qualities of nominate contracts. Such 'naked' or 'bare' agreements [*pacta nuda*], as they were sometimes called by medieval jurists, were all unenforceable by ordinary legal actions (and, for this reason, regarded as 'incomplete' – *imperfecta*), even if they were technically obligatory under the *ius gentium* and the *ius naturale*.[63]

Contract	Obligation	Remedy
Ius naturale and *ius gentium* contract [*pacta nuda*]	*Obligatio naturalis* and *obligatio iurisgentium*	
Ius civile contract	*Obligatio civilis*	*Actio*

The medieval notion of a 'naked' or 'bare' agreement originates in a famous text by Ulpian in the *Digest*: *Nuda pactio obligationem non parit, sed parit exceptionem*.[64] It was meant to indicate a formless agreement based on consent alone and, therefore, unactionable. Medieval civilians readily exploited this metaphor of nudity by suggesting that such formless agreements could theoretically be 'clothed' [*vestita*]

[61] The four principal types of 'nominate' contracts identified classically by Gaius were *literis*, *verbis*, *re* (real contracts), and *consensu* (contracts of sale, hire, partnership, mandate, *negotiorum gestio*).

[62] Civilians generally treated *pactum* and *conventio* (or the combined *pactum conventum*) as equivalent, based on D.2.14.1.3. Cp. *Gloss. Ord.* on D.2.14.1, s.v. *Conventionis*: *Omne pactum est conventio et conventio est genus*. Cp. D.50.12.3. Klaus-Peter Nanz, *Die Entstehung des allgemeinen Vertragsbegriff im 16 bis 18 Jahrhundert* (München: J. Schweitzer, 1985) 45.

[63] Bartolus on D.2.14.7.4; Antonio da Butrio on X.1.35.1. Cp. D.44.7.52.9. One notable dissenting opinion to the principle that a *nudum pactum* activates a *naturalis obligatio* was the French legal synthesist, François Connan, whose theory of synallagmatic contracts would influence Bodin.

[64] D.2.14.7.4.

with a civil remedy.[65] In this way, all agreements, or *pacta*, could theoretically be classified according to this so-called 'theory of the clothes' [*vestimenta pactorum*] as either 'naked' [*pacta nuda*] or 'clothed' [*pacta vestita*].[66] What's striking, however, is how far medieval civilians were willing to 'clothe' ostensibly 'naked' pacts with garments, thereby making them actionable.[67] It marked a decisive shift away from classical Roman law which generally denied that *pacta nuda* and the natural obligations arising from them were actionable by ordinary remedies.

Contract	Obligation	Remedy
Ius naturale and *ius gentium* contract [*pacta nuda*]	*Obligatio naturalis* and *obligatio iurisgentium*	*Vestimenta pactorum*
Ius civile contract	*Obligatio civilis*	*Actio*

This theory of the clothes became a cardinal doctrine of the later medieval civil law of contracts, passed on to later generations of lawyers of the *ius commune* through its preservation in the *Ordinary Gloss* to the *Digest* and in the legal scholarship of the Bartolist Commentators. But it became a target of fierce criticism in the law schools of sixteenth-century France, the centre of the humanist style of jurisprudence.[68]

Bodin was first exposed to these developments in the law of contract during his time as a law student at Toulouse, where his teachers and contemporaries included Jacques Cujas and Étienne Forcadel, leaders of French legal humanism, the *mos gallicus iuris docendi* (the French method of the teaching of law). Both led the charge against the Bartolist theory of the clothes and sought to restore an allegedly pristine classical doctrine that *obligatio naturalis* was unenforceable by any civil remedy.[69]

[65] The glossator, Accursius, for example, 'clothed' the *pacta praetoria* and *pacta legitima* by the *vestimentum legis auxilio*. Another example is Azo who, unlike classical Roman jurists who treated the innominate real contract of *donatio* as a *pactum nudum*, recategorized *donatio* as a *pactum vestitum* because donations were actionable. *Donatio* is exceptional in this discussion because it was classically regarded to be both actionable and a *pactum nudum*. Zimmermann, *Law of Obligations* 538–39.

[66] *Gloss. Ord.* and Bartolus on D.2.14.7.5. Zimmermann, *Law of Obligations* 538–39; Bart Wauters, '*Ius Commune* and Contract Law', *Uniform Rules for European Contract Law?: A Critical Assessment*, ed. Francisco de Elizalde (Oxford: Hart Publishing, 2018) 40.

[67] Decock, *Theologians and Contract Law* 115 has described this gradual process of clothing bare agreements as a 'denaturation' of classical Roman contract law.

[68] Zimmermann, *Law of Obligations* 539, however, argues that even the French humanists such as Duarenus, Connan, Cujas, and Donellus were inclined to abandon the principle, *nuda pactio obligationem non parit*. Lothar Seuffert, *Zur Geschichte der obligatorischen Verträge* (Nördlingen: C.H. Beck, 1881) 108–14; Nanz, *Die Entstehung des allgemeinen Vertragsbegriff* 65.

[69] Henri Gilles, 'La Faculté de droit de Toulouse au temps de Jean Bodin', *Annales d'histoire des facultés de droit et de la science juridique No.* 3 (1986): 23–36; Pierre Mesnard, 'Jean Bodin à Toulouse', *Bibliothèque d'Humanisme et Renaissance* 12 (1950): 31–59.

But it was more than simply a staid academic interest. Bodin had a very specific reason for participating in these academic debates on the law of contractual obligations, and that is because of his view that even sovereigns can, in its public capacity on behalf of states, enter, and be party to, contractual obligations.[70] And as parties to contracts, sovereigns can, in principle, be legally bound to perform their contractual duties, as required by the *ius naturale* and *ius gentium*. As Bodin put it, sovereigns, just like everyone else, are always bound by their 'lawful and reasonable agreements' [*conventions justes et raisonnables*] and 'required to observe their promises' [*promissa servare tenetur*].[71]

This was, needless to say, one of Bodin's fundamental teachings on sovereignty. Sovereigns are legal subjects of the *ius naturale* and the *ius gentium*, from which sovereigns not only derive duties, but also their rights. Being so duty-bound to the requirements of the *ius naturale* and the *ius gentium*, not even sovereigns can exempt themselves from having to perform their contractual duties owed to others.

The legal reasoning for this was based on Bodin's view that contractual agreements involving sovereigns were structurally 'synallagmatic' [from συνάλλαγμα] in form.[72] Indeed, most genuine contracts, Bodin thought, were synallagmatic, involving some reciprocal exchange of legal 'consideration' [*causa*] between contracting parties, a *quid pro quo* achieved by the 'giving' [*causa dandi*] of something valuable or by the 'doing' [*causa faciendi*] of some valuable act.[73] Any transaction of goods or services taking the form of a *do ut des* ('I give so that you give' such as

[70] Bodin, thus, anticipates the doctrine of sovereignty and obligation established in *S.S. Wimbledon* (United Kingdom, France, Italy, Japan v. Germany), 1923 P.C.I.J. (ser. A) No. 1 (August 17): 25.

[71] *République* 134; cp. *De Republica* 86 [1.8]; cp. *De Off.* 3.24.92: *Pacta et promissa servare*. Grotius, *De Iure Belli ac Pacis* at 2.14.1, and 2.16.16 cites Bodin specifically by referring to this passage. Bodin connects this to the rule of natural equity, D.2.14.1, which Kelsen has notably suggested as the *Grundnorm* of international law.

[72] Cp. *Distributio* fol. B, s.v.: *Conventio: Contractu cui synallagma*. The Greek συνάλλαγμα was a generic term indicating any type of commercial transaction or exchange giving rise to mutual obligations. It was Aristotle's preferred term in the *Nicomachean Ethics* to designate 'transaction' in crafting his theory of commutative justice. The Roman jurists at D.50.16.19, however, used it generally to mean what, in Roman law, were classified as 'consensual contracts' – such as the contracts of sale, hire, and partnership – all of which activated mutual obligations, such as the mutual obligations of *emptor* and *vendor* in the *emptio-venditio* contract of sale. And there is textual evidence in the *Digest* (D.2.14.7.2; cp. D.19.5.5) suggesting that συνάλλαγμα also included all varieties of 'innominate contracts' – unnamed contracts that, in effect, say *dedi tibi rem ut mihi aliam dares* (I give this thing to you, so that you give something else to me), or *dedi ut aliquid facias* (I give this to you, so that you do something for me). Nicholas Theocarakis, '*Nicomachean Ethics* in Political Economy: The Trajectory of the Problem of Value', in *History of Economic Ideas* 14 (2006): 9–53.

[73] Bodin's list of synallagma in *Distributio* fol. B included all nominate contracts of Roman law, such as the consensual contracts of sale, hire, partnership, and mandate, as well as innominate real contracts. Also included were the nominate real contracts such as loan for use [*commodatum*], deposit [*depositum*], and pledge [*pignus*], which he labelled as contracts based on 'trust' [*creditum*]. Bodin would later, in the *République*, use these contracts to explain the notion of 'public trust' or 'public credit' central to the holding of public office. Sovereigns and their subordinate magistrates holding a public office vested with some degree of *imperium* engage in a synallagmatic contract, in which both sovereign and magistrate are tied by mutual obligation and the *imperium* itself is the consideration. The *De Republica* frequently speaks of *imperium depositum* and describes *imperium* as a *res commodata*.

sale), a *do ut facias* ('I give so that you do' such as hire), or a *facio ut facias* ('I do so that you do'), constituted a valid synallagmatic contract.[74]

What all such transactions, whether a simple purchase of goods in a marketplace or a complex treaty negotiation, shared in common was the mutual or 'bilateral' structure of obligation resulting from all such engagements.[75] All parties, even sovereigns, are bound and required to perform the contracted act, whether a *causa dandi* or *causa faciendi*, as consideration for the others. This is how, for example, Bodin interpreted the mutually obligatory structure of international treaties, whether between sovereigns of equal standing [*aequo foedere*] or between sovereigns of unequal standing [*iniquo*], such as a protectorate created by a 'treaty of protection' between a patron and client-state (see Chapter 1).[76] So too did Bodin interpret feudal bonds of homage and fealty between lord and vassal in similarly synallagmatic terms, such that both parties were said to be 'reciprocally bound' [*réciproquement obligés*].[77]

The principle of συνάλλαγμα extended even to contracts enacted between sovereigns and their own subjects, taking specifically the synallagmatic exchange of a *facio ut facias* ('I do so that you do').[78] Just as subjects are duty-bound to obey their sovereign, sovereigns too are duty-bound to do justice (sometimes Bodin adds *garde, & protection*) for their subjects.[79] The specific services being exchanged as 'consideration' between sovereign and subject are less important to Bodin than the reciprocal structure of these duties. What really matters is that all parties, even sovereigns, are required under the *ius gentium* and *ius naturale* to perform their respective ends of such a bargain.

There's a strikingly egalitarian quality in this contract doctrine. The fact that one of the contracting parties is a sovereign makes no difference at all in adjudicating the bindingness of the sovereign's synallagmatic duties, nor does it confer any special advantage to the sovereign over the subject. As Bodin put it:

[74] *Distributio* fol. B, s.v.: *Negotium*. Bodin specifically remarks that the number of synallagmatic contracts taking the form, *facio ut facias*, is *infinitae*.

[75] This indicates the influence of François Connan who controversially, among the major French humanists, argued that συνάλλαγμα was the essence of all valid and actionable contracts. *Commentariorum de Iure Civili*.

[76] *République* 104, 106; *De Republica* 68, 579 [1.7; 5.6].

[77] *République* 104; *De Republica* 68 [1.7], citing L.F. 2.6 and 2.26.1.

[78] This is how Bodin chose to interpret the Aragonese *leges pactionata* which, properly speaking, were not 'laws' at all, but contracts.

[79] *République* 19, 85, 610–11; *De Republica* 14 [1.3: *imperandi ac parendi mutuis officiis*], 56 [1.6], 450 [4.6: *obligatio mutua est & utrinque contracta, ut non magis principi parere subditi debeant, quam princeps subditis ius dicere*]. While monarchs are duty-bound to do justice for their subjects, failure to perform is an offence, *not* so much to their subjects, but to God, as a third-party surety to whom the oath is sworn. What Bodin is suggesting here with his synallagmatic analysis, however, is that a sovereign's obligation is due to subjects, particularly when subjects have an 'interest' (*République* 133) in the obligor's performance.

> An agreement between a sovereign prince and his subjects creates a mutual obligation which binds the two parties reciprocally and from which neither can withdraw without the mutual consent of the other. In this respect, the sovereign is in no way to be seen superior to the subjects.[80]

Not even the 'absolute' power of sovereignty, which otherwise could release and absolve subjects from legal obligation, can be sufficient to release them from the obligatory bond of contract by legislative fiat (for reasons we will see in Chapter 4). On this point, however, Bodin was crystal clear: a sovereign 'cannot derogate from contracts simply by an assertion of sovereign power'.[81] Like any private person, sovereigns too must secure the permission and consent of their 'creditors' (even creditors who happen also to be their subjects) in order to be released from their valid contractual duties.[82] Since it is the consent of two or more [*pactio duorum pluriumve*] to engage in an exchange that initially creates a reciprocally binding obligation in the first place, it can only be by the performance of those duties or by a contrary act of consent that such mutual obligation can be amended or dissolved [*contrario consensu dissolvitur*].[83]

Even sovereigns, then, are expected and required to perform their contractual duties, including duties owed to their own subjects. And the reason for this is that the law enjoining performance of contractual duties is ultimately an equitable rule of natural law, binding sovereign and subject alike, without differentiation.[84] While Bodin marshalled evidence from numerous medieval civilian and canonistic authorities to make this fundamental point, it was ultimately the canonistic jurisprudence of the medieval Decretalists, the canon law commentators on the *Decretals* of Gregory IX [*Liber Extra*], which apparently had the greatest influence on Bodin.[85]

[80] *République* 135: *La convention est mutuelle entre le Prince & les subjects, qui oblige les deux parties reciproquement & ne peut l'une des parties y contrevenir au prejudice, & sans le consentement de l'autre*; *De Republica* 87: *Conventio inter cives, ac principem mutuam habet obligationem, a qua discedi sine mutuo consensu non potest. In quo genere Princeps nihil habet, quod subditis superior esse videatur* [1.8], citing D.15.16.19, 2.14.58 (which is the same passage Bodin cites at *Distributio* fol. B, s.v.: *Conventio*: *Contractu cui synallagma*), 50.17.35.

[81] *République* 153; *De Republica* 100 [1.8]. Cp, *République* 133; *De Republica* 86 [1.8], where Bodin identifies the exceptional circumstances where sovereigns can be released from contracts that involve an invalid diminution of sovereignty [*iis quae ad iura maiestatis imminutae*], just as in private law, individuals can be released from contracts for reasons of fraud [*dolus*], error, or fear [*metus*]. Grotius comments upon this passage in *De Jure Belli ac Pacis* 2.14.1.

[82] *Distributio* fol. D, s.v.: *Liberatio est obligationis solutio*, citing D.2.14.62.

[83] D.2.14.1.2; 50.17.35. I have called this the 'principle of symmetry' in 'Unmaking Law' 273–79. Bodin applies the principle in explaining how feudal obligations mutually binding lords and vassals and how political obligations mutually binding sovereigns and subjects can be dissolved by mutual consent. *République* 89; *De Republica* 59 [1.6].

[84] D.2.14.1, which Bodin cites at *De Republica* 99–100 [1.8]. His use of the phrases, *promissa servare tenetur* and *iusta promissa servare*, suggests that he was also thinking of *De Off.* 3.92.

[85] *De Republica* 87 cites Cino da Pistoia, Bartolus, and Baldus on C.1.14.4, Giasone del Maino on C.1.14.1, and Felino Sandeo on X.1.2.3. Bodin's use of *ius commune* authorities clearly signals his

And it's not hard to see why. Not only was this Decretalist literature of applied canon law on the cutting edge of developing a general theory of contract, it directly addressed the theoretical question whether sovereigns are bound by their legally valid pacts and contracts. Their answers (deployed as commentaries on X.2.19.1) were uniform: 'A sovereign prince who has entered into a contract with his subject is bound at least by natural law' [*saltem naturaliter*].[86] One consequence immediately follows: a sovereign cannot arbitrarily cancel [*tollere non potest*] natural obligations arising from contracts entered into with subjects, but instead is presumed to be under a valid obligation due to subjects.[87]

Bodin, who cited these sources at length, evidently found the Decretalists far more useful than the humanists in framing his own ideas.[88] This Decretalist influence is clearest in the *République*, where Bodin neatly (if somewhat inaccurately and incompletely) summarized the canonistic position: a sovereign 'can only be bound by a natural obligation' (i.e. *obligatio naturalis* arising from the *ius naturale*), but not by a civil obligation (i.e. *obligatio civilis* arising from the *ius civile*).[89] Unlike private persons, then, sovereigns were generally immune from being sued without their consent and from being compelled to perform contractual duties by an ordinary civil *actio* litigated in a regular court.[90] That is because civil obligations and civil actions, just like civil contracts (often exemplified by the Roman verbal contract of *stipulatio*), were all part of the civil law [*obligations sont de droit civil; iuris civilis propria sit*] which ultimately is a product of a sovereign's positive legislation.[91] As the

rejection of the humanist theory. Mesnard, 'Jean Bodin à Toulouse' 54–59 argues that Bodin's theoretical writings during his Toulouse period indicate a substantial doctrinal break from Cujas and the influence, instead, of Connan.

[86] Nicolas de Tudeschi [Panormitanus], *Commentaria in Secundam Secundi Decretalium Libri Partem* (Venice, 1571) fols. 2_{vo}–3_{ro} [on X.2.19.1]; Antonio da Butrio, *Super Secunda Secundi Decretalium Commentarii*, vol. 4 (Venice: Apud Iuntas, 1578) fol. 2_{ro} [on X.2.19.1]. This discussion is the inspiration for Grotius' own analysis in *De Iure Belli ac Pacis* 2.14.6.

[87] Francesco Zabarella, *Consilia* (Venice: Apud Ioannem Baptistam a Porta, 1581) fol. 152_{ro} [*Consilia* 147]; Felino Sandeo, *Commentariorum Pars Secunda* (Venice, 1601) fol. 67_{vo} [on X.2.19.1, §3], citing C.1.22.6.

[88] It is less clear how charitably or accurately Bodin represented the Decretalist position. Lloyd, *Jean Bodin* 100, 121, has expressed doubt on how well Bodin actually knew his legal sources and suggests that he may have, as was a common practice among lawyers writing *consilia*, simply mined the sources he consulted for relevant citations. Two of Bodin's favourite canonist authorities were evidently Alessandro Tartagni da Imola and Felino Sandeo, whom Ralph Giesey, in 'Medieval Jurisprudence' 174–75, describes as the 'masters of applied Roman and canon law'.

[89] *République* 153; *De Republica* 100 [1.8]. Siding with Innocent IV, Bodin rejected the medieval doctrine that a 'sovereign prince can derogate from the law of nature', which he attributed to Accursius and Cino da Pistoia on C.1.22.6, D.1.4.1, and X.1.2.7. What they really meant by 'law of nature' was actually the 'law of nations', from which sovereigns *can* depart. *De Republica* 290 [3.4].

[90] Such sovereign immunity could, and even should, be voluntarily waived by the sovereign and consent to subjecting itself to the jurisdiction of an ordinary court. *République* 619, 621, 627; *De Republica* 456, 458, 463 [4.6], citing D.2.1.10 and C.3.5.1: *neminem sibi esse iudicem vel ius sibi dicere debere*.

[91] *République* 153; *De Republica* 100 [1.8].

author of the *ius civile*, a sovereign authority could always exempt itself from obligations arising from a suit, whether by derogation, or even by a sovereign legislative act aimed at abrogating entirely the law under which a contract and civil remedy are created.

Such sovereign immunity, however, did not extend to natural obligations. On this point, both civilians and canonists could agree in principle: sovereigns, just like everyone else, are bound by natural obligations, including obligations arising from 'naked' contracts and agreements of *ius naturale* based on mere consent. The key question really was a more practical one of legal process: can a sovereign be sued for failure to perform a natural duty? The civilians (following the Glossatorial principle) were clear: natural obligations, though binding, are not actionable. And that is because actions, strictly speaking, are creatures of the *ius civile*, not the *ius naturale* or *ius gentium*.[92]

Canonists, however, arrived at a different conclusion.[93] They rejected the Glossatorial doctrine that *actiones sunt a iure civili*, arguing instead that actions are ultimately derived 'not from civil law, but from natural law or the law of nations'.[94] In this way, canonists proved to be creatively adept at providing for extra-civil remedies to enforce such obligations. One of the first to do so was the canonist, Huguccio, who introduced the remedy of the *officium iudicis* as an equitable tool to enforce imperfect rights deriving from formless, or 'naked' agreements [*pacta nuda*] that would otherwise be unactionable in civil law.[95] Although, in the medieval polity of Christendom, it was a remedy intended to be used by confessors in the court of conscience [*in foro interno*], it established the canonistic principle that even natural and *ius gentium* obligations were theoretically actionable.

Canonists of the later Middle Ages further built upon Huguccio's basic insight. Probably the most influential in developing this doctrine was the canonist, Sinibaldo Fieschi, an accomplished Decretalist in his own right who would, in 1243, become Innocent IV, one of the most accomplished and influential of the medieval canonists. A commentary by Innocent on the *Decretals*, well known among *ius commune* lawyers and cited twice by Bodin in the *République*, laid out the essentials of the canonistic position on notional actions of the *ius naturale*:

[92] *Gloss. Ord.* on D.1.1.5; cp. 1.2.2.6.

[93] Two of these *doctores utriusque iuris* were Baldus de Ubaldis and his student, Paul de Castro, on D.1.1.5.

[94] Pennington, *Prince and the Law* 148–49. Cp. *De Republica* 100: *Nulla fere conventio nulla obligatio cogitari potest quae non sit et naturae et gentium omnium communis.* The shift toward a *ius naturale* and *ius gentium* source of *actiones* and guarantees of legal process in canonistic argument reflected the growing concern for the rights of defendants and the integrity of legal procedure, all threatened by the arbitrary use of torture.

[95] Decock, *Theologians and Contract Law* 123–24.

While it might be sustained that a prince can theoretically withdraw an actionable remedy, he in fact can never take away the duty to deliver justice, since this would be against natural law.[96]

The importance of this text lies in Innocent's acknowledgement that, while the specifics of legal remedies may be technical matters of civil law, the general principle that wrongs must be righted through *some* kind of legal process and remedy is ultimately a matter of natural law, and therefore cannot simply be erased by negative legislation.[97] For this reason, later civilians and canonists alike have suggested, contrary to the Glossators, that *actiones* can't be exclusive to civil law. They belong as much to the *ius naturale* and to the *ius gentium* (as Guido of Suzarra, Jacob de Arena, and Paul de Castro suggest) as they do to the *ius civile*.[98]

Taken together, the Decretalist theory of canon law looked strikingly different from the humanist theory of civil law:

Contract	Obligation	Remedy
Ius naturale and *ius gentium* contract [*pacta nuda*]	*Obligatio naturalis* and *obligatio iurisgentium*	*Officium iudicis in foro interno*
Ius civile contract	*Obligatio civilis*	*Actio in foro externo*

From Bodin's point of view, the humanists were simply wrong to insist that contractual obligations of the *ius naturale* and the *ius gentium* were unactionable. They just weren't imaginative enough to see that the *ius naturale* and *ius gentium* provided for a different type of remedy to be sought outside the walls of an ordinary courtroom and, instead, in the confessor's court of equity, which, in medieval canon law, held jurisdiction even over sovereign princes.[99] While Roman law purists might balk at such suggestions of an *actio naturalis* or *actio iuris gentium* to enforce contractual obligations, canon lawyers of the medieval Church had no problem assigning to confessors in the *forum animae internum* (court of

[96] Innocent IV, *Commentaria Super Libros Quinque Decretalium* (Frankfurt am Main, 1570) fol. 3_{vo} [on X.1.2.7], citing C.1.22.6: *Licet sustineatur quod auferat actionem tamen quin reddat iustitiam auferre non potest, cum esset contra ius naturale.* Bodin cites this passage in *République* 150, 414.

[97] Pennington, *Prince and the Law* 150 comments that, 'I do not know of other jurists who maintained that a prince could not abolish the juridical process or ignore an action because he was bound by natural law to render justice ... Innocent's brief comments provided a *pièce justicative* to establish a right of due process' for the later Middle Ages. Bodin knew and cited this legal literature on X.1.31.1 and 2.1.13.

[98] Guido of Suzarra on D.17.1.22.5, Jacob de Arena on Inst.4.6, in Pennington, *Prince and the Law* 154–55; Paul de Castro on D.1.1.5, §2, §§14–15: *actiones de iure gentium.*

[99] Cp. D.2.14.7.

conscience) the jurisdictional authority to enforce obligations and protect rights arising from the *ius naturale* and *ius gentium*.[100]

Where did Bodin find himself in this debate? A concise, but revealing remark, in the *République* shows that Bodin generally favoured the Decretalist position over the legal humanists: Contract, obligation, and action are all concepts cut from the same legal cloth.[101] Those who deny that naked pacts are actionable fundamentally misunderstand how the three are supposed to go together:

> Obligation as well as contract are of the same nature. Therefore, if a contract arises from the *ius naturale* and the *ius gentium*, it logically follows that the corresponding obligations and actions must also be of the same nature.[102]
>
> It is very certain in terms of law that if the contract is of natural law or of the common law of mankind, then the corresponding obligation and the action will also be of the same nature.[103]

To wit: if a contract is legally valid, then there must also be, as legal consequences of that contract, a binding obligation as well as *some* remedy, the 'subjective right', which can theoretically be invoked to enforce that obligation.[104]

But Bodin stopped short of a full ringing endorsement of the Decretalist position. He demanded something more than simply the confessor's *officium iudicis* of canon law. It's not enough, he thought, to leave it to a sovereign's confessor to ensure that a penitent sovereign keeps its pacts and promises [*pacta et promissa servare*]. There must be a real concrete remedy, actionable even for breaches of naked pacts, just as there are remedies for breaches of nominate contracts of civil law. This is precisely where, Bodin thought, 'the interpreters of canon law err and go astray' [*intelligitur labi et errare pontificii iuris interpretes*].[105]

[100] Even among later medieval civilians, jurists recognized that a strict adherence to classical Roman law was no longer practical and contributed to what Wim Decock has termed a 'denaturation' of classical Roman law, *Theologians and Contract Law* 107.

[101] On this point, Bodin cites Bartolus, Baldus, and Angelus de Ubaldis (Baldus' brother) on D.12.6.15 (on *condictio indebiti*), C.5.21.2 (on *actio rerum amotarum* in divorce), and D.1.1.5 (on the different sources of 'obligation' and 'action').

[102] *De Republica* 100: *Obligatio eiusdem sit naturae atque conventio. Igitur si conventio naturalis est, ac gentium omnium communis, obligationes quoque, et actiones, eiusdem esse naturae consequens est.*

[103] *République* 153: *Car il est bien certain en termes de droit que si la convention est de droit naturel ou de droit commun a tous peuples, et l'obligation et l'action seront de mesme nature.*

[104] Bodin went even further, *De Republica* 100: 'Hardly any [civil] contract or obligation can be imagined which does not originate in the *ius naturale* and the *ius gentium*'. This passage evidently had some resonance among early modern readers. The author of the 'Political Education', reprinted in *The Dutch Revolt*, ed. Martin Van Gelderen (Cambridge: Cambridge University Press, 1993) 212–13 evidently relied on Bodin. Bodin is not cited, but the sequence of citations and the overall argument indicate that the author was referencing this passage. Grotius too must have had this passage in mind while crafting his own analysis at *De Iure Belli ac Pacis* 2.14.6.

[105] *De Republica* 100.

Bodin's solution was, in effect, to 'confiscate' the confessor's equitable jurisdiction of *officium iudicis* and to transfer it into the hands of judges staffing civil courts. In doing so, Bodin empowered judges with the judicial tools to enforce performance, not only of civil duties, but also of natural duties. But most important of all, this widened scope of jurisdiction over matters of both law and equity effectively positioned sovereigns *under* the equitable jurisdiction of the very judges they've appointed.

Doesn't this contradict the very idea of sovereignty? Bodin didn't think so. And that is because, in his view, courts don't really 'belong' to sovereigns, nor do judges 'work' for sovereigns, in the same way that subordinates in the hierarchy of public administration do.[106] While courts and judges [i.e. *magistratus*] may initially be constituted and appointed by sovereigns, they are not so much agents of sovereigns as they are agents of equity – or, to borrow from Ulpian, 'priests of justice'.[107]

Bodin repeatedly made this observation in identifying the dual function of judges in a well ordered state, which he termed *legis actio* and *officium iudicis*.[108] While their legally defined [*lege definita*; *legitima*] jurisdiction empowered judges to provide civil remedies [*legis actiones*] to enforce civil obligations as the law provided, their very role as judge additionally empowered them, Bodin argued, with *officium iudicis*, the discretionary [*nobile*] power as 'trustees of equity' to provide equitable remedies of the *ius naturale* and *ius gentium*, by 'supplementing or moderating laws' [*quum leges supplet, quum leges moderatur*], where the law is somehow deficient or silent.[109]

But Bodin was prepared to go even further and acknowledge that, where appropriate in exceptional cases, judges might even need to go 'beyond the law' [*praeter legem*] and even 'contrary to the law' [*contra legem*] to do what justice

[106] For this reason, judges cannot be arbitrarily removed from office in a *droit* government, in the same way that a sovereign can remove an official appointed on extraordinary commission. Indeed, arbitrary removal, for Bodin, is one of the classic signs of despotic, or *seigneurial*, rulership. See Daniel Lee, 'Office Is a Thing Borrowed: Jean Bodin on Offices and Seigneurial Government', *Political Theory* 41 (2013): 1–32.

[107] D.1.1.1. Bodin identifies the right of creating judgeships and appointing judges to fill those seats – the *ius magistratuum creandi* – as one of the chief *marques* of sovereignty. But since even sovereigns are required to do justice, they may also be seen as agents of equity. See also Vittor Ivo Comparato, 'La teoria del *magistratus* nella *Methodus* di Jean Bodin', *Annali della Facolta di Scienze Politiche: Materiali di Storia* 17 (1980): 204; Vittor Ivo Comparato, 'Sulla teoria della funzione pubblica nella *République* di Jean Bodin', *Il Pensiero Politico* 14 (1981): 93–112; Anna Maria Lazzarino Del Grosso, 'Le Magistrature in Bodin', *Il Pensiero Politico* 40 (2007): 394–409.

[108] *Distributio* fol. E, s.v.: *Legis Actio*; fol. F, s.v.: *Iudicis Officium*; *Methodus* 263; *République* 440; *De Republica* 304–5 [3.5]. The distinction between *legis actio* and *officium iudicis* is ultimately traceable to the Bartolist analysis on D.2.1.1 on the *officium mercenarium* and the *officium nobile*.

[109] Bodin uses the phrase, *lege definitum*, to define the officer [*officialis*] at *De Republica* 259 [3.2], in contrast to the commissioner [*curator*] whose public function is conferred *extra ordinem sine lege imperantis arbitrio*. *Distributio* fol. A, s.v.: *Ius*: *Humanum*: *Gentium*: *Aequitas ius est arbitrio statuentis permissum* (cp. D.1.1.7). Cp. *De Republica* 288 [3.4] on the equitable *officium nobile* of magistrates empowered to correct and supplement the laws [*leges supplere, emendare, corrigere posset*].

requires.[110] Not only, then, was Bodin prepared to promote a robust notion of judicial independence, he saw that independence as essential to ensuring that sovereigns perform their obligations.[111]

Legibus Solutus: Liberty from the Laws

There's an important reason why Bodin gets caught up in this technical debate on contractual rights, obligations, and remedies, deriving from the *ius naturale* and the *ius gentium*. It illustrates the basic principle that all sovereigns are legal subjects of the *ius naturale* and the *ius gentium*.[112] And it is from these higher laws of the *ius naturale* and the *ius gentium* that all sovereigns ultimately derive not only their duties, but also their sovereign rights.

This is, needless to say, a core principle undergirding the entire design of Bodin's theory of sovereignty. Not only did it effectively burden sovereigns under obligations of the *ius naturale* and the *ius gentium*, it also, at the same time, empowered them theoretically with 'subjective' rights deriving *from* those same 'objective' laws. This marked the real novelty of Bodin's approach to his theory of sovereignty: the Bodinian right of sovereignty presupposes and entails an anterior system of objective law.

This constituted an unorthodox opinion. By the time Bodin started his studies of sovereignty, it already became commonplace in the law schools to say that sovereignty was best to be characterized as a kind of a negative permissive 'liberty' from the laws – and more specifically, 'liberty from obsolete laws and bad customs'.[113] For so many of these *docteurs* of law, being sovereign was nothing other than being *legibus solutus*, like the Roman emperors, 'free from the laws'.[114]

[110] *Methodus* 264. The *praeter legem/contra legem* distinction appears in nominalist literature such as in John Duns Scotus, *Quaestiones in Lib. III Sententiarum*, Tomi Quinti, Pars Secunda (Lyon: Sumptibus Laurentii Durand, 1639) 1368, 1370 [1, Distinctio 44, Quaestio 1]; Francis Oakley, 'Jacobean Political Theology: The Absolute and Ordinary Powers of the King', *Journal of the History of Ideas* 29 (1968): 338.

[111] *République* 153; *De Republica* 100 [1.8]. As Bodin points out, even God is bound by promises.

[112] *République* 131 [1.8]: *tous les Princes de la terre sont subiects aux loix de Dieu, & de nature, & a plusieurs loix humaines communes à tous peuples;* cp. *De Republica* 84.

[113] Brian Tierney, *The Origins of Papal Infallibility, 1150–1350* (Leiden: Brill, 1972) 30. However, cp. *Popular Sovereignty* 27–35, where I show that *legibus solutus*, in connection with the *lex regia* and the *leges de imperio*, could be understood to mean that one has become so free *through* the operation of the laws.

[114] I choose to translate *solutus* as 'free' in the sense of a Hohfeldian permissive liberty-right, being 'exempt' or 'released' from some legal duty. To be *legibus solutus* means, then, that one is not required or obliged to obey the laws [*leges*], or, in short, $\sim O(\varphi)$. The point that Bodin will make is that the Hohfeldian liberty of *legibus solutus* isn't the same as sovereignty.

Bodin discusses the *legibus solutus* principle at *République* 131, *De Republica* 85. On the significance of D.1.3.31, see Adhemar Esmein, 'La maxime *princeps legibus solutus est* dans l'ancien droit public français', in *Essays in Legal History*, ed. Paul Vinogradoff (Oxford: Oxford University Press, 1913); Tierney, 'Prince Is Not Bound By the Laws'; Dieter Wyduckel, *Princeps Legibus Solutus: Eine*

The original inspiration for this analysis was, not surprisingly, the *Digest* of Roman law, which cited Ulpian's famous description of the emperor's own relationship to the laws: *Princeps legibus solutus est* (D.1.3.31).[115] And following Ulpian's authority, it became customary in the juridical literature of the *ius commune* to define sovereign authority as *legibus soluta*, so much so, that the two became, in effect, mutually synonymous and functionally equivalent. Kings and princes were *legibus soluti*. Popes were *legibus soluti*.[116] Even God, as *princeps naturae* and *naturae legislator*, was *legibus solutus* from his own divine and natural laws.[117]

Bodin, probably grudgingly, followed this convention in his own writing. As early as the *Distributio*, Bodin connected the concept of sovereignty [*ius maiestatis*] specifically to the juridical condition of being free from law [*lege soluta*].[118] And again, in the Latin *De Republica*, Bodin famously defined sovereignty in Ulpian's language, as a public power of state that is *legibus soluta*, free from the laws.[119]

It is clear, however, that he was very uneasy about defining sovereignty in terms of the *legibus solutus* doctrine of Roman law, for a variety of reasons. One problem was vagueness in the doctrine. It was not clear, at first glance, from *which* laws, specifically, a sovereign was said to be free. Could a sovereign be free from the higher laws? Could a sovereign be free from God's divine laws? Could a sovereign even be free from *all* laws, *legibus omnibus solutus*?

These questions became a point of intense academic debate among theologians, philosophers, and lawyers of the European *ius commune*. Bodin was evidently familiar with this literature, based on the authorities cited in the *marginalia* of the *République*. Among these sources, however, Bodin found the Decretalists most troubling. They allowed that the *legibus solutus* doctrine could be (mis)understood as signifying something like a proto-Schmittean total lawlessness, a liberty from all laws [*legibus omnibus solutus*], whether human, natural, or divine. That is, in fact, exactly what happened among early modern publicists and lawyers partial to the

Untersuchung zur frühmodernen Rechts- und Staatslehre, Schriften zur Verfassungsgeschichte 30 (Berlin, 1979); Pennington, *The Prince and the Law*.

[115] *Legibus solutus* also occurs at D.32.(1.).23, C.6.23.3, Inst.2.17.8(7). In general, Ennio Cortese, *La norma giuridica: Spunti teorici nel diritto comune classico*, 2 vols. (Milan: Giuffrè, 1962–64).

[116] VI.1.2.1.

[117] Bodin's voluntaristic juridical theology in *The Colloquium of the Seven about Secrets of the Sublime* [*Colloquium Heptaplomeres*], trans. Marion Leathers Kuntz (University Park, Pennsylvania: Pennsylvania State University Press, 1975) 31 [Toralba: 22] positioned God as *naturae legislator suis legibus solutus*. And as a legislator who is *legibus naturae semper solutus*, God can *fixit ac iussit* the laws of nature as well, as Bodin argued in *Universae Naturae Theatrum* (Lyon: Apud Iacobum Roussin, 1596) 40; cp. 206. Cp. *Methodus* 367. God can 'occasionally change these laws at will' [*voluntate arbitrioque suo interdum mutat*]. Calvin, himself a civilian, famously proclaimed that *Deus legibus solutus est, sed non exlex*. *Exlex* was a technical term reflecting the teaching of 1 Corinthians 9:21. Dan Edelstein, *The Terror of Natural Right: Republicanism, the Cult of Nature, and the French Revolution* (Chicago: University of Chicago Press, 2009) 157, n.111.

[118] *Distributio* fol. F, s.v.: *Sententia*.

[119] *De Republica* 14 [1.3].

Machiavellian politics of the 'reason of state'; some were led to believe that sovereigns were subject to no law (except perhaps, as Cicero put it at *De Legibus* 3.8, the *suprema lex – salus populi*) and, thus, free to do whatever they pleased.

Bodin, for his part, felt compelled to clarify his own view in explaining the relationship between sovereignty and the law. And it was precisely against this extreme expansive view of sovereign lawlessness that Bodin framed his response. Sovereigns were certainly, in a sense, free [*soluti*] from the laws, but they were free – *only* – from civil laws [*ius civile*], positive legislation whether of their own making or of their precedessors (for reasons we will see in Chapter 4). Yet, all sovereigns remained bound and 'subject,' just like everyone else, to the higher laws of the *ius naturale* and, to a more limited extent, the *ius gentium*.[120] It was therefore, in his view, highly misleading to characterize sovereignty, as the Decretalists intimated in their description of Papal sovereignty, as the quality of being 'free from *all* laws' [*legibus omnibus solutam*].[121]

Indeed, sovereigns could not, as Bodin famously stated at one point in the *République*, unilaterally exempt [*derogare*] themselves or dispense others from the obligatory force of those higher laws simply by asserting sovereignty.[122] No sovereign, according to Bodin, can alter, abrogate, or even partially derogate from obligations deriving *ex iure naturale*, in the same way that sovereigns could alter their own positive legislation.[123]

Viewed in context, then, Bodin's position on the scope of a sovereign's permissive liberty from the laws was comparatively moderate. Bodin has typically been described in the academic literature as an 'absolutist' with respect to sovereignty (if we are to understand 'absolutism' as a political doctrine promoting political rulership unlimited by any law). But, as we'll see in Chapter 4, Bodin himself disavowed such absolutism, which he invariably identified with canonists and, especially, the Decretalist doctrine concerning papal *potestas absoluta*. Canonists, it turns out, were the real 'absolutists,' and Bodin took deliberate steps to distance himself from the Papal absolutism their jurisprudence of 'absolute power' championed.[124]

[120] *République* 131, 149; *De Republica* 84, 97 [1.8]. In the *République/De Republica*, he will further specify that sovereigns are subject also to divine law. This was already recognized in the German scholarship on public law and state as one of Bodin's major contributions: Hermann Rehm, ed., *Handbuch des Öffentlichen Rechts* (Freiburg: Mohr, 1896) 249.

[121] The phrase appears at *De Republica* 84.

[122] *De Republica* 100 [1.8]; cp. *République* 150, *De Republica* 97.

[123] Bodin, citing the *Gloss. Ord.* and Cino da Pistoia on C.1.22.6 and commentaries on D.1.4.1 and X.1.2.7, specifically singles out canonists who allow that a sovereign may derogate even from obligations arising *ex iure naturale*. Bodin does allow, however, that sovereigns can issue a command contrary to the *ius gentium*, so long as it complies with the *ius naturale* and *ius divinum*: *République* 414 [3.4].

[124] This conclusion is confirmed in the literature by Tierney, *Origins of Papal Infallibility*; Ralph Giesey, 'Medieval Jurisprudence'; Kenneth Pennington, *Prince and the Law*; Jane Black, *Absolutism in Renaissance Milan: Plenitude of Power under the Visconti and the Sforza, 1329–1535* (Oxford: Oxford University Press, 2009); Joseph Canning, *Ideas of Power in the Late Middle Ages, 1296–1417* (Cambridge: Cambridge University Press, 2011). As Bodin put it at *De Republica* 102, citing Angelus de Ubaldis on D.2.2.3.3, the canonists were the most 'dangerous flatterers' [*perniciosis*

Imperium: Power Over the Laws

There was another interpretive problem with the *legibus solutus* doctrine.

It failed to capture what Bodin regarded as the essential quality of sovereignty. And that is because being *legibus solutus* – free from legal duties – was not the same as being sovereign.[125] As Bodin put it, 'It is possible for one to be released [*solutus sit*] from all the laws of one's state [*omnibus civitatis suae legibus*] and even from the authority of all magistrates [*magistratuum omnium imperiis solutus*] and yet lack the rights of sovereignty [*iura maiestatis*]'.[126]

To illustrate the point, Bodin gave the example of first-century Roman dictators who were, at certain times, given an extraordinary commission to exercise powers outside the ordinary legal constraints of office. In this regard, Bodin was especially interested in the critical period of late Roman Republican history, when the Roman senate, by law (through a senatorial action classified as a *solutio legibus*), frequently exempted individual persons from ordinary legal constraints of public office, in order to invest them with a legally unlimited dictatorial power for a definite period of time.[127] Bodin cited the Roman general, Pompey, whose military commission was said to be 'exempt from the laws' [*legibus solutus est*] for a five-year period by statute (the *lex Gabinia de piratis persequendis*), so that Pompey might 'wage war against pirates' while freed from the ordinary legal restraints governing the conduct of military leaders on the field.[128]

Another illustration appearing only in the Latin *De Republica*, references the so-called *lex regia*, the legendary Roman statute traditionally thought to have

adulatoribus] of princes and popes and their absolute powers. He then proceeds to cite the numerous canonists who were willing to acknowledge, *bona privatorum suo iure diripere posse* (popes and princes can by their right to assert absolute power legally seize private property), and thereby violate a cardinal rule of natural law prohibiting the taking of private property, including, inter alia, Nicolas de Tudeschi, *Commentaria in Tertium Decretalium Librum* (Venice, 1571) fol. $94_{\text{ro-vo}}$ [Panormitanus on X.3.13.2]; Felino Sandeo, *Commentaria in V.Lib. Decretalium* (Venice: Apud Iacobum Picaiam, 1570) cols. 123–26 [Felinus Sandeus on X.1.2.7, §§128–32].

125 The full text of D.1.3.31 serves to illustrate this point: *Princeps legibus solutus est: Augusta autem licet legibus soluta non est, principes tamen eadem illi privilegia tribuunt, quae ipsi habent.* Ulpian is clear that the emperor and empress can both be *legibus soluti*, precisely because it is a privilege that can be extended to others.

126 *République* 131; *De Republica* 84 [1.8].

127 Bodin would later call this penchant for using extraordinary commissioners as one of the key destabilizing features that would lead to the collapse of the Republic. Benjamin Straumann, *Crisis and Constitutionalism: Roman Political Thought from the Fall of the Republic to the Age of Revolution* (Oxford: Oxford University Press, 2016) 280–86, 295–302. On the senatorial *solutio legibus*, A. Arthur Schiller, *Roman Law: Mechanism and Development* (The Hague: Mouton Publishers, 1978) 44.

128 *République* 131; *De Republica* 84; Turchetti 467 [1.8], citing Plutarch, *Plutarch's Lives: Agesilaus and Pompey, Pelopidas and Marcellus*, trans. Bernadette Perrin, vol. 5, Loeb Classical Library 87 (Cambridge: Harvard University Press, 1917) 176–81 [Pompey, §25].

The senate's use of the *solutio legibus* was increasingly viewed as a senatorial usurpation of a power thought to belong rightfully to the popular assemblies. The result was the statute, *lex Cornelia de legibus solvendo* regulating and limiting the use of such dispensations.

authorized the full (and arguably irrevocable) transfer of Roman *imperium* from the people to the *princeps*.[129] Because Augustus was traditionally regarded as the first Roman *princeps*, jurists believed that the *lex regia* must have somehow corresponded to the various legal acts, which empowered Octavian with high powers of state such as the *maius imperium* and *tribunicia potestas* traditionally distributed in the Republic across various magisterial offices.[130]

Bodin, however, took a different view of these enabling acts of the late Republic, which 'exempted Augustus from all laws of his country in perpetuity' [*omnibus patriae legibus in perpetuo solutus sit, ut Augustus*].[131] Even though he was technically a *princeps* (specifically, *populi Romani princeps*: the 'first citizen of the Roman people') who was legally made *legibus solutus* by popular legislation of the *lex regia*, Augustus was not properly sovereign. And that is because Augustus lacked the power to make and unmake law which (in Bodin's reading of Roman constitutional history) remained with the Roman senate and people even into the early years of the Principate.[132]

Bodin doggedly refused to call these dictators and *principes*, who were technically *legibus soluti*, 'sovereigns' over Rome. Why not? The reason, he explains, is that sovereignty was more than just liberty from the laws; it was a licit power *over* the laws as well and, by implication, a power over everyone bound by those laws.[133] Bodin's point was a proto-Hohfeldian one: one can certainly enjoy legal liberty without legal power. But there's no reason for us to think that enjoyment of such a permissive Hohfeldian liberty, like the one conferred upon Pompey by the *lex Gabinia*, or upon Augustus by the *lex regia*, necessarily entailed a Hohfeldian power as well.[134]

What Bodin was trying to articulate here was the fine juridical distinction between a 'liberty-right' and a 'legal power', a distinction traceable, in modern Anglo-American analytic jurisprudence, to the legal theory of Jeremy Bentham and Wesley Newcomb Hohfeld. As Bodin saw it, the *legibus solutus* doctrine meant

[129] Cp. *Gloss. Ord.* on C.6.23.3, s.v.: *lex imperii* (i.e., *lex regia* of D.1.4.1, Inst.1.2.6). The text in the *Code* indicates the exceptional quality of this *lex* which 'frees' [*solverit*] the *princeps* from the 'solemnities of the law'. This is the same language Bodin uses at *De Republica* 85: *Idcirco lex ipsa principem legibus solvit.*

[130] Clifford Ando, 'The Origins and Import of Republican Constitutionalism', *Cardozo Law Review* 34 (2013): 917–35.

[131] *De Republica* 85 [1.8].

[132] Bodin's view is that Vespasian, not Augustus, was the first proper sovereign emperor of Rome, and that is because he thinks the transfer of authority only finally occurred with the *lex de imperio Vespasiani*.

[133] *République* 131. Sovereignty thus functions as, what Lars Lindahl has described, a positional concept.

[134] Consider tax exemptions as an analogy: The state legislature may have enacted a new law granting a tax exemption, releasing me from the obligation to pay taxes on, say, rental properties. I am, even as a private citizen, *lege solutus* with respect to that particular *lex*. But even though I enjoy a Hohfeldian liberty with respect to that tax obligation, I do not, as a private citizen, have any legal power with respect to that legislation. I cannot directly amend that law or abrogate that law of my own will: Only the legislature can.

nothing more than a permissive liberty-right concept, the condition of being exempt, or released, from positive legal duties. This was, moreover, largely consistent with Ulpian's original meaning in D.1.3.31: the emperor enjoyed a liberty-right, in the sense that he was not obliged [*solutus*], and thus, free from the duty to comply with his own positive laws.[135]

This *legibus solutus* doctrine was not, however, the same as a legal power, nor did it entail the conferral of such a power. Of course, one could enjoy the liberty-right of being *legibus solutus* along with the legal powers associated with sovereignty. As we'll see, Bodin himself understood sovereignty in this way, as both a liberty-right and legal power. But (and this is the key point) one is not automatically vested with such powers, solely on account of being *legibus solutus*. One could be *legibus solutus* even without such powers (just as one could be vested with legal powers without also being *legibus solutus*).

All this pointed to a need for a proper examination of a sovereign's legal powers (or 'plenary competence', as Judge Crawford has put it), separately from liberty-rights.[136] And that required shifting away from a narrow liberty-rights model of the *legibus solutus* doctrine, which presupposed a sovereign's liberty *from* the law, towards an alternative theory, one that pictured sovereignty in terms of a sovereign's licit powers *over* the law, a notion that Bodin captured with the term, *imperium*.

What exactly was *imperium*? Most lawyers, like Bodin, trained in Roman law would instantly recognize *imperium* as a term of public law, functioning as a catch-all term signifying public magisterial authority. In the Roman context, *imperium* indicated the formal constitutional powers of high magistrates – above all, the magisterial 'power of the sword', codified in Justinian's *Digest* as the *merum imperium*.[137] So closely associated was the *imperium* with magisterial power that it eventually became indistinguishably synonymous with other terms indicating the public functions of Roman magistrates – above all, the related term, *iurisdictio*.[138]

[135] As Tierney has pointed out, the Glossatorial interpretation of D.1.3.31 generally understood *legibus solutus* in this way, to be a permissive liberty-right. Accursius' example in the *Gloss. Ord.* on D.1.3.31, s.v.: *Princeps legibus* illustrates with the law of testaments in C.6.23.3.

[136] James Crawford, *The Creation of States in International Law*, 2nd ed. (Oxford: Oxford University Press, 2007) 89, largely following the analysis of C. Rousseau, 'L'indépendence de l'État dans l'Ordre International', *Hague Recueil des Cours* 73 (1948): 171–253, which distinguishes between the independence of statehood and sovereignty.

[137] D.1.21.1.1; 1.21.5; 2.1.3. In the last of these entries, Ulpian explains that *merum imperium* is the 'power of the sword' [*gladii potestas*], which is also simply called 'power' [*potestas*] (not unlike the paterfamilial *patria potestas* of *ius vitae necisque* over children) and is to be differentiated from *mixtum imperium* which includes those functions of magistrates which concern legal process – broadly, *iurisdictio*. The *merum-mixtum* distinction is needed because a private person can be selected to serve as a judge and exercise a delegated *iurisdictio*, yet have no enforcement powers of *merum imperium* which remains with the magistrate.

[138] D.50.16.215. D.1.21.1.1 specifically suggests that *imperium* is attached [*cohaeret*] to *iurisdictio*, so that when the praetor appoints a judge and delegates *iurisdictio*, one can say that the praetor is actually delegating a share of public *imperium* as well. Paul's reason for this is found in D.1.21.5.1: *Iurisdictio sine modica coercitione nulla est.* However, he specifies that *merum imperium* is never delegated with *iurisdictio*. Papinian makes the same point in D.1.21.1.1, which prohibits delegation of *merum imperium* because magistrates (as well as dictators) are entitled to hold it by special legal authorization

But it wasn't always this way. As a product of the new humanistic attitude toward jurisprudence, Bodin was attentive to the historicity of the legal vocabulary in the *Digest*, which, he recognized, was really an artefact of the late Roman Empire.[139] By that time, during the age of Justinian and Tribonian, *imperium* acquired an expansive colloquial sense in later Latin literature beyond legal discourse, such that it became possible, for example, for Varro to speak of the '*imperium* of the bees', or for Cicero to reference the '*imperium* of the mind', or the *imperium domesticum* of the *paterfamilias*.[140]

By contrast, in the earliest Republican sources, centuries before Tribonian was commissioned by Justinian to compile the texts making up the *Corpus Iuris Civilis*, *imperium* was a narrow technical term specifically indicating the extramural military command of high magistrates beyond the Roman *pomerium*.[141] The contrast between *imperium* and *iurisdictio*, thus, might be compared to the modern distinction between military and civilian authority. It was possible for one to have *iurisdictio* without *imperium*; *imperium* without *iurisdictio*; and to have both *imperium* and *iurisdictio*, as did the consuls and praetors whose *imperium* was legally conferred upon them by a formal legislative enactment, a *lex de imperio*.

Bodin sought to recapture this original (and apparently neglected) notion of *imperium*, understood as the military command of a superior *imperator* over his inferiors. He did so because, in its original non-juridical meaning as military command, *imperium* (from *imperare*: 'to command') usefully illustrated what he regarded as the essentially relational character of sovereignty, as a normative relation of command and obedience. In this respect, sovereignty was not unlike the *imperium* of an *imperator* commanding a legion of soldiers.[142]

This relation of command and obedience intrinsic to *imperium*, patterned on the example of Roman military discipline, proved to be a usefully elastic model for Bodin. *Imperium*, Bodin thought, could be used to explain a diverse range of asymmetrical relations based on command such as the *paterfamilias* over the family, the

[*lege datur*]. Papinian is referring to the legal instrument of a *lex de imperio* promulgated by an authorizing vote of the *comitia curiata*. One of Bodin's earliest works in legal theory was an unpublished work entitled, *De imperio et iurisdictione*, a treatise devoted specifically to this interpretive problem of isolating what, if anything, might be the distinctive quality of magisterial *imperium* and why some believe it can't be delegated.

139 Fred Drogula, 'Imperium, Potestas, and the Pomerium in the Roman Republic', *Historia: Zeitschrift für Alte Geschichte* 56 (2007): 427.

140 Drogula, 'Imperium, Potestas, and the Pomerium in the Roman Republic' 420–1, citing Marcus Tarentius Varro, *On Agriculture*, trans. William Davis Hooper, rev. Harrison Boyd Ash, Loeb Classical Library 283 (Cambridge: Harvard University Press, 1934) 500–1 [*De Re Rustica* 3.16.6]; Cicero *De Re Publica* 1.60; *Pro Caecina*, trans. G. Grose Hodge, Loeb Classical Library 198 (Cambridge: Harvard University Press, 1927) 148–49 [18, §52].

141 Cicero, *Philippics 1–6*, ed. and trans. D.R. Shackleton Bailey, rev. John Ramsey, Gesine Manuwald, Loeb Classical Library 189 (Cambridge: Harvard University Press, 2010) 286–87 [*Philippic* 5, 6.45].

142 We can be reasonably confident that this was Bodin's construction of *imperium* from his deliberate choice to stipulate its French equivalent to be *commandement*.

procurator over the *collegium*, and the magistrate over the inhabitants of a legally defined jurisdiction. All of these were different species of *imperium*. What they all shared in common was the command, or *imperium*, of some superior positioned over inferior addressees of those commands.

Sovereignty too belonged to this category of *imperium*. It was, like these other examples of *imperium*, a vertical relation of command, positioning the 'highest', or supreme [*souverain*; *summum*], authority of a state (whether *princeps populusve*, as Bodin would repeatedly say) over subjects, of all ranks and conditions, making up that state. Bodinian subjecthood, thus, ultimately was marked by a question of Hohfeldian liability to someone else's *imperium*. What made one a subject really was whether or not one was an 'addressee' of – and, thus, *liable* [cp. *obnoxium*] to – a sovereign's commands.

Taken together, Bodin understood *imperium* to be a genus with numerous species of *imperium*, which he illustrated visually in the tabular representation of the *Distributio*:[143]

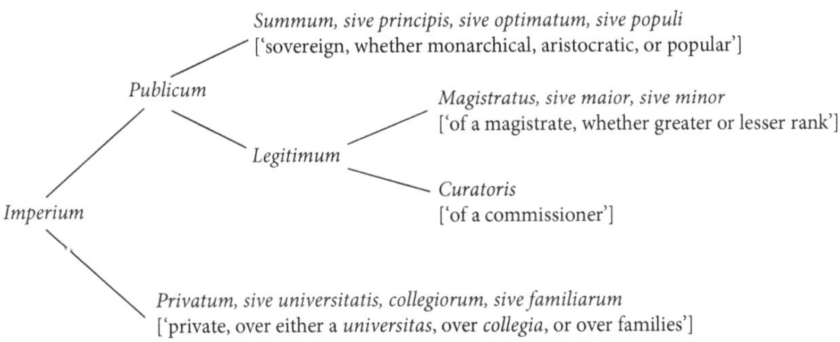

Imperium was a genus, first, divided into species: 'private *imperium*' and 'public *imperium*'. The latter was further sub-divided, giving rise to 'lawful [*legitimum*] *imperium*', designating the legally circumscribed authority of subordinate public authorities, 'magistrates' and 'commissioners' [*curator*], charged with the day-to-day exercise of government functions.[144] Bodin reserved the title, *summum imperium*, exclusively to designate this final category of sovereignty, underlining the crucial point that this wasn't just any generic *imperium*, but a specific kind of *imperium*.[145] It was public *imperium* of the highest [*summa*] rank, high-ness itself, whether in a monarchy, an aristocracy, or a democracy.

[143] *Distributio* fol. E, s.v.: *Imperium*; cp. *République* 19; *De Re Publica* 14 [1.3].

[144] On the difference between 'officer' and 'commissioner', *République* 372, 378; *De Republica* 259, 263 [3.2]; Lee, 'Office Is a Thing Borrowed'; *Popular Sovereignty* 208–15. Carl Schmitt regarded this Bodinian distinction 'an extraordinarily clear and detailed juridical foundation' for the analysis of dictatorship in *Dictatorship: From the Origin of the Modern Concept of Sovereignty to Proletarian Class Struggle*, trans. Michael Hoelzl and Graham Ward (Cambridge: Polity, 2014) 25. Cp. Bonney, 'Bodin and the Development of the French Monarchy': 43–61.

[145] *Methodus* 256, 260–61.

Bodin's redirected attention on command and command-relations as the substance of sovereignty raises another question about command in general: what happens when a commander expresses a command to those addressees liable to that command? The short answer, for Bodin, is that the command somehow alters the duties of the commander's addressees, whether by creating new duties [*ligandi*] or eliminating preexisting ones [*solvendi*].[146] Or, to put it in other words, commanders can bind and unbind and, as a result, change the relations between those in command and those subject to command, whether by tightening or loosening duties. And, for this reason, we might characterize all commands (and countermands: negations of commands) as *binding-devices.*

Ius Imperii: The Right of Command

Observe, however, that one must first *be* a commander in order to command.[147] I can't, as a random private individual, stand in the middle of Sproul Plaza and order random passers-by to do as I say. Why not? I have no right, no authority, no 'standing' as a private individual to do so.[148] Passers-by would be fully within their right to ignore me, just as I, as a civilian standing outside the military chain of command and not subject to the jurisdiction of the Uniform Code of Military Justice and its courts, would be fully within my right to disregard commands of a senior military officer addressed to subordinate addressees inside the military chain of command.[149] Something more, therefore, needs to be said about how one acquires (and loses) such standing and becomes a commander in the first place, one entitled to issue binding commands to others as addressees with the expectation of dutiful compliance.

Before proceeding further on this point, however, I should note that one influential solution to this problem has already been supplied by English jurists of the early nineteenth century – most notably, by John Austin. What makes one a commander (or 'superior', as Austin put it) is nothing other than the effective capacity to use coercive force to subdue and induce others to comply with one's wishes.[150] For Austin, this capacity to use coercive force as sanction alone was the *sine qua non* of a genuine command.

[146] Hohfeld labelled this idea as 'power' in his fourfold scheme of incidents in 'Some Fundamental Legal Conceptions' 44–54.

[147] Likewise, one must first *be* an addressee of those commands in order to be liable to them.

[148] Margaret Gilbert, *Rights and Demands: A Foundational Inquiry* (Oxford: Oxford University Press, 2018) 57–59, 62–64, 70–71 offers an interpretation of rights in terms of the 'standing to demand' actions of others.

[149] Even if I were armed and became Hart's gunman, I'd still have no right.

[150] Austin uses the language of harm: 'If you are able and willing to harm me in case I comply not with your wish, the expression of your wish amounts to a command … A command is distinguished from other significations of desire by this peculiarity: that the party to whom it is directed is liable to evil from the other, in case he comply not with the desire'. Austin, *Province of Jurisprudence Determined* 21–2.

Austin's theory is typically regarded in the academic literature as the exemplar of the so-called 'command theory of law', what H.L.A. Hart would derisively characterize simply as nothing more than the law of the 'gunman'.[151] Legal theorists recovering the intellectual roots of this command theory have tried to portray Bodin (with limited success) as a type of command theorist, likening his theory to Austin's. And that is because, like Austin, Bodin too defined positive legislation [*loi*; *lex*] as 'the command of a sovereign' [*sanctio seu iussum principis aut summae in Republica potestatis*].[152] For this reason, it has become common, especially among anglophone legal theorists, to treat Bodin as a primitive (and often caricatured) ancestor of the modern command theory of law.[153]

But it's less clear whether Bodin really deserves to be treated as a proto-Austinian command theorist. And that is because there is, in fact, a huge semantic and conceptual gap separating Bodinian *imperium* from Austinian 'command' (and, likewise, Benthamite 'imperation'), as it functions in the standard command theory doctrine.[154] The reason for the difference is this: whereas Bodinian *imperium* was grounded in a normative concept of right [*droit*; *ius*], Austinian 'command', by contrast, was intended to be a value-neutral concept of rightless force [*vis*].[155]

This is a vital, though easily overlooked, distinction in the juridical analysis of command that deserves a closer and more critical investigation. Consider, first, force. Force is, in a fundamental way, thoroughly democratic and egalitarian, in that anybody can use or threaten force to hold sway over others.[156] But, needless to say, not all uses of force are lawful or licit. Bodin turned to Cicero for his favourite examples illustrating such illicit force – the violence associated with brigandage and piracy [*latrocinia*]. Brigands and pirates, which modern courts have compared to modern-day slave traders and terrorists, hold a special place in the history of

[151] Hart, *Concept of Law* 6–7.

[152] *Distributio* fol. A, s.v. *Ius*: *Humanum*: *Civile*; *République* 216; *De Republica* 150 [1.10]. Bodin concedes that, while all laws must be understood to be commands of a sovereign, not all sovereign commands take the form of law. His discussion of *lettres de commandement* illustrates formal commands addressed to magistrates that are injunctive, but not statutory.

[153] An egregious example is Pavlos Eleftheriadis, 'Law and Sovereignty', *Law and Philosophy* 29 (2010): 535–69.

[154] Jeremy Bentham, 'Source of a Law' [from Bentham Mss., UCL, Box 88b: 229–37] in *Bentham's Political Thought*, ed. Bhikhu Parekh (London: Croom Helm, 1973) 162.

[155] This is why Bodin qualifies his definition of law as the *recta summae potestatis iussa*; *le droit commandement*: It is not just *any* command or order that counts as law, but the 'lawful' command of a properly sovereign authority, something that no robber, brigand, pirate, gunman, or (as we'll see in Chapter 5) tyrant, can have. Turchetti 684–5 [1.10.7]. The rightless character of Austinian command was by design, in order to enable a supposedly scientific, value-neutral way of talking about the force of law.

[156] It could be argued that this capacity to use force is a Hobbesian 'right of nature'. Hobbes' natural right, however, is fundamentally a liberty-right concept. Bodin's theory, by contrast, is a claim-right. One's *right* to command is correlative to, and entails, someone else's duty to obey that command.

Austin's position is more problematic. He acknowledges that 'the term *superiority* … is implied by the term command'. But elsewhere he explains that 'the term *superiority* signifies *might*: the power of affecting others with evil or pain, and of forcing them, through fear of that evil, to fashion their conduct to one's wishes'. Austin, *Province of Jurisprudence Determined* 30.

international law and political thought as representing those totally outside the boundaries of law, what Cicero would call (and Bodin would borrow from him) 'the common enemy of mankind' [*communis hostis omnium*].[157] What sets their brazen acts of force apart from the proper *imperium* of an official authority is the former's explicitly lawless character. Theirs was, as Cicero taught, the inhumane way of beasts, exercising an illicit force to which they had no right.[158]

Would it be sensible to characterize such illicit, bestial force as commands, comparable to the *imperium* of the senior officer commanding her inferiors in the military chain of command? From what can be extrapolated from his original statement of the command theory, Austin would likely have had no serious objection.[159] And that is because, for him, all true commands were ultimately coercive orders backed by force of sanction.[160] Even laws, which he defined as the commands of sovereigns, held sway, not because of some overriding sense of duty, but because of the lawmaker's capacity to use force – or, in a word, their 'might'.[161]

Bodin's view on the matter was, needless to say, somewhat different and challenged this foundational axiom of modern Anglo-American jurisprudence.[162] To wit: no act of brigandage or piracy may ever be regarded as a proper act of command, or *imperium*, in Bodin's view. The reason for this was to be found in what he regarded as the essentially obligatory character of command: a true act of command should *oblige* those to whom the command is addressed. But, for Bodin (and *contra* Austin), mere acts of brigandage and piracy – or 'brute force' as legal theorists sometimes call it – never oblige and, thus, can never be obligatory in their effects. Even if such force, or threat of force, is successful in inducing habitual obedience from among those subject to it, it can't be regarded properly as *imperium*, for its lack of right.[163]

This was why Bodin found the Ciceronian tropes of brigandage and piracy so useful for his analysis (and also why they recur throughout his theoretical corpus). They epitomized in the extreme the sort of illicit force that, in Bodin's view, could

[157] For example, *Filartiga v. Peña-Irala* 630 F.2d 876 (2nd Cir., 1980) ¶54. Cicero, *De Off.* 3.107. Cicero's purpose is to distinguish 'lawful enemies' from enemies outside the law, such as brigands and pirates. See Chapter 5 on how Bodin includes tyrants among his list of 'the common enemies of mankind'.

[158] The comparison to beasts, the force and fraud of lions and foxes, can be found in *De Off.* 1.13.41.

[159] For a defence of Austin against Hart's criticisms, see Russell Hardin, 'Sanction and Obligation', *The Monist* 68 (1985): 403–18.

[160] Austin's explanation for the officer's command over her inferiors would have to involve the officer's threat of force over them, since superior force is what obliges others, in Austin's view.

[161] Austin, *Province of Jurisprudence Determined* 30.

[162] I say 'foundational' because, even though modern legal theorists have thoroughly challenged the Austinian command theory of law, no one seems to have really challenged Austin's model of command as orders backed by force.

[163] Victims of brigandage and piracy are, thus, entirely free and within their right to resist. Unlike Hobbes' or Austin's analysis, no wrong or injury would be done through the non-compliance of such captives because nothing is due to their captors. Contrast this Bodinian thesis against the Austinian/Hobbesian doctrine on the legal effects of force. Whereas the juridical effect of force is obligation in the Austinian/Hobbesian theory, force neither binds nor unbinds in the Bodinian theory.

not possibly be *imperium*, precisely because such violent outlawry can neither oblige anyone under any duty, nor enfranchise brigands and pirates, by such act of force, with any correlative right of conquest [*droit de conquête*], as the *ius gentium* typically allowed.

Unlike Austin, then, Bodin insisted on making a basic category distinction between *imperium*, which he regarded as a proper relation of command, and *latrocinium*, the brigandage and piracy which he explicitly excluded from the former. Austin lumped all these together into one generic category of 'command', disregarding altogether the historical question of one's right to assert a command to other duty-bound addressees. But Bodin resisted such a move because he wished to preserve and highlight the especially normative quality of *imperium*.

In this respect, what really distinguished *imperium*, above all else, was the obligatory relation of right and duty – the bond or *vinculum* – which it entailed. To wit: one must first have the right to command [*droit de commandement*; *ius imperii*] in order to command at all, just as the addressee of that command must first be obliged under a correlative duty to obey and perform what is commanded.[164] Without that anterior obligatory bond creating and constituting the roles of right-holding commanders and duty-bound addressees of commands in the first place, no act of command is possible. No one can issue a command, nor can anyone be the addressee of that command.

Now, at first glance, this may seem puzzling and implausible. If we think again of brigands and pirates, don't they, in a way, 'command' their captives when they threaten force to extract their captives' compliance? Suppose, as an example, that brigands show up as I'm walking across Sproul Plaza. These fearsome brigands pull out their firearms and order me to hand over my money. Fearing for my safety, I would, as I suppose almost everyone would, comply with the brigands' threats of coercive force and surrender my money.

But while it is true that I comply with the brigand's threat, compliance is the most that I can give to the armed brigand. What I cannot give is obedience, for the simple reason that I haven't accepted the brigand's right to command me. *Contra* Austin, then, I am in no measure duty-bound to obey the brigand (and that is why *non-compliance* with the brigand's orders isn't *disobedience*: no wrong is done to the brigand).

What compels me to comply with the gunman's order isn't duty, correlative to some putative right of the gunman to command. Rather, it's the gunman's Smith &

[164] This theory operates on the presumption that sovereigns will not command anything contrary to divine law and natural law. *République* 414; *De Republica* 289 [3.4], citing Baldus on D.1.9.12, 2.1.3 and Innocent IV on X.1.2.7. Sovereign commands must always be obeyed, unless they are *notoirement fausses ou nulls ou contre les loix de nature*. *République* 413; *De Republica* 289; *Stato* 2:149–50 [3.4], citing *Decisiones Rotae Novae de exceptione III* fol. 211, Felino Sandeo, *Commentaria in V.Lib. Decretalium* cols. 370–88 [Felinus on X.1.3.3]; Alexander Tartagnus Imolensis on X.1.3.24 and the *Clementine Constitutions* 2.11.1, Bartolus, *In I^am^ Partem Digesti Novi Commentaria* (Basel: Ex Officina Episcopiana, 1588) fols. 353_{ro}–362_{ro} [on D.42.1.15]; X.1.3.14.

Wesson. Were the brigand to be disarmed, the compulsion to comply would evaporate instantly. My outwardly observable compliance, thus, shouldn't be taken as an act of dutiful obedience, as Austin suggests, because there is no obligation tying me to the gunman. He has no right to command me, any more than some bossy unarmed stranger on Sproul Plaza trying to order me around. Just as I can ignore the stranger, so too can I ignore the brigand, were it not for his firearm.

So, while the brigand may certainly be able to use force to get their way with others, such force, by itself, wasn't *imperium*. Nor could the brigand be properly called a 'commander' [*imperator*] over those who've been coercively subjugated, for the simple reason that they haven't earned the right or the title. Whatever entitlement to *imperium* they did have was, at best, a 'defective title' [cp. *ex defectu tituli*], a term of art that lawyers deployed to characterize the legal status of tyrants (see Chapter 5).[165]

The importance of this example, which is inspired by H.L.A. Hart's famous 'gunman situation', is in the interpretive claim that the Austinian command theory of law is merely the 'gunman situation writ large', wherein the Austinian sovereign is comparable to a gunman.[166] Seeing that Bodin conceptualizes sovereignty as a species of command, it is tempting to think of Bodin as a proto-Austinian command theorist, in which a Bodinian sovereign may be comparable to a gunman – or, to use Bodin's own examples, a brigand or a pirate – all willing to use force to get their way with others.

When we recall, however, Bodin's categorical exclusion of rightless brigands and pirates – and we may reasonably conjecture, gunmen – as models for commanders, we are obliged to conclude that Bodinian *imperium* must be more than simply brute force, just as the state must be more than a band of robbers and pirates. And the reason for this is simple. Unlike the rightless force of lawless brigands and pirates, which never oblige anyone, the right of command [*droit de commandement*; *ius imperii*] was *always* obligatory.

Indeed, what sets Bodin's *imperium* apart from the coercive force of brigands, pirates, and gunmen is obligation. And that is why Hart's depiction of the command theory as the gunman situation writ large, simply isn't going to work for Bodin's *imperium*. We require instead a new metaphor: Bodin's sovereign isn't so much a gunman (commanding compliance from a captive hostage), as it is a creditor (demanding performance from a debtor or obligor owing some service).[167] What differentiates the gunman from the creditor is entitlement – that is, the right (the *droit*, the *ius*), the standing to demand and require performance from others, something that robbers, pirates, and gunmen don't have. Whereas the Austinian

[165] Bodin will develop the point at *République* 299; *De Republica* 208 [2.5], with reference to civilian and canonistic authorities on the *actio quod metus causa* (legal remedies for transactions done out of fear): C.2.19.11; D.4.2.22; D.15.4.1; X.4.6.7.

[166] Hart, *Concept of Law* 7.

[167] I would, therefore, amend the Austinian theory and re-label it as the 'demand theory of law'.

sovereign *commands* another by force, the Bodinian sovereign *demands* from another by right.

In order to make some sense of this interpretive claim, it's vital to recall, first, that *obligatio* in the civil law was ultimately a relational concept. In the English-speaking world, we are accustomed to treating 'obligation' as a synonym for duty which, as moral philosophers have argued, needn't be relational at all. But, as the eminent English scholar of Roman law, Peter Birks, once explained, an *obligatio* is essentially relational and double-sided. To speak of duty in connection with *obligatio* captures only one half of the concept, for *obligatio* is as much a concept of right as it is a concept of duty.[168] That is, indeed, the point of Justinian's definition of *obligatio* as a *vinculum iuris* – a legal bond (or, literally, a 'legal chain'), tying [*ligandi*] duty-bound 'obligors' (those who owe some service or performance) to right-holding 'obligees' (those who, as beneficiaries, are *owed* the obligor's performance, as a Hohfeldian claim-right).

Bodin's point was that, like *obligatio*, *imperium* was also a relational concept of obligation – an *in personam*, or 'special obligation' as modern moral philosophers now like to say. It was a bond tying inferiors to superiors and assigning to each their respective duties and rights. To the superior was assigned the subjective right to command inferior addressees – what Bodin called *droit de commandement* and *ius imperii*. And to the inferior was assigned the correlative duty to obey those commands.

Needless to say, all of these elements constitutive of *imperium* are lacking in brigandage and piracy. That is why captives subdued under the violence of brigands and pirates never owe any duty to their lawless captors. It is also why captives can never be said to 'wrong' their captors, in the same way that an inferior's failure to perform one's duty to obey *can* be said to 'wrong' the superior of an *imperium*-relation.

A similar point can be made about the right of the superior. Whereas brigands and pirates are, in Bodin's view, totally rightless over their subdued captives (who, in turn, are under no duty to obey their captors), the superior in an *imperium*-relation, by contrast, enjoys the right to command the inferior and benefit from the inferior's performance of the commanded (or, more specifically, 'legislated') duty.

But perhaps the most important point of all to stress is the juridical structure of the superior's right to command inferiors. This 'right of command' – what Bodin called *droit de commandement* and *ius imperii* – is also a *droit subjectif*, a 'subjective right' belonging to anybody in a lawful position of command.[169] Earlier,

[168] Birks, *Roman Law of Obligations* 5.

[169] Bodin limits his analysis to two basic types of commanders: (1) sovereigns invested with the right of sovereignty [*ius maiestatis*; *ius summi imperii*; *droit de souveraineté*]; and (2) magistrates invested with the legally subordinate right of magistracy [*ius magistratus*; *ius imperii*; *droit de commandement*]. While both indicate *imperium*, the first (1) type of *imperium* is *summum legibus ac magistratuum imperio solutum* and *proprium maiestatis*, whereas (2) the second is *legitimum quod legibus obligatur* and *magistratuum proprium*. *De Republica* 300 [3.5].

we encountered this concept of *droit subjectif*, along with its related counterpart of *droit objectif*.[170]

Some analogies may help illustrate the nature of these *droits subjectifs*. Take, for example, driving. The legal right to drive is a permissive right conferred to qualified drivers by way of a permissive licence, as the state traffic law (the corresponding *droit objectif*) allows.[171] The function of the licence is to make the licensee's act of driving licit or permissible – and, therefore, rightful. Another illustration is the *ius suffragii*, the right to vote conferred upon citizens by way of a registration procedure, as voting laws (the corresponding *droit objectif*) allow. The function of registration is to enfranchise citizens and make their act of voting licit or permissible – and, therefore, rightful. What makes these activities, whether driving or voting, licit is the permissive 'objective' law [*droit*; *ius*] that carves out specific 'subjective' rights [*droits*; *iura*] and confers them, whether by licensing or by enfranchising, to particular individuals, as 'subjects' of the 'objective' law.

Something similar happens with Bodin's *droit de commandement*. Like driving or voting, commanding [*commandement*; *imperium*] is, in Bodin's analysis, an *acte juridique* and 'subjective' right bestowed upon magistrates by way of some legal act of license or authorization. We can easily observe this, Bodin thinks, in the classical model of Roman law, which not only governed the creation of permanent public offices but also regulated how officers of all ranks were to be appointed to those offices and invested with their *imperium*.

Bodin never failed to point out in his studies of Roman public law that a magistrate's *imperium*, along with all the rights attached to magistracy, was always traceable to some anterior legal authorization, licensing the appointed magistrate to exercise such *imperium* licitly over others. In classical Roman law, that authorization typically took the form of a curiate statute, a formal *lex* passed by the Roman curiate assembly [*lex curiata de imperio*].[172] Take, for example, the *ius gladii*, the Roman magisterial right to inflict capital penalties reserved exclusively

[170] Lindahl, *Position and Change* 195–96; Alf Ross, *Directives and Norms* (London: Routledge & K. Paul, 1968) 130. Hans Kelsen, 'What Is a Legal Act?' *American Journal of Jurisprudence* 29 (1984): 199–212. Jurists, predominantly in Continental schools of jurisprudence, have variously called this abstract notion of an 'act-in-the-law' *Rechtsgeschäft, rechtliche Können, acte juridique*. Alois von Brinz, *Lehrbuch der Pandekten*, vol. 1 (Erlangen: Andreus Deichert, 1873) 211 [§65: Das rechitliche Dürfen und Können; licere, posse]; Ernst Rudolf Bierling, *Zur Kritik der juristischen Grundbegriffe* (Gotha: Friedrich Andreas Perthes, 1883) 49–51.

[171] Literature one finds at the local DMV routinely points out that driving is a 'privilege', not a 'right', presumably to disabuse drivers of the thought that driving might be a fundamental civil or constitutional claim-right, imposing correlative duties on state authorities. What this popular DMV refrain misunderstands, however, is that even privileges are Hohfeldian rights. I am entitled to certain rights, so long as a I hold my licence.

[172] Cicero, *De Re Publica* 2.31. The conferral of *imperium* upon the consul by the *comitia curiata* through a *lex curiata de imperio* during the Republican period mimicked the archaic precedent of the Monarchy, during which kings were chosen in the interregnal curiate assembly.

to magistrates of the highest rank with *merum imperium*.[173] Such a fearsome right could only be lawful, if conferred by a curiate statute.

Statute, however, wasn't the only legal instrument through which the investiture of a legal right of *imperium* could be formally authorized.[174] Bodin pointed out that one-time extraordinary and irregular commissions of authority, such as dictatorships and generalships, could also theoretically confer plenary rights to command even without any accompanying positive legislation creating a permanent office and formally defining the powers of office. By way of such extraordinary commissions, the Roman state could directly delegate and entrust certain public functions of state, including even the exercise of *imperium*, to designated private persons as agents or mandataries of state. In this way, through delegation, any private citizen could be empowered *specialiter* with the right of *imperium*, even for just one day.[175]

Observe, however, that, without such a lawful conferral of *imperium*, whether conferred by statute or by some other extraordinary commission, upon a designated recipient, there can be no licit right to exercise *imperium*. What really struck Bodin was just how fastidiously the Romans insisted upon this point, especially concerning Roman constitutional practice in authorizing the legal use of force in war. One of his favourite illustrations, taken from Plutarch, involved Caesar's allegedly unauthorized and illegal use of force in his conquest of Gaul. Even though Caesar, as proconsul, successfully subdued Gaul, he did so, according to his political rival, Cato the Younger, illegally and without proper authority [*iniussu Senatus ac populi*]: Caesar, in Cato's view, lacked the legal right empowering him with the lawful *imperium* to wage war and conclude peace on behalf of Rome.[176] What

[173] *Merum imperium* was distinguished from the *imperium* that was thought to be 'mixed' with *iurisdictio* [*mixtum imperium*]. Whereas *iurisdictio* applied properly within the city walls [*pomerium*] of Rome, *merum imperium* applied beyond the city walls, in the provinces and among conquered peoples. The latter was originally associated with the extralegal military command of an *imperator*, such as a consul or a provincial governor, with authority over an army or a province. But one needn't hold high public office in order to be vested with *merum imperium*. Peter Garnsey, 'The Criminal Jurisdiction of Governors', *Journal of Roman Studies* 58 (1968): 51–59.

[174] Papinian's comments on the Roman law on delegated jurisdiction in D.1.21.1 further elaborated on the variety of legal instruments used to authorize special conferral of *imperium*, such as a *lex*, a *senatus consultus*, or a *constitutio principis*. Livy, *History of Rome*, vol. 7, trans. Frank Gardner Moore, Loeb Classical Library 367 (Cambridge: Harvard University Press, 1943) 80–81 [*Ab Urbe Condita* 26.21.6–8] indicates that *plebiscitum* might also confer *imperium*. Whereas *iurisdictio* (the right to preside over a trial and declare a verdict) can be conditionally delegated from the praetor to an agent or mandatary, the praetor's authority cannot.

[175] The term, *specialiter*, is Papinian's term in D.1.21.1.pr. Bodin cites the example of Mamercus Aemilius Mamercinus, the one-day dictator, at *République* 124, 377; *De Republica* 80, 262 [1.8, 3.2].

[176] *Methodus* 266; *République* 224; *De Republica* 155; Turchetti 703 [1.10], cites Caesar's violence during the Gallic Wars as a usurpation establishing an illegitimate tyranny, a pattern that would be repeated in Rome itself. Plutarch, *Cato the Younger*, in *Lives: Sertorius and Eumenes, Phocion and Cato the Younger*, vol. 8, Loeb Classical Library 100, trans. Bernadotte Perrin (Cambridge: Harvard University Press, 1919) 8:358–59 [51.1–2]; *Caesar*, in *Lives: Demosthenes and Cicero, Alexander and Caesar*, vol. 7, Loeb Classical Library 99, trans. Bernadotte Perrin (Cambridge: Harvard University Press, 1919) 7:496–99 [22.1–5].

Cp. Grotius, *De Iure Belli ac Pacis* 1.3.5, possibly reading this passage from Bodin, cites this mutual hostility between Cato and Caesar leading to his conclusion that, in waging war without proper authorization against the Germans in Gaul, Caesar had illegally stepped beyond the boundaries of

Caesar accomplished, therefore, wasn't so much a legal extension of Roman sovereignty by right of conquest, as it was instead an illegal usurpation comparable to the violence of brigands and pirates.

The constitutional lesson here can be extended beyond the specific classical example of Rome. In all states, public authority ultimately is a 'subjective' legal right whose legitimacy originates in some 'objective' legal authorization. While this applies at all ranks, it is especially apposite at the highest rank of sovereignty, whose right of authority likewise derives in some 'objective' law, a *ius summi imperii*.

Ius Summi Imperii: The Right of Sovereignty

Bodin's thesis is that a magistrate's *ius imperii* – the legal right to exercise authority over others – is always traceable to some anterior 'objective' act of authorization, such as a curiate *lex de imperio* bestowing *imperium* upon an officer with some public charge. What about a sovereign's legal right to exercise sovereign authority? Where is the 'objective' legal authorization conferring such a *ius summi imperii*?

The difficulty in answering this question lies in the crucial difference between the *imperia* of sovereigns and of magistrates. Whereas a magistrate's *imperium* was defined and limited precisely by those laws which originally create, bestow, and regulate the magistrate's authority (like a curiate statute), the sovereign's *imperium*, as we've seen, was *legibus solutum*. Sovereignty, indeed, can't be traceable to some authorizing piece of positive legislation, in the same way magistracy can, for the simple reason that sovereigns are themselves the authors of the positive legislation that create magistrates and confer upon them their magisterial *imperium*. To suggest that ordinary positive legislation can create and confer sovereignty would be to introduce a basic contradiction in the logic of sovereignty, by allowing one to be, at the same time, both *legibus solutus* and *legibus obligatus*.

Consider a metaphor: when a sovereign legally creates a new magistracy and bestows upon the newly appointed magistrate a share of their public *imperium*, as a trustee of the public interest, a legal debt is thereby created between the sovereign and the magistrate. While the magistrate has the legal right to exercise authority, he doesn't 'own' it. It is, instead, merely a 'borrowed' [*commodata*] power, which the magistrate is under a legal obligation to return to its proper owner, the sovereign, once the magistrate's legally defined term of office has expired.[177] If you were, thus,

his proconsular authority over Gaul. Bodin explains this point at *République* 227; *De Republica* 158; Turchetti 709 [1.10], with reference to D.3.3.48, 2.14.28, 12.6.6, Baldus on C.4.35.15, Giasone del Maino on Inst.4.6.28, D.17.1.5, 17.1.46, 17.1.51, 29.2.25.7.

[177] Observe that magistrates are also subjects. So, they are under a double-obligation to their sovereign. They are, first, bound under the general political obligation binding indifferently on all subjects to obey their sovereign. They are, additionally, bound under the special obligation arising from the debt incurred by the sovereign's bestowal of *imperium* upon the magistrate.

to imagine authority as a kind of deliverable asset, or *res*, sovereigns and magistrates are in the analogous position of creditors and debtors. And we know that this is precisely how Bodin understood the juridical relationship between a sovereign authority and a subordinate magistrate because he says so explicitly, dressed in juridical language that would be obvious to any lawyer of the *ius commune*, that the subordinate magistrate is, legally speaking, a mere depositary, a lessee, a pledgor of a public power belonging properly to someone else.[178] In Bodin's political theory, all magistrates of all ranks are legally burdened by this 'debt' which must be repaid – whether by lawfully 'laying down' [*deponit*] and returning their authority at the end of their term of office, by removal from office, or by death.[179]

What differentiates sovereigns from magistrates is this debt: only genuine sovereigns are truly 'debt-free' so to speak, in respect of their *imperium*. Unlike magistrates who are encumbered by obligations and owe the repayment and return of *imperium* to their sovereign 'creditor' on demand or expiry of the term, sovereigns, by contrast, own their *imperium* and, therefore, are under no such duty as magistrates are.[180] To be clear, Bodin isn't suggesting that a sovereign literally 'owns' sovereignty, as if it literally were a commodity that can be bought and sold, lent and hired, or placed on deposit.[181] He is instead simply suggesting a legal analogy: just as ownership indicates an owner's exclusive right and title to use (or 'abuse') one's property [*ius utendi et abutendi re sua*], we can likewise think of sovereignty also as a sovereign's exclusive right and title to rule. What both share in common is the 'exclusivity' of right and title, something that is, as lawyers say, *suo proprio*. Just as there can be only one owner with exclusive title over some piece of property, so can there be only one sovereign with exclusive title to rule over a state.

How, then, does one legally acquire an exclusive title?[182] Consider, first, how one can come to own property in the first place. Classical jurists allowed that property can be acquired through formal legal methods defined in the positive legislation of the *ius civile* (such as the *cessio in iure* and *mancipatio*). But these 'civil' methods were technically available only to *cives*, or Roman citizens, rendering impossible

[178] *Popular Sovereignty* 204–15. Perhaps the most well-known passage in Bodin's text illustrating this idea is *De Republica* 79, 81 [1.8], where high magistraterial offices and commissions (such as dictatorships) are compared to *depositum*, *commodatum*, *pignus*, and *precarium*.

[179] On *deponere*, see *Popular Sovereignty* 185, 213 on D.1.17.1 on the Prefect of Egypt 'laying down *imperium* [*deponit* ... *imperium*]'. Bodin observed the criticism of Andrea Alciato on the *deponere* being applied to public offices, *Opera Omnia*, vol. 4 (Basel: Thomas Guarinus, 1582) 39 [*Paradoxa*, Book II, §§3–5]. Bodin felt it was necessary to combat the emerging legal theories used to defend the venality of office, whereby offices and honours were sold and held as property by private individuals.

[180] And the reason for this, according to Bodin, is simple: one cannot owe a debt to oneself.

[181] That is because sovereignty, just like any form of authority, is an obligatory relationship giving rise to an *in personam* (or, to use Hohfeld's vocabulary, 'paucital') right – that is, the sovereign's right to benefit from the subject's service or performance of a duty owed. Ownership, by contrast, gives rise to an *in rem* (or 'multital') right against the whole world, reflecting an owner's exclusive title over some property. Wesley Newcomb Hohfeld, 'Fundamental Legal Conceptions as Applied in Judicial Reasoning', *Yale Law Journal* 26 (1917): 712.

[182] Grotius famously answers this question in *De Iure Belli ac Pacis* 2.3.4.

any *ius civile* property transaction with non-Roman peregrines, lacking 'civil' status.

What is a non-Roman to do? The solution was to look to the *ius gentium*, the law observed and shared in common by the many peoples and nations making up humanity, which allowed property transactions through methods (such as *occupatio*, *traditio*, and *specificatio*) widely recognized as valid. The *ius gentium* permits anyone, whether Roman or not, to acquire property and the title of ownership, *dominium*, in these ways.[183]

Like property, sovereignty too could be lawfully acquired by means recognized near universally by all peoples and nations in the *ius gentium*. Just as the many nations and peoples of the world observe that property can be acquired lawfully through occupation, prescription, or simple delivery, so too do the many nations and peoples of the world observe that a state's sovereignty also can be acquired lawfully through such means recognized in the *ius gentium*.[184] Bodin identified some of these means, *passim*: title of sovereignty could legally be acquired, for example, by voluntary consent, by election [*par voye d'election*; *suffragio populi vel optimatum*], by lot [*par sort*; *sorte*], by right of succession [*par droit successif*; *legitime successione*], and even, in limited cases, by prescription of time [*praescriptio*].[185]

Most striking about the *ius gentium* was its permissive quality. As Bodin reminds us, all sovereigns are legal subjects of the *ius gentium*, and so, sovereigns, like everyone else, find themselves placed under legal obligations, requiring or prohibiting certain actions. But the *ius gentium*, just like any legal system, wasn't simply meant to be strictly obligatory in its effects. It was also understood to be a 'permissive' body of law which, in carving out special legal permissions and liberties, defined what was legally permissible and, therefore, 'rightful'.[186]

By indicating what was legally permissible by many nations, the *ius gentium* recognized a range of subjective rights. It was, for example, permissible by the *ius gentium* for one to acquire a valid title of ownership simply by taking possession of a previously unowned thing as first occupant, just as it was permissible for one to acquire a valid title through simple delivery.[187] In this way, we could understand

[183] D.1.1.5.

[184] *Distributio* fol. D, s.v.: *Antecedentia*: *Acquisitio*: *Dominii*: 'Acquisition of ownership is done in more or less nine ways: By just force [*vi iusta*] namely of arms, when engaged in lawful war, or in licit hunting of wild animals, birds, and fish . . . occupation [*occupatione*] . . . natural accession . . . by art . . . by transfer with a just cause [*traditione ex iusta causa*] . . . ' Cp. D.41.1.9.3.

[185] *République* 299; *De Republica* 208 [2.5], citing D.43.20.3; Cp. *République* 215; *De Republica* 149; Turchetti 683 [1.10]. On the theme of imprescriptibility, Bodin cites, inter alia, Baldus de Ubaldis, *Consiliorum sive Responsorum*, vol. 3 (Venice: 1575) fol. 76_{ro} [3:274]; fol. 85_{ro} [3:303]; Claude de Seyssel, *Speculum feudorum* (Basel: Thomas Guarinus, 1566) 110.

[186] My argument here follows Brian Tierney's analysis of the 'permissive' quality of natural law. Just as jurists found natural law to be obligatory and permissive in its juridical effects, so too did they find the law of nations likewise to produce obligatory and permissive effects.

[187] Cp. Grotius, *De Iure Belli ac Pacis* 2.2.4 cp. D.41.1.3.

property ownership as an exclusive right and title arising *ex iure gentium*, through the permissions recognized by all.

We can say something similar about Bodin's understanding of sovereignty. Like property, sovereignty too was an exclusive right and title arising *ex iure gentium.*[188] It derived its legal validity from the normative order of the *ius gentium*, which recognized and permitted multiple ways one can come to have a right to rule over another who is, correlatively, duty-bound to obey.

But by far, the most important of these was the derivative title of conquest resulting from victory in a legal war [*par juste guerre*; *iusto bello*], a principle which Bodin derived from the cardinal doctrine of the *ius gentium* that victory in war confers upon the conquering party the 'seigneurial' right of *dominium* – that is, the legal right to enslave the vanquished party.[189] War, in Bodin's view, was the catalyst that could transform states and create new juridical relations, including even relations of slavery [*dominium*] and sovereignty [*imperium*]. In the next chapter, we will begin to see how war can be both a destructive as well as a creative force in Bodin's legal imagination.

[188] In this respect, Bodin anticipates (and may even have been an inspiration for) a principle articulated in Hans Kelsen's own pure theory of law: 'The statement that sovereignty is an essential quality of the State means that the State is a supreme authority. Authority is usually defined as the right or power to issue obligating commands. The actual power of forcing others to a certain behaviour does not suffice to constitute an authority. The individual who is, or has, authority must have received the right to issue obligating commands so that other individuals are obliged to obey. Such a right or power can be conferred upon an individual only by a normative order' (Kelsen, *General Theory of Law and State* 383). Kelsen traces that normative order to a *Grundnorm*. Bodin calls it the *ius gentium*.

[189] Cp. *De Iure Belli ac Pacis* 3.8.1. Chapters 3 and 5 will trace the right of conquest in more detail in Bodin's thought.

3

Slaves, Subjects, Citizens

In the previous chapter, I argued that Bodinian sovereignty was fundamentally conceptualized as a relational concept of *imperium*, modelled on a private law obligation.[1] Sovereigns and subjects were, in Bodin's theory, much like obligees and obligors, in that they were tied together by an obligatory bond assigning rights and duties to each. While sovereignty assigns to subjects the duty to obey the sovereign's command, it assigns to sovereigns the right to issue those commands to subjects [*ius subditos imperandi*] who are so duty-bound [*obligantur*].[2]

The essence of this obligatory relationship between sovereign and subject was command [*commandement*; *imperium*].[3] And while such command theoretically could (and historically did, as we'll see) take the form of the sovereign's bare will [*arbitrium*], as he evidently thought it did among those oriental despots exemplified by the personal seigneurial rulerships of the Ottoman sultans and the Muscovite tsars, it was far more appropriate and equitable for the expression of that sovereign command to take the form of positive legislation.[4] Whatever the vehicle for the rightful expression of a sovereign's command, whether through the rule of will or the rule of law, the effect in both types of regimes remains the same: the 'subject' [*subditus*] is to be defined strictly and only in terms of that obligatory duty to obey that command.

This is an epoch-making moment in the history of political thought, one that has not been properly recognized by political theorists. Just as Bodin was the first modern theorist to isolate the distinctive character of sovereignty (an achievement for which he is well known in political science and jurisprudence), Bodin was also the first modern theorist to try and isolate the distinctive character of political

[1] On sovereignty as a 'relational concept' in legal theory, see the seventh tenet of sovereignty in Loughlin, *Idea of Public Law* 83–7.

[2] Bodin uses the term 'subject' [*sujet*; *subditus*] as genus and species, and we can see this most easily in the opening of *De Republica* 1.9 which lists the nine degrees of subjection [*novem genera tenuiorum*] (*République* has six degrees, so I argue that the Latin text is the more comprehensive to use in making this point). The seventh degree of subjection at *De Republica* 109 is the *subditus*; the corresponding passage at *République* 163, with a different numbering, calls it *le subiect naturel*.

[3] This also shows why sovereignty must necessarily be a relational concept. If sovereignty is about commanding, it must be about commanding others, since, on Bodin's reading, at *De Republica* 85, of D.45.1.108.1, self-binding is impossible: One cannot 'command' and 'oblige' oneself.

[4] The distinction between these two chief instruments for the expression of sovereign command – whether *arbitrio* or *legibus* – marks a key point of difference between Bodin's theory of law, and the later 'command theory' formulated by Austin. In the background to this distinction is Bodin's belief in the autonomy of law and the legal system from politics. More on this in Chapter 4.

The Right of Sovereignty. Daniel Lee, Oxford University Press. © Daniel Lee 2021.
DOI: 10.1093/oso/9780198755531.003.0004

subjecthood as well, what it means to be *subject* to a sovereign authority.[5] And it's no surprise why: subjecthood and sovereignty are conceptually symbiotic and correlative, in that each is defined in terms of, and entails, the other.[6] Because of this, Bodin saw the task of defining subjecthood as necessarily connected to the task of defining sovereignty.

The results of this analysis are striking. For, just as statehood is *sui generis* (irreducible to other comparable forms of human association such as the family or corporation, as we saw in Chapter 1), so too is political subjecthood *sui generis*, also irreducible to other related concepts that are, Bodin thought, too often mistaken for subjecthood, such as slavery, vassalage, and clientage.[7] It's true, as Bodin observes, that subjects might *also* be slaves to masters, vassals to lords, clients to patrons. Subjects of the sultan, Bodin observes, are commonly said to be his slaves.[8] And enfeoffed subjects, to take another example, can also be said to be vassals and tenants *in capite* of their liege lord.

But Bodin's key point is that subjects *need not* also be slaves, vassals, clients, or any other type of bondsman. And, correspondingly, sovereigns need not also be masters, lords, or patrons in order to be sovereign. We might, indeed, read Book I of the *République*, largely as his attempt to sharpen these distinctions (and, in doing so, also to sharpen the distinctions between sovereignty [*summum imperium in subditos*], paterfamilial power [*patria potestas in liberos ac adversus uxores*], despotic mastery [*dominium in servos*], feudal lordship [again, *dominium* – but *in vassallos*], and patronage [*patrocinium in clientes*]).

My goal in this chapter will be to isolate, from among these varieties of asymmetrical juridical relations, Bodin's 'pure' concept of political subjecthood – 'pure' in the sense that it is segregated from neighbouring concepts with which subjecthood has (Bodin thinks) historically been associated and confused, such as slavery, vassalage, and clientage.[9] There are two reasons why this will be a useful exercise for anyone studying Bodin's theory of sovereignty. First, because subjecthood is

[5] Keechang Kim, *Aliens in Medieval Law: The Origins of Modern Citizenship* (Cambridge: Cambridge University Press, 2000) 202–3 suggests that the real innovation in Bodin's *République* is not so much the analysis of sovereignty, but of subjecthood.

[6] To wit: sovereignty entails the highest right [*summum ius*] of commanding subjects [*in subditos*], whether *arbitrio principis* or *legibus*. Reciprocally, subjecthood entails a sovereign who can act as an 'obligee' – i.e. a party to whom obligation is owing.

[7] On the family-state comparisons in Bodin's theory, see Odorisio, *La famille et l'état dans la République de Jean Bodin*; Becker, *Gendering the Renaissance Commonwealth*.

[8] Guy Le Thiec, 'Le droit de conquête en guise de constitution: Jean Bodin et les penseurs protestants face au régime politique ottoman', *Il Pensiero Politico* 39 (2007): 353–55 explains that the claim of ownership over enslaved subjects was a mark of nobility and extended to children who were taken from conquered populations through the Ottoman practice of *devchirmé* and, after being brought into the sultan's household, called 'sons of tribute'.

[9] My argument in this chapter, thus, overlaps some with the sensible study of E. Grosso, 'Dal suddito del signore al suddito dello stato', *Le Vie della Cittadinanza* (Padua: CEDAM, 1997) 141–85. Bodin's earliest readers understood this aspect of Bodin's project. Cp. Pierre Charron, *De la Sagesse Trois Livres* (Paris: Robert Fuge, 1632) 265–69 [1.48] on *Seigneurs & esclaves, maistres & serviteurs*, cited in Henry Heller, 'Bodin on Slavery and Primitive Accumulation', *Sixteenth Century Journal* 25 (1994): 63.

so intimately connected to sovereignty, whatever clarity we can reach in understanding 'pure' subjecthood will spill over in our attempt to reach clarity in isolating a 'pure' concept of sovereignty (note that Bodin's famous chapters on sovereignty emerge towards the end of *République* I, only after he has conceptually sanitized subjecthood and sovereignty from these conceptual contaminants).

The other reason is that this will give us some insight into Bodin's Ramist-influenced method of analysis.[10] When Bodin conducts his conceptual analysis, he typically approaches the task by negation. Instead of trying to answer the question of the form, 'What is *x*', Bodin first answers the (implied) inverse question, 'What isn't *x*'.[11] The bulk of *République* I is organized in this way, as an extensive treatise of negation, following the Ramist method of *dispositio*, where the sequence of questions is key. He is trying to show what pure political subjecthood is, first, by showing what it isn't, before offering an affirmative proposition indicating what it is.[12]

The opening sections of this chapter will discuss the two major categories that he eliminated in his search for the pure subject – foreigners and slaves. What makes the pure subject distinctive is an apparent contradiction, whereby a person is, at once, free (that is, not a slave: whether *ingenui* or *liberti*) and unfree (that is, *imperio obligatur*), an uncertain condition that Bodin struggles to describe as one whose default 'natural liberty' (that is, equal liberty under the *ius naturale*) has been 'diminished to some extent' [*quodammodo deminuta*], but not so much that the person is a slave. This pure, or 'free subject' (as Bodin designates this category), is what he calls 'citizen', a state-centric classification of persons defined not in terms of civil rights (let alone *equal* civil rights), nor by any other 'thick' source of common civic identity such as ancestry, religion, custom, law, or residence.[13] The one and only point that fundamentally mattered in making a 'sovereign' citizen-body, or

[10] The influence of the logician, Pierre Ramus, and 'Ramism' in Bodin's thought has been the subject of several studies, including Kenneth McRae, 'Ramist Tendencies in the Thought of Jean Bodin', *Journal of the History of Ideas* 16 (1955): 306–23; Lloyd, *Jean Bodin*; 31–3, 53-62, 69–71, 129–30, 185; Cesare Vasoli, *Armonia e giustizia: Studi sulle idee filosofiche di Jean Bodin* (Florence: Olschki, 2008).

[11] Thus, the famous definition of sovereignty in *République* 1.8 is finally stated only after Bodin has eliminated a range of competing alternatives. The usefulness of this approach can be observed in its continuing use in contemporary political philosophy, such as in Samuel Scheffler, *Equality and Tradition: Questions of Value in Moral and Political Theory* (Oxford: Oxford University Press, 2012) 331. I thank Eric Beerbohm for sharing the reference.

[12] I do not believe, however, Bodin has committed the fallacy of affirming a definite conclusion from negative premises. He's only eliminating possibilities to narrow the field of consideration.

[13] On this distinction between subjecthood and citizenship, see also Pietro Costa, 'La celebrazione della sovranità: Jean Bodin', in *Civitas, storia della cittadinanza in Europa, I: dalla civiltà comunale al settecento*, ed. Pietro Costa (Rome/Bari: Laterza, 1999): 73–80; Georges Ferrière, 'Sujets et citoyens selon Bodin', in *Sujet et Citoyen: Actes du Colloque de Lyon, 11–12 Septembre 2003*, ed. J.-L. Harouel (Aix-en-Provence: Presses Universitaires d'Aix-Marseille, 2003) 99–113. I'd argue that Bodin has a good claim to be the first theorist of 'multicultural citizenship' – and even of the 'multicultural state', as he thought Rome – a state made up of many *gentes* – surely was.

state, is shared subjection to a common sovereign; indeed, sovereignty is what solves the so-called 'boundary problem' in recent democratic theory.[14]

Note the one element, however, that Bodin did *not* believe to be fundamental to the making of a sovereign state: territory. While it has become customary in modern public international law and political science to treat sovereignty chiefly as a territorial concept – as the supreme uncontested authority over some geographically bounded area and its inhabitants – Bodin never conceptualized sovereignty in territorial terms: Bodinian sovereignty was *not* territorial sovereignty.[15] Sovereignty, for Bodin, extended, *not* over land (as an *in rem* right), but over persons (as an *in personam* right), wherever they happened to be physically located.[16] This is, I argue, a common error made by modern readers of Bodin, who perhaps unintentionally import a Westphalian bias in assuming that Bodinian sovereignty must have been territorial in nature. Once we expose and expunge that territorial bias, however, it becomes possible to imagine what might be described as extraterritorial statehood, obviating the need for a bounded civic spatiality for politics.[17]

Foreigners and Subjects

Bodin approached the problem of defining political subjecthood by presenting a series of contrasts distinguishing between subject [*subiect*; *subditus*], foreigner [*l'estranger*; *peregrinus*], and slave [*esclave*; *servus*, *famulus*].[18] By showing (1) how

[14] Frederick Whelan, 'Democratic Theory and the Boundary Problem', in *Nomos 25: Liberal Democracy*, ed. J.R. Pennock and J.W. Chapman (New York: New York University Press, 1983): 13–47; Ian Shapiro, *Democratic Justice* (New Haven, Connecticut: Yale University Press, 1999); Sarah Song, 'The Boundary Problem in Democratic Theory: Why the Demos Should Be Bounded by the State', *International Theory* 4 (2012): 39–68; Arash Abizadeh, 'Democratic Theory and Border Coercion: No Right to Unilaterally Control Your Own Borders', *Political Theory* 36 (2008): 37–65.

[15] Of course, states in practice require territorial space of *some* kind to exist and thrive. Thus, my position is entirely consistent with the conclusion in Miglietti, 'Sovereignty, Territory, and Population' 17–34, which treats territory not so much as a matter of sovereignty, but rather as a matter of government. What Bodin denied, in my view, is what political theorists have dubbed the 'particularity thesis' that sovereign states are entitled, as one of their essential sovereign rights, to claim exclusive territorial use-rights over some specific lands, such as Stilz, *Territorial Sovereignty*. Indeed, Bodin's associational conception of statehood (discussed in Chapter 1) suggests that geographically defined territory is in fact inessential. For a persuasive explanation of why territoriality quickly becomes attached to sovereignty in the sixteenth-century, see Jordan Branch, *Cartographic State: Maps, Territory, and the Origins of Sovereignty* (Cambridge: Cambridge University Press, 2013) 77–95.

[16] Andrew Fitzmaurice drew this distinction as 'territorial sovereignty' and 'personal sovereignty', the latter of which was 'comparable with the feudal societies of medieval Europe': *Sovereignty, Property and Empire, 1500–2000* (Cambridge: Cambridge University Press, 2014) 6. An analogous point can be made about the Bodinian family: what makes a family isn't common residence within one household, but obligatory ties of familial relations, all ultimately under one common head of household.

[17] This is one of the key themes emerging from Annabel Brett, *Changes of State: Nature and the Limits of the City in Early Modern Natural Law* (Princeton: Princeton University Press, 2011).

[18] The structure of *République* I is best illustrated in the opening paragraphs of Chapter 9, listing the 'degrees of subjection'. *République* 162–3 lists *six degrés de subiection*; *De Republica* 108–9, by contrast, lists nine.

subjects differed from foreigners and also (2) how subjects differ from slaves, Bodin felt he could specify the distinctive quality of political subjecthood which would be defined exclusively in the relational terms of allegiance requiring one to obey the command of some specific sovereign with the right to command.

It's important to stress at the outset that Bodin is articulating (at least) two different sets of contrasts (i.e. the subject/foreigner contrast and the subject/slave contrast), each of which is not equivalent to each other. What makes a subject different from a foreigner is not going to be the same as what makes a subject different from a slave. Whereas the first is a question concerning (what we'd today call) nationality or citizenship, the other is a question concerning legal status. Needless to say, these are different questions being asked and answered.

The first is a simple, but fundamental, distinction: whereas the subject [*subditus*] is defined as one who is duty-bound under a bond of allegiance owing to a sovereign, the foreigner [*peregrinus*] is under no such duty to the same sovereign.[19] It is, therefore, logically impossible to be a subject and a foreigner (with respect to the same sovereign state) at the same time because it would involve a basic contradiction (it would mean that one could be duty-bound and duty-free at the same time).[20] Of course, a foreigner in one state may nevertheless be the subject of some *other* sovereign, as was the Frenchman Bodin, for example, during his 1581 visit to England. Owing no allegiance to Elizabeth I or to any other sovereign other than his own, he remained a French subject during his foreign travels.[21] Bodin even raised the theoretical possibility, for sake of argument, that the foreigner might even be (as Hannah Arendt put it) 'stateless', bound to *no* sovereign on earth and, thus, a member of no state, like brigands and pirates. One could simply remain *in libertate naturali* – or, as Bodin revealingly suggests at one point, in *anarchia*.[22]

There's a political purpose for introducing the foreigner at this early stage of Bodin's argument. Because the foreigner is free of the duty (otherwise binding on subjects) to obey the sovereign, foreigners are legally free, in a permissive Hohfeldian sense, to do certain things that subjects may not.[23] Indeed, Bodin hints at various places in his writings on the importance of this distinction between

[19] *De Republica* 61. *République* 93 has *la difference essentielle du bourgeois á l'estranger.*

[20] It's not clear whether Bodin allows anything like dual citizenship, but he addresses some related cases in 1.9 in connection with vassalage, so that it is possible for one to be a subject of a sovereign, while also being a vassal to another, foreign sovereign, strictly in a feudal relationship.

[21] This point will become important in Bodin's analysis of foreign residence, denaturalization, and expatriation. Bodin's trip to England in 1581 with François, the Duke of Anjou, intending to propose marriage to Elizabeth I, is covered in Lloyd, *Jean Bodin* 189–91.

[22] *De Republica* 49 [1.6]. Hannah Arendt, *The Origins of Totalitarianism*, new edition (New York: Harcourt, 1976) 276–80.

[23] Note, however, that foreigners and subjects alike are all bound under obligations arising from the *ius naturale* and the *ius gentium*. What gives a court – and a sovereign – jurisdiction over a foreigner, then, is its equitable judicial duty [*officium iudicis*] to enforce the *ius naturale* and *ius gentium* norms over both subjects and foreigners alike.

subject and foreigner, but its full implication will only be observed later in his treatment of tyrannicide and resistance, a topic to which I will return in Chapter 5.[24]

Of course, the subject/foreigner contrast itself was not especially innovative. As Keechang Kim has persuasively argued, Bodin was simply relying on the medieval law of aliens:

> Bodin, like his contemporaries in England, was assuming that human beings must first of all be divided into citizens and foreigners and that this division must turn on the political submission (allegiance) to the ruler. Also, like Coke and Bacon who saw the division between subjects and aliens as an eternal and everlasting division grounded upon nature and reason, Bodin was convinced that his understanding of citizenship was of universal and permanent validity transcending time and place.[25]

The real innovation, instead, was in the presentation of the contrast and how it fitted together with the other major distinction he introduced, the subject/slave contrast.

Slaves and Subjects

The subject/foreigner contrast could be resolved simply by determining whether or not one was duty-bound under allegiance to a particular sovereign authority. The subject/slave contrast, however, was more difficult because both were, in a sense, 'subjects' under someone's power.[26] Whereas slaves are defined by their subjection to their masters [*seigneur*; *dominus*; cp. δεσπότης], political subjects are defined only by their subjection to their sovereigns.[27] While simple enough in theory, Bodin recognized an interpretive difficulty owing to the historical point that, in many ancient slaveholding societies, sovereigns *were* masters, such that subjecthood and slavery (and, correspondingly sovereignty and mastery) were treated as equivalent to, or indifferently from, each other. As Bodin put it, one

[24] For example, *République* 152, 300–1; *De Republica* 99, 208–9 [1.8, 2.5].

[25] Kim, *Aliens in Medieval Law* 203–4. Kim places Bodin's reasoning in the same category of English arguments used in *Calvin's Case* in defining subjecthood in terms of allegiance.

[26] The Roman jurisconsults recognized this equivocation. D.50.16.215: *Potestatis verbo plura significantur: in persona magistratuum imperium ... persona servi dominium.* Note also that those *in potestate magistratuum* or *sub imperio* are never called 'subjects' in Rome. After Caracalla, who granted citizenship to all free persons in the Roman Empire, they are 'citizens'.

[27] As you can see, there is an equivocation attached to the term 'subject' [*subditus*; or one who is *subiectus* to one who can *subiicere*]. The latter formulation of subjection to sovereigns is a modern interpolation: The classical Roman law of Justinian makes no mention of such subjection, although it speaks frequently of being 'under the power' of others, such as D.1.6.1.1 (*in potestate dominorum*).

could theoretically be 'doubly-bound' [*duplici obligando*] as hybrid slave-subjects in states where one's sovereign was *also* one's personal master.[28]

Because of this confusing conceptual overlap, especially in the laws and customs of ancient slaveholding societies, Bodin observed how easy it was (as early modern republican ideologues discovered) to overlook these fine-grained distinctions. What Bodin stressed was that, despite the conceptual overlap, these were different types of legal relationships, each of which called for its own differentiated analysis – as different as obligor/obligee, debtor/creditor, promissory/stipulator, client/patron. Bodin took it as his mission to disentangle and salvage a 'pure' concept of subjecthood, distinct from slavery.

In pursuing this mission, however, Bodin had an uphill battle to fight. Separating 'subject' from 'slave' correspondingly required separating sovereignty from mastery. But early modern lawyers, during this crucial period when ideas of private law and public law were mixed together in forming the fundamentals of modern public international law, were addicted to the habit of intermingling concepts of *imperium* and *dominium* together as legal analogy.[29] The juridical intermingling of *imperium* and *dominium* was a troublesome vestige of medieval legal science and feudal practice on the vital question of 'jurisdiction' in D.2.1.1, and it was well-established (though highly un-Roman) dicta, taught in all the law schools of the Continent, that *imperium* was a kind of *dominium*.[30] Kicking that habit required dismantling that dicta.

The origin of the dicta can be traced to Glossatorial interpretations (and especially the Bolognese doctors, Martinus and Bulgarus) on two Roman law sources, the *Lex Rhodia* (D.14.2.9) and the *Bene a Zenone* (C.7.37.3). Both of these sources

[28] Bodin occasionally uses the phrase, *duplex obligatio*, to stress this notion of the double-bond. That there are two separate bonds is indicated at *République* 273; *De Republica* 189: *unius imperio ac dominatu omnia tenebantur* (in the earliest states).

[29] This intermingling of private *dominium* and public *imperium* and jurisdiction was a central feature of medieval legal thinking on sovereignty, explored in the classic studies of Francesco Calasso, *I glossatori e le teoria della sovranità: Studio di diritto commune pubblico* (Milan: Giuffré, 1951); Ennio Cortese, *Il problema della sovranità nel pensiero giuridico medioevale* (Rome: Bulzoni, 1982). It is now central to modern international law. See Hersch Lauterpacht, *Private Law Sources and Analogies of International Law* (London: Longmans, Green and Co., 1927) and the more recent paper of Randall Lesaffer, 'Argument from Roman Law in Current International Law: Occupation and Acquisitive Prescription', *European Journal of International Law* 16 (2005): 25–58.

[30] *Popular Sovereignty* Ch. 3 retraces this doctrinal history in detail, including the feudal doctrine of divided *dominium*. In the literature, the best and clearest explanations of this background for a general readership, in my view, are to be found in Constantin Fasolt, *The Limits of History* (Chicago: University of Chicago Press, 2004) 155–218; Garnsey, *Thinking About Property* 177–203. More technical treatments are to be found in Francesco Calasso, '*Iurisdictio* nel diritto comune classico', *Annali di Storia del Diritto* 9 (1965): 89–110; Pennington, *Prince and the Law* 18–24; Robert Feenstra, '*Dominium* and *Ius in Re Aliena*: Origins of a Civil Law Distinction', *New Perspectives in the Roman Law of Property: Essays for Barry Nicholas*, ed. Peter Birks (Oxford: Clarendon Press, 1989), and the classic, though dated, study of Edouard Meynial, 'Notes sur la formation de la théorie du domaine divise', in *Mélanges Fitting*, ed. Herman Fitting (Montpellier: Impr. Générale du Midi, 1907). There's also a good, though technical, discussion of the problem in J.H. Burns, *Lordship, Kingship, and Empire 1400–1525* (Oxford: Clarendon Press, 1992); Canning, *Ideas of Power* 139–64. The topic is investigated again in Fitzmaurice, *Sovereignty, Property, and Empire* 33–51.

fed into an interpretive tradition that sees anybody with the title of *princeps* (even, as Bartolus of Sassoferrato famously declared, a *populus liber* or *civitas quae sibi princeps*) to be a *dominus* (whether as lord, master, owner), so that sovereigns, even popular sovereigns, have both rights of *imperium* and of *dominium* over their subjects.

But, as Bodin recognized, the effect of this intermingling of *imperium* and *dominium* together in describing the sovereign qualities of a *princeps* only caused further confusion in describing the corresponding qualities of political subjecthood – specifically because the language of *dominium* introduced the possibility that political subjecthood was really just a kind of slavery or serfdom.[31] And so, Bodin began the *République* with an extended discourse aimed at disentangling the public from the private. And for good reason; as Bodin put it, here in a snide comment on Plato, 'nothing can be public, where nothing is private'.[32]

Where does one begin in isolating the 'slave' from the 'subject'? For Bodin, the logical starting point, at least as good as any other classical source, was Roman law. One of the most famous passages in all of Justinian's *Digest* is taken from Gaius' *Institutes*, where his *summa de iure personarum divisio* is quoted: 'All persons are either free or slave'.[33] Gaius' *divisio*, always part of the first-year university curriculum in civil law, was foundational to the law of persons, even long after the Roman Empire dissolved and its practices of slavery fell into desuetude. And, as much recent scholarship in the theory and history of the republican tradition of politics has revealed, Gaius was treated as an indispensable Roman authority in articulating that distinctive 'third' concept of liberty that is, by convention, now called in theoretical scholarship 'non-domination'.[34]

The impression one takes away from the title, *De statu hominum*, under which Gaius' *divisio* appears in the *Digest*, is that slavery was a permanent, if not necessarily a natural, feature of humanity. There's a legal reason for this; as Florentinus famously put it, slavery is legal by a 'decree of the law common to all nations, by which one is, contrary to (the law of) nature, made subject to someone else's *dominium*' [*constitutio iuris gentium qua quis dominio alieno contra naturam subicitur*].[35] Florentinus' point here is that slavery is universal and lawful, *not* because Roman law made it so, but because the law of nations, shared in common by all peoples, whether Roman or not, made it so. All historical nations – whether Hebrew, Egyptian, Persian, Greek, or any other *gens* – observe the legality of slavery and were legally entitled under that shared *ius gentium* to enslave [*dominare*]

[31] Cp. Lee, 'Sovereignty and *Dominium*'.

[32] *République* 15; *De Republica* 11 [1.2].

[33] D.1.5.3.

[34] Skinner, *Liberty Before Liberalism* 38–41; Pettit, *Republicanism* Ch. 2.

[35] D.1.5.4. *Constitutio* is a technical term in Roman law signifying a type of Emperor-promulgated positive legislation in the Empire (described in D.1.4.1: *Quod principi placuit*), a unilateral decree or enactment aimed at some kind of legal change or reform, analogous to a Papal bull (i.e. an 'Apostolic Constitution') with the full force of law.

others. Of course, a nation may choose not to exercise this legal right (like France, a significant example as we'll see below) as permitted by the *ius gentium*, but non-exercise of a right does nothing to change its legal validity.

What Bodin observes is that, historically speaking on a grand scale, slavery was not at all permanent and, in fact, *unnatural*. Humans were once all free and equal.[36] Bodin makes frequent, if oblique, mention of this primaeval age of 'natural liberty' (cp. *De Republica* 14: *libertas naturalis*) throughout his writings, and he probably took the idea from a number of different sources and traditions.[37] One such source was Ulpian in the opening rubric of the *Digest*, *De iure et iustitia*, who describes this primaeval world as one where 'all people were by the law of nature born free' [*iure naturali omnes liberi nascerentur*]. In this slaveless world, slavery and manumission were both 'unknown' [*incognita*].[38] Since all humans were naturally free, humans 'were called by one name' [*uno naturali nomine homines appellaremur*] without distinction of status: there was no need for a Gaian division of persons into free and slave, since everyone was naturally free.

But, at some point, someone took the audacious step of introducing slavery into the world, such that only some retained their original freedom, while others lost it when they were enslaved. Ulpian observes that primitive enslavement made possible Gaius' and Ulpian's standard legal division of all persons into free [*liberi*], slave [*servi*], and 'freedmen' [*liberti*], as well as the invention of manumission, all of which were interpolations of the *ius gentium*.

Tracing the historical origins of slavery under the *ius gentium* to some discrete moment in history of primitive enslavement would have been hard enough. But Bodin made his task even harder by adding a complicated twist to his inquiry. Not only was the archaic age of natural liberty a slaveless age, it was also (he posits) a stateless age, a pre-political time before states.[39] Stateless and slaveless were, then, the two key features of this original world of natural liberty governed only under the *ius naturale*, through which 'all humans are equal' [*quod ad ius naturale attinet, omnes homines aequales sunt*].[40] We might ask how humanity moved from a stateless world to a world full of states, just as we might ask how humanity moved from a slaveless world to a 'world full of slaves' [*le monde est rempli d'esclaves*].[41] Observe

[36] D.50.17.32.

[37] Bodin's search for this primaeval natural liberty displays the especially syncretic quality of his historical reasoning, using multiple sources and traditions – in this case, Roman law, Hebrew Scripture, classical histories, and Patristics – to arrive at what he thought was the most reliable account of the historical origins of the sovereign state in documented human history. On Bodin's comparative historical method, Julian Franklin's early study still ranks among the best studies. Julian Franklin, *Jean Bodin and the Sixteenth-Century Revolution in the Methodology of Law and History* (New York: Columbia University Press, 1963) 68–73.

[38] D.1.1.4.

[39] However, despite the absence of states, there were families, whose paterfamilial heads [*chef des familles*] held the supreme domestic power of life and death over their wives and children [*in liberos*], *République* 477; *De Republica* 330 [3.7].

[40] D.50.17.32.

[41] *République* 46; *De Republica* 31 [1.5].

that these are separate questions being asked, and it's not unreasonable to think that two separate stories should be told in response.

But for Bodin, only one story is necessary, and that's because it's the same story. The origin of slavery is inextricably connected to the origin of statehood. Bodin acknowledges this fundamental point of history when he postulates, following 'the unmistakable testimonies of the most reliable historians' [*par le tesmoignage indubitable des plus veritables historiens*], that the first sovereign in human history must have been a slaveholder.[42] And it was by this slaveholder's original title of *dominium* that he also derived his original title of sovereignty.

The most important source documenting this transition from a primitive slaveless and stateless world of natural liberty to a world full of slaves and of states was the 'testimony of sacred history' [*tesmoignage de l'histoire sacree*; *testis ... historia sacra*], in Scripture where we learn from Bodin's reading of the Table of Nations that the first slaveholder-sovereign with both *dominium* and *imperium* in history was the Biblical figure of Nimrod the hunter.[43] Nimrod, whose name Bodin thinks means 'fearsome master' [*seigneur terrible*; *dominus metuendus*], features prominently not only in Bodin's reconstruction of the primitive mythological origins of the state, but in the Western historical imagination. Described in the canonical Mosaic account as 'a mighty hunter before the Lord' [*robustus venator coram Domino*], Nimrod plays a pivotal role because he is regarded as the founder and sovereign of the first state in recorded human history, in Assyria. And not just any state; Nimrod established what Bodin, following Le Roy's translation of Aristotle, classified as a *monarchie seigneuriale* or *dominatus* – so called because of Nimrod's role as a conquering master [*seigneur*; *dominus*] commanding his subjects not by laws [*droits*; *legibus*], but by will [*volunté*; *arbitrio*].[44]

Despite the brief mention of Nimrod in four verses of Hebrew Scripture (Genesis 10:8–9, as well as 1 Chronicles 1:10 and Micah 5:6), he became the object of extensive commentary in classical and later humanist Biblical scholarship, two of which Bodin cites – the Greco-Jewish commentator, Philo of Alexandria (c. 20 B.C.E.–40 C.E.), and the Roman Jewish commentator, Titus Flavius Josephus (37/38–100 C.E.).[45] For Josephus, Nimrod was in fact the tyrant responsible for the

[42] *République* 69; *De Republica* 46 [1.6]. Bodin attributes this statement to Thucydides [*Proemium*], Plutarch [*Theseus*], Caesar, and Solon (via D.47.22.4).

[43] *République* 68, 273; *De Republica* 46, 189 [1.6, 2.2]; 350 [3.8, only in the Latin *De Republica*]. Cp. *Colloquium* 184 [142]. Mary Nyquist, *Arbitrary Rule: Slavery, Tyranny, and the Power of Life and Death* (Chicago: University of Chicago Press, 2013) 130–31.

[44] *République* 272–3; *De Republica* 189 [2.2]. Bodin, following convention, renders δεσπότης/δεσποτεία into Latin as *dominus/dominium* and, following Le Roy's translation of Aristotle's *Politics*, in French with *seigneur/seigneurie*. Thus, the category of *monarchie seigneuriale/dominatus* described in *République/De Republica* 2.2 is a king ruling as a *seigneur/dominus*/δεσπότης. Bodin is likely thinking of the 'fifth type of kingship' described in *Politics* 3.14, 1285^{b}30–33, which LeRoy translates as *Seigneur*. Cp. Le Roy, *Politiques* 164 [*Politics* 3.6, 1279^{a}19–21] distinguishing *droits republiques* from *seigneuriales*.

[45] Nimrod pops up in various places in post-medieval philosophy and literature by Dante, Fortescue, Milton, Bacon, Marvell, Filmer, and Locke. Edward Elgar's *Enigma Variations* includes a variation

construction of the Tower of Babel, the ultimate primitive relic of humanity's rebellious nature and contempt for God. His reading inaugurated a tradition of Biblical scholarship that would later inspire Augustine to read the relevant verse in Vulgate Scripture, describing Nimrod's presence 'before the Lord' [*coram Domino*] instead (following the *Vetus Latina* text of the Bible) as rebellion 'against the Lord' [*contra Dominum*], reflecting Nimrod's disobedience.[46]

For Bodin, who was particularly interested in the fashionable early modern science of Biblical chronology, identifying Nimrod as the world's first sovereign made a lot of sense. One of Bodin's first published works was *De venatione* ('On hunting'), a translation of Oppian's *Κυνηγετικά*, a work revealing not only his youthful literary ambition as a classical scholar but also his interest in seeing hunting as a sort of divine bequest permitting primitive brigandage of animals at the earliest stages of humanity.[47] The description of Nimrod in Scripture as a hunter provided what Bodin thought was compelling documentary evidence that Nimrod most likely would have been the first sovereign, to whose *imperium* and *dominium* all those conquered were first doubly-bound [*unius imperio ac dominatu omnia tenebantur*].[48]

In this chronology, Nimrod's date corresponds with the emergence of slavery (and therefore sovereign states) in the immediate postdiluvian period.[49] Whoever introduced slavery (and states) to the world, thus, couldn't be any older than Noah. The 'mighty hunter' fits nicely into this chronology. Scripture identifies Nimrod in Genesis and 1 Chronicles as the son of Cush and the great-grandson of Noah. Bodin further specifies that he was a direct 'descendant of [Noah's accursed son] Ham' [*Chami nepotem*], to stress that Nimrod was only a few generations removed from the Flood. It is not unreasonable, in Bodin's genealogy, to think of Nimrod, given his reputation, as both the world's first *seigneur* and *souverain*.

Most important was *how* Nimrod was thought to have established his sovereignty and *dominium* over his enslaved Assyrian subjects. He was 'the first to have subjugated men under his *imperium* by force and violence' and, in so doing, the first also 'to have established sovereign rule in his kingdom in the land of Assyria' [*le*

entitled 'Nimrod', which is said to be Elgar's dedication to a German music critic, August Jaeger [German for 'hunter'].

[46] Augustine, *City of God*, vol. 5, trans. Eva Sanford, William Green, Loeb Classical Library 415 (Cambridge: Harvard University Press, 1965) 16–17 [*De civitate Dei* 16.3]: *gigans venator contra Dominum Deum* which is based, not on the Vulgate [*robusus venator coram Domino*], but on the *Vetus Latina* text that seems to be influenced by Jewish interpretive tradition. Christoph Uehlinger, 'Nimrod', in *Neues Bibel-Lexikon*, ed. Manfred Görg and Bernhard Lang, vol. 2 (Zurich: Benziger, 1995) 929–32.

[47] Jean Bodin, *Oppiani de Venatione* (Paris: Apud Michaëlum Vascosanum, 1555). Cp. *République* 273; *De Republica* 189 [2.2]: *potentissimum venatorem appellant, loquendi genus Hebraeis familiar, quo verbo latronem significari volunt.*

[48] *République* 272–3; *De Republica* 189 [2.2]. Bodin even observed that *ante Nimerodi aetatem, aequa erat omnium libertas*, coinciding with the remark of D.1.1.4. Cp. *Apologie de René Herpin* fol. $15_{\text{ro-vo}}$, which criticizes Ferrier of mistakenly claiming that Nimrod was a virtuous and heroic prince.

[49] *République* 49; *De Republica* 33 [1.5].

premier qui assubiectit les hommes par force & violence, establissans sa principauté au pays d'Assyrie; primum omnium homines sub imperium vi subiungxisse, ac dominatus fundamenta in Assyria iecisse].[50] The example of Nimrod refutes the contrary thesis, attributed to Aristotle, Demosthenes, Cicero, and Herodotus, that 'the first kings were chosen on account of their greatness of integrity and reputation for doing justice'.[51] Nimrod shows that what mattered more than anything else was, as Bodin put it, 'force and violence'.

This primitive act of enslaving violence was a world-historical moment accomplishing two things at once. Nimrod not only introduced slaves [*servi*] into a world where previously there were none, but, by that very same act, he also introduced subjects [*subditi*], a conceptually distinct category, but historically bundled together with slavery.[52] The following key passage explains how this happened:

> Before there were any cities or forms of state, every *paterfamilias* held the supreme right of life and death [*summum ius vitae ac necis*] over his children and his wives. After some time, however, violence and lust for power, as well as avarice and desire for revenge, pitted all against all [*aliis in alios*]. The outcome of those wars had made some conquerors [*victores*], while forcing the conquered into slavery [*servire cogebat*] by the more powerful. The one who conducted himself bravely in combat as leader [*ducem*; *chef et capitaine*] commanded [*imperebat*] his comrades even after bringing about victory, but not as a *paterfamilias*: Some he commanded were loyal subjects [*loyaux subjects*; *amicis*], others slaves [*esclaves*; *servis*]. Those 'slaves' were completely deprived of that full liberty bestowed by nature upon everyone to live as each pleased. But even among 'subjects,' natural liberty was still diminished to some degree [*quodammodo deminuta*], by the one they chose [*elegerant*] as their leader. And this was because each was required as a private individual to acknowledge [*prestoyent obeissance*; *agnoscere*] their chosen leader's sovereignty. Those who did not so acknowledge and agree to obey the sovereign's laws and command [*loix & commandement*] ended up losing all their liberty. Thus was the origin of the words, 'slaves' [*servitutis*] and 'subjects' [*subditorum*], 'citizens' [*civium*] and 'foreigners' [*peregrinorum*], 'sovereign prince' [*principis*] and 'tyrant' [*tyranni*].[53]

This succinct account shows that the first sovereign, Nimrod, actually acquired two distinct legal titles by conquest – the titles of mastery [*seigneurie*; *dominium*] and of sovereignty [*souveraineté*; *imperium*] – by that original act

50 *République* 69; *De Republica* 46 [1.6].

51 *République* 69; *De Republica* 46 [1.6]. On this point, Bodin's marginalia refers the reader to his discussion on this topic of primitive kingship in *Methodus* 471–72.

52 A similar conclusion is reached by Le Thiec, 'Le droit de conquête en guise de constitution': 356–59.

53 Based on a synthesis from *République* 68 and *De Republica* 46 [1.6]. Becker offers a reading of this passage in *Gendering the Renaissance Commonwealth* 118–19.

of conquest (as we'll see in Chapter 5, a perfectly valid legal title *ex iure gentium*). Any university-educated lawyer can tell that Bodin is simply patterning his analysis on Florentinus' statement that, under the *ius gentium*, one is said to become a slave instantly when 'one is captured by enemies' [D.1.5.5.1: *ab hostibus (capitur)*] in a lawful war and to be, thereafter, subject to his new masters [*in potestate … dominorum*] with the lawful power of life and death [D.1.6.1.1: *vitae necisque potestatem*] over their newly acquired slaves.[54] They are, moreover, called 'slaves' [*servi*], not because their purpose is 'to serve' [*dominos servire*] their masters, but instead because they have been 'saved' [from *servare*] – saved from death by conquerors trying to profit by selling their captives into slavery (D.1.5.4.2). It is an etymology that Bodin apparently endorsed, belittling its unnamed critics (probably Jacques Cujas) as 'unskilled grammarians' [*grammaticis imperitis*].[55]

Bodin, however, is doing something more novel with Florentinus. Traditionally, Florentinus was only talking about how the enslavement of captives in war might be legally permissible – and, thus, a legal 'right' of conquerors – under the *ius gentium*. Bodin took this traditional analysis a step further in saying that the *ius gentium* allowed something even more: victors (like Nimrod) acquired not only a private right of *dominium in servos*, but also a public right of sovereignty [*ius summi imperii in subditos*].[56]

From the very moment of conquest, then, it was legally possible to differentiate between three distinct parties: (1) Nimrod whose sovereign and seigneurial rights were acquired through the *ius gentium*; (2) those who were subject under Nimrod's sovereign right of *imperium*; and (3) those who are subject under Nimrod's seigneurial right of *dominium*. The architecture of Bodin's chronology and the constitutional structure of Nimrod's Assyrian state might be represented visually:

[54] Bodin always reads D.1.5.5.1 in connection with D.49.15.24 and 50.16.118, which specify that the term, 'enemy' [*hostis*], is to be read as one formally named by the Roman *fetiales* in a formal declaration of *bellum publicum*. Slaves (and not to mention new titles of sovereignty) can be acquired only *in bello licito*, and not through any act of unauthorized violence of 'robbers and pirates'. Likewise, the legal protections of a *bellum licitum* (or, what is the same, a *bellum iustum*), such as the right of postliminy, can be claimed only by legal belligerents, and not by mere bands of robbers. Cp. *Gloss Ord.* and Baldus on D.1.1.5 s.v.: *Ex hoc iure*.

[55] *République* 50; *De Republica* 33 [1.5]. *Gloss. Ord.* on D.1.5.4.2, s.v.: *servare*, however, challenges this etymology deriving *servus* from being 'saved' from death. He is most likely thinking of Jacques Cujas whom Bodin knew from his days at Toulouse and, ever since, often belittled in his writings as a grammarian but without proper scientific knowledge of civil law. One example appears at *République* 468–69 [3.6].

[56] This is why the Roman wars were essential to Bodin's account of Roman expansion, the despotic seignurial nature of provincial government, and how Roman sovereignty grew to the cover the entire Mediterranean world. He uses the same model of conquest to explain the acquisition of a seigneurial title of sovereignty in the context of early modern imperialism and the founding of colonies.

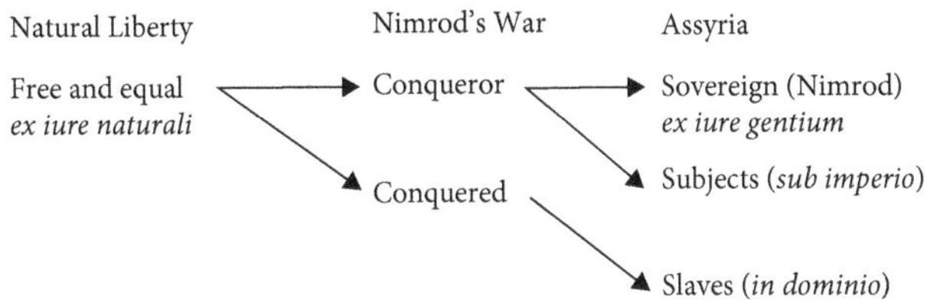

Observe that Nimrod's Assyrian state is, in effect, a *hybrid state* populated by two distinct populations, 'subjects' and 'slaves'.[57] Note what these two population groups share in common. They are, first, all subject to one common sovereign, Nimrod, and it is this common subjection that makes them members of one state. Moreover, they have all suffered what lawyers called *deminutio*, in that they have lost the original natural liberty and equality they enjoyed *ante bellum*.[58]

But just as the civil law recognized varying degrees of *capitis deminutiones*, so too did Bodin argue that the degree of liberty lost was similarly variable. Slaves, not surprisingly, lost the most. 'Those conquered in war', Bodin explains, 'were completely deprived' [*victis omnino adempta fuit*] of 'that full liberty granted by nature to everyone to live as one might wish' [*plena illa & a natura cuique tributa libertas vivendi vt vellet*]. These individuals suffered a *deminutio maxima* losing all their liberty to become Nimrod's personal slaves, thereby sinking to what Bodin would identify as the ninth and lowest degree of subjection.

'Subjects', however, represented an unusual case. Unlike slaves who represented the population conquered in war, Nimrod's subjects weren't slaves at all. They were still technically free even though they were *obligantur imperio Nimerodi*. In Bodin's history above, these subjects originated as Nimrod's *amici* (Chapter 1), his fellow colleagues and trustworthy comrades in arms whom he led in war. While their original natural liberty was, to be sure, 'diminished to some extent' [*quodammodo deminuta*], it was not the kind of total deprivation of liberty that resulted in enslavement. Rather, Nimrod engineered a new kind of relationship with his fellows whereby those of equal standing [Bodin's Latin text describes them as *aeque et sociis*] entered into a relationship whereby one, as a free (i.e. non-slave) private individual [*privatim*], voluntarily recognizes and accepts another's sovereignty [*summum alterius imperium agnoscere*].

57 'Subjects': *République* refers to the *fideles & loyaux subiects*; *De Republica* calls them *amici* of the conquering sovereign. Bodin is likely thinking about Aristotle here: Assyria was, at once, both an οἶκος and a πόλης, and Nimrod seems to represent what Aristotle designated in *Politics* 3.14 as the 'fifth kind of kingship' – the 'despot', or, as Le Roy translated it in *Politiques* 190, the *Seigneur*. On this topic, see the study of Vittor Ivo Comparato, 'Note su Bodin e Aristotele, sovranità e proprietà nella definizione di Stato', *Materiali di storia: Annali della Facoltà di Scienze politiche di Perugia* 18 (1982): 7–13.

58 Bodin's loose reference to the term, *deminutio*, at *De Republica* 46 [*quoddam modo deminuta*] and 47 [*libertas potestate domini deminuatur*] is a clear gesture towards the *capitis deminutio* in Roman law which Gaius defines as a *status permutatio*, at D.4.5.1. *Deminutio* can be of varying degrees, whether minimum, medium, or maximum. Bodin's idea is that, while both subjects and slaves have suffered a *deminutio*, slaves suffered a *deminutio maxima*, while subjects suffered a *deminutio* of a lesser degree.

All early states followed the pattern of Assyria and were unambiguously seigneurial states, ruled by one *seigneur* or *dominus*. But Bodin's grand narrative suggests that humanity eventually found a way to disaggregate and separate *imperium* over subjects from *dominium* over slaves, so that sovereigns of later ages no longer needed to rule their states as masters ruled their households, or to treat their subjects as personal slaves dependent on their *arbitrium*.[59] While a sovereign certainly *could* rule as a *dominus*, it's just bad politics to do so. Far more advisable is it to eliminate slavery and establish states made up of 'free persons' [*liberi homines*] who were, nevertheless, obliged and bound lawfully as 'subjects' [*subditi*] tied together only by obligations of *imperium* (but not *dominium*).

There is an unexpectedly 'republican' quality to Bodin's political anthropology, a grand narrative of human development that is also a liberation story. And while I'm not prepared to argue, as a point of interpretation, that we should be reading Bodin as a 'republican' theorist or a theorist of republican liberty, it's hard to avoid the conclusion – given the textual evidence of his antipathy towards slavery, Ottoman despotism, and the oriental style of seigneurial rulership creeping into French politics – that Bodin favoured a politics of 'non-domination' which can only be experienced in free states with 'free subjects'.[60]

The Free Subject

How do slave states, like Assyria, become free states, like France? The modern scholarship on the early modern revival of republican politics indicates that there's

[59] The key to this transformation, according to Bodin, was the invention of positive legislation [in the sense of *lex*; *loi*], as a tool of (what he called) *droit* government, indeed, a divinely-inspired invention that Bodin, following Josephus' *Contra Apionem*, attributes to Moses. This is because law is what made possible the constitution of magisterial offices and independent courts that exercised a *legitimum imperium*, whose powers and terms of office were strictly defined by legislation, rather than by the arbitrary will of the sovereign. *République* 393; *De Republica* 272 [3.3], citing Book II of *Contra Apionem*: *Mosem primum omnium mortalium leges scripsisse.* Bodin cites Pomponius' *Enchiridion* (always reproduced in the *Digest* at D.1.2.2.1): *Et quidem initio civitiatis nostrae populus sine lege certa, sine iure certo primum agere instituit omniaque manu a regibus gubernabantur.* Cp. *République* 621; *De Republica* 458 [4.6].

[60] Bodin saw this creeping seigneurialism especially in the French courts of Parlement. The Parlement originated as an extraordinary seigneurial body, an annual ambulatory [*ambulatoire*] court of servile peers whose commissions were 'precarious', in that they were *révocables au plaisir du Prince* and its members 'like natural slaves' [*les subiects en la monarchie seigneuriale, comme esclaves naturels*]. In the later Middle Ages, however, Parlement was made a sitting court with a legally defined jurisdiction [*Cour ordinaire ... avec puissance resort, & iurisdiction ordinaire*]. Most important in this institutional history were the decrees of Louis XI and Philip V who, Bodin argued, assured judicial independence by guaranteeing life tenure for judges (and perhaps an unintended consequence, the sale of judicial offices), a key sign of France's move away from *seigneurie* to a constitutional monarchy with the rule of law, or *droit monarchie*. *République* 599; *De Republica* 441–42 [4.4]; cp. *République* 379–80; *De Republica* 264 [3.2]. Bodin is, however, anxious that the personal rulership characteristic of oriental despots was gradually making a comeback in French royal politics, and he pointed to the Parlement, where the Valois monarchs of the sixteenth-century, especially Charles IX, began to institute policies chipping away at that independence, so that judges serve, like slaves, at the pleasure of their prince, ruling seigneurially like a sultan, *République* 387; *De Republica* 269 [3.2].

only one way to do this: eliminate kings, since (so goes the republican logic) kingship is the source of enslaving *dominium*. Free states, in this republican theory, require kingless rule: they must be popular states with popular sovereignty.

Bodin didn't see it that way. It's a mistake to equate kingship with *seigneurie* or *dominium*, since kings can eliminate the offensive *dominium* without also relinquishing their title of sovereignty. Monarchs, Bodin thought, could be champions of liberty and agents of liberation.[61] Of course, Bodin readily acknowledges that kings certainly *could* be 'despotic' or master-like in their rulership, as Nimrod supposedly was. But this was by no means necessary. Kings can choose to rule over free people.

Key to this argument was manumission. In the law of persons, slavery was described as a complete loss of liberty, a condition of total domination under a master. But it wasn't, legally speaking, a permanent condition.[62] Nor was it, for that matter, a 'natural' condition.[63] Any slave could, in theory, be released from the bondage of servitude and have their liberty restored (or 'vindicated' as civilians say, as in *vindicatio in libertatem*). This is accomplished by manumission, the formal legal release from the power of *dominium* through which a slave can, thereafter, become a 'freedman' [*libertinus*]. As Ulpian puts it in D.1.1.4, manumission is a 'bestowal of liberty' [*datio libertatis*] by which slaves are 'released from another's power' [*liberatur potestate*].

It's important to note that the legality of manumission, like the legality of slavery, is established not by the law of nature, but instead, by the law of nations. Manumission, as a legal tool to release from bondage, only exists because we now live in a world where the *ius gentium* has permitted slavery also to exist. But in the slaveless world of primaeval natural liberty, there'd be no need for manumission (just as in a world without cars, there'd be no felt need for traffic laws).

But if the function of manumission was to restore liberty, what sort of liberty was restored? Could manumission also be used to release subjects from their political subjecthood under a sovereign, in the same way that manumission can release slaves from their slavery from under a *dominus*?

Consider again the case of Nimrod: Nimrod acquired his title of sovereignty over Assyria by conquest in a licit war (as we shall see in Chapter 5, a perfectly legal method to acquire a new sovereign title under the *ius gentium*). But by that very same act of conquest, Nimrod acquired an additional title of *dominium* as well, so that his conquered Assyrian subjects were also, at least initially, his personal

[61] At *République* 69; *De Republica* 46 [1.6], Bodin observed that the 'West Indies were discovered full of slaves' [*les Isles Occidentales furent trouvés remplies d'esclaves*]. Imperial expansion, in Bodin's view, could potentially be justified as a mission of liberation, to use sovereignty to end, or at least limit, modern slavery.

[62] There are even several unusual cases of 'slaves without masters' [*servus sine domino*], such as the 'abandoned slave' [*servus derelictus*] which Justinianic law treated as effectively freed and *res nullius*.

[63] D.1.5.4.1.

slaves.[64] Nimrod's Assyrians, then, were actually doubly bound under two distinct bonds of obligation [*duplici obligando*], *imperium* and *dominium* both created by one juridical act of conquest.[65]

Now suppose that Nimrod, in an act of grace, voluntarily renounced his personal right and seigneurial title of *dominium* and decided instead to enact a general release, an emancipation proclamation, so to speak, effectively manumitting all of his subjects from their servile status, so that they were now all 'freedmen', or *libertini*. Were they, despite this newly acquired 'free' status, of like standing as Nimrod's *amici*, still unfree?

For a classical jurisconsult, the answer is no.[66] Manumission makes a slave free, and that's the end of the matter. But Bodin, needless to say, isn't a classical jurisconsult. For him, the answer to the question must be yes (i.e. Assyria's manumitted *libertini* are still unfree), and for a simple reason: manumission is a release dissolving only the one bond of *dominium*, but it leaves untouched the other preexisting bond of *imperium*, which remains fully active even in this hypothetical Assyrian free state populated by newly-freed *libertini* [*quoque civibus omnibus aliquid de libertate naturali detrahitur, ut summae alterius potestati subiicia*[*n*]*tur*].[67] Some other form of release, therefore, is necessary to dissolve the residual bond of *imperium*. Despite manumission, they're still duty-bound subjects.[68]

But subjects of a specific kind: Bodin classifies them as 'free subjects' [*franc subjects*], which the freedmen become 'at the moment of manumission' [*manumissi momento*].[69] At first glance, you might ask, as was suggested earlier, whether a contradiction is involved in this scenario, since it requires one to be free (as a *libertinus*) and unfree (as a duty-bound subject) simultaneously. But Bodin can easily shield himself from that charge simply by pointing out the double-bond structure of Nimrod's rule, given that there are two separate obligatory bonds in question; the free subject is 'free' from the bond of *dominium*, but 'unfree' from the bond of *imperium*.

[64] D.1.5.4-5.

[65] *République* 273; *De Republica* 189 [2.2]: They were *unius* [1] *imperio ac* [2] *dominatu tenebantur*. The corresponding passage at *République* omits this formulation of the double-bond of seigneurial sovereigns. Bodin often talks about double-bonds in various contexts, and describes them as a *duplex obligatio*, to stress the basic legal point that an obligor's release from one bond, whether by performance or otherwise, doesn't entail release from the other bond, *De Republica* 99–100, 114.

[66] That is because, in the Roman context, the status *cives, Latini Iuniani, peregrini, dediticii*, were conceptualized less in terms of subjection/non-subjection, and more in terms of the possession of special legal rights, such as the *ius suffragii* or *commercii* and others in *ius Quiritium*.

[67] *De Republica* 47 [1.6].

[68] And, therefore, Nimrod's manumission does not restore the default natural liberty, only liberty from *dominium*. For true statelessness, Nimrod would, in addition, need to release from *imperium*. One other important point of difference: Bodin argues, at *République* 70; *De Republica* 47 [1.6] that, upon manumission, the *libertinus* is immediately a 'citizen'. That is by no means certain in classical law, since manumission can sometimes produce various categories of non-citizens, such as Junian Latins or *dediticii*.

[69] *République* 70; *De Republica* 47 [1.6], citing D.49.15.5; D.50.1.7; Inst.1.6; C.10.40.7.

But in this apparently innocuous response, Bodin has done something revolutionary and heterodox, with the introduction of something like a new priority rule in the law of persons. Every university-trained lawyer (as Bodin was) in medieval and early modern Europe, whether of civil, canon, or common law, knows that the foundational division in the law of persons concerns status: all persons are either 'free' [*liberi homines*] or 'slave' [*servi*].[70] All other legal classifications of personality are parasitic on, and flow from, this primary question, what Gaius has called the *summa de iure personarum divisio.*[71]

What's important to note is the priority rule as it operates in classical Roman law. Gaius' *divisio* is anterior to all other legal questions about personality (including the question whether or not one is a subject). It must be answered first before addressing any other question about personality. This priority rule remained unchanged in the medieval jurisprudence of the Italian Glossators and was well-established dicta among Bodin's legal humanist contemporaries in France. Even the most technically gifted academic lawyers in Bodin's day – François Baudouin, Hugues Doneau [Donellus], and François Connan – continued to insist on the primacy of Gaius' *summa divisio*, and textbooks of civil law always began with Gaius.

Bodin's presentation eliminated this primacy entirely.[72] He reversed the sequence of priority, such that the *summa divisio* is no longer the question of *dominium*. Instead, it was the question of *imperium* – whether one is a subject or foreigner.[73] Only once this has been decided, Bodin thinks, can it then be possible to address downstream legal questions about free or slave status, or other questions about personal status, rank, or dignity.[74]

We can see this because, in Bodin's mind, it's possible to be a subject without being a slave [*le franc subject*; *liber homo*], but it's impossible to be a slave without also being someone's subject, whether of the same *dominus* (as in the case of Nimrod) or of some other sovereign (as was enslaved Joseph, whose *dominus* was Potiphar and whose sovereign was Pharaoh). Slavery, for Bodin, is possible only in a world where there are states and where the boundaries separating subject from foreigner are already established, a point confirmed by Bodin's observation that the

[70] Even the English judge, Bracton, once a student of the Bolognese doctor Azo, observes the classical priority of the division between free and slave.

[71] D.1.5.3.

[72] Keechang Kim, 'L'étranger chez Jean Bodin', *Revue historique de droit français et étranger* 76 (1998): 78 gives several examples in the humanist legal scholarship documenting the priority given to the free/slave distinction even during Bodin's life. François Hotman is one example cited, in *Partitiones iuris civilis elementariae* (Basel: Apud N. Episcopium Iuniorem, 1560) 8–9, which states that despite the *multiplex* ways of dividing persons, one remains ... *summa & prima, quae bipartita est: ut alii liberi, alii servi dicantur.*

[73] This change is reflected in the section, 'Of Persons', in the Napoleonic *Code Civil* which treats, first, the question who is and isn't French (and therefore, capable or incapable of French civil rights). *The Code Napoleon, or The French Civil Code* (London: William Benning, 1827) 3–5 [1.1.1, §§7–16].

[74] I disagree, however, with Kim's treatment of liberty. He seems to confuse liberty as a strictly non-interference concept with liberty in the sense of exceptional privileges or immunities secured through formal licensing instruments such as charters and letters patent.

antediluvian world was a world of families marked by a *libertas naturalis*, without masters or slaves.[75]

In one fell swoop, then, Bodin has managed to upend centuries of legal doctrine. One commentator goes further, arguing that 'Bodin's solution amounts to nothing less than erasing the past'.[76] The result was a radical shift on concepts of personality and political membership that very few commentators on Bodin – and almost no political or legal theorist on citizenship and nationality – have fully appreciated or understood the technical details of the legal argument.[77]

Why would Bodin want to allow such a fundamental shift in the legal understanding of personality? Bodin, unlike his contemporaries who fetishized it, felt no special attachment to the classical jurisprudence of the Roman law (even though he was trained in the civil law, taught it, and used it in his legal practice in the Parlement).[78] As we've already seen in Chapter 2 concerning contractual obligations, he was instead a system-builder and aimed at articulating legal fundamentals to be found, not just in Rome, but in all states in history.[79]

While recognizing the historical importance of Roman law in Western legal history and its usefulness in teaching law, he nevertheless was willing to do what so many of his contemporaries could not, which was to extract himself from the dead hand of Justinian. Roman law, as Bodin would put it in the *Methodus*, was simply the accumulated legal experience of one ancient civilization – but only one among many others. The legal wisdom of Gaius, Ulpian, and Papinian, however much a model worthy of emulation, can't possibly claim to be a universal law for all peoples, just as Latin, however useful in teaching rules of grammar, rhetoric, and eloquence in prose and poetry in the schools, can't possibly capture the linguistic rules and usages of all tongues.[80]

[75] It is theoretically possible to restore one *in statu naturali* by double-release from the double-bond of *dominium* (by manumission) and *imperium* (by denaturalization or exile).

[76] Kim, *Aliens in Medieval Law* 205.

[77] The argument in *République* 1.5–6 is presented in the unwelcoming lawyerly style of a legal *consilium*, generally inaccessible to the modern reader. Its value and significance, however, have been recognized in a range of historical studies, including Peter Riesenberg, *Citizenship in the Western Tradition: Plato to Rousseau* (Chapel Hill, North Carolina: University of North Carolina Press, 1992); Charlotte Wells, *Law and Citizenship in Early Modern France* (Baltimore, Maryland: Johns Hopkins University Press, 1995); Quaglioni, 'Les citoyens envers l'État'; Kim, *Aliens in Medieval Law*; Peter Sahlins, *Unnaturally French: Citizens in the Old Regime and After* (Ithaca: Cornell University Press, 2018) 19–23.

[78] *République* 154–55; *De Republica* 101 [1.8] stresses that, even though Roman law is taught, France is by no means bound by it, except insofar as the French sovereign (or his agents) has consented to its use in courts.

[79] Alberto Ribeiro de Barros, 'Bodin et le projet d'une science du droit: La *Juris universi distributio* (1578)', *Nouvelle revue du XVI*ᵉ *siècle* 21 (2003): 57–70.

[80] Bodin's relationship with the humanist legal scholarship is a complicated one, but on this specific point, he seems to be in consensus with legal humanists such as Hotman who, in *Anti-Tribonian* and *Francogallia*, criticized servile Roman law as a legal system based on slavery and, instead, argued that French legal practice was not of Roman, but primarily Germanic origin. Ralph Giesey, 'When and Why Hotman Wrote the *Francogallia*', *Bibliothèque d'Humanisme et Renaissance* 29 (1967): 581–611; Donald Kelley, *François Hotman: A Revolutionary's Ordeal* (Princeton: Princeton University Press, 1973).

If the goal was to formulate general principles essential to all legal systems, and not just the Roman system, Bodin would have had to seek non-Roman sources of law (Greek, Egyptian, Hebrew, Persian, etc.), in addition to Roman, and apply a consistent method of comparison across sources.[81] In practice, that would require abandoning certain fundamentals of Roman law – including Gaius' priority rule in the law of persons.

We can already see an early indication of this move in the *Distributio*, where Gaius' *divisio* between free persons and slaves becomes one among several possible, equally valid, ways of dividing legal categories of personality, as follows.

Divisio personarum ex dignitate
(Bodin, *Distributio* fol. A, s.v.: *Personæ*)

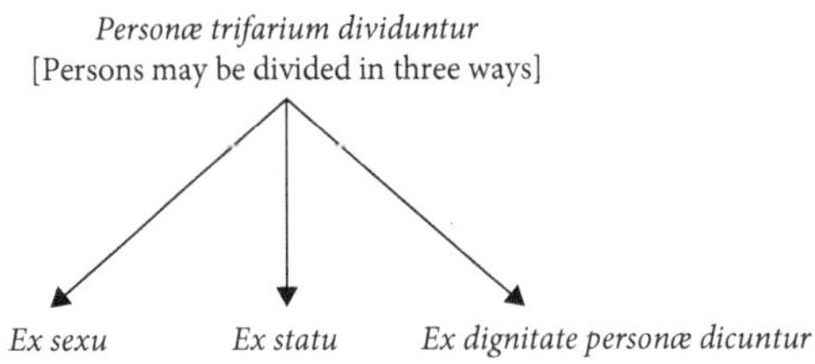

But in this presentation, there is no obvious priority rule at work. Among the three divisions – *ex sexu, ex statu*, or *ex dignitate* – there is no indication which of these is supposed to take precedence. My sense is that Bodin is cautiously experimenting with alternatives to Gaius, but without committing himself to any particular priority rule.

That early apprehension displayed in the *Distributio* is gone in Bodin's later treatments in the *Methodus* and the *République*, both of which require a new priority rule that treats the subject/foreigner contrast and the question of *imperium* – and *not* the free/slave contrast and the question of *dominium* – as the new *summa divisio*. One reason for this shift is due to the deliberately state-centric orientation of Bodin's first extended treatment of political subjecthood in the *Methodus*. Ostensibly a text about comparative historical methodology and interpretation, the *Methodus* represents Bodin's first attempt at formulating the main elements of his general theory of state and of those who are subject to its sovereignty. He turns to the state for a strictly practical reason: the state, whether of the Assyrians, the Hebrews, the Egyptians, the Persians, the Romans, serves as Bodin's principal unit of historical analysis. Answering that question necessarily requires us to specify the boundaries of political membership in the state – those who are 'inside' it and those who are 'outside'.

There's another reason why Bodin felt he had to upstage Gaius and introduce a new priority rule: Not all states were slaveholding societies as Rome (or Nimrod's

[81] Donald Kelley, 'Development and Context of Bodin's *Method*', in *Verhandlungen der Internationalen Bodin Tagung in München*, ed. Horst Denzer (München: Beck, 1973).

Assyria) was, a point that Bodin pursues at some length in the *République*. His native France, a land once reduced in antiquity to slavery under Caesar's *dominium*, was case in point. Slavery, Bodin wrote, had long since vanished in France (the land of *franc* and free people), and so, it would seem there's no need for Gaius' *divisio* between free and slave in a land where (as a famous maxim puts it) 'there are no slaves'. While civilians continued to insist on the primacy of Gaius' *summa divisio* even in the universities of slaveless France, Bodin pointed out that Roman law was still, and always had been, a foreign artefact of Roman *imperium* on French soil – even in the so-called *pays du droit écrit*.[82] For these reasons, he proposed instead the heterodoxy that perhaps a different *divisio*, indigenous to French law and custom, might be more appropriate.

The most important advantage in this new scheme was that Bodin was now able to isolate subjecthood from slavery. You do not need to be a slave (or any other kind of bondsman like a serf, a vassal, a client, a tributary), in order to be a proper 'subject'. Nor, for that matter, does one need to have *dominium*, in order to assert *imperium*. The one and only thing that matters is the bond of obligation – or 'allegiance' – that establishes the moral boundary separating subject from foreigner. For Bodin, then, sovereignty alone is what solves the so-called 'boundary problem' of political theory. Nothing else – whether one's ancestry, class, language, religion, custom – is relevant in settling political membership.

Taken together, we can now make some sense of the earlier hypothetical example concerning Nimrod's generous act of manumission transforming the 'slave subject' to a 'free subject'. The 'free subject' is no contradiction in terms, but the logical result of a new priority rule in the division of persons. Nor is this mere conjecture. The textual evidence is to be found in the opening of the French *République* I, 6. There, he carves out the category of the 'free subject' [*le franc subiect*]: it is one who 'holds the sovereignty of another' [*tenant de la souverainete d'autruy*].[83]

But it is only in the Latin *De Republica* which finally clarifies this point and synthesizes the result of the new priority rule that Bodin had introduced in the law of persons: the free subject is a 'free person who is duty-bound to the sovereign power of another' [*liber homo, qui summae alterius potestati obligatur*].[84] This is the duty-bound subject in the purest conceptual form, stripped of all sources of domination, save for sovereignty.

Bodin recognizes that this notion of the free subject is *sui generis* and immediately senses that he requires a new term to specify this category. He chooses the term, 'citizen' [*citoyen*; *civis*].

[82] *République* 154; *De Republica* 101 [1.8]. On Roman law in the *pays du droit écrit*, see Ralph Giesey's study, *The Juristic Basis of Dynastic Right to the French Throne*, Transactions of the American Philosophical Society No. 51 (Philadelphia: American Philosophical Society, 1961).

[83] *République* 68 [1.6].

[84] *De Republica* 45–6; 47 [1.6].

The Citizen

Bodin uses the terms, 'subject' [*subject*; *subditus*] and 'citizen' [*citoyen*; *civis*] interchangeably. And now we can see why he does this: The Bodinian citizen is a *kind* of Bodinian subject – more specifically, *le franc subject*. So, while not all subjects must be citizens, all citizens are, by definition, subjects – those subject to some sovereign's *imperium*.[85] All the qualities of subjecthood necessarily apply even to the category of 'citizens', who are, despite their 'free' status, whether as 'freeborn' [*ingenui*] or as 'manumitted' [*libertini*], bound by obligation of political allegiance.

It's difficult to stress just how much Bodin's treatment of citizenship marked a monumental achievement in the intellectual history of the concept. Shared subjection – the passive (though not servile) condition of being tied by common allegiance to one sovereign power – has now become the essence of political membership.[86] Citizenship is marked, not by *vita activa*, but (one might say) by *vita passiva* – to be *subditus*.

In (re)defining citizenship in terms of subjection, it's no mystery that Bodin's primary target was Aristotle. The citizen was, as Bodin summarized Aristotle, 'one who may share in the administration of justice, may hold office, or act in a deliberative capacity'.[87] Bodin observed, however, that Aristotle's treatment of civic membership in *Politics* III was 'suitable only for democratic states' – specifically, in the kind of popular rule to be found in democratic 'Athens in the time of Pericles', after the Solonic and Cleisthenic reforms.[88] For Aristotle and others who followed his influential analysis (Bodin singled out, by name, Gasparo Contarini, Carlo Sigonio, and Girolamo Garimberto), citizenship was to be understood in the participatory terms of *vita activa*.[89]

The problem here, Bodin argued, was that Aristotle (and his followers) tried to make a faulty generalization. Aristotle may have been correct in saying that Athenian citizens were distinguished by office-holding, jurisdiction, and deliberation. He might even have been right to say this about Hellenic states in general. But to then say that office-holding, jurisdiction, and deliberation are to be the essential

[85] Rejecting Aristotle, Bodin turns instead to another classical model for this analysis of citizenship: the Antonine Constitution, referenced in D.1.5.17, is the decree of Caracalla that extended Roman citizenship to all free persons under Roman *imperium*. See Lee 'Citizenship, Subjection, and the Civil Law'.

[86] The extension of citizenship was, thus, an efficient technique of empire-building, a tool of domination to mark conquered peoples uniformly as subjects of a common imperial power. This is a central theme in Ando, *Antonine Constitution*.

[87] *Methodus* 232, citing *Politics* 3.1, 1275^{b}19: *Civem definit Aristoteles, iudiciorum, magistratus, & consilii capiendi potestate.*

[88] *Methodus* 232.

[89] *Methodus* 232. Gasparo Contarini, *De Magistratibus et Republica Venetorum Libri V* (Basel, 1547) 29–32; Carlo Sigonio, *De Republica Atheniensium Libri IV* (Bologna, 1564) 40; Girolamo Garimberto, *De Regimenti Publici de la Citta* (Venice, 1544) fol. xi. Bodin renews his complaint at *Methodus* 249 but targets also Petrus Soderinus as another humanist Aristotelian.

characteristics of citizenship *everywhere* in all states is *non sequitur*. Such characteristics were, as he put it, not at all essential but purely *casuelles, & accidentaires*.[90]

To illustrate this criticism, Bodin asks whether the Aristotelian analysis could make any sense of Roman citizenship under the Antonine Constitution of 212 C.E., whereby citizenship was extended universally to all free persons in the Roman Empire. 'What is to be done', Bodin asks, 'in the case of Emperor Antonine [Caracalla], who in a proclamation ordered that all free men … should be Roman citizens?'[91] For Bodin, Aristotle's theory of citizenship in the πόλης was fundamentally flawed, for two critical reasons. First, Aristotle cannot explain the legal status of Roman provincials following the universal grant of citizenship in the Antonine Constitution. Nor could it explain differences in citizenship status such as the *civitas cum suffragio* and *civitas sine suffragio*. As he argues, if we were to follow Aristotle's analysis, free inhabitants of Roman provinces would be 'aliens because they had been denied civil rights … [i.e. they were] debarred from honours, judicial matters, and public counsels' – a result he described to be both 'absurd and dangerous'.[92] It was absurd because a classical Aristotelian analysis would allow one to be 'partly citizens' [*partim cives*] and 'partly foreigners' [*partim peregrinos*].[93] And it was dangerous, because harbouring such a large domestic population of disenfranchised outsiders could function as 'an excellent pretext for civil war'.[94] Were we to apply Aristotle's analysis, such individuals would hold what Bodin described as the unenviable and uncertain position of being 'exiles or foreigners in their own countries' [*in sua civitate exules aut peregrini*].

As a result, Bodin argued that Aristotle failed to explain practices of citizenship in sufficiently general terms, far outside the classical context of Athenian democracy.[95] And so, for this reason, Bodin dismissed the Aristotelian theory as entirely unsuitable for what he wanted: a general theory of state.

The root of the problem was conceptual; Aristotle 'never defined sovereignty'.[96] If he only had defined sovereignty and recognized its binding obligatory force,

[90] *République* 93 [1.6]. On the significance of office-holding and accountability in Athenian politics, see Melissa Lane, 'The Idea of Accountable Office in Ancient Greece and Beyond', *Philosophy* 95 (2020): 19–40.

[91] *Methodus* 232 ('132').

[92] *Methodus* 232 ('132'). He is thinking of the category of *civitas sine suffragio*, where the question of citizenship is determined separately from the question of civil right.

[93] *Methodus* 245.

[94] *Methodus* 232 ('132').

[95] Bodin even suggests that Aristotle's theory cannot consistently be applied even to Athens itself because it does not count the invisible under-class population who were nevertheless inhabitants subject to the rule of the Athenian *polis*. *Methodus* 232 ('132').

[96] Bodin explains at *Methodus* 235 that Aristotle confused the *summum imperium* for the *administratio* [or *gubernatio*] *Reipublicae*, a distinction that reappears in *République* 272; *De Republica* 189 [2.2], and in discussions of the form of government best suited for each form of state that only a 'harmonic' balance or mixture of aristocratic and popular government is best for the lawful government of a monarchy. On the theme of sovereignty and government, see Tuck, *Sleeping Sovereign*; Sophie Nicholls, 'Sovereignty and Government in Jean Bodin's *Six Livres de la République* (1576)', *Journal of the History of Ideas* 80 (2019): 47–66. See also Ann Blair, 'Authorial Strategies in Jean Bodin', *The Reception of Bodin*, ed. Howell Lloyd (Leiden: Brill, 2013) 152.

Bodin thought, Aristotle might have seen that citizenship isn't really about the possession of civil rights – since, even rightless persons can (so long as they are 'free subjects') technically still be citizens. The only essential criterion in identifying a citizen is shared subjection 'under one and the same authority' [*esse sub unum & idem imperium subiecta*]. Indeed, if citizens of a state can be said to share anything at all, it is only this fact of 'free subjection' that differentiates the citizen from both the foreigner and the slave.[97] But beyond this essential requirement of common subjection, citizens needn't share anything else in common with each other, nor must citizens cultivate anything like civic friendship, civic culture, or mutual identity or recognition: 'Citizens may differ mutually from each other in their laws, languages, customs, religions, and the endless number of nations [*gentium*]' to which they can belong.[98]

Consider, then, the many things that citizens do *not* share with each other and, thus, is (purposely) left out of Bodin's ultra-minimal definition of citizen. There's no mention of shared bloodline, ancestry, language, custom, or even (especially striking in Bodin's era of religious violence) religion.

Nor must citizens share the same body of law. A state need not have one *ius civile*. It can have (so long as the sovereign permits it) many coexisting *iura civilia*, a point he illustrates with the legal pluralism characteristic of empires (what we might today describe as multinational states), such as that of the Ottomans and of the Romans, who freely used Greek laws and customs and allowed conquered peoples to keep their own customs while recognizing the *maiestatem Romani populi*.[99]

Above all, Bodinian citizenship didn't require attachment to any particular territory or homeland. As Bodin put it, a geographically scattered citizenry – 'however scattered their lands may be' – can still, in theory, be one state, 'provided they are controlled by the same authority'.[100]

The result was an astonishingly pluralistic conception of citizenship, one allowing pluralism of all kinds. So long as there was subjection under one common sovereign, Bodinian citizenship could be pluralistic along any number of dimensions – multinational, multilingual, multi-faith, and even potentially (to borrow from Will Kymlicka) multicultural.

Perhaps most striking is the remarkably *inegalitarian* quality of Bodin's theory of citizenship. Bodin makes no requirement that citizenship entail civil equality (that is, strict equality of civil rights). For him, civil inequality is entirely permissible, and even desirable, in the citizen-body of a Bodinian state. Of course, states

[97] *Methodus* 247.

[98] *République* 72; *De Republica* 48 [1.6].

[99] Bodin's target was Cicero whose definition of the state as kind of *societas* [an association or partnership made up of equals, *socii*] at *De Re Publica* 1.39 required, in part, shared consensus on law. Cicero's theory of state is referenced at *Methodus* 237–38. On the legal pluralism of the Turks and the Romans, see *Methodus* 238 and 249, respectively.

[100] *Methodus* 237–38.

(most likely, Bodin thought, a democracy) certainly *could* distribute civil rights on a principle of strict equality. But this was by no means necessary, as he developed in his theory of harmonic justice.[101]

Possession, or lack, of civil rights – 'honours' or 'privileges' as he, very revealingly, calls them – are not proxies for citizenship status: 'Privileges', he says, 'cannot make one a citizen. Only the mutual obligation of the sovereign to the subject can'.[102] And so, *civil status* (whether or not one is a subject of a state) can be entirely divorced from *civil rights*. As perverse as it may sound to the modern liberal ear, he is perfectly willing to admit that even disenfranchised rightless persons within the state (i.e. those without any privileges) are nevertheless technically citizens, so long as they are free subjects – 'second-class' citizens, no doubt, but still citizens. And that's because 'citizens are not to be defined by the greatness of their civil rights [*beneficiorum amplitudine definiendi*]'.[103] To the modern liberal theorist, Bodin would simply respond that there's just no good reason why *lack of civil rights* should be taken as evidence for *lack of citizenship*, which, in his view, was a separate juridical question.[104]

Losing Citizenship

Citizens are, at once, free and unfree. They are, on the one hand, free in status, free from the servile condition of slavery [*dominium*] under the power of a master [*seigneur*; *dominus*]. Yet, on the other hand, they remain bound by the obligations of political subjecthood, constitutive of sovereignty [*imperium*].

101 Bodin's theory of justice is, in large part, developed as a criticism of Aristotelian theories of what is *aequale*. Rejecting both the commutative justice modelled on arithmetic ratios (the *ius strictum* he characterized as democratic) and the distributive justice modelled on geometric ratios (justice he characterized as aristocratic), Bodin proposed instead a third concept of justice called 'harmonic justice', modelled on the harmonic ratio (the form of justice associated with monarchy). See also Michel Villey, 'La justice harmonique selon Bodin', *Archives de philosophie du droit* 15 (1970): 301–15; Simone Goyard-Fabre, 'Jean Bodin et les trois justices', in *Aequitas, Aequalitas, Auctoritas: Raison théoretique et légitimation de l'autorité dans le XVIe siècle*, ed. D. Letocha (Paris: Vrin, 1992). Johannes Kepler's political treatise in the *Harmonices Mundi* is a direct response to Bodin's theory of justice.

102 *République* 85; *De Republica* 56 [1.6].

103 *De Republica* 87 [1.6]: *qui plures habeant immunitates, magis cives quam caeteri sint appellandi.* The Latin text has a marginal citation to Book X of Pliny's *Epistles*.

104 Nor would he be likely to endorse recent theories of 'differentiated citizenship', as proposed in a body of theoretical scholarship by Will Kymlicka, *Multicultural Citizenship* (Oxford: Oxford University Press, 1995); Joseph Carens, *Culture, Citizenship, and Community* (Oxford: Oxford University Press, 2000); and Iris Marion Young, 'Polity and Group Difference', *Ethics* 99 (1989). While such theories of 'differentiated citizenship' are sceptical of liberal egalitarianism and argue instead for recognition of group memberships (whether linguistic, cultural, ethnic, or otherwise) in pluralistic societies, they nevertheless argue for group differentiation for egalitarian reasons. Moreover, group-differentiated citizenship is still measured in terms of the distribution of civil rights.

We have seen how, through manumission, a slave can be released from another's *dominium* to become a freedman. Could a citizen, on analogy to manumission, also be released from the political obligations of *imperium*?[105]

Bodin's answer was yes: there's nothing permanent or natural about *imperium* (just as there's nothing permanent or natural about *dominium*). And that is because all sovereign-subject relations are, in theory, ultimately artificial creations of will.[106] Whatever is wilfully made can always be wilfully unmade, including those political obligations tying subjects to the *imperium* of their sovereigns. If the political will is there, there's no reason why a sovereign couldn't also release subjects from their political obligations.

How such obligatory bonds are to be dissolved, however, was a separate, more technically difficult question. Could a subject simply renounce one's citizenship or abjure one's obligations unilaterally, or must a subject obtain permission first? Could foreign residence be taken as equivalent to loss of citizenship? Can one lose citizenship by committing treason or some other crime?

To address these questions, Bodin thought, we need to know, first, a little bit more about how one comes to be a citizen in the first place. As we've seen in Chapter 2, the sovereign-subject relationship of *imperium* ultimately was an obligatory bond, and so, Bodin felt he could apply the general principle of the *Nihil tam naturale* in the *Digest* which concerns the symmetrical structure of all obligations: all valid obligations are to be dissolved in the same manner in which they are originally contracted.[107] The same principle, Bodin thinks, applies for obligations between sovereigns and subjects. Dissolution of the sovereign/subject bond must somehow approximate the original constitution of that bond.

But that raises another question: how is that obligatory bond of allegiance originally constituted? He distinguishes as follows.[108] Some subjects are simply 'natural', in that they are born into subjecthood.[109] Others, however, are *assumpti* or *creati*: foreigners (or even naturally free persons) are 'made' into subjects, whether by conquest or by creating a new bond and admitting, even 'enrolling' (Bodin calls them *ascripti*), them into political membership – in other words, by naturalization.

Most remarkable is the essential function of mutual consent for such 'enrollment' to take place. For a prospective subject to be naturalized, one must not only voluntarily submit or 'subject oneself to another's sovereign power' [*se alterius*

[105] *République* 131; *De Republica* 84 [1.8] discusses the example of *lex Gabinia* of 67 B.C.E. which released Pompey from all legal and political duties, so that he was *omnibus civitatis suae legibus solutus* and *magistratuum omnium imperiis solutus*.

[106] In the case of natural-born citizens [*cives nati*], Bodin operates on a theory of tacit consent.

[107] D.50.17.35. Thus, *nudi consensus obligatio contrario consensu dissolvitur*.

[108] See Bartolus on D.41.3.15 and also Julius Kirshner, '*Ars Imitatur Naturam*', *Viator* 5 (1974): 313; Julius Kirshner, '*Civitas sibi faciat civem*: Bartolus of Sassoferrato's Doctrine on the Making of a Citizen', *Speculum* 48 (1973): 694–713; Peter Riesenberg, 'Citizenship at Law in Late Medieval Italy', *Viator* 5 (1974): 333–46. Bodin is following the Bartolist distinction between *cives ex pacto* and *cives originarii*.

[109] Bodin models this clearly on D.1.5.5.1, stating that, *ex iure gentium*, one acquires the status of the mother at the time of birth.

summae potestati subiecit], one also must be 'accepted' [*accipiatur*] by the receiving citizen-body, by formally being 'enrolled among the number of citizens' [*in numerum civium conscriptus*].[110] The same principle of mutual consent operates at the time of exit: since mutual consent creates the sovereign-subject bond, it can only again be 'by mutual consent' [*mutuo consenso*] between sovereign (or one of the sovereign's authorized agents: a court) and subject for any amendment to, or even dissolution of, that solemn bond.[111]

Requiring some formal expression of consent for a subject's release presented, Bodin thought, a safeguard against denaturalization (where forced exile, *proscriptio*, could be used as an arbitrary punitive measure) as well as a more equitable alternative to novel legal theories of how citizenship might be – without the subject's consent – lost or transferred.[112] Some of these novel theories[113] were actually being tested in French courts at the time that Bodin was developing his own theory of citizenship, and so, an added sense of urgency drove Bodin's argument (and a major reason why *République/De Republica* I, 6 reads much like a *consilium*).

One set of cases involved the so-called *droit d'aubain*, a feudal prerogative of the French crown entitling the cash-strapped monarch to confiscate the estate of deceased foreigners, whether or not they died intestate, thereby potentially devastating the inheritance rights of the deceased's heirs.[114] Who exactly counted legally as an *aubain* (*albinatus*; cp. '*alibi-natus*'), or 'foreigner', under the *droit d'aubain* was less clear and became a contentious matter that was litigated extensively in the early modern Parlements.

One celebrated test case litigated before the Parlement of Paris caught Bodin's attention, and he commented upon it in the *Methodus* and *République*. It involved a Frenchman, Pandolphe de Cenamy, who reportedly resettled in Venice and lived there for fifty years, until his death. Although he took up residence, remarried, and raised a family in Venice, it was unclear whether Cenamy was actually a Venetian citizen (and, therefore, an *aubain* in French customary law).[115] When the crown

[110] *De Republica* 48 [1.6]; *Methodus* 247. Bodin cites D.50.1.6; C.10.40.7; D.50.16.239.4.

[111] Bodin frames the mutual consent to acquire or change citizenship in terms of a *donatio inter vivos*, which requires consent from donor and donee: *Car tout ainsi que la donation ne vaut rien si le donateur n'a presenté, & le donataire accepté l'offre a luy faicte: aussi l'estranger n'est point citoyen ny subject du Prince estranger, & demeure tousiours subject de son Prince naturel*: *République* 51. Bodin also cites the Roman law rule making it illegal for one unilaterally to renounce or forsake one's native country. Turchetti 366–67: D.50.1.1–2; 50.1.6.

[112] *Distributio* fol. F, s.v.: *Poenale*, which lists *proscriptio* and *relegatio* as penalties available to the magistrate.

[113] D.50.1.20. Key sources for these theories include Baldus on C.6.37.2, s.v.: *habitus*; Bartolus on D.34.7.1; Paul de Castro on D.30.1.41, 49.14.3.2 (Turchetti 371); Alessandro Tartagni da Imola, *Consiliorum Alexandri Tartagni Imolensis* (Venice: Ex Officina Damiani Zenari, 1578) 4: fols. 22_{vo}–23_{ro} [4, *Consilium* 29], 5:fols. 40_{ro}–40_{vo} [5, *Consilium* 32].

[114] Wells, *Law and Citizenship in Early Modern France* 15–16. As I discuss in the Conclusion, the monarchy was drowning in sovereign debts and tried to find novel ways to raise revenue quickly to repay their creditors. Capitalizing on the *droit d'aubain* was one strategy.

[115] Bodin cites a Venetian law which says that fourteen years of residence qualifies one for citizenship: *République* 90; *De Republica* 59 [1.6].

attempted, through assertion of the crown's *droit d'aubain*, to expropriate Cenamy's heirs of their French properties, they filed suit which ultimately made its way to the Parlement to decide whether or not Cenamy actually was a foreigner and, thus, deprived of immunity from *droit d'aubain*.

Bodin reported the Parlement's judgment: 'By a decree made 14 June 1554, the court of Parlement ruled that a Frenchman [Cenamy], despite having lived abroad for fifty [*cinquante*; *quinquaginta*] years in Venice, nevertheless remained subject to the French king', and thus his heirs were still French and immune from arbitrary expropriation by the sovereign's claim of *droit d'aubain*.[116]

But it was Bodin's reasoning that was most striking. Even after fifty years of foreign residence, Cenamy retained his French citizenship, all because he had never 'expressly renounced it' [*patriam repudiasset*], whether before the king directly or before one of the king's courts.[117] The mere fact of residency abroad (even residency for long periods of time), by itself, can't alter the civic bond of obligation tying subject to sovereign, and for a simple reason: it would be grossly inequitable and prejudicial to both sovereign and subject.[118] Drawing upon Roman and canon law, Bodin rejected the sovereign's argument that residence abroad could be taken as signalling something like a legally valid, though tacit, consent to loss of citizenship.[119] Something as serious and potentially prejudicial as that should never be permissible by tacit consent. As he put it, 'tacit consent [*consentement taisible*; *tacita consensio*] can never be valid in a prejudicial matter [*chose preiudiciable*]', especially when it is entirely possible for 'one to express openly what one wishes, whether by words or by deeds' [*aperte quid velit verbis aut factis expresserit*].[120]

What this case (among the several others that Bodin discusses) also shows is that, so long as the conditions for expressing mutual consent between sovereign and subject are satisfied, there's no reason in principle why a bond of *imperium* can't be dissolved, in the same way that a bond of *dominium* can be dissolved via manumission. Had Cenamy expressed outwardly his intention to renounce citizenship and were it accepted by the sovereign (or an agent of the sovereign), he could have been released fully from all residual obligatory ties to the French sovereign and free thereafter to subject himself to another sovereign, including Venice.

[116] *République* 92; *De Republica* 60 [1.6]. The Latin has an apparent typo, dating the decision in '1584', which is not possible, given that the French text (published prior to 1584), already comments on the case. Other accounts report that Cenamy was in Venice for fourteen years. *Methodus* 248 briefly mentions the case.

[117] *De Republica* 60. Bodin also hints that one can lose citizenship by denaturalization or *bannissement perpetuel*.

[118] *République* 91–2 [1.6], citing Baldus on C.8.51.2 and on D.1.5.2; Bartolus on D.25.3.1.

[119] *République* 92 [1.6]; Turchetti 373, citing canonistic authorities on VI.5.12.5.reg.43, and D.11.1.11.4; 27.7.4.pr.

[120] *République* 92; *De Republica* 60 [1.6].

Sovereignty, Territory, and Extraterritorial Statehood

Bodin's political theory of the state intertwines what Annabel Brett has once described as the 'two competing narratives' of state.[121] The one narrative, of classical origin, imagines the state as a kind of association or body politic made up of citizens, a *societas civium* as Cicero once put it.[122] And, as we saw in Chapter 1, Bodin fundamentally saw the state in this way, as a kind of pluralistic association – *un corps parfaict de republique* made up of citizens, grouped in their families and corporate collegiate bodies, all united together as one *communauté civil* or *societas civilis*.[123]

There is another narrative of state, however, that visualizes the state as a hierarchical order of command and obedience, inspired ultimately by the Roman experience of imperial rule. Bodin also subscribed to this other vision which was expressed in the form of sovereignty and the relation of dutiful subjection it entailed.

Yet, while most early modern political theorists tried to disentangle these two narratives, Bodin deliberately sought to integrate them together into one grand unified theory of state.[124] What enabled Bodin to do so was his treatment of citizenship, by redefining the citizen, not so much as a bearer of civil rights and privileges, but as a special kind of subject – namely, a 'free subject'. Shared subjection under one common sovereign authority (and not the enjoyment of special privileges or civil rights) was what made any group of individuals a *universitas civium*. The concept of sovereignty, thus, did double-duty in Bodin's theory, not only by performing a 'commanding' function over duty-bound subjects, but also, at the same time, by performing a 'uniting' function; it was the sovereign authority which 'united all the members and parts, and all families and colleges into one civil body' [*qui unit tous les membres & parties d'icelle, & tous les mesnages & colleges en un corps*].[125]

There is, however, a third potential narrative of state that is conspicuously missing in Bodin's political theory – territoriality. As Lauren Benton observed, 'Bodin's sixteenth-century tract on sovereignty is notable for its utter lack of attention, and

[121] Brett, *Changes of State* 122.

[122] *De Re Publica* 1.49; cp. *Politics* 3.6, $1278^{b}10$–12; 3.9, $1280^{b}29$–$1281^{a}1$.

[123] *République* 14; *De Republica* 10 [1.2]. *République* 474; *De Republica* 327 [3.7].

[124] As Brett observes in *Changes of State* 131–32, the German publicist, Henning Arnisaeus, in *De Jure Majestatis Libri Tres* (Frankfurt: Typis Andreae Eichorn, 1610) 223–25 [2.1.1, §5], also attempted to blend these two narratives together, following the models of Aristotle and Bodin.

[125] Bodin doesn't deny, however, that individuals could come together on their own, whether out of natural sociability or some other natural desire for the company of others. But unlike Aristotelians and Ciceronians, Bodin denies that a natural spontaneous coming-together of people, simply by natural sociability or desire for happy fellowship with others, is sufficient to make a state. Without sovereignty, the most they can be is a loose association – variously, a *societas*, a *confoederatio*, a *universitas* – based on ties of friendship, but not on obligation.

even mention of, territory'.[126] It's not that Bodin was oblivious to the concept of territoriality. On the contrary, he was witness to the rapid process of territorialization and land reform that had already started taking place in the decades before Westphalia, as the practical problems arising from the hollowed-out remnants of feudal jurisdictions, increasingly mobile populations, and international commerce all added to the feeling that 'territory had to be re-conceptualized in relation to sovereignty'.[127] He specifically observed how the territorialization of law and politics reified political membership and authority, not only in the juridical terms of obligation owed to, and rights held by, sovereigns, but in the spatial terms of territoriality, whether one is physically 'inside' or 'outside' a territory, a physical space, demarcated by borders.

Bodin's sensitivity to matters of territoriality can be observed specifically in his treatment of concrete legal cases concerning technical questions of territorial or 'praedial' jurisdiction, especially jurisdiction over foreigners and over fiefs.[128] For example, Bodin cited a case litigated on appeal before the Parlement of Paris concerning the principle of international comity and extraterritorial jurisdiction. Here, a Venetian merchant sued and obtained judgment against a French merchant for contumacy, or contempt, in the Venetian courts.[129] But because the French defendant was physically located in France, the Venetian plaintiff was required to obtain formal letters from the Venetian authorities formally requesting the French authorities to enforce the Venetian court's sentence. The Parlement ultimately ruled in favour of the Venetian plaintiff and reportedly put into execution the foreign court's judgment, but without any retrial or reexamination of the facts established in Venice. Bodin disagreed with the Parlement's conclusion, arguing instead that judgments of foreign courts must not be enforced by domestic authorities without first holding a retrial and *de novo* examination of the facts.[130] Venetian jurisdiction, it seems, only goes so far as the seigniorial borders.[131]

[126] Lauren Benton, *A Search for Sovereignty: Law and Geography in European Empires, 1400 1900* (Cambridge: Cambridge University Press, 2009) 287. This is maybe a bit too extreme: in this respect, I agree with Sara Miglietti's remark on Benton's characterization of Bodin at 'Sovereignty, Territory, and Population in Jean Bodin's *République*': 18. Stuart Elden points out that, while Bodin rarely uses the Latin, *territorium*, he uses the French term, *territoire*, and the Latin, *fines*, in a number of places. Bodin also shows awareness of D.50.16.239.8, which supplies Pomponius' famous etymology of 'territory' from one's capacity to inspire fear or 'terrorize' [*terrendi*] those within one's borders [*intra fines*].

[127] Brett, *Changes of State* 170. Jordan Branch has suggested that one visible sign of this change was manifest in the technological advances in the early modern science of cartography which began to emphasize spatial boundaries, rather than spatial relations. Jordan Branch, *The Cartographic State: Maps, Territory, and the Origins of Sovereignty* (Cambridge: Cambridge University Press, 2013).

[128] Bodin sometimes refers to the feudal jurisdiction attached to fiefs, such as at *République* 398 [3.3]; 431–32, 436 [3.5].

[129] Notably not a matter of the law merchant or *lex mercatoria*.

[130] *République* 470–71; *De Republica* 325 [3.6]; *Stato* 2:240, citing the principle of D.48.3.6. Borrowing from the analysis of Ulrich Huber, *De conflictu legum*, Joseph Story, *Commentaries on the Conflict of Laws*, 3rd ed. (Boston: Charles Little and James Brown, 1846) 43 [2, §33] famously characterizes comity an 'imperfect obligation' between sovereigns. Ernest Lorenzen, 'Huber's De Conflictu Legum', *Illinois Law Review* 13 (1918–19): 397; Alan Watson, *Joseph Story and the Comity of Errors* (Athens, Georgia: University of Georgia Press, 2012).

[131] Borders or boundaries may not even be the conceptually appropriate term, insofar as Italian city-republics and principalities are concerned. Luciano Piffanelli, 'Crossing Boundaries: A Problem of

Elsewhere, in explaining the territorial limitations of magisterial jurisdiction, Bodin cites the Roman rule that the authority of provincial governors is active and valid only when he remains within the legally defined boundaries of the province. Such authority, however, ceases just as soon as the governor steps outside his province, at which point he becomes *privatus* without authority.[132] He similarly affirms the principle of criminal law, *ubi peccaverit, ibi puniendum esse*, establishing that criminal defendants are to be prosecuted, tried, and punished in the location where the offence had occurred.[133] And, partly for this reason, he endorses, on grounds of natural and divine law, the practice of extradition between states.[134]

Perhaps the closest that Bodin came to articulating something approximating a notion of territorial sovereignty occurs in *République* I, 9, where Bodin handled the topic of fiefs and the scope of feudal jurisdiction. One particular case capturing Bodin's attention concerned the Duchy of Lorraine, legally a fief of the Holy Roman Empire. Enclosed within Lorraine were minor seigneuries, such as the County of Apremont, which claimed a dubious title of sovereignty based on various grants of regalian prerogatives. Commenting on the constitutional question whether a new title of sovereignty could arise from subinfeudation, Bodin observed that the case of Apremont isn't sovereignty, but merely a limited jurisdiction.[135] The scope of the subvassal's jurisdiction (in this case, the Comte d'Apremont's), moreover, is limited to the territory [*territoire limité*] of the fief. Within those territorial limits, however, the count's jurisdiction extended equally over every individual subject [*particuliers*], as well as over all of them as a whole [*en general*].[136] Although his point isn't specifically about sovereignty, but rather about jurisdiction, it's not

Territoriality in Renaissance Italy', *Viator: Medieval and Renaissance Studies* 49 (2018): 245–75, suggests instead 'spheres of influence'.

[132] *République* 464; *De Republica* 321 [3.6], citing D.1.18.3 and 2.1.20; cp. *De Republica* 324. *République* 467; *De Republica* 323, citing D.42.1.15.1, indicates conversely how the provincial boundaries define the governor's obligation to carry out commands in his province if commanded to do so by Rome [*si hoc iussi*]. Bodin has a readymade answer to explain why jurisdictional boundaries can apply for magistrates, but not for sovereigns: sovereigns ultimately have complete control over where boundaries of provinces or lesser jurisdictional units are to be drawn. But in the relations between states, that is precisely the sort of unilateral boundary-making control they lack. One sovereign cannot decide for another sovereign, without consent, where an international boundary is to be drawn.

[133] *République* 466; *De Republica* 322; *Stato* 2:231 [3.6], citing Felino Sandeo on X.1.29.21; Panormitanus on X.1.33.16.

[134] *République* 471–72; *De Republica* 325 [3.6], against the *opinio communis* of Baldus, Odofredus, Alexander Tartagnus Imolensis, Fulgosius, Felino Sandeo, among others. However, Bodin acknowledges the duty of *non-refoulement* that innocent refugees seeking asylum must not be extradited and returned to tyrants, at 473.

[135] *République* 211 [1.9] concludes with the general point that *les Princes feudataires ne se peuvent qualifier Rois, ni les Ducs, Marquis, Comtes, Princes, user du titlre de Majesté*.

[136] *République* 185; *De Republica* 126–27; Turchetti 607 [1.9], citing D.50.1.30; 50.15.4.pr; Jean de Roussines Faure [Iohannes Faber], *In Iustiniani Imperatoris Codicem* (Lyon, 1550) on C.4.66.1, C.1.1.1; D.50.16.239.8; Marianus and Bartolommeo Soccini [Socinus], *Consiliorum seu Potius Responsorum*, vol. 1 (Venice: Apud Franciscum Zilettum, 1579) fol. 158_{ro}–158_{vo} [*Consilium* 86, §6]; fols. 215_{vo}–216_{vo} [*Consilium* 127]; Soccini, *Consiliorum seu Potius Responsorum*, vol. 2 (Venice: Apud Franciscum

difficult to see how the territorial quality of feudal jurisdiction could potentially be extended to imagine the territorial quality of sovereignty.[137]

Taken together, then, there is plenty of evidence to suggest that Bodin at least apprehended the theoretical possibilities of territorial statehood and sovereignty, modelled on the territorially limited jurisdiction of seigneuries, fiefs, and provinces, as well as the classical model of Roman provincial government. And yet, despite this territorializing trend, Bodin nevertheless chose to conceptualize the state in purely juridical terms as an interpersonal construction of obligation and rights, in a way that was not supervenient on territory. Bodin's definition of the state, as a *civium omnium coetus sub eiusdem imperii summa potestate*, makes no reference whatsoever to territory.[138] And that is because the only thing uniting the citizens of a state as one union is a sovereign, not territory or anything else.

This allowed, in theory, the possibility of a geographically scattered pluralistic state, as we saw in Chapter 1, a state made up of a heterogeneous citizenry with diverse customs, languages, and religions, all subjects under one sovereign. Bodin, of course, did acknowledge that, in practice, citizens of a state certainly could share more in common than just their sovereign. They might share the same laws and customs, in which case they would become a *civitas*. They might share the same creed or the same tongue. And they might even share the same permanent territory, in which case they would become an *urbs*.

None of these, however, were necessary for statehood, a point he developed with reference to the vast empires of antiquity. The Roman Empire, for example, was a heterogeneous state made up of conquered peoples, each with their own customs, scattered across the Mediterranean world. What made them all Roman and one state, however, was their subjection to one Roman emperor as their sovereign. Even the early modern empires of the Ottoman Turks, the Tartars, and the Spanish, whose boundaries [*finibus*] were marked by the 'course of the sun' [*solis cursus*], could be seen as one unitary state, solely on account of the unifying sovereignty of their sultans, khans, and kings.[139] Bodin's point was that states – and specifically the citizens making up states – do not need to share the same permanent territory or space. As he put it in the *De Republica*, states are not to be defined by their walls [*moenibus*], nor by the territorial space they enclosed.[140] Nor must the borders of

Zilettum, 1579) fols. 30_{ro}–32_{ro} [*Consilium* 169]; D.18.1.73; VI.1.16.7; Baldus de Ubaldis, *In Usus Feudorum Commentaria* (Lyon, 1550) on L.F. 1.5 [*Quibus modis feudum amittatur*].

[137] Cp. Bartolus on D.2.1.1, §15, on the categories, *iurisdictio sine territorio, territorium sine iurisdictione*, and the legal analogy of *iurisdictio* with *dominium*.

[138] *De Republica* 10 [1.2]. The corresponding passage at *République* 13 expresses the point as *l'union d'un peuple sous une seigneurie souveraine*.

[139] *De Republica* 10 [1.2]; cp. *Methodus* 238.

[140] *De Republica* 10 [1.2], likely a reference to Aristotle, *Politics* 3.3, 1276^{a}25–7.

a well-ordered state, as Bodin put it, be 'limited by swords', but only 'by justice' [*Reipublicae bene constitutae fines non gladiis . . . sed iustitia terminantur*].[141]

Why did Bodin omit territory from his theory of state? This was a deliberate choice. His chief aim, as Stuart Elden put it, was 'to separate out the polity from its mere location or population'.[142] In this respect, Bodin was motivated by a thorough-going anti-Aristotelianism.

> Aristotle defined the city [*la cité*; *civitatem*, citing *Politics* 3.9] as a company of citizens, [*une compagnie de citoyens*; *civium multitudinem*] who have everything necessary for living well. But he does not differentiate the 'state' from the 'city' [*République et cité*; *Rempublicam a civitate*] and insists that there can be no 'city' unless all citizens inhabit one and the same place [*en mesme lieu*; *uno et eodem loco*], which is absurd.[143]

It made no difference, for Bodin, *where* the citizens of a state were geographically located. The one and only thing that mattered, for Bodin, was the interpersonal obligatory bond of *imperium* tying sovereign and subject together – wherever they happen to be. As Bodin put it, even while the people of a state may be 'scattered across various locations' [*in diversa loca dissipari*], the state itself continues to exist as one whole.[144] This is what Bodin's commentary on the famous Cenamy case demonstrated. Pandolphe de Cenamy didn't become a foreigner, or *aubain*, simply by living abroad in Venice for many years, as the judges of Parlement ruled. Only a deliberate and lawful act by both sovereign and subject, mutually agreeing to dissolve the bond of obligation, could accomplish that.

This is why Bodin regarded terms indicating statehood, such as *république/respublica* and *cité/civitas*, to be chiefly juridical concepts [*mots de droit*], rather than terms, like *ville/urbs*, signifying a particular geographical territory or location [*cité est un mot de droit, qui ne signifie point un lieu, ny une place*].[145] In this respect, Benton notes that Bodin's theory was 'consistent with an early modern construction of sovereignty as spatially elastic. Because subjects could be located anywhere, and the tie between sovereign and subject was defined as a legal relationship, legal authority was not bound territorially'.[146]

[141] *République* 756; *De Republica* 560 [5.5].

[142] Elden, *Birth of Territory* 264.

[143] *République* 74; *De Republica* 49 [1.6]. The phrase, *une compagnie de citoyens*, is taken from Le Roy's translation of the *Politics* which likewise defines the *cité* as a *compagnie* and as a *communion de citoyens*, at *Politiques* 156 [*Politics* 3.3, 1276^{b}2], and *communion de bien vivre, par maisons & familles* at *Politiques* 168 [*Politics* 3.9, 1280^{b}34–35]. We can be reasonably sure that Le Roy is the source because Bodin's citation (on *République* 74, n.8: 'lib.3.cap.6.Politic'. = *Politics* 3.9) uses the older numbering scheme for the *Politics*. It is evident that much of Bodin's vocabulary in the French *République* is taken from Le Roy: Le Roy's translation of *Politics* 3.9 is especially strong evidence for this.

[144] *De Republica* 10 [1.2].

[145] Bodin's comment on the destruction of Carthage, at *République* 77 [1.6], is apposite: The *ville/urbs* was destroyed, but the *cité/civitas* survived.

[146] Benton, *Search for Sovereignty* 288.

Abstracted, then, from the outward physical limitations of geography, population, and space, Bodin's *respublica* emerges as a spatially fluid juridical construction. And for this reason, territoriality becomes merely a contingent, rather than an essential, element of sovereignty. Put another way, Bodin furnishes us only with a theory of 'personal sovereignty', but not a theory of 'territorial sovereignty'.[147] It would be a mistake, therefore, to impress upon Bodin's theory the modern Westphalian bias of territorial sovereignty.

None of this is to suggest that Bodin ignored the importance of territory as a matter of effective sound government. Permanent territory was, without doubt, a 'desirable attribute' for states, whose cultivation would be necessary for any well-ordered state to thrive.[148] And, as Sara Miglietti persuasively argues, much of the *République* was devoted to addressing these practical questions concerning the optimal size of a state's territory and strategies for achieving maximal territorial expansion even through war if necessary.[149]

Territories and boundaries, however, change over time, especially in the pre-Westphalian world that Bodin inhabited. Land belonging to one sovereignty today may belong to another sovereignty tomorrow. And so, he concluded that statehood mustn't be anchored in unfixed things like territory, but rather in only those things that can remain reliably permanent over time. Bodin found this in the mutual obligations tying sovereigns to subjects.

But even the most permanent of obligations can be dissolved. In the next chapter, we will investigate what Bodin designated to be the means by which obligations can be dissolved within a state: absolute power.

[147] Using Fitzmaurice's distinction in *Sovereignty, Property and Empire* 6.

[148] Elden, *Birth of Territory* 264.

[149] Miglietti, 'Sovereignty, Territory, and Population' 24–5. The political question of territory is directly related to the population demographics of the state, in a proportional relation. Miglietti's reading of *République* IV and V suggests territory is a practical question of government concerning the different challenges of governing a small state [*petit République*] and large state [*grand République*], as well as the different challenges of governing princely states and popular states.

4

Absolute Power: Law, Sovereignty, Absolution

Bodin's notoriety in political theory rests singularly upon his thesis that sovereignty is an 'absolute power'.[1] Our task in this chapter is to elucidate the function of 'absolute power' in Bodin's theory of sovereignty.

This is, in my view, an urgent task. If sovereignty is, as Bodin stipulates, an 'absolute power' and essential to the sovereignty of all states, it's only sensible to ask what this 'absolute power' actually is, if only to understand how constitutional democracies, which are also sovereign states, might also be said to have 'absolute power' as Bodin postulated. For political theorists studying Bodin, this may well be the most important question to investigate.

But strikingly, it never has been asked or investigated *de novo* in any thorough or systematic way in the modern scholarship on Bodin. Instead, commentators, almost invariably anglophone, have relied on the cursory assumption that 'absolute power' must reliably signal some non-trivial commitment to political 'absolutism'.[2] As a result, it has been all too easy to brand Bodin as a crude 'absolutist' and to dismiss his theory of sovereignty as a deeply unattractive relic of a bygone age, totally inappropriate for a modern politics built upon the basic constitutional axiom that institutions are to be designed to tame and contain the exercise of public power and protect the rights of individuals.

But that assumption of absolutism is precisely what must be questioned. Bodin's invocation of 'absolute power' wasn't supposed to be an affirmation of 'absolutism' (if, by 'absolutism', one intends to evoke connotations of, as John Locke put it, 'absolute arbitrary power' or the 'purely despotical power' of a 'conqueror over the subdued').[3] Indeed, it couldn't be, considering that the term, *absolutisme*, was coined

[1] *République* 122 [1.8]: *Souveraineté est la puissance absolue & perpetuelle d'une Republique.*

[2] This is the guiding assumption of the most important monographic study of Bodin's political thought in English, Franklin's *Jean Bodin and the Rise of Absolutist Theory*, which purportedly charts a sudden shift in Bodin's thought during the French Wars of Religion from a medieval 'constitutionalism' to a modern 'absolutism'.

[3] John Locke transformed the meaning of 'absolute power' (or 'absolute, arbitrary power') in his *Two Treatises of Government* 284 [II, §23] by effectively likening 'absolute power' to the 'purely despotical' power of a 'lawful conqueror . . . over the subdued' at 387 [II, §178] in war and domestic power of masters over slaves and fathers over children. Through Locke's influence, then, 'absolute power' became a convenient term capturing everything that liberalism would come to fear, as Judith Shklar once influentially suggested – the 'arbitrary power' of despotic slavemasters and the 'force without right' of monstrous tyrants: Judith Shklar, 'The Liberalism of Fear', in *Liberalism and the Moral Life*, ed. Nancy Rosenblum (Cambridge: Harvard University Press, 1989). But in doing so, Locke jumbled together

The Right of Sovereignty. Daniel Lee, Oxford University Press. © Daniel Lee 2021.
DOI: 10.1093/oso/9780198755531.003.0005

relatively recently in the history of ideas, in the aftermath of the French Revolution (it didn't even gain widespread currency until the nineteenth century). For Bodin, 'absolute power' wasn't 'absolutist'.[4]

We can be reasonably confident in this conclusion because Bodin himself was careful to disavow and preemptively dissociate himself from ideas of arbitrary rule that would eventually be associated with the term, 'absolutism'.[5] Bodin's trenchant criticism of despotic 'seigneurial' rule (exemplified in his day by Ottoman and Muscovite oriental despotisms) and his avowed preference for *droit gouvernement* (so-called because it is the form of rulership where a sovereign governs by impartial law [*lex*], rather than by the naked arbitrary will [*arbitrum*] of a *seigneur* or *dominus*, like a δεσπότης over a slave) shows just how much he valued the rule of law. His acknowledgement of sovereignty's democratic possibilities also underlined his strict view that 'absolute power' needn't take the form of an absolute monarchy.[6] Even constitutional democracies, in Bodin's view, have 'absolute power' and regarded it as constitutionally essential for an independent people to exercise democratic self-determination. And as we've seen in Chapter 2, Bodin insisted that, despite their 'absolute power', all sovereigns are nevertheless subject to the requirements of divine law, natural law, and the law of nations, a position which differed sharply from the radical lawlessness envisioned by the Decretalists who positioned the Pope above all laws, whether human, natural, or even divine.[7] When Bodin is compared against the canonists, it becomes pretty clear who the real 'absolutists' were.[8]

Still, Bodin stubbornly retained the notion of 'absolute power' in his political vocabulary. We are confronted, then, with an interpretive problem of the first order: what *was* absolute power really supposed to be in Bodin's theory, if not the arbitrary seigneurial rulership of tsars or sultans or the lawless force of brigands and pirates? What would a non-absolutist concept of absolute power look like?

what Bodin meticulously laboured to keep distinct in his theory of public law and state. The semantic transformation of 'absolute power' and 'absolute monarchy' in early modern English political thought is traced in James Daly, 'The Idea of Absolute Monarchy in Seventeenth-Century England', *Historical Journal* 21 (1978): 227–50 and, more generally, in Burgess, *Absolute Monarchy*.

[4] The category of 'absolutism' – like most '-isms' of political science such as 'socialism', 'capitalism', 'liberalism', and 'constitutionalism' – was an invention of modern French historical scholarship, introduced in the aftermath of the French Revolution to reinterpret the institutions of the ancien régime. One of the earliest uses of the term, *absolutisme*, is attributed to François-René de Chateaubriand, who used the term in his 1797 *Essai sur les revolutions*, over two centuries after Bodin's death. The historiographical point here is that Bodin could not possibly have used the term, 'absolutism', to signify the cluster of ideas it would represent in modern liberal thought.

[5] Bodin, *Apologie de Rene Herpin* fol. 4_{vo}; *République*, Epistola [sig. $b4_{vo}$].

[6] Lee, *Popular Sovereignty* 217–23.

[7] *République* 131; *De Republica* 84 [1.8].

[8] As Bodin put it at *De Republica* 102, the canonists were the most 'dangerous flatterers' [*perniciosis adulatoribus*] of princes and popes and their absolute powers. Among the canonists cited are Baldus and Angelus de Ubaldis, Panormitanus, Felino Sandeo, Raphael Fulgosius, Johannes Faber, Alexander Tartagnus Imolensis, Albericus de Rosate, Dino de Mugello, and Paris de Puteo.

A short, probably forgettable, passage in what remains perhaps the most-read chapter in Bodin's *République*, 'De la souveraineté' (1.8: *De iure maiestatis*) answers this question directly and gives a glimpse of what 'absolute power' was intended to be. For this purpose, Bodin pointed his readers to the medieval Decretalist, Sinibaldo Fieschi (c.1195–1254), who would become Innocent IV, one of the great legal minds of the thirteenth century whom Bodin called 'the most skilled jurist in both canon and civil laws' [*iuris utriusque peritissimus*].[9] It was Innocent IV who, in Bodin's words, 'best understood what absolute power [*puissance absolue*; *iura maiestatis*] is ... It is nothing but the power of overriding ordinary law [*deroger au droit ordinaire*; *ordinario iuri* [Bodin glosses this as *patriis legibus*] *derogare potest*]'.[10]

Innocent IV's observation on X.1.6.20 was inspired by a provision of the *Decretals* handling a technical aspect of canonistic regulations governing episcopal elections. But his main point extended this Papal 'plenitude of power' – *potestas absoluta*, as some canonists called it – far beyond the narrow administrative details of Church election law, empowering the Pope to dispense with and set aside rules of canon law governing all sorts of legal matters such as marriage law and monastic vows.[11] Ordinarily these rules were rigidly inflexible and had to be followed to the letter. An exception, however, was always made for the Pope who, by an exceptional exercise of 'absolute' power [*potestas absoluta*] – his 'authority to transcend his normal jurisdiction and executive authority' [*potestas ordinaria*] – could dispense with 'ordinary' rules of canon law. While binding for everyone else, the law was, in the Pope's hands, plastic and even soluble.

What Bodin ultimately found in Innocent IV's commentary was confirmation of his own thesis that sovereignty must include absolute power, understood strictly as the power of overriding, dispensing with, or setting aside ordinary positive legislation. There's a simple reason for this, as the Decretalists

[9] Innocent IV [Sinibaldo Fieschi], *Commentaria Super Libros Quinque Decretalium* (Frankfurt am Main, 1570) 49_{vo}–50_{ro} [Innocent IV on X.1.6.20, s.v.: *Ordinatione*].

[10] *République* 133; *De Republica* 86 [1.8]; cp. *République* 156; *De Republica* 102 [1.8]. Bodin targets the canonistic doctrine that private property can be legally seized by the Pope, contrary to natural law, by invoking *absoluta potestas*. Bodin characterizes the canonistic opinion as an illegal seizure 'by force and by arms' [*par force, par armes*; *vi & armis*]. In the French text, he describes the canonist view as *le droit du plus fort*, a phrase that will appear in Rousseau, *Social Contract* I, 3. Here, the French *République* specifies again that 'absolute power is nothing other than the power of derogating civil laws' [*le puissance absolue n'est autre chose que derogation aux loix civiles*]. Dan Edelstein has suggested that Bodin may have been the first to use this phrase in 'Rousseau, Bodin, and the Medieval Corporatist Origins' 18.

[11] Pennington, *Prince and the Law* 66–7 cites the discussion of Hostiensis. On the theology of absolute power, Oakley, 'Jacobean Political Theology', and Massimiliano Traversino Di Cristo, 'The Mediaeval Distinction of God's *Potentia Absoluta/Ordinata* as an Archaeology of the Early Modern Investigation of Power', in *The Theology of Potentia Dei and the History of European Normativity*, *Divus Thomas* 115 (Bologna: Studio Domenicano, 2012): 35–82; 'The Classic Age of the Distinction between God's Absolute and Ordered Power: In, Around, and After the Pontificate of John XXII', *Franciscan Studies* 76 (2018): 207–66.

acknowledged in their analysis of Papal plenitude of power: a Pope deprived of this absolute power to unmake or set aside the force of law would effectively be constrained by those very laws, a conclusion that would contradict the very point of sovereignty as a plenary power that is 'free from the force of the laws' [*legibus soluta*].[12] Borrowing from Innocent IV and repurposing the Pontifical theory of absolute power for his own theory of sovereignty, Bodin anticipated a central tenet of modern legal positivism: every independent legal system must have the 'derogatory' power of negative legislation – that is, the capacity to undo and annul its own positive legislation.[13]

Absolute power turns out, then, to be interwoven into the heart of Bodin's theory of law and legislation. Indeed, it is precisely for this reason that Bodinian sovereignty often is described specifically as 'legislative sovereignty'.[14] Legislation was the quintessence of sovereignty. Bodin specifies, however, that legislation has a double aspect, both positive and negative. Legislation isn't just about making new laws. It is also about *unmaking* existing laws. The effect of legislation, then, is both obligatory and permissive. It can bind and unbind.

Given its specifically juridical function, absolute power turns out to be a much more limited power than is typically appreciated: It is a power, *not* so much over men, but a power over the laws that govern men. Modern Legal Realists will perhaps argue that this is a bogus distinction without a real difference. But it *did* make a huge difference for Bodin. And we shall see why in this chapter.

Making and Unmaking Law: Bodin's Theory of Legislation

Bodin famously writes in the *République*:

> The principal right of sovereign majesty and absolute power consists principally in giving law to subjects in general without their consent.[15]

[12] For example, Hostiensis, *Summa Aurea* (Venice: Ad candentis Salamandrae insigne, 1570) fols. 232$_{vo}$–234$_{ro}$; 205$_{vo}$–218$_{ro}$ [on X.3.8.4; 2.28.4]. Bodin makes the same point at *République* 131; *De Republica* 85 [1.8]. Black, *Absolutism in Renaissance Milan* 11–12.

[13] Kelsen, *General Theory of Law and State* 268; Hart, *Concept of Law* 95–6.

[14] A notable example is the study of A. London Fell, *Origins of Legislative Sovereignty and the Legislative State*, 5 vols. (Cambridge: Oelgeschlager, Gunn and Hain, 1983). Fell's thesis credits Jean de Coras [Corasius], who taught civil law at, inter alia, Toulouse, as the source of many of the ideas that would be attributed to Bodin. Fell's narrow focus on Coras overlooks the broader influence of medieval legal science, and especially the centrality of canonistic jurisprudence.

[15] *République* 142: *Le poinct principal de la maiesté souveraine, & puissance absolue, gist principalement à donner loy aux subjects en general sans leur consentement*; *De Republica* 92: *Ex quibus efficitur summum ius maiestatis in eo potissimum versari, cum non modo singulis, sed etiam universis leges dantur, iisque imperator* [1.8]. Notably, Bodin's example in the very next sentence highlights the French monarch's power to have certain customs 'repealed' [*abolies*; *abrogatas*] without consent of the assembled Estates.

Legislation – the sovereign act of making and giving law to subjects, or, in a word, command [*imperium*] – was the essence of Bodinian sovereignty.[16] Everything a sovereign did, by right of sovereignty and in the official public capacity of a sovereign, was, according to this Bodinian theory, a legislative act – which is the same as saying a formal command addressed to all subjects.

Seeing the connection between legislation and sovereign command, Bodin made one of the most controversial and memorable statements in all of the *République*, which was his thesis that all the rights constitutive of sovereignty – that is, the various *droits* and *marques* of sovereignty – were ultimately and indivisibly reducible to this one sovereign right of legislation.

> This same power to make and unmake the law [*mesme puissance de donner & casser la loy*; *iubendae ac tollendae legis summa potestate*] includes all the other rights and marks of sovereignty, so that we can properly say that there is only this one mark of sovereignty, since all the others are included in this.[17]

According to this analysis, then, all the major sovereign rights, the *regalia maiora*, identified by Bodin – such as the right to declare war and conclude peace, the right of final appeal, the right to appoint and dismiss magistrates, and the right to grant pardons and other dispensations against the rigour of the law – were indivisibly bundled together and really just various 'legislative' acts, precisely because they were formal expressions of sovereign *imperium*.

[16] Earlier generations of American scholarship on Bodin – John Brown, Beatrice Reynolds, and Julian Franklin – have argued that defining sovereignty in terms of legislation was an 'absolutist' innovation in the *République*, marking a sharp break from an earlier, more moderate, more 'liberal' or 'constitutionalist' position in the *Methodus*, which allegedly prioritized other executive and judicial functions of sovereignty. This thesis has been thoroughly criticized in the literature which stresses the continuity from the *Methodus* to the *République*. Preston King, *The Ideology of Order: A Comparative Analysis of Jean Bodin and Thomas Hobbes* (New York: Barnes and Noble, 1974) 300–10; Lee, *Popular Sovereignty* 187; Tuck, *Sleeping Sovereign* 31–35; Sara Miglietti, Introduction, *Methodus ad facilem historiarum cognitionem*, ed. and trans. Sara Miglietti (Pisa: Edizioni della Normale, 2013) 31–48. An earlier body of French scholarship affirms this continuity thesis, Henri Baudrillart, *J. Bodin et son temps: Tableau des theories politiques et des idées économiques au XVIe siècle* (Paris: Librairie de Guillamin, 1853) 145; Roger Chauviré, *Jean Bodin, auteur de la République* (Paris: É. Champion, 1914) 271; Pierre Mesnard, Introduction in *Jean Bodin, La méthode de l'histoire: Traduite pour la première fois et presentèe* (Paris: Société d'édition 'Les Belles lettres', 1941) xvi.

[17] *République* 223; *De Republica* 155 [1.10]. This was a doctrine that would become central in shaping the theoretical debate on sovereignty for the following two centuries after Bodin. Hobbes, for example, accepted and restated Bodin's thesis, at one point in the *Elements of Law* 167, even citing Bodin by name (the only time he cited Bodin by name). Rousseau, by contrast, took aim directly at Bodin in the passage at *Basic Political Writings*, 154–55 [*Social Contract* 2.2] (as one of 'our political theorists unable to divide sovereignty'), arguing that 'acts of declaring war and making peace have been [wrongly] viewed as acts of sovereignty, which they are not, since each of these acts is not a law but merely an application of the law'. Part of the reason why we, reading Bodin in the twenty-first century, may have doubts about his thesis is because of the powerful influence of Rousseau on our thinking about what ought to count as proper legislation.

To make some sense of Bodin's theory of legislation, we need to begin first with the fundamentals of Bodin's theory of law and recall that what Bodin called 'law' [*loi*; *lex*] was simply the formal expression of a sovereign command:

> The word, 'law' [*loy*; *leges*], understood simply on its own without any embellishment, signifies the lawful command of a sovereign authority [*le droit commandement... qui ont toute puissance*; *recta summae potestatis iussa*], whether of one person, of the many, or the few [*de celuy ou ceux*; *sive unius, sive omnium, sive paucorum*], over others without exception. That law can either bind all subjects in general [*touche tous les subjects en general*; *omnes cives ... complectatur*], or a particular group of subjects [*en particulier*; *certe maximam civium partem*: 'privilege'], except for the one who gives the law.[18]

And, for this reason, Bodin famously defined law [*loi*; *lex*] as 'the command of a sovereign authority' [*summae potestatis iussum*; *sanctio seu iussum principis aut summae in republica potestatis*].[19]

One of law's definitive qualities was the very fact that it was 'posited' or enacted.[20] Positive legislation doesn't just appear out of nowhere, nor is it a permanently fixed

[18] *République* 216 (cp. 155); *De Republica* 150 [1.10]. Observe that 'privilege' [*privi-legium*] is a kind of positive legislation; it is the command of a sovereign authority addressed to, and binding on, one or several [*unius ... aut paucorum*], but not all, subjects, *République* 216; *De Republica* 150 [1.10]. It is, therefore, *ius singulare*, as at D.1.3.16, cp. *Distributio* fol. A, s.v.: *Lex Singularis*. Crucial to privilege was its 'derogatory' quality, in that privileges 'derogate from the force of an existing law' [*derogatur legi*] by partially cancelling [*pars detrahitur*] or nullifying the full force of a statute otherwise binding on others, D.50.16.102. Thus, 'all privileges are contrary to the laws' [*legibus contraria*], *République* 424; *De Republica* 296 [3.4]; on the deontic logic of privilege, Audun Stolpe, 'A Theory of Permission Based on the Notion of Derogation', *Journal of Applied Logic* 8 (2010): 97–113. Anticipating Rousseau's criticism of privilege, in *Basic Political Writings* 161 [*Social Contract* 2.6], Bodin characterized privileges as 'odious' and 'against the law', in part because the charters or letters-patent creating privileges contain language that grants are made in perpetuity and, thus, seem to shackle a sovereign's ability to revoke or cancel privileges, *République* 424; *De Republica* 296 [3.4], citing C.3.28.35, D.43.8.2.10, 1.3.14, 1.3.16; *République* 132; *De Republica* 85 [1.8], cited a case involving the Chancellor Michel de l'Hôpital who refused to seal the privileges granting a perpetual tax exemption to St. Maur des Fossez. They also divide a citizenry into the privileged and the unprivileged, necessitating Bodin's statement that 'privileges do not make one a citizen, but only the mutual obligation of the sovereign to the subject', *République* 85; *De Republica* 56 [1.6].

[19] *Distributio* fol. A, s.v.: *Sanctio*. Note that the sovereign is not the only legislator (only the 'sovereign' legislator), since subordinate government officials with a lesser degree of *imperium* – 'magistrates' – can also issue legally binding commands and create rules within the scope of their defined jurisdiction. These are not properly 'laws' but 'edicts' [*magistratus iussum*]. Cp. Bodin, *De Republica* 150–51 and *République* 216–7 on the variety of Latin words in Roman law meaning 'law' and the abuse of language in early modern legal theory. Bodin's caution might still apply to modern commentators on Bodin who fail to observe the semantic gap between the capacious meaning signalled by the modern English word, 'law', and the narrower meaning signalled by the French *loi* and the Latin *lex*.

[20] Although Bodin recognized the difference between *ius scriptum* and *ius non scriptum*, he seems to have assumed that a proper *lex* should take a written and published form. *République* 420–21; *De Republica* 293 [3.4] discussed the practical problem in French constitutional practice of assessing the obligatory force of legal commands in the form of *ordonannces* and *édits* that have not yet been properly 'enregistered' and published by the Parlement. Cp. *République* 146–48, 375, 387; *De Republica* 95, 261, 268 [1.8, 3.2], on Parlement's use of green wax with red and green silk ties on sealing and enregistering

feature of nature. A *lex* must be promulgated, authored, created, or (as Bodin prefers) commanded [*iussum*, as a verbal participle from *iubere*: to 'order' or 'command'] by a lawmaker with the competent legislative authority – that is, with the legal right and the standing – to do so, as we have seen in Chapter 2.[21]

In likening law to a command addressed generally to subjects, Bodin understood law to function as a kind of *binding-device*, in that its essential juridical effect was obligatory. Law obliges [*ligat*], whereas the absence of law releases [*solvit*]. Positive legislation, insofar as it is a command of the sovereign, binds subjects under a legal duty to φ (or $\sim\varphi$), as the sovereign's *lex* requires.[22] Like *obligatio* in private law, then, legislation addressed by a sovereign to subject functioned as a 'legal chain' [*vinculum iuris*] whose function was to bind and oblige [*ligare*] subjects to their sovereign by requiring them to perform specified legal duties or (as Bentham once put it) 'services'.[23] In this way, a subject is duty-bound to perform particular acts, 'services' required by the sovereign, in just the same way a debtor was thought to be duty-bound to perform particular acts as her creditor required: non-performance of one's obligation (whether to obey the sovereign's legislation, or to repay one's creditor) would result in some sanction – monetary damages, imprisonment, a pound of flesh.

Taken together, Bodin was deliberately connecting three different ideas together into one unified theory of sovereign legislation:

(1) lawmaking;
(2) command (or, to borrow from Benthamite legal vocabulary, 'imperation');
(3) placing of subjects under a specific legal duty (specifically, a legal duty of the *ius civile* arising from an *obligatio civilis*: see Chapter 2).

legislative documents to indicate their permanence, unlike edicts. Cp. *République* 410; *De Republica* 287 [3.4].

[21] However, *imperium* need not be the only form in which sovereignty is expressed. Citing the authority of Josephus, Bodin stipulates, in his reading of Scripture at *République* 393; *De Republica* 272 [3.3], that legislation originated with the Mosaic law. Before that point, however, Bodin thinks sovereignty could only be expressed in a non-statutory form, as an unmediated expression of sovereign will [*arbitrium*].

What makes a sovereign legislative authority 'competent' in the first place is a topic discussed earlier in Chapter 2. What the sovereign really has is the standing and the right to *demand* of its subjects performance of required acts. Instead of a 'command theory', Bodin's theory should be treated instead as a 'demand theory' of law. The concept of a demand-right based on one's *standing* to demand performance is explored in Chapter 4 of Gilbert, *Rights and Demands*.

[22] A command encompasses both requirements $O(\varphi)$ and prohibitions $O(\sim\varphi)$. Both have sometimes been grouped under the category of 'preceptive laws' [*leges praeceptiva*], because they require performance or non-performance.

[23] Jeremy Bentham, 'Power and Right' [Bentham Mss., UCL, Box 88a: 120–32, 'Exposition'], in *Bentham's Political Thought*, ed. Bhikhu Parekh (London: Croom Helm, 1973) 190–91. In the *Distributio*, Bodin recognizes that *lex* can perform both a *preceptive* function (by requiring or prohibiting actions) as well as a *permissive* function (by permitting a juridically defined space of free and licit actions). The source for this is likely D.1.3.7 and the *Decretum* Dist. 3, c.4. I will return to this preceptive/permissive distinction below.

All three elements, in Bodin's theory, go together and even entail each other. But clearly the most important element in this triad of ideas was the third, which was the *legal effect* of a positive sovereign command: making a new law was, effectively, the making of a new duty.

Bodin, thus, envisaged the legal system of a sovereign state – whether the law of Rome or the law of France – as a networked structure of sovereign-authored duties, the obligatory bonds by which subjects were tethered to their sovereigns. All legal systems, in Bodin's view, were really just intricate patterns of duties, which were, in principle, attributable to the handiwork and legislative craftsmanship of sovereigns.

What Bodin wanted to stress, however, was the point that these patterns of positive legal duties, as well as the laws which created them, weren't meant to be static. They were dynamic and can (even should) change substantially over time.[24]

Note, however, that legal change moves in both directions – in the direction of more laws as well as in the opposite direction of fewer laws. Just as a legal system changes by the introduction of *new* laws burdening subjects under new duties through *positive* legislation, so too can a legal system change by the repeal of *existing* laws thereby releasing subjects from duties through what (borrowing from Hans Kelsen) might be called *negative* legislation.

This negative legislative power of repeal is, of course, vital to any theory of legislation. Sometimes, the public weal requires the repeal of deleterious legislation. But it raises a key interpretive question: can such acts of repeal, which alter the structure and aggregate pattern of legal duties binding subjects, be characterized properly as 'legislation'? This has been the subject of an ongoing debate in modern jurisprudence. Needless to say, some of the most influential voices in the English command-theory school of jurisprudence, who, like Bodin, have characterized law as commands of sovereigns, have nevertheless been loath to characterize negative acts of repeal as legislation.

John Austin's analysis is canonical on this point. For him, the repeal of legislation isn't really legislation at all. It is, instead, merely the *negation* of legislation, which, in his view, isn't the same thing.

> Laws to repeal laws, and to release from existing duties, must . . . be excepted from the proposition 'that laws are a species of commands'. In so far as they release from duties imposed by existing laws, they are not commands, but revocations of commands. They authorize or permit the parties, to whom the repeal extends, to do or to forbear from acts which they were commanded to forbear from or to do. And,

[24] Lee, 'Unmaking Law' 279–87; *République* 575–76; *De Republica* 426 [4.3] distinguishes between first-order ordinary positive legislation and second-order fundamental laws [*leges quae ad statum Reipublicae pertinent*].

> considered with regard to *this*, their immediate or direct purpose, they are often named *permissive laws*, or, more briefly and more properly, *permissions*.[25]

A fundamental asymmetry between the making and unmaking of law (and, correspondingly, between obligation and permission), thus, undergirds the Austinian command-theory of legislation, wherein only the positive making of a new law – and thus, of a new duty – counts as genuine legislation. The negative unmaking of an existing law, by contrast, can't, according to Austin, be counted as legislation because its effect is just the opposite: it is *permissive*, instead of *obligatory*. Austin's analysis insists on a strict distinction between command and countermand.

What sets Bodin apart is how he handles this theoretical question, centuries before Bentham and Austin. To wit: sovereign acts of repeal – those negative countermanding acts of 'de-imperation', whereby a sovereign *unmakes* law and, consequently, releases [*absolvit*] subjects from preexisting legal duties – *are* acts of legislation. Even if the juridical effect is, as Austin points out, permissive by unbinding and releasing subjects, Bodin insists they still should count properly as legislation.

Command and countermand, in Bodin's interpretation, are thus juridically equivalent. And the reason is this: unmaking law by negative countermand, just like the making of new law by positive command, directly alters the structure of duties under which subjects are bound.[26] Indeed, unmaking law, Bodin insists, is as much an essential, though typically overlooked, aspect of legislation as the making of new law:

> Also included in this power of making and unmaking the law [*puissance de conner et casser la loy*] is the power of its declaration and correction.[27]

Yet, the negative power of unmaking law is essential. Without it, the theory of legislation – and, by implication, of sovereignty – is incomplete.[28]

[25] Austin, *Province of Jurisprudence Determined* 32. It should be remembered that Austin studied Roman law in Germany, and the principal ideas that informed his command theory doctrine are ultimately of civilian origin.

[26] Bodin has thus anticipated the Hohfeldian incident of the legal 'power'.

[27] *République* 223; *De Republica* 154–5 [1.10]: *Cuius autem potestatis est legem iubere, eiusdem est abrogare, derogare, obrogare, subrogare*; cp. *République* 131, 134, 151. *De Republica* 85, 87, 98 [1.8]. The marginal note refers to the Roman law authorities, C.1.14.1, 1.14.3, 3.1.8, D.1.4.1, 37.5.6. On 'derogation' and 'abrogation', D.50.16.102. Bodin may be targeting Cicero, *De Re Publica* 210 [3.33], where Cicero declares that a 'true law' [which is defined as *recta ratio naturae congruens*] cannot be altered, partially repealed, or entirely abolished [*nec obrogari ... neque derogari ... neque tota abrogari*].

[28] Carl Schmitt, in his reading of Bodin, recognized this point in *Political Theology*: 'The authority to suspend valid law – be it in general or in a specific case – is so much the actual mark of sovereignty'. *Political Theology: Four Chapters on Sovereignty*, trans. George Schwab (Chicago: University of Chicago Press, 2005) 9.

Why incomplete? Bodin proposes a thought experiment. Suppose a prince is empowered to enact new positive legislation, but *disempowered* from amending or repealing existing legislation – say, by a solemn oath requiring princes to swear to keep and uphold the laws.[29] Could such a prince still be said to be sovereign, despite this legislative disability? Bodin doesn't think so: 'The prince who swears to keep [unchanged] the civil laws either is not sovereign, or else becomes a perjurer [*pariure*] if he violates his oath, which a sovereign prince will have to do in order to annul, change, or correct the laws'.[30] A prince who is limited in this way simply indicates that sovereignty rests elsewhere, and that, more likely, the state's constitution was aristocratic or democratic in form.

The problem wasn't unique to monarchies. Oligarchies and democracies, where sovereignty resides in a collective body of citizens rather than in one individual, also could potentially diminish and even forfeit their right of sovereignty through burdensome constitutional devices (for example, by onerous supermajority requirements for amendment) entrenching legislation in perpetuity, thereby binding not only themselves in the present, but also their future selves. While this constitutional logic of entrenchment is intended to respond to the fear of democratic majorities, as one often finds in modern defences of constitutional democracy, it potentially threatens to undermine the very sovereignty that made popular rule possible.

Bodin illustrated this point by way of a crucial moment in Athenian constitutional history which he described as one of the causes of the Peloponnesian War – the enactment of the Megarian Decree.[31]

> The Peloponnesian War started because of a law [*édit*; *Atheniensium lex*] enacted by the Athenians, which prohibited Megarian ships from docking in the port of Athens. The Megarians complained to their ally (the Spartans), arguing that the law of nations had been violated [*outrage contre le droit des gens*; *iura gentium violari*]. The Spartans subsequently dispatched an ambassador to Athens, requesting that this law be repealed [*lex abrogaretur*] at once. Pericles, who was then said to be the supreme authority in Athens by permission of the people, responded to the ambassadors that, by ancestral custom, Athenian laws are irrevocable [*immutabiles*], once approved by the people and published.[32]

[29] *République* 144; *De Republica* 93 [1.8]. Bodin's comment on Pliny, who observes Trajan's oath to keep the laws, suggests that this was merely customary and entirely supererogatory, in order to serve as an 'example of scrupulous observance'. Trajan remains *legibus solutus*, even though he swears this oath. The words of Trajan's oath, thus, have no performative effect in transforming his exemption from the laws.

[30] *République* 145; *De Republica* 94; Franklin 27 [1.8].

[31] The Megarian Decree was an economic sanction prohibiting commerce between Athens and Megara. Bodin cites two separate accounts of this episode, one from Thucydides, *History of the Peloponnesian War* 1.139–41, the other from Plutarch, *Life of Pericles* 29.4–30.1.

[32] *République* 146; *De Republica* 94–95 [1.8].

For Bodin, Pericles' reply, essentially suggesting that his hands were tied by custom, was a lame excuse. If it were true, it would mean the Athenian people could no longer be sovereign, since they would be bound by their own laws.

But no law is really perpetual or irrevocable; it only appears so when those with legislative authority continuously make the free political choice to leave the laws untouched. But nothing legally stopped Pericles or the Athenian people from repealing the Decree.[33] Pericles could have, if the political will was strong enough and if he so chose, formed a democratic majority to revoke the original Megarian Decree.[34] His refusal to do so was a deliberate political choice.

Taken together, disabling sovereign princes and peoples from amending or repealing their own laws effectively entrenches and hardens legislation, immunizing them from change, so that they become perpetual and immutable. The problem with such putatively immutable laws, however, was their implication for sovereignty. Such perpetual laws, were they really to exist (Bodin didn't believe they did), would essentially nullify and disable the right of sovereignty, for it would suggest that there were some first-order positive laws which sovereigns cannot touch and over which sovereigns have no power to change. Of course, it is entirely within a sovereign's right *voluntarily* to refrain from amending or even repealing a law. It may even be good public policy to refrain from changing the laws too often, as Bodin intimated at one point.[35] But to deny to a sovereign the legal ability and right to change – or even unmake – its own law is, thus, to deny its very sovereignty, precisely because sovereignty is constituted by that very 'absolute' power, whether exercised or unexercised, to make and unmake the laws. It would render a sovereign, who is supposed to be master *over* its laws, instead a slave *to* its own laws.[36]

[33] *République* 148; *De Republica* 96 [1.8].

[34] This is consistent with the account given in Thucydides, *History of the Peloponnesian War* 1.67, 1.139–40. His own rejoinder, at *République* 148; *De Republica* 96 [1.8], discusses the Athenian γραφη παρανομων, a form of action to prosecute those proposing an unconstitutional law, and invokes Plutarch. Isnardi Parente, *Stato* 1:383a–b, proposes the sources to be Plutarch, *Pericles*, in *Lives: Pericles and Fabius Maximus, Nicias and Crassus*, vol. 3, Loeb Classical Library 65, trans. Bernadotte Perrin (Cambridge: Harvard University Press, 1916) 106–7 [37.2], and Cicero's *Letters to Atticus*, vol. 1, Loeb Classical Library 7, ed. and trans. D.R. Shackleton Bailey (Cambridge: Harvard University Press, 1999) 140–41 [*Ad Atticum* 23.2–3]. On the γραφή παρανόμων in Athenian procedure, see Melissa Schwartzberg, 'Was the *Graphe Paranomon* a Form of Judicial Review?' *Cardozo Law Review* 34 (2013): 1049–62; Martin Ostwald, *From Popular Sovereignty to the Sovereignty of Law: Law, Society, and Politics in Fifth-Century Athens* (Berkeley: University of California Press, 1986) 125–29, 135–36; Josiah Ober, *Mass and Elite in Democratic Athens* (Princeton: Princeton University Press, 1989) 95–6.

[35] In Lee, 'Office Is a Thing Borrowed' 418–19, I suggested that there are 'transaction costs' associated with legislative change. While sovereigns may have the right to change the laws, they must also weigh the costs associated with the exercise of that sovereign right. It is much better policy, Bodin concludes, to 'endure' an unjust law so that it loses its force 'little by little' [*peu à peu*] than to 'break it by sudden violence'. *République* 577 [4.3].

[36] Mario Turchetti, 'Une question mal posée: la qualification de perpétuel et irrévocable, appliquée à l'Édit de Nantes de 1598', *Bulletin de la Société d'Histoire du Protestantisme Français* 139 (1993): 41–78; 'Nota su Bodin e la tirannide: il diritto di revoca e gli editti irrevocabili', *Il Pensiero Politico* 30 (1997): 325–338.

In Bodin's view, then, this sovereign ability to unmake law is essential to his entire theory, precisely because this, more than anything else, is what ensures that a sovereign authority can't be enslaved or limited by laws of its own making. What emerges from Bodin's theory of legislation is a principle of legislative symmetry, in which *positive* acts of making new law mirror *negative* acts of unmaking law.[37] Because both types of legislative acts effect changes in the overall pattern of legal duties burdening subjects, whether by binding [*ligandi*] or unbinding [*solvendi*] them, Bodin concludes that the right of sovereignty itself correspondingly consists of both a positive (obligatory) and a negative (permissive) aspect. And he often specifies this double aspect of a sovereign's legislative power in the way he spells out the juridical essence of sovereignty as the power of making – *and unmaking* – law.[38]

Absolute Power as the Power of Release

A sovereign's command and countermand – or, equivalently, the making and unmaking of law – are, thus, meant to be paired inseparably together in Bodin's theory of legislation. So are the corresponding juridical effects of legislation – the binding [*ligandi*] and unbinding [*solvendi*] of subjects resulting, respectively, in legal obligations and legal permissions.

But even having identified this juridical symmetry, Bodin nevertheless placed special priority on the negative aspect of repealing or 'unmaking' law, and that is because the sovereign's ability to emend or unmake any of its laws was the definitive aspect of sovereignty. Given this distinctive quality, Bodin introduced – and, actually, repurposed – a specific term of canon law, the priestly *potestas absolvendi*, to designate this negative power of unmaking law and releasing subjects from anterior legal duties. That term was 'absolute power' [*puissance absolue*; *potestas absoluta*].[39]

Bodin is (in)famous for having defined sovereignty as 'absolute power'. In what is probably the most famous sentence in his entire corpus he defined sovereignty as *la puissance absolue & perpetuelle d'une République* – 'the absolute and perpetual power of a state'.[40] Bodin points out here that one of the essential qualities of sovereignty is its *puissance absolue*, a term that is typically translated into English as

[37] Lee, 'Unmaking Law' 274.

[38] *République* 131: *qu'ils puissent donner loy aux sujects, et casser ou aneantir les loix inutiles pour en faire d'autres*; *De Republica* 84 [1.8]: *Non modo singulis sed etiam universis leges dare, et latas abrogare: quod ab eo fieri non potest, qui alterius iussis ac imperiis teneatur*; cp. *Methodus* 234: *leges iubere et tollere*.

[39] There are some instances where Bodin uses *puissance absolue* to indicate a preterlegal *patria potestas*, such as at *République* 36 [1.4].

[40] *République* 122 [1.8]. The corresponding passage in *De Republica* 78 uses the more legalistic expression, *potestas legibus soluta*, but elsewhere he uses the canonistic term, *potestas absoluta*, and often with direct reference to canonistic sources, especially Panormitanus.

'absolute power'.[41] This is, needless to say, a troublesome term. 'Absolute power', Lord Acton once famously declared, 'corrupts absolutely', and Bodin's conspicuous invocation of this power has led so many commentators to conclude that Bodin must have been some kind of 'absolutist', and, thus, an arch-enemy of those political values represented in modern doctrines of liberalism, constitutionalism, and the rule of law.[42]

I don't believe that was Bodin's intent. Most likely, Bodin acquired this reputation through the work of his most ardent early modern readers – Michel de la Serre, James VI/I, Pierre Grégoire, William Barclay, Robert Filmer, Thomas Hobbes, Jacques-Bénigne Bossuet – whose genuine absolutist and royalist commitments led them creatively to repurpose and exploit Bodin's theoretical writings on absolute power for royalist polemical purposes favouring 'absolute monarchy' over 'mixed' or 'limited monarchy'.[43]

Consider, first of all, the kind of power this 'absolute power' was supposed to be. It is a power, *not* so much over men, but a power over the laws that govern men. It was simply the higher-order power of a sovereign to annul, repeal, rescind, revoke positive legislation and, therefore in effect, to release subjects from prior legal duties. Bodin, who used a more antiquated Ciceronian vocabulary, expressed the same idea as the power of 'derogation', 'abrogation', 'obrogation', or 'subrogation' of an existing statute or custom.[44] Every legal system, if it is to remain independent and autonomous, requires absolute power, for the simple reason that legal reform and change necessitates the ability to unmake law.

Before proceeding any further, though, we need to consider a point about language: why did Bodin choose to call it 'absolute' power, a term that has led generations of commentators to conclude that Bodin must have been a prophet of 'absolutism'? The answer, I think, requires us first to examine more closely the word, 'absolute', itself – as it functioned in Bodin's French *absolue puissance* and in the Latin *potestas legibus soluta* and *potestas absoluta*.

The English word, 'absolute', masks an important linguistic feature that is far easier to observe in Latin and French, which is that the word, 'absolute', isn't properly an adjective; it is a verbal participle.[45] 'Absolute' shares a similar characteristic with other related words such as 'dissolute', 'resolute', 'definite', and 'requisite',

[41] Knolles, *Commonweale* 84.

[42] John Emerich Edward Dalberg-Acton [Lord Acton], 'Letter of Lord Acton to Bishop Creighton, 5 April 1887', in *Historical Essays & Studies*, ed. John Neville Figgis and Reginald Vere Laurence (London: Macmillan and Co., 1907) 504.

[43] On Bodin's influence on early modern absolutists, see Salmon, *French Religious Wars*; Oakley, 'Jacobean Political Theology'; Sommerville, 'English and European Political Ideas': 168–94; Salmon, 'The Legacy of Jean Bodin': 500–22; Burgess, *Absolute Monarchy and the Stuart Constitution*; Lloyd, *Reception of Bodin*; Evrigenis, 'Sovereignty, Mercy, and Natural Law': 1073–88.

[44] *De Republica* 154–5, referencing Cicero, *De Re Publica* 3.22; *De Inventione* 2.54.134. D.1.3.32, 50.16.132.

[45] *Absolutus* is the participle of *absolvere* (and ultimately, *solvere*). *Absous* (as in *République* 131: *dispense et absous de toutes les loix, ordonnances et coustumes*) is derived from the verb, *absoudre*.

in that, despite appearances, they function as verbal participles. To wit: just as 'dissolute', 'resolute', and 'requisite' are derived, respectively, from transitive verbs 'to dissolve', 'to resolve', 'to define', and 'to require', so too is the word, 'absolute', also derived from a transitive verb, 'to absolve'. The same pattern is found in Latin, where *absolutus* is the verbal participle derived from *absolvere* and, ultimately, from the transitive verb, *solvere*, a term of monumental importance in medieval law and theology.

What is the meaning and significance of this verb, *solvere*? We've already encountered it in connection with the law of obligations. The classical image suggested by the term is loosening, untying, and releasing someone from some bond or fetter. The bond might be a physical one, like the iron chains [*vincula*] constraining a prisoner.[46] (Indeed, *ab-solutio* in Roman court procedure is the term for acquittal, to signify release from the constraint of a sanction like imprisonment.)[47] The bond could also be abstract, like the artificial chains of obligation, the *vincula iuris*, that were said to bind [*ligare*] debtors to their creditors. Another related signification of *solutio* is payment, as when a debtor pays off [*solvit*] a debt owing to a creditor.[48]

Chains and debts, however, were not the only bonds from which one might be 'released' [*solvitur*]. The language of release was central to the Catholic theology concerning the bond of sin and, more specifically, the means by which one might be released [*solvitur*] from sin, just as one is released from debt. Absolute power, in this context, was specifically a priestly power, the 'power of releasing someone from the bond of sins' [*potestas absolvendi a peccatis*], a power lawfully wielded only by priests as confessors sitting *in foro interno*.[49] Even Reformation theologians in Bodin's lifetime framed the doctrine of original sin specifically in terms of a bond, from which a sinner, like a debtor, could also be pardoned and released [*solvitur*], but with a twist: just as a debt could be repaid to a creditor and 'satisfied' by a specially designated third-party, rather than by the original debtor, so too could the bond of sin, requiring a 'payment' in blood, be satisfied by an 'anointed' third-party to stand in for the sinner and remit payment [*solvit*] vicariously to satisfy the original blood-debt.[50]

[46] And, for this reason, *solvere/solutio* has often been connected to a sense of liberation. Indeed, *solutio*, which literally is the paying-off or discharge of a debt obligation, has been described by Bodin as a *liberatio obligationis*. *Distributio* fol. D shows that Bodin was using the various forms of discharge, catalogued under the title, *De solutionibus et liberationibus* (D.46.3) in the *Digest*, as a principal source in illustrating performances or releases from debt obligations.

[47] Cp. *Distributio* fol. E: s.v. *Sententia*: *Absolutoria*. Bodin comments on the A.C.N.L. (= *Absolvo, Condemno, Non Licquet*), the three possible verdicts in Roman criminal trials, at *Methodus* 264 and *République* 433; *De Republica* 301 [3.5]. Cp. *Distributio* fol. F, s.v. *Sententia*, where Bodin observes that judicial sentence can only be either *absolutoria* or *condemnatoria*.

[48] Inst. 3.13.pr. Bodin is more explicit in the *Distributio*, where he defines *solutio* as a *liberatio obligationis*.

[49] Decock, *Theologians and Contract Law* 89.

[50] The Vulgate uses *solvere* in a number of key verses: Matthew 5:17–18 (Christ fulfilled, but did not abolish [*solvit*] the law); Mark 11:4 (the disciples releasing a bound colt); Ephesians 2:14–15 (Christ

For his part, Bodin takes no clear position in these theological debates, but he questions the absolute power that, it seems, the priesthood has arrogated unto itself. His late writings on theology explore some of these aspects of absolution and the priestly absolute power to pardon and release from sin. In the *Colloquium Heptaplomeres*, Bodin's last and perhaps most controversial work on theology, for example, one of the interlocutors in the *Colloquium*, the Jewish Salomon Barcassius, declares that 'nothing seems more detestable ... than for the priests of the Roman church to claim the power of pardon for sins or to forgive [*ignoscere*] those who confess their sins, since this is fitting for immortal God alone in behalf of the right of His sovereignty [*pro iure suae maiestatis*]'.[51] Salomon's criticism is directed at the medieval doctrine of 'the power of the keys', the Scriptural source used to justify the power of priests – and ultimately the Papal *plenitudo potestatis* – to pronounce absolution in the Tridentine liturgy, which is summarized by the Catholic Paulus Coronaeus: 'Christ most openly bestowed this power upon His disciplines so that whatever things they might bind or unbind [*vincirent et solverent*] on earth the same would be unbound and bound [*soluta et colligata*] in heaven'.[52] The Calvinist interlocutor, Curtius, however, responds with a typically anticlerical criticism of this reading of Scripture: 'I do not know why the Roman priests have twisted the words for "binding" and "unbinding" [*ligandi et solvendi*] to mean the abolition of sins [*scelerum abolitionem*], unless they thought they would be more important if they took possession of things which were communicable to no creature according to the right of divine sovereignty [*in iure divinae maiestatis*]'.[53]

One can, thus, be released [*solutus*] from chains, from debts, and from sins. Bodin extended this line of reasoning to one more bond, the most important bond from which one can be released – positive legislation [*loi*; *lex*]. I mentioned earlier that Bodin thought of law as a kind of abstract bond or chain, a *vinculum* whose practical function was to tie [*ligat*] subjects to sovereigns. The irresistible image for Bodin pictured subjects, duty-bound to obey their sovereign's commands, to be not unlike prisoners, debtors, and even sinners. And just as prisoners were bound by iron chains, tethering them to their taskmasters, and just as debtors were

breaking [*solvens*] down walls separating Christians). Colossians 2:14 is also noteworthy in the metaphor of debt-cancellation. Most important, however, is Matthew 16:19, 18:18, which documents Christ's commission of Peter. This notion of vicarious atonement is the subject of an interesting theological work, *De Satisfactione*, by Grotius who, in part, uses legal concepts drawn from the Roman law of obligations to argue against the controversial 'Socinian' doctrine (after theologian Faustus Socinus, a grandson of the Bartolist, Marianus Soccini) that Christ's suffering and death was unnecessary for the atonement. The theological controversy is studied in Debora Shuger, *The Renaissance Bible: Scholarship, Sacrifice, and Subjectivity* (Berkeley: University of California Press, 1994). Socinianism has been the topic of several recent studies such as Sarah Mortimer, *Reason and Religion in the English Revolution: The Challenge of Socinianism* (Cambridge: Cambridge University Press, 2010).

[51] *Colloquium* 456 [347].

[52] This is a reference to Christ's commission of Peter in Matthew 16:19 and 18:18.

[53] *Colloquium* 456; cp. *De Republica* 98 [1.8]: *Qui a Pontifice maximo legibus divinis solutus sit, huic apud Deum immortalem satis esse.*

bound by moral chains of obligation, tethering them to their creditors, so too were subjects bound by legal chains, tethering them to their sovereigns.[54] Dissolving this obligatory chain calls for a solvent that only sovereigns may use – through negative legislation.

Forms of Unmaking Law: Abrogation and Derogation

Absolute power then just was the sovereign's negative power of unmaking law. But it was the juridical effect of this negative power that really mattered for Bodin. Through a sovereign's assertion of absolute power, subjects, whether individually or collectively, can be released and freed from legal duties (or, in other words, they can be *legibus soluti*). What really is 'unmade' by absolute power is the obligatory force of some law or legal norm, which a sovereign, or an authorized agent (such as a judge), can deactivate, whether partially or in full.[55]

This absolute power could be asserted in a variety of ways. One direct and obvious way, of course, was simply by 'abrogation', the formal legislative repeal of some existing *lex* or legal norm in full.[56] Repealing a law immediately dissolved the bond of obligation tying all subjects under a legal duty to perform (or forbear) some specified act, thereby releasing them.[57]

This absolute power of emending or even abrogating any of its own laws [*leges emendantis ... legibus solventis*] was entirely within the right of a sovereign and, for Bodin, the quintessence of its sovereignty.[58] In principle, it could be asserted (or unasserted) anytime by a sovereign, as it pleased, so long as it was formally expressed legislatively as a 'contrary law expressly repealing' [*loy contraire portant derogation expresse*; *nisi contraria lege ac singulari derogatione sublata fuerit*] some existing law.[59] Ideally, the power was intended specifically to be used as a corrective,

[54] Hobbes uses a similar imagery depicting civil laws as 'bonds' or 'chains' in *De Cive* 156 [14.3]; *Leviathan* 147.

[55] *République* 420–21; *De Republica* 293 [3.4].

[56] In principle, any and all positive legislation can be repealed by 'absolute power'. Bodin, thus, disallows any notion of an 'immutable' or 'perpetual' law or legal entrenchment devices, immunizing laws from amendment or repeal.

[57] Releasing a subject from a legal duty *doesn't* necessarily mean that the subject is released from subjecthood; it is *not* a return to natural liberty of the state of nature. In Bodin's view, one can be a subject to a sovereign, even while being released from *all* legal obligations. This is illustrated with the example of the Emperor Augustus, at *De Republica* 84–5 [1.8] who, Bodin claims, was *legibus omnibus patriae legibus in perpetuo solutus*, yet remained technically a subject of the Roman state. Had Bodin known Bracton, he might have considered Bracton's own example in making the same point: the 'singular privilege' of Mary who was *legibus soluta*, by virtue of Immaculate Conception. Gaines Post, 'Bracton as Jurist and Theologian on Kingship', *Proceedings of the Third International Conference of Medieval Canon Law, Strasbourg, 1968*, ed. Stephan Kuttner (Rome: Biblioteca Apostolica Vaticana, 1971) 123–9.

[58] *Distributio* fol. A, s.v.: *Ius sine sanctione:Aequitas.*

[59] *République* 36; *De Republica* 24 [1.4], cp. C.8.52(53).2.

to repeal outdated laws still on the books, especially laws and customs deemed to be inequitable.[60]

Bodin supplied numerous examples of the sovereign assertion of absolute power, aimed at repealing and abrogating laws and customs. Not surprisingly, many of his examples were taken from Roman legal history. He frequently cited Late Republican legislation (both civil and praetorian), such as the *lex Aebutia*, aimed at repealing large portions of the then-outdated XII Tables, the foundation of Roman civil law.[61]

Some of these legislative reforms reflected the rapid pace of social change in the Late Republic and underlined how the strict application of archaic rules of the XII Tables could itself be a source of injustice. He cited a provision of the XII Tables (Table VIII), which imposed a penalty of twenty-five coins [*XXV asses*] for unlawfully inflicting bodily injury upon another.[62] Bodin observed that, at the time of the Decemvirate (which promulgated the XII Tables), twenty-five coins was a draconian penalty, ensuring that the impact would be felt by any Roman, wealthy and poor alike, daring to violate the law. By the Late Republic, however, twenty-five coins was a relatively light fine, particularly for the very wealthy who could afford to pay without any financial hardship. Bodin even referred to a comment by Labeo on the XII Tables concerning the 'exceptionally rude' [*egregie improbus*] jurist, Neratius who reportedly 'struck people's faces by the palm of his hand for his own amusement' [*delectamento os hominis liberi manus suae palma verberare*]. Undeterred by the civil penalty set in the XII Tables, he made his slave follow him with a money bag, immediately paying his victims the twenty-five coins. The injustice of the situation forced the praetors, acting on behalf of the state, to repeal [*absolvere*; *abrogandae legis XII praebuit occasionem*] this portion of the XII Tables and leave the penalty instead to the equitable discretion of the courts.[63]

Bodin also explored numerous cases of legal abrogation in his native France, including some notable cases and orders of the Parlement of Paris where the reigning sovereign decided to undo and repeal their former legislative actions. He cited, at one point, an *arrêt*, or decree, of Charles V, which repealed a former law [*legem abrogavit*], effectively dismantling all corrupt public offices in one fell swoop [*in una lege*].[64] Another concerned an amendment to the law on royal gifts promulgated by Philip VI in 1333. Originally intended to protect the fisc, it turned out to

[60] *République* 133; *De Republica* 87 [1.8], citing Baldus on C.1.14.8 and Guido da Baisio, *Super Sexto Decretalium* (Lyon: Apud haeredes Iacobi Guintae, 1547) fol. 2_{ro-vo} [Archidiaconus on VI.1.2.1].

[61] *République* 36, 577, 1028; *De Republica* 24, 426, 756–57 [1.4, 4.3, 6.6]. The *lex Aebutia* empowered the praetors to reform civil procedure and modify the scope of *patria potestas*.

[62] XII Tables, 8.4; cp. Inst. 4.4.7; Gaius 3.220, 3.223.

[63] *République* 1038; *De Republica* 763–64 [6.6]. Cp. Jakob Spiegel, *Lexicon Iuris Civilis* (Basel: Apud Ioan. Heruagium, 1554) col. 74 [*De iniuriis, aliis que delictiis*]. Bodin saw this as a shift from strict arithmetic justice to harmonic justice.

[64] *République* 579; *De Republica* 428 [4.3]. This was supposed to illustrate the dangers of radical legal change.

be far more damaging [*incredibile detrimentum*] than anticipated and so 'was repealed only two years later' [*biennio post abrogata est*].[65]

One interesting case even illustrated the scope of the French sovereign's absolute power with respect to canon law in France. Indeed, the legal pluralism of later medieval France routinely gave rise to jurisdictional conflicts between canon and civil law, and their respective episcopal and royal courts.[66] The coexistence of these legal systems in France encouraged strategic forum shopping, as Bodin illustrated by a case involving a priest who, being convicted for lewdness and fraud in the civil courts, nevertheless obtained absolution for his crimes, as canon law allowed, instead in the episcopal court of the Papal legate, thereby escaping punishment from the French civil authorities.[67] On appeal, the Parlement of Paris ultimately decided to punt (partly to avoid being accused of repealing Papal legislation) and referred the case to Council, the *Conseil du Roi*, for a final judgment – effectively, to the then-sovereign, Charles IX.[68] The sovereign's response through Council, ultimately took the form of the *Ordonnance de Moulins* of 1566, a comprehensive reform of the legal system championed by the Chancellor Michel de l'Hôpital.[69] As Bodin described it, the sovereign 'finally promulgated legislation abrogating that specific principle of canon law' [*tandem lege apud Molincos lata, decretum illud pontificii iuris apud nos sublatum est*], a dramatic show of French absolute power over canon law and Papal influence in France.

Formal abrogation, however, wasn't the only way a sovereign could release subjects from a legal obligation. Nor must a sovereign be the sole or even primary agent of absolute power. Like any of its powers concerning the law, a sovereign could conditionally delegate and mandate its exercise to agents and mandataries, including the absolute powers of abrogation and derogation.[70]

In locating the operation of absolute power in the interstices of state and society, Bodin turns instead to the courtroom. Why courts? Bodin's view was that courts, and the judges who staff them, perform a vitally important function in any law-governed state.[71] Not only are they tasked with the consistent application of the law

[65] *République* 745; *De Republica* 554 [5.4].

[66] *De Republica* 278–79 [3.3]; *Stato* 2:141–42. This passage only appears in the Latin text. Bodin, noting that some of these cases were *me presente apud iudices*, claims to have observed these trials firsthand.

[67] X.2.1.4, 1.3.25.

[68] Judgment of the Parlement of Paris, reportedly from 26 February 1569. Bodin points out that the specific problems in the case were discussed *copiose* by Felino Sandeo on X.2.1.4. Felino died in 1503, so it is impossible for him to have commented on a decision from 1569. Bodin likely meant to say that it touched on matters discussed by Felino.

[69] Charles IX, 'Ordonnance sur la réforme de la justice, No. 110' (1566), in *Recueil général des anciennes lois Françaises*, vol. 14, Part 1, eds. Isambert, Decrusy, Taillandier (Paris: Belin-Leprieur, 1829) 199 [§39].

[70] *République* 223; *De Republica* 154 [1.10] gives the example of Solon and Lycurgus and elsewhere makes the same point about the Decemvirate.

[71] *République* 415; *De Republica* 289 [3.4] discusses cases where a sovereign orders a judge to repeal an existing law that is more just and profitable [*le plus iuste ou le plus profitable edict*] and replace it with

on behalf of the sovereign, but, by virtue of their judicial office, they interpret and judge *how* those laws are to be applied or not applied.

This is not an insignificant power. Judicial activity in the courtroom is precisely where one observes up close the mechanics of absolute power at work, especially where judges, in exercising their *iurisdictio*, transform the law from within by exercising what Bodin, following Papinian, calls the judicial 'power of correcting, moderating, and supplying the laws' [*potestas … leges corrigenda, moderandi, suplendi*] on equitable grounds.[72] Indeed, even 'judges of the lowest rank [*les moindres iuges*] have this power to judge according to the equity of the cause'.[73]

Bodin illustrated this idea with numerous examples taken from Roman private law. One was the *lex Laetoria* which addressed a problem arising from underage minors (under the age of twenty-five) who, despite their minority, were nevertheless *sui iuris* (legally independent) and succeeded to the role of *paterfamilias*, making them legally responsible for the family estate. This Laetorian law provided a legal remedy for these vulnerable minors defrauded into entering exploitative and potentially ruinous transactions. While the Laetorian law ostensibly protected minors by empowering them with the right to sue for fraud, it didn't actually reverse or undo the harmful, fraudulent transactions. Praetors, however, judged this to be inequitable and, thus, introduced an additional equitable remedy [*auxilium*], the *restitutio in integrum*, designed specifically to undo the transaction and restore [*restituere*] the minor to his former condition, as if the transaction had never taken place.[74] Citing this Praetorian *restitutio in integrum*, Bodin explained that the praetor merely 'supplemented and corrected' the law – but didn't abrogate the Laetorian law, nor did he legislate from the curule seat.[75]

It's not entirely surprising that Bodin would turn to the judiciary, rather than to the sovereign authority itself, as the principal engine of legal change. As a professionally trained civil lawyer (and, briefly, a professor of civil law at Toulouse), Bodin was deeply fascinated by the forensic nature of litigation and the casuistical methods of legal science and saw the activities of ordinary judges, rather than that of sovereigns, as the primary catalysts of legal change. Indeed, he says it is from his own experience in the courtroom – *apud iudicem* ['in the presence of the judge'] as it were – as a young lawyer pleading before the Parlement that he

a less just and less profitable law [*moins iuste et moins proffitable au public*]. In these cases, the judge may stay the order [*il peut tenir l'execution de l'edict ou mandement*] temporarily.

[72] *Distributio* fol. F, s.v.: *Officium Iudicis*; *République* 438; *De Republica* 304 [3.5], on the urban and peregrine praetors; cp. D.1.1.7.1. Bodin shies away from articulating a more forceful power of judicial review to strike down legislation, but he comes very close to it.

[73] *République* 1023; *De Republica* 754 [6.6].

[74] D.4.4.1.

[75] *République* 223; *De Republica* 155 [1.10], citing D.37.5.6, 48.19.11, 40.9.12, 48.18.1, 48.16.1, 42.1.32, 1.1.7, 37.1.1. Bodin implicitly refers to the *auxilium restitutionis* in *De Republica* 86, where he observes cases where one can be released from invalid obligations and restored [*in integrum … restitui potest*] where the obligation is based on error, fraud, or fear.

'at last ... understood that a real and solid knowledge of the law is found not in the dust of the law schools, but in the battleground of the forum [*non in scolastico pulvere, sed in acie forensi*]'.[76]

But there is a special difficulty in the case of judges. Judges of all ranks in a sovereign state, whether the lower-court seneschals or baillis or high court judges sitting in Parlement, are themselves creatures of the law. They occupy legal roles and wield legal powers defined and limited by law and exercise their *iurisdictio* only as the sovereign's law allows.[77] So, it seems that judges are, in an important sense, legally subordinate to the sovereignty of the state, in just the same way as any other government official, bound to exercise authority only as the law allows. From the perspective of the state's sovereignty, they are no different in status from that of mere *scribas, lictores, cornicularios, apparitores, carnifices* (Bodin's examples) who are likewise appointed to perform certain legally defined public functions of state.[78]

In a fundamental way, then, judgment is a legally regulated act, existing within the laws that sovereigns legislate. When a judge issues a ruling, she can only do so as the law prescribes, without adding to, or subtracting anything from, the severity or lenience of the law [*nec in iudicando legis acerbitati aut lenitati detrahere, aut addere quicquam*].[79] What this might suggest is that judges in their official capacity don't really have much independence or discretion at all. They are merely cogs in the legal machinery of the state, enabling the law to take its course of due process.

But clearly judges were more than simply cogs in the legal machinery of the Bodinian state, and that is because, unlike the 'servile' dronelike function of scribes, lictors, and adjutants, judgment involved something substantially more than simply following instructions in some rulebook authored by some superior. It involved interpreting, applying, amending, updating, and potentially even correcting and rewriting that rulebook.

So, it seemed to Bodin, judges actually bore a double-identity – one which was *intralegal*, another which was *extralegal*, empowering the judge to exercise judgment literally 'beyond the law' [*praeter legem*] and 'even sometimes against the law' [*etiam interdum contra legem*], when equity required it.[80] And the same was true for sovereigns: 'The sovereign [when sitting as judge] must bear two contrasting persons [*deux personnes contraires*; *utramque personam*] ... that of a merciful father [*pere misericordieux*; *parentis clementissimi*] and that of an upright judge [*magistrate entier*; *integerrimi iudicis*]'.[81]

[76] *République*, Epistola [sig. $b3_{vo}$]; Kenneth McRae, 'Appendix A: Bodin's Prefaces', in *Commonweale* A71.

[77] In discussion of this point, Bodin often refers to Papinian's analysis in the rubric in the *Digest* on 'mandated' or 'delegated jurisdiction' at D.1.21.1.

[78] *Methodus* 254–55.

[79] *Methodus* 264.

[80] *Methodus* 264.

[81] *République* 622; *De Republica* 459 [4.6].

Bodin called the equitable, extralegal function of judges the *officium iudicis nobile*, which he saw not so much as a competitor or alternative to the strict application of the law [*legis actio*], but rather, as supplementary or even as a corrective to it (Chapter 2).[82] Judges, not simply as agents of the law, but also as agents of 'equity', performed this 'noble' function of repairing deficiencies in the law by, for example, 'supplying' rules to fill deficiencies in the law or 'moderating' the force of the laws, as equity demands.[83]

Suppose, for example, a judge is presented with a case where, based on the bare facts, *prima facie* it appears the defendant is liable and the law should run its course. While the judge could condemn, it is within the competence of the judge to make equitable exceptions and release the defendant from legal liability. By acquitting – or 'absolving' – a defendant of legal wrongdoing, the judge is doing something extraordinary: She is carving out an exception to the legal rule and partially 'derogating' from the law's full force.[84] She is, for reasons of equity, preventing the legal machinery from running its course in *this particular* case. In doing so, the judge is not only deactivating the operation of a legal duty, the effect of which is 'derogatory'. The judge is also creating a body of higher-order rules of equity – rules that signal to other judges, and even the sovereign, the conditions under which some law should and should not apply, the sort of exceptions, or defences, that can be pleaded, and so forth.

Essential to this emerging picture of praetorian equity and judicial power, however, was the background assumption that, despite their power of jurisdiction, ordinary judges, even of the highest rank, never have the final word; only the sovereign authority, to whom final appeal [*provocatio*] can (in theory) always be made, does. Indeed, Bodinian sovereignty, which is almost always understood in terms of the legislative power to make and unmake law, is just as much to be understood in terms of judicature.

[82] *Distributio* fol. E, s.v.: *Legis actio*: *est ipsius legis executio, vis, ac potestas*, citing also D.11.1.4 and D.1.1.12; *Distributio*, fol. F, s.v. *Officium Iudicis*; cp. Inst. 4.17; Bartolus on D.2.1.1. Ernest Metzger, 'Outline of Roman Civil Procedure', *Roman Legal Tradition* 9 (2013): 1–30. The classic modern study is Max Kaser, *Das Römisches Zivilprozessrecht* (München: C.H. Beck, 1966).

[83] *Distributio* fol. A, s.v.: *Ius sine sanctione*; cp. D.1.1.7.1; fol. F, s.v.: *Officium Iudicis*; *Methodus* 264; *De Republica* 155, citing D.48.19.21. Bodin does not seem to allow courts to exercise a power of judicial review. On the other hand, he absorbed the Ciceronian worry (Cicero, *De Re Publica* 3.17, on the *lex Voconia*; cp. *République* 719; *De Republica* 535 [5.2] on Augustus' derogatory exemption from the Voconian law for Livia) concerning *leges iniustae*, unjust laws or laws whose strict execution would result in an inequitable consequence. So, while judges can't, on their own judicial authority, abrogate or derogate from the laws, they *can*, as agents of equity, supplement, correct, and amend [*supplere, corrigere, emendare*] them, so long as they don't 'break' the law. And as a result, even judges, through judicial orders or 'edicts', can release subjects from obligation or alter how legal rules are to be applied, all without altering the law itself. Bodin at *République* 415; *De Republica* 289 [3.4] observes that judges may even stay the operation of the law [*il peut tenir l'execution de l'edict ou mandement*] temporarily. On these themes, see François Saint-Bonnet, 'La notion d'exécution chez Bodin', *Revue Français d'Histoire des Idées Politiques* 34 (2011): 231–44.

[84] See, in general, Luis Duarte d'Almedia, *Allowing for Exceptions: A Theory of Defences and Defeasibility in Law* (Oxford: Oxford University Press, 2015).

Modern constitutional norms separating legislative and judicial powers will likely complicate and prevent us from seeing these two as related. But, for Bodin, these sovereign powers of legislation and judicature were merely two sides of the same coin of sovereignty. When exercised to reshape the law and its application so as to make it more equitable, judicial power becomes a *kind* of legislative power – not because judges are *making* law, but because they are *unmaking* and *remaking* law.[85] In Bodin's view, judges *do* legislate, negatively, from the curule seat, or the bench, as the case may be.

It is, for this reason, that Bodin insists on emphasizing the sovereign's appellate jurisdiction, as an ultimate court of final appeal with the power to pardon, especially 'to pardon those condemned to death' [*capitis damnatos absolvere*] and 'to restore' their civil status [*potestatem damnatos restituendi*].[86] It is in this judicial role as a supreme court that the sovereign authority of a state, whether a prince or a popular citizen-assembly of some kind, transforms the obligations that bind subjects under the law.

The Limits of Absolute Power

Even though absolute power is a negative power of unmaking law and dismantling its obligatory effects on subjects, it is important to remember that Bodin always intended to limit the scope of this power's application. Though it was a power over law, it was understood to be a power only over a specific category of law, *leges* – the sovereign-authored positive legislation and legal norms that, together, made up a state's *ius civile*.

That's certainly an enormous power that shouldn't be underestimated. But not all laws take the statutory form of positive legislation, or *lex*, a point he tried to stress through his typology of law (see Chapter 2), or *divisio iuris*, distinguishing between ordinary positive legislation authored directly by a sovereign (or indirectly through a sovereign's agent) from higher law which, though just as obligatory as positive legislation, were not the product of sovereign legislative command. Indeed, some laws needn't even be enacted formally by a sovereign through legislative means to be valid and binding. Such laws, Bodin conjectured, were permanently fixed and

[85] This analysis, it must be stressed, makes Bodin fundamentally different from someone like Montesquieu and Madison who treat legislative and judicial powers as different categories of power altogether. They are both of a kind, for Bodin.

[86] *République* 231, 237; *De Republica* 160, 164 [1.10]; *Methodus* 261 [*in extrema provocatione*]. Only the *République* separately identifies the power of pardon as a distinct mark of sovereignty, *République* 621; *De Republica* 458. The model invoked by Bodin is the *lex Valeria*, which gave any Roman citizen condemned to death the right to appeal [*provocatio ad populum*] the court's decision to the assembled sovereign *populus* for pardon. Bodin sees this as analogous in the French case to appeals from Parlament personally to the monarch.

obligatory, not because some sovereign lawmaker has commanded it, but instead, because their natural 'equity' demanded it.

Bodin is recalling a foundational distinction in jurisprudence originating in Aristotle and Cicero, who both, each in their own ways, tried to articulate this distinction between positive legislation and higher law. Aristotle, for example, in a passage of the *Nicomachean Ethics* that would prove to be crucial to Grotius' theory of *ius*, distinguished between a permanently fixed 'natural' [φυσικὸν] justice and a 'conventional' [νομικὸν] human justice.[87] Cicero, likewise, distinguished between the natural law [*ius*] of right reason by which 'human society is bound together' [*devincta est hominum societas*] and the positive 'laws of nations' [*populorum ... legibus*].[88]

The most important source in developing this typology for Bodin was Ulpian. The first rubric of the *Digest* of Roman law, 'On law and justice' [*De iure et iustitia*], attracted voluminous commentaries by academic lawyers because it contained Ulpian's standard typology of the three principal species of law – natural law [*ius naturale*], the law of nations [*ius gentium*], and civil law [*ius civile*]. Ulpian drew the tripartite division in the following way:

> Natural law is what nature has taught all animals. For that law is not exclusive to humankind, but common to all animals.[89]

> The law of nations is the law which the nations of humanity use.[90]

> Civil law is that which neither entirely diverges from the natural law and the law of nations, nor follows them in all things. And so whenever we add anything or take anything away from the law common to all [*iure communi*], we make a law specific [*ius proprium*] to our citizen-body, that is the 'civil'.[91]

This tripartite division of law was the first lesson that aspiring lawyers learned in the law curriculum of Renaissance universities.[92] It is, indeed, the first substantive

[87] Aristotle, *Nicomachean Ethics* 5.7, 1134b18.

[88] *De Legibus* 1.42.

[89] D.1.1.1.3: *Ius naturale est, quod natura omnia animalia docuit: Nam ius istud non humani generis proprium, sed omnium animalium.*

[90] D.1.1.1.4: *Ius gentium est, quo gentes humanae utuntur.*

[91] D.1.1.6.pr: *Ius civile est, quod neque in totum a naturali vel gentium recedit nec per omnia ei servit: Itaque cum aliquid addimus vel detrahimus iuri communi, ius proprium id est civile efficimus.*

[92] Straumann, *Roman Law in the State of Nature* 91, n.27 observes, however, that D.1.1.1.3–4 is 'often viewed as an interpolation', citing Paul Vander Waerdt, 'Philosophical Influence on Roman Jurisprudence? The Case of Stoicism and Natural Law', in *Aufstieg und Niedergang der römischen Welt*, vol. 2, ed. Wolfgang Haase (Berlin: De Gruyter, 1994): 4891–92 and Laurens Winkel who traces the origins of *ius naturale* and *ius gentium* respectively to Peripatetic and Stoic sources in 'Die stoische *oikeiosis*-Lehre und Ulpians Definition der Gerechtigkeit', *Zeitschrift der Savigny-Stiftung für Rechtsgeschichte, Romanistische Abteilung* 105 (1988): 669–79.

topic to appear in both Justinian's *Institutes* (Inst.1.2: *De iure naturali gentium et civili*), the standard introductory textbook of Roman law.[93] So, it is not surprising that lawyers would preserve this classical tripartite typology.

Bodin, who almost certainly would have been exposed to this typology during his period of legal studies in Toulouse, belonged to a generation of humanistic lawyers that began to challenge openly the inherited traditions of legal analysis.[94] One area that attracted Bodin's attention, as well as the attention of his contemporaries, was this tripartite typology of law. Why, he asked, should law be divided immediately into three categories, as Ulpian did? Wouldn't it make more sense, Bodin conjectured, to identify a *summa divisio*, before proceeding to make the specific technical distinctions that Gaius and Ulpian proposed?

This was the basic insight that drove Bodin's attempt at what he thought was a more systematic and accessible reordering of the law. He initially recorded his criticism in the *Distributio*, a principal purpose of which was to reexamine critically the way Gaius and Ulpian drew their distinctions. Bodin's style of analysis in this work, notable for its tabular presentation, was shaped by the then-fashionable 'Ramist' method of analysis, so named after the Parisian logician and rhetorician, Pierre Ramée [Ramus].[95]

Bodin's proposal in the *Distributio*, while perhaps more orderly and in line with humanist principles, was nevertheless unorthodox and un-Classical. Instead of the tripartite division in Ulpian's system, 'a dichotomy [διχοτομεῖν] is more convenient, and, as far as possible, one-to-one distinctions; thus, Aristotle and Plato divide justice into natural [φυσικὸν] and legal [νομικὸν], which is the division Paul followed'.[96]

Bodin likewise sought to dichotomize law into a bipartite typology: *Id* [= *ius*] *duplex est, naturale, et humanum*.[97] The invented category of 'human law', in turn, is then further subdivided into the more familiar categories of *ius gentium* and *ius civile*. The original tabular version of Bodin's *Distributio* organized these types of law as follows:

[93] Gaius' *Institutes*, only rediscovered in the nineteenth century as a palimpsest, was unavailable to Bodin, but some crucial parts of Gaius' division were reproduced in the *Digest* at D.1.1.9 (Gaius 1.1). Gaius, guided instead by a Stoic approach, avoids the tripartite typology by treating the *ius gentium* as a juridical expression of *ratio naturalis*, so that, unlike Ulpian, there is no meaningful difference between *ius gentium* and *ius naturale* as one expansive category. The passage is also useful in Gaius' restatement of the distinction, separating *ius commune* from *ius proprium*.

[94] Franklin, *Jean Bodin and the Sixteenth-Century Revolution* 59–79; Donald Kelley, 'Civil Science in the Renaissance: Jurisprudence Italian Style', *Historical Journal* 22 (1979): 777–94.

[95] Goyard-Fabre, 'Commentaire Philosophique' 100–105; McRae, 'Ramist Tendencies'.

[96] *Distributio* fol. A. Aristotle, *Nicomachean Ethics* 5.7, 1134^{b}18; Plato, *Laws* 2, 653^{d-e}; cp. *Gorgias*, 488^{b}2–3, 488^{e}4; D.1.1.11. Goyard-Fabre, 'Commentaire Philosophique', in *Exposé* 101.

[97] *Distributio* fol. A; s.v.: *Ius*. It is possible that Gratian, and canon law more generally, may have been another source, although Bodin doesn't rely on canonistic sources in the *Distributio*. Gratian's *Decretum* D.1, c.1 opens with the statement of Isidore of Seville that 'all ordinances [*leges*] are either divine or human'.

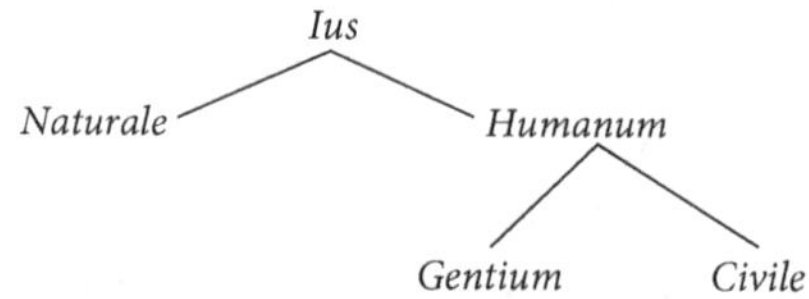

The purpose of this conceptual reordering was to stress a vital theoretical point in Bodin's jurisprudence, which was to prioritize the distinction between 'natural' and 'human' law, but without eliminating entirely the three distinct categories of law in Ulpian's original typology.[98] He didn't want to reduce Ulpian simply to Aristotle or Cicero; rather, he wanted to syncretize them.

What, then, was the difference between 'natural' and 'human' law? It was this: whereas human laws can be traced to some original human act of legislation, natural law, by contrast, is permanently fixed and beyond the scope and jurisdiction of any human lawmaker. Such natural laws can neither be made by any human lawmaker or court, nor can they – crucially – be *unmade* by any human lawmaker or court exercising absolute power.[99]

A sovereign's absolute power, thus, turns out to be a *limited* power – limited, specifically, in its scope of application. By no means was it understood to be a power over the higher laws to which even sovereigns were bound. While a sovereign *can* use its absolute power to amend or repeal its own positive legislation, no sovereign, however powerful, can use that same absolute power to repeal or derogate from the requirements of the natural law and the divine law.[100]

The implication is that sovereigns cannot, by their absolute power, unilaterally exempt, or unbind, themselves from an obligation derived from those higher laws (Chapter 2), for the simple reason that such absolute power gives them no legal competence to do so. It would be a profound mistake to think that

[98] This is why Bodin's system in the *Distributio* does not fully correspond to the strictly bipartite division of Gaius and Paul. It is also worth noting the similarity between the system in the *Distributio* and the third division of *ius* in Grotius' *De Iure Belli ac Pacis* 1.1.9, which proceeds first by dividing *ius* into *ius naturale* and *ius voluntarium*, and then, secondarily, subdividing the latter into divine positive law, the law of nations, and civil law.

[99] It is an open question, however, whether a divine lawmaker could, in principle, unmake higher law. Leaving open this possibility, Bodin deliberately changes his legal vocabulary in the *République/De Republica*, where, instead of the traditional *ius gentium* and *ius naturale*, Bodin renders these categories as *lex gentium* and *lex naturalis* and, additionally, adds the category of *lex divina*. Accordingly, *Colloquium* 31 [Toralba: 22] positions God as the *naturae legislator suis legibus solutus*. Cp. Cesare Vasoli, 'Il tema dell'assoluta potenza divina nell'*Universae naturae theatrum* di Jean Bodin', in *Potentia Dei: l'omnipotenza nel pensiero dei secolo XVI e XVII*, ed. G. Canziani, M.A. Granada, and Yves Charles Zarka (Milan: Franco Angeli, 2000).

[100] *République* 415; *De Republica* 290 [3.4] contrasts Innocent IV's view, on X.1.29.31, with the view of other jurists (Bodin singles out Baldus on X.1.3.17, and the *Gloss. Ord.* and Cino da Pistoia, *Lectura Super Codice* on C.1.22.6; D.1.4.1; X.1.2.7) that a 'sovereign prince can derogate from the law of nature' [*principem iuri naturae derogare posse*]. Cp. X.3.8.4, a decretal of Innocent III, which invokes the power of dispensation as part of the Papal plenitude of power.

sovereignty somehow gives sovereigns a special license, an advantage or edge, over ordinary subjects, by exempting them from the requirements of the *ius naturale*.[101] These higher laws bind all humans indifferently, whether sovereign or otherwise.

As we've already seen in Chapter 2, Bodin illustrates this basic principle with an investigation of one of the most important obligatory requirements of the *ius naturale*, the principle that everyone is duty-bound to honour and perform one's contractual agreements [*pacta conventa*]. Even sovereigns, who are, by definition, empowered with the absolute power to unmake law and release subjects from legal duties, are, as legal subjects themselves bound under the *ius naturale*, required to perform *their* contractual duties. In fact, as we've seen already in Chapter 2, Bodin goes even further to say that sovereigns are 'even more tightly bound [*tellement oblige*; *arctius obligari*] to perform their contractual duties than private subjects are'.[102] The reason for this, Bodin explains, is that sovereigns who enter into contracts, whether with foreigners or with their own subjects [*sive cum exteris sive cum civibus contraxerit*], end up burdened under a 'double bond of obligation' [*obligation double*; *duplex obligatio*].[103] The one bond is simply the equitable rule of the *ius naturale*, binding on everyone, that *conventions & promesses* must be performed.[104] The other bond, however, is unique to sovereigns and traceable to their oaths. In effect, it is an obligation to their future selves to ensure that the sovereign's credit and good faith as the guarantor and enforcer [*garand formel*; *vindex*, *ultor*] will remain valid in the future as it is in the present.

For these reasons, sovereigns can't unilaterally release themselves from contracts they've voluntarily agreed to enter with others, simply by an exercise of absolute power, as we already saw in Chapter 2. Indeed, no sovereign can simply 'legislate' its way out of contractual duties on its own. The only lawful way that a sovereign (or anybody, for that matter) can be released from their contractual duties is either by performing its duties or by obtaining release through the mutual consent of the other parties who were involved in originating the contract:

> An agreement between a sovereign prince and his subjects creates a mutual obligation which binds the two parties reciprocally and from which neither can withdraw without the mutual consent of the other.[105]

[101] *République* 135; *De Republica* 87 [1.8]. On this principle, Bodin targets Cino da Pistoia, Baldus, and Bartolus on C.1.14.4, Giasone del Maino on D.1.4.1, and Felino Sandeo on X.1.2.3.
[102] *République* 153; *De Republica* 100 [1.8].
[103] *République* 152–53; *De Republica* 99 [1.8].
[104] Bodin cites the rule of D.2.14.1.pr.
[105] *République* 135: *La convention est mutuelle entre le Prince & les subjects, qui oblige les deux parties reciproquement & ne peut l'une des parties y contrevenir au prejudice, & sans le consentement de l'autre*; *De Republica* 87: *Conventio inter cives, ac principem mutuam habet obligationem, a qua discedi sine mutuo consensu non potest* [1.8], citing D.15.16.19, 2.14.58, 50, 17.35.

Bodin's reasoning in support of this principle points to an influential rule of the *ius naturale*, recorded in the last title of the *Digest* (*De diversis regulis iuris antiqui*) as an extract of a text by Ulpian:

> Nothing is as natural as the legal rule that every obligation should be dissolved in the same way that it is contracted. Thus, a verbal obligation can only be cancelled by words [*verbis*]; and an obligation based on bare consent [*nudi consensus*] can only be dissolved through their contrary consent.[106]

What Bodin finds in Ulpian's dicta is a principle of symmetry; bonds of obligation are to be dissolved, or unmade, only in the same manner that they are originally created. Insofar as contracts are concerned, it is only fair and consistent with natural equity that contracts entered into by the mutual consent of all parties should be amended or dissolved again by mutual consent of all affected parties.[107]

Suppose, then, that a sovereign authority makes a contract with its subjects. Because the structure of contractual obligation is bilateral (or 'synallagmatic') and reciprocally binding, the sovereign cannot unilaterally withdraw or alter the contract merely by asserting 'absolute power'. The consent of all parties bound by the agreement, both sovereign and subject, is legally required, since it is, in principle, by the consent of parties that a contractual obligation is first constituted.[108] Bodin has no problem with this doctrine, insofar as it applies to contractual obligations.

Laws [*lois*; *leges*] are different. Unlike contracts which are collective acts of consent, laws are unilateral acts of command. And the difference between consent and command is in the structure of obligations arising from each; whereas consent binds all consenting parties, a command binds only the addressees of the command, but not the commander. Command binds and unbinds, one might say, asymmetrically.

This is true even for 'commands of sovereigns' – in other words, laws. Unlike contracts, which oblige mutually and omnilaterally, the obligatory force of laws [*lois*; *leges*] is non-mutual and unilateral; at least one party always remains 'free' or 'exempt' [*solutus*] – or, we may now say, 'absolute' – from the binding force of that created law. And that one party, of course, is the lawmaking sovereign itself, which – as the supreme 'commander' in a state – can bind subjects, while remaining free, or *solutus*, from the force of its own legal commands.[109]

106 D.50.17.35: *Nihil tam naturale est quam eo genere quidque dissolvere, quo colligatum est. Ideo verborum obligatio verbis tollitur: nudi consensus obligatio contrario consensu dissolvitur.*

107 *République* 151; *De Republica* 98 [1.8]. On the 'natural equity' of keeping one's contracts and performing one's contractual duties, Bodin cites D.2.14.1 to establish the principle that such obligations derive not from the *ius civile* of a state, but from the *ius naturale* and especially the *ius gentium*, as indicated at D.1.1.5, both of which are binding even on sovereigns, D.2.14.1.2; 50.12.3; 50.17.27.

108 Tacit consent: D.2.14.2.pr; 2.14.4; 2.14.57; cp. D.1.3.32.

109 *Distributio* fol. D, s.v.: *Liberatio est obligationis solutio*, citing D.2.14.62; cp. D.50.16.176 on the meaning of *solutio* and *solvere*.

It is for this reason, then, that Bodin invokes the famous doctrine of Roman law in his own analysis of sovereignty: *Princeps legibus solutus/le Prince est absous de la puissance des loix* (D.1.3.31), 'the sovereign is exempt from the binding obligatory force of its own legislative enactments'.[110] Since the sovereign, who is by definition exempt from its own laws [*legibus solutus*] and enjoys a maximal liberty-right, does not need anybody else's consent or permission to make law and, in effect, to bind subjects under legal obligation, neither does the sovereign need, by parity of reason, anybody's consent to *unmake* [*absolvere*] law, or (what is the same thing) to release subjects from the bond of legal obligation. The sovereign's absolute power of negative legislation is entirely sufficient to derogate from, or abrogate fully, an existing law and release subjects from duty, all on the sovereign's own initiative. This is precisely why Bodin explicitly insists that law can be made and unmade *without anybody else's consent*.[111] Consent of subjects, while it may be a nice additive by enhancing a law's legitimacy and acceptability, is ultimately inessential to legislation, whether positive or negative.

Bodin adamantly insisted upon stressing this structural difference between law and contract. At first glance, it's probably not clear to a modern lawyer how one could possibly confuse the two. It seems fairly obvious in a modern legal system that a contract, which belongs in private law, isn't the same as a legislated statute, which resides in the realm of public law. Still, he claims that many easily (and perhaps wilfully) confuse one for the other.[112]

Why the confusion? Bodin thinks it arises from the point that laws and contracts are both binding-devices. Their juridical effects are obligatory. Because of this shared obligatory quality, some commentators have (mistakenly, Bodin thought) been led to categorize contracts, which are the product of 'common consent' between sovereigns and subjects, as though they were 'laws', such as the so-called 'pactionary laws' [*loix pactionnees; leges pactionatas*] of Aragon.[113]

But this basic category mistake obscures a vital structural difference between the two: whereas contracts bind omnilaterally, laws bind only unilaterally. Given this, we can see why Bodin would have been so troubled by the Calvinist theory of legislation. If, as the Calvinists argue, 'law' originates by an act of consent between sovereign and subjects, it would follow, on the principle of symmetry, that such 'law' can only be amended or repealed by a subsequent contrary act of consent between sovereign and subjects.[114]

But this only confuses laws and contracts – more specifically, it confuses the *means* by which laws and contracts are constituted and dissolved. Only consent

110 *République* 131; *De Republica* 85 [1.8].
111 *République* 221; *De Republica* 153 [1.10].
112 *République* 135; *De Republica* 87 [1.8].
113 *République* 134; *De Republica* 86 [1.8]. In general, see Ralph Giesey, *If Not, Not: The Oath of the Aragonese and the Legendary Laws of Sobrarbe* (Princeton: Princeton University Press, 1968).
114 This is simply an extension of the principle in D.50.17.35.

can activate and dissolve a contract, just as only an act of command or countermand can enact or abrogate a law. It would, therefore, be a mistake to think, as Calvinists did, that an act of consent could enact law. It would likewise be a mistake to think, as the more radical canonists did, that a unilateral act of countermand or what Bentham would call 'de-imperation' – in other words, an assertion of absolute power – could unilaterally dissolve a contract, or any obligation arising from higher law norms. Such errors in juridical reasoning, Bodin concluded, reflected an elementary failure to detect these fundamental differences in the structure of obligations potentially involving sovereigns.

Why Absolute Power?

I will conclude by addressing a more general question: why must a sovereign have absolute power?

If my analysis in this chapter is correct, it's *not* because Bodin was an adherent to some political doctrine of 'absolutism'. Rather, Bodin's doctrine is presented as an analytically-true proposition, following from anterior premises about the nature of commands and obligations: It is *necessarily true* that the sovereign authority of a state, as a commander over subjects, is *legibus solutus* and absolute – free from the binding force of its own legislation. It is what makes the sovereign a sovereign.

The sovereign *must* be *legibus solutus* because it is conceptually incoherent otherwise. For a sovereign *not* to be *legibus solutus* and not be absolute would mean that a sovereign could, in principle, impose binding legislation on itself and require of itself (or its future self) the performance of some legal duty, as if it were itself a subject. It is impossible for a sovereign to give a law unto oneself, for exactly the same reason that it is impossible to give a command unto oneself.[115] Both scenarios create, Bodin argues, the absurd situation where one is supposedly bound under an obligation owed to oneself – which is to say that it is no obligation at all. It would be, in Bodin's view, just as absurd as a situation where one owes a debt to oneself, or where one makes a promise to oneself. One cannot be both a creditor and a debtor, nor can one be both a stipulator and a promissory. Likewise, one cannot both be both sovereign and subject.

To explain why, Bodin recalls a well-known passage in the *Digest*, a text originally formulated by the Roman jurist, Pomponius, that Rousseau would later describe as a fundamental 'maxim of civil law': 'No promise can be valid if it lies

[115] D.4.8.51. The incoherence of sovereign auto-limitation in Bodin's theory places Bodin in opposition to modern neo-Kantian theories of *Selbstverpflichtung* formulated by jurists such as Georg Jellinek. On this theme, see Diego Quaglioni, *I limiti della sovranità: Il pensiero di Jean Bodin nella cultura politica e giuridica dell'età moderna* (Padova: CEDAM, 1992) and Diego Quaglioni, 'Sovranità e autolimitazione: Rileggendo la *Dotttrina Generale del Diritto dello Stato* di Georg Jellinek', in *Crisi e metamorfosi della sovranità*, ed. Maurizio Basciu (Milan: Giuffré, 1996).

wholly within the choice of the promissory'.[116] The point of this important text is to illustrate the absurdity and impossibility of self-binding or self-obliging acts. It would be absurd to think one can make a promise to oneself, or owe a debt to oneself. One could, of course, certainly try – just as one could try and self-legislate by means of an ambitious new year's resolution or a self-regulated diet. But Javolenus' (and Bodin's) point is that none of these can be binding. This is why there is no injury (and, thus, no cause of action) if one breaks one's own new year's resolution or cheats on a self-imposed diet, just as there is no consequence if one breaks a promise to oneself or fails to repay a debt owed to oneself (or, rather, to one's future self). One can't 'wrong' oneself, nor can one sue oneself in court. By the same reasoning, this is also why sovereigns can never really be bound by their own laws.[117]

Readers approaching Bodin's theory from a constitutionalist perspective may find this perhaps the most worrisome aspect of his theory, since it undermines the very point of the rule of law and potentially leaves public authorities of state beyond the scope of public accountability. If sovereigns can arbitrarily exempt themselves from their own laws, it would be just as if there were no laws at all.[118] Why give such an 'absolute power' to sovereigns?

There are several responses to assuage this constitutionalist (and particularly Anglo-American constitutionalist) worry. Perhaps the first point to underline is just how much Bodin, anticipating Montesquieu, actually valued and praised the rule of law as a normative ideal, a notion he captured under the term, *droit gouvernement.* While he acknowledged that some states were governed in a despotic manner – that is, in the seigneurial manner of the Turks and Muscovites whose sultans and tsars were commonly imagined in Western thought to have ruled their subjects as master (cp. *seigneur*, *dominus*, δεσπότης) lording over their slaves – he categorically rejected such lawless, despotic regimes, favouring instead the impersonal *droit gouvernement* of states applying the rule of law.[119]

But as much as Bodin valued *droit* government, he was mindful of the shortcomings of the law itself – warts and all – and for this reason, refused to fetishize the rule of law. Bodin was especially worried that early modern states, like France, were weighed down by (inherited) and allegedly perpetual legal enactments, particularistic privileges and customary laws, from which they cannot easily free themselves. Such legal enactments may, Bodin acknowledges, once have performed a genuinely valuable social function in some bygone age. But what can we do when their utility has since expired?

[116] *République* 132; *De Republica* 85: *Nulla … obligatio consistere potest, quae a voluntate promittentis statum capit* [1.8], citing D.45.1.108.1 and 32.1.22.pr. This is the 'maxim of civil law' that Rousseau has in mind at *Social Contract* I, 7, ¶1. Hobbes makes reference to the doctrine at *Leviathan* 184. See Quaglioni, '*Les citoyens envers l'État*' 269–79.

[117] Specifically, this is because any sovereign command can be 'unmade' by a sovereign countermand.

[118] Locke, *Two Treatises of Government* 400 [II, §202]: 'Wherever law ends, tyranny begins'. Cp. Lon Fuller, *The Morality of Law*, rev. ed. (New Haven: Yale University Press, 1969) 79–81.

[119] Straumann, *Crisis and Constitutionalism* 300; Lee, 'Office Is a Thing Borrowed' 415.

Bodin's insistence that sovereigns are free to *unmake*, as well as *remake*, the law, is driven principally by a reformist agenda, aiming to reform and reconstitute a legal order burdened by the dead hand of the past. It is, indeed, what differentiates him from the legal thought of later social contract theorists whose starting point is the anarchical legal vacuum of the state of nature. Whereas Grotius, Hobbes, and Locke see legislation as the primary tool to create new laws where previously there were none, Bodin, by contrast, sees the sovereign's absolute power of negative legislation as the tool to *unmake* old laws – especially customary laws – that need to be discarded and replaced.

What these considerations illustrate is the general point that the supposed value of any law is always relative and conditional, not absolute. And it is precisely this conditionality or contingency that makes entrenchment – making legal change either difficult or practically impossible – a highly risky and dubious legislative strategy. A sovereign can never know for sure how valuable a law will really prove to be over time. This reflects, in large part, Bodin's own background worry about the inescapable epistemic limitations of legislators: lawmakers – even the best lawmakers – are just no good at forecasting how the laws they've enacted will function at a later date.

In this respect, Bodin is appealing to a worry once formulated by Aristotle about an inbuilt limitation intrinsic to the rule of law:

> Law is always a general statement, yet there are cases which it is not possible to cover in a general statement … This does not make it a wrong law; for the error is not in the law nor in the lawgiver, but in the nature of the case: the material of conduct is essentially irregular. When therefore the law lays down a general rule, and thereafter a case arises which is an exception to the rule, it is then right, when the lawgiver's pronouncement because of its absoluteness is defective and erroneous, to rectify the defect by deciding as the lawgiver would himself decide if he were present on the occasion, and would have enacted if he had been cognizant of the case in question … This is the essential nature of the equitable: it is a rectification of law where law is defective because of its generality.[120]

Even in the best possible scenario, a Bodinian legislator can't legislate for every possible case in advance or anticipate every possible dispute or legal problem. By its very nature, any law enacted by a sovereign legislator will suffer from some degree of imperfection and inexactitude, a point Bodin recognizes in the *Distributio* when he observes that a law enacted with the best of legislative intentions and authored by the best of legislators – a Moses, a Lycurgus, a Solon, a Justinian – may turn out

[120] Aristotle, *Nicomachean Ethics* 5.10, 1137^{b}16–29; cp. *Politics* 3.15, 1286^{a}10–22. Plato, too, expresses this worry about the rule of law in *Statesman*, 294^{b-d}; 295^{a}–296^{a}. On law and equity in Aristotle's legal thought, see Allan Beever, 'Aristotle on Equity, Law, and Justice', *Legal Theory* 10 (2004): 33–50.

to be 'excessively obscure' [*nimis obscuré*] in meaning, or it may be simply 'unfair' [*iniqua*] in its application to specific contexts.[121] Given these practical difficulties, Bodin recognizes the need for some degree of elasticity or flexibility in the law, as a corrective remedy to the inescapable shortcomings intrinsic to any legal system. Without a sufficient degree of reflexive elasticity, a legal order risks its own ossification, whereby static legal rules harden and fossilize into onerous juridical artefacts, becoming what Plato once described as an 'ignorant and obstinate tyrant'.[122]

However, Bodin's plea for legal elasticity is tempered by prudential considerations concerning the pace of legal change, and he turns out to be mildly conservative, on practical questions of legal change. For example, as a general principle of legislation, he advises that, in situations where it is necessary to introduce 'new laws' [*nouvelles ordonnances*], it is crucial that such legislation be introduced 'little by little' [*petit à petit*; *peu à peu*] and 'not suddenly' [*non pas tout à coup*], lest the state authorities inadvertently introduce a popular 'contempt of all other laws' [*un mespris de toutes loix*] and 'kindle ... a fire of sedition' [*feu de sédition*] setting ablaze the whole state.[123] He also differentiates between the *kinds* of law that can be changed – specifically, between what he calls (1) 'laws concerning ordinary policy' [*qui concernent la police ordinaire*] and (2) 'laws which pertain to the constitutional form of the state' and its sovereignty [*loix qui touchent l'estat*; *qui touche l'estat*; *leges quae ad statum Reipublicae pertinent*; *legibus quae statum civitatis continent*].[124] Whereas the former can be changed readily, even within a relatively short period of time [*parvo momento mutabiles*] if necessary, Bodin treats the latter as if they were 'immutable' [*quas si fieri possit, immutabiles esse*], while admitting that even these fundamental laws may be changed when necessity of state [*salus populi*] demands it. Still, he stresses the practical risks of exercising this particular sovereign right and warns sovereigns: 'To change the laws that affect the state [*mutare* (*leges*) *salva*

[121] *Distributio*, fol. F, s.v.: *Iudicis Officium*.

[122] Plato, *Statesman*, 294[c]; Bodin cites *Laws* VII, 797[c] at *République* 575; *De Republica* 426; *Stato* 2:470–71 [4.3]. Cp. Hart, *Concept of Law* 95–6.

[123] *République* 577, 579; *De Republica* 427 [4.3]. In these passages, a state with a broken legal system is compared to a diseased body. The remedy of bloodletting, allowing the release of humours, though necessary, must not be too sudden: such is 'not the way to cure the diseases, but to kill the diseased'.

[124] *République* 575, 576; *De Republica* 426 [4.3]. Bodin is anticipating a distinction introduced by J.L. Mackie between 'first order laws' and 'second order laws' in 'Evil and Omnipotence', *Mind* 64 (1955): 211. Concerning ordinary laws, such as those concerning commerce or 'the lenity or severity of punishments' [*de poenarum acerbitate aut lenitate*], Bodin writes it is entirely proper that they be changed when necessary, even within a short time [*parvo momento mutabiles sunt*]. The second type of laws are the *leges imperii* or fundamental laws. In a monarchy, such as France, these might include the Salic Law and the legal prohibition on alienation of the royal domain, which are 'conjoined to the sovereignty itself'. In a democracy or aristocracy, these might be the laws governing elections. Bodin declares that *Princeps nec eas* [i.e. the *leges*] *abrogare, nec iis derogare possunt*, at *De Republica* 88. It's not clear if he actually meant to say that the sovereigns actually cannot abrogate – or simply that they should not. But the examples he cites suggest that, as a point of historical fact, sovereigns violate these laws all the time, even though they shouldn't. On *la police* and its connection to the constitutional thought of Claude de Seyssel and Louis Le Roy, see Nicholls, 'Sovereignty and Government' 51: *La police* is 'a particular type of rationality, or prudence, determining the oversight of day-to-day administration in a commonwealth'.

Republica conatur; de changer les loix qui touchent l'estat] is just as dangerous as disturbing the foundations or cornerstones that support the weight of a building'.[125]

But as a general principle, Bodin must allow the possibility of equitable legal change because an uncompromisingly rigid adherence to the letter of the law can itself become a source of profound injustice. What Bodin visualizes ideally, then, is not the elimination of the rule of law altogether, but a supplement to law derived from equity, so that a 'harmonic' blend of law and equity might enable the realization of a higher-order form of justice that would otherwise be impossible in a state slavishly bound to its own unchanging laws.[126]

One implication immediately follows: since it has been shown that legal change – i.e. the capacity to amend or repeal [*abrogare, derogare, subrogare, obrogare*] a law – requires and entails a (Bodinian) notion of sovereignty, sovereignty itself turns out to be fundamental to the very idea of the rule of law.[127] The point is worth underlining: sovereignty, and its absolute power to make and unmake law, is *integral* to, and inseparable from, the rule of law. So, it seems that commentators who have attempted to cast Bodin as an 'absolutist' diametrically opposed to the rule of law have relied on a false opposition between sovereignty and legality. Sovereignty entails legality, a thesis that will have profound implications for Bodin's understanding of the international legal order.

125 *République* 576; *De Republica* 426 [4.3].
126 *Distributio* fol. F, s.v.: *Finis, Iustitia.*
127 Bodin, *De Republica* 98. In this way, Bodin anticipates ideas that would be central to the twentieth century German jurist, Hermann Heller, especially the doctrine that 'positivization' of law is impossible without sovereignty. I am grateful to Diego Quaglioni and David Dyzenhaus for this insight.

5

The Common Law of Mankind, the Common Enemies of Mankind

Sovereignty inhabits the interstices between legality and extralegality. On the one hand, sovereigns are understood to be *legibus soluti*, in that they are exempt from obligations arising from their own positive legislation. And, as we've seen in the previous chapter, sovereigns enjoy this privilege of exemption precisely because it is entailed by their 'absolute power' to unmake law. On the other hand, they are also understood to be *legibus imminuti* as legal subjects of obligations arising from the higher legal norms of natural and divine law.

Natural and divine law are not, however, the only bodies of law to which sovereigns are subject. Sovereigns are also said to be legal subjects of the *ius gentium* – what Bodin has sometimes described as the law shared in common by all peoples [*omnium populorum*]. This chapter will explore specifically how Bodin understood that relationship between sovereignty and the *ius gentium*.

We might begin, first, by asking what the *ius gentium* was supposed to be, or how it differed, if at all, from the *ius naturale*. (Indeed, in classical Roman law, some jurists such as Gaius, though certainly not all, often treated the *ius gentium* and *ius naturale* as equivalent.) Since the time of Vattel, the *ius gentium* was uniformly translated as the *droit des gens*, or 'the law of nations', and was interpreted explicitly to mean that body of law governing the relations between sovereign states, in times of war and peace, concerning treaties, embassies, high seas, and warfare. Jeremy Bentham would eventually introduce a new term, 'international law', to serve as an anglicization of *ius inter gentes*, and to replace the more old fashioned term, 'law of nations'.[1]

[1] Jeremy Bentham, 'Preface', in *The Collected Works of Jeremy Bentham: An Introduction to the Principles of Morals and Legislation*, ed. J.H. Burns and H.L.A. Hart (Oxford: Oxford University Press, 1970) 6. *Ius inter gentes* as a term for international law appears in Francisco de Vitoria, *De Indis et De Iure Belli Relectiones*, trans. John Pawley Bate, ed. Ernest Nys (Washington: Carnegie Institution of Washington, 1917) 151 [*De Indis* §3, 386]. Vitoria cited Gaius' classical formulation in Inst. 1.2.1 (D.1.1.9 and Gaius 1.1) that the *ius gentium* is the legal expression of *naturalis ratio inter omnes homines*, but crucially replaced *homines* with *gentes*, thereby yielding *ius inter omnes gentes*. This usage would be adopted by Alberico Gentili, Francisco Suarez, *Selections from Three Works*, trans. Gwladys Williams, Ammi Brown, John Waldron, and Henry Davis (Oxford: Clarendon Press, 1944) 347 [*De Legibus, ac Deo Legislatore*, 2.19.8], and eventually by Richard Zouch, *Juris et Judicii Fecialis Sive Iuris Inter Gentes* (The Hague: Johannes Verhoeve, 1659) 2–3. Rafael Domingo, *The New Global Law* (Cambridge: Cambridge University Press, 2010) 22–24; David Armitage, 'Globalizing Jeremy Bentham', *History of Political Thought* 32 (2011): 72–3.

The Right of Sovereignty. Daniel Lee, Oxford University Press. © Daniel Lee 2021.
DOI: 10.1093/oso/9780198755531.003.0006

Bentham wasn't simply trying to update an outdated legal vocabulary. He was trying to correct a well-known ambiguity captured by the term, *ius gentium*, which could mean both international law, as well as the law shared in common by all nations. Bentham himself relied on an earlier analysis by the French chancellor, Henri François d'Aguesseau, who likewise observed the ambiguity between the *Droit des Gens* [*Ius Gentium*] and the *Droit entre les Nations* [*Ius inter Gentes*].[2]

Bodin, by contrast, used the term, *ius gentium*, in the more old-fashioned way that d'Aguesseau, Bentham, and many others in the era of baroque jurisprudence, tried to repudiate, or at least bracket aside. For Bodin, the *ius gentium* was a body of law whose function was to license certain types of action so that they are covered by a juridical shell of legality. In Roman private law, the appeal to the *ius gentium* was often a useful tool to enable simple commercial transactions between Romans and peregrines. It allowed, for example, Roman courts to bypass the burdensome *mancipatio*, a *ius civile* procedure limited only to Romans, and allow a property transaction to be concluded with the far more versatile *traditio*, a recognized *ius gentium* procedure open to Romans and non-Romans alike.

But the *ius gentium* covered far more than just commerce. Indeed, the most important topic of the *ius gentium*, by far, was war. In the *Digest*, Hermogenian's canonical description of the matters concerning the *ius gentium* (D.1.1.5) lists war first, and that is because of all the legal effects or consequences that follow from a lawful war – conquest, enslavement of the vanquished, and potentially the acquisition of a new title of sovereignty. The idea was this: if war is recognized to be legal according to the *ius gentium*, then so must all these legal effects following from war. War, thus, turns out to be the creative force that can generate new sovereignties and new states. In this way, war and conquest become one of the principal legal methods of acquiring a derivative title of sovereignty.

But this derivative method of acquiring sovereign title by conquest comes with an important qualification. Not all wars activated these legal effects. Only 'legal wars' did – that is, wars legally permissible under the *ius gentium*. And the key element in determining whether a war is legally permissible, so that it is more than simply the raw violence of pirates and brigands [*latrocinium*], was formal public declaration of war, a right Bodin has explicitly reserved to sovereigns as one of their exclusive prerogative *marques*. States – and only states – can wage war and legally reap the spoils of war.

The importance that Bodin attached to this sovereign right to declare war (and conclude peace) was inspired by a well-known rule of Roman law, the *lex Hostes* (D.49.15.24), which treated public declarations of war as a kind of illocutionary speech-act through which a state of war can be lawfully initiated. As we've already

[2] Henri François d'Aguesseau, 'Essai d'une institution au droit public', in *Discours et oeuvres mêlées de M. le Chancellier D'Aguesseau*, nouvelle édition, 2 vols. (Paris: Chez les Libraires Associés, 1786) 2:294 [§7].

seen in Chapter 1, public declaration, through the *rerum repetitio*, was the quasi-ritualistic means by which erstwhile friends and allies can become public enemies of state – *hostes*. And, as public enemies, they could be, according to the *ius gentium*, defeated in war and lawfully converted to slaves and subjects of the victorious combatant.

Not all wars, of course, were publicly declared in this way. Lacking the legitimacy of the *ius gentium*, such undeclared – and therefore, illicit – wars counted for nothing more than the mere force and violence of criminal brigands and pirates, what Ulpian called *latronculi et praedones*. While such violent outlawry could potentially result in the successful creation of a new regime, by effectively seizing or stealing someone else's sovereignty in an act of usurpation, Bodin was unprepared to admit that such illicit regimes based only on brute force, rather than any right originating in the *ius gentium*, could deserve the title of sovereignty. They deserved instead another title – tyranny. And because their unlawful title fell outside what was permissible under the *ius gentium*, such outlaws weren't properly enemies of state, but rather, 'enemies of all mankind' [*hostes humani generis*].

In this chapter, we will explore how the *ius gentium* established those legal boundaries, separating not only what was legally permissible from what was legally impermissible, but also separating those belonging to humanity and those outside humanity. The chapter will open with an exposition of the *ius gentium* in classical jurisprudence, what Gaius famously defined, not so much as 'international law', but as 'the law common to all of mankind' [*communi omnium hominum iure*]. Of the various provisions of the *ius gentium*, war was the most consequential of the legal rights permitted under the *ius gentium*, specifically because of its juridically transformative effects. Not only could a lawful war create slavery [*dominium*], as a spoil of war, it could also activate a new lawful title of sovereignty [*imperium*].

But, as Bodin pointed out, those spoils can be enjoyed, only if the war conforms to the recognized principles and requirements of the *ius gentium*. Falling short, force without such legal right [*latrocinium*] yields something very different, in Bodin's analysis. Following Cicero, Bodin often compared such violence to the mere brute force of pirates, brigands, and robbers, all acting without right, and therefore outside the permissible boundaries of the *ius gentium*. While these unlawful 'enemies of mankind' may be effective in using their force to extract compliance to their will, like any highwayman or gunman, they have no right to demand such compliance, and, correlatively, there can be no duty to obey.

As we'll see, Bodin had one more item to add to this list – tyrants. In Bodin's mind, tyranny, most often manifest in the illicit usurpation of someone else's lawful title of sovereignty by force or fraud, belongs in the same company as piracy and brigandage. And because tyrannical force cannot give rise to any rights or duties attached to a valid obligation, Bodin allows the legality of tyrannicide. This will be a surprising conclusion, especially for many readers who have typically interpreted Bodin as a zealous opponent of radical tyrannicidal politics. But, as I'll show, Bodin draws a crucial distinction between (what I will call) seigneuricide and tyrannicide, a distinction often overlooked in the interpretive scholarship. Recovering that distinction will reinforce a side of Bodin that has been overlooked, his abiding concern for political legitimacy.

The *Ius Gentium*: The Common Law of Mankind

What exactly was the 'law of nations' [*ius gentium, droit des gens, Völkerrecht*]?[3] Modern lawyers typically assume that the *ius gentium* was simply a synonym for public international law, a *ius inter gentes*, governing the legal relations between independent peoples. That's probably because the foundational modern treatises on international law – Gentili, Grotius, Pufendorf, and Vattel – were framed explicitly as treatises on the *ius gentium* – or, in Vattel's case, the *droit des gens*.[4] As commentators on the *ius gentium*, these jurists addressed standard topics in the *ius gentium* that would become central to modern international law, such as the law of war and the law governing embassies and postliminy.

But even in this literature, the founding fathers of modern international law observed that the archaic term of classical jurisprudence, *ius gentium*, didn't quite fully capture the notion of public international law, as it is understood in modern jurisprudence. While some aspects of the *ius gentium* dealt with matters involving the legal rights, duties, and the relations between states (such as on matters of war and embassies), they observed that this body of law also covered matters, having nothing directly to do with what we would now regard as international law. Suarez, for example, recognizing the multifaceted aspects of the *ius gentium* in classical jurisprudence, found it necessary to distinguish between *ius inter gentes* and *ius intra gentes*.[5] Grotius likewise distinguished between the *ius gentium*, as used in classical Roman jurisprudence, and the *ius illud gentium proprie dictum*, signifying what he envisioned, the modern international law governing the society of states.[6] Vattel identified no fewer than three different forms of the *droit des gens* – voluntary, conventional, and customary – some of which covered core matters of private

[3] For a general overview, see Dante Fedele, 'Ius Gentium: The Metamorphoses of a Legal Concept', *Empire and Legal Thought: Ideas and Institutions from Antiquity to Modernity*, ed. Edward Cavanaugh (Leiden: Brill, 2020).

[4] Consider, for example, Grotius' *magnum opus* whose full title, it will be recalled, was *De iure belli ac pacis libri tres, in quibus ius naturae et gentium, item iuris publici praecipua explicantur* [On the law of war and peace in three books, in which the law of nature and of nations, and likewise the particulars of public law are set forth].

[5] Genc Trnavci, 'The Meaning and Scope of the Law of Nations in the Context of the Alien Tort Claims Act and International Law', *University of Pennsylvania Journal of International Economic Law* 26 (2005): 208, citing Suarez, *Selections from Three Works* 347 [2.19.8].

[6] *De Iure Belli ac Pacis* 2.8.1.

law.[7] Indeed, it is precisely because of this historical ambiguity attached to the *ius gentium* that Bentham felt compelled to coin a new term, 'international law'.[8]

All this points to a deeper interpretive puzzle concerning the meaning and function of the *ius gentium*. If *ius gentium* wasn't simply a synonym for 'international law', then what else could it be? One approach to answering this question involved recovering the original meaning and function of the *ius gentium* in classical Roman law, where the term originally appears.[9] The opening title of the *Digest* identifies the *ius gentium* as one of the principal forms of law that govern Romans. Together with the *ius naturale* and the *ius civile*, the *ius gentium* is one of the three principal sources of law governing Romans. Ulpian famously defines it as that part of the *ius naturale* specific to humanity.[10]

Henry Wheaton, the American author of the first modern treatise of international law in English, explained it this way:

> The law of nations, *ius gentium*, in its most ancient and most extensive acceptation, as established by the Roman jurisprudence, is a law founded upon the general usage and tacit consent of nations. This law is applied, not merely to regulate the mutual relations of states, but also of individuals, so far as concerns their respective rights and duties.[11]

It was that body of law whose legal rules and principles were understood to be common to the legal systems of all (or, at least, the most 'civilized') states.[12] As Grotius put it in explicitly Ciceronian terms, such a shared *ius gentium* was the foundation for a common 'bond of human fellowship' [*societatis humanae vinculum*] across many peoples.[13]

Jeremy Waldron once provided a useful analogy drawn from the scientific method and 'the established body of scientific findings' to explain the function of this *ius gentium* in classical jurisprudence:

[7] Vattel, Preliminaries 68.

[8] Mark Weston Janis, 'Jeremy Bentham and the Fashioning of International Law', *American Journal of International Law* 78 (1984): 405–18.

[9] Henry Sumner Maine recovers the classical meaning of *ius gentium* and distinguishes it from what he regards as the 'classical expression for international law ... Jus Feciale' in *Ancient Law*, 4th ed. (London: John Murray, 1870) 53.

[10] D.1.1.1.3–4. Straumann, *Roman Law in the State of Nature* 91, n.27.

[11] Henry Wheaton, *Elements of International Law*, 6th ed. (Boston: Little, Brown, and Company, 1857) 14, citing the German jurist Heffter.

[12] What counted as 'civilized' and capable of law is a central theme in Martti Koskenniemi, *The Gentle Civilizer of Nations: The Rise and Fall of International Law, 1870–1960* (Cambridge: Cambridge University Press, 2001) and Jennifer Pitts, *Boundaries of the International: Law and Empire* (Cambridge: Harvard University Press, 2018).

[13] *De Iure Belli ac Pacis* 2.8.26.

> [Just as] existing scientific claims ... stand as a repository of enormous value to individual researchers as they go about their work ... similarly, the law of nations is available to lawmakers and judges as an established body of legal insight, reminding them that their particular problem has been confronted before and that they, like scientists, should try to think it through in the company of those who have already dealt with it.[14]

The *ius gentium*, thus, identified points of juridical convergence through time and across many different legal cultures and systems. Such observable convergence on specific points of law, including even in private law, across diverse legal systems was standardly described as a 'consensus' – as Bodin put it, the *consensus omnium populorum*, an overlapping 'consensus of all peoples'.[15]

For Bodin, demonstrating such a 'consensus' functioned as a distinctive method of proof confirming the universal veridicality and the validity of a legal norm shared in common. Such *argumentum consensus gentium* was a common rhetorical technique used in ancient law by which some legal norm could be verified [*probatur*] as authoritative, though not by reference to an abstract reason, but instead, by empirical reference to the accumulated legal experience and practices of many peoples.[16] This technique of verifying legal validity by showing *consensus gentium* was, in fact, one of the methodological problems of comparative analysis framing Bodin's study of law and history in the *Distributio* and the *Methodus*. It would be, he thought, *absurdum* 'to establish from Roman law the whole universal law' of humanity [*ex Romanis legibus ... de universo iure statuere*] – that is, the *ius gentium*.[17] That grand task would require gathering 'the laws of all states, or those of the most famous states' – the Persians, the Greeks, the Egyptians, the Hebrews, the Turks, in addition to the Romans – so that 'the wise may compare them ... and forge the best type of state from among them' [*optimum genus ex iis conflarent*]'.[18]

The *ius gentium*, thus, was *sui generis*. A large part of the interpretive difficulty in making sense of the *ius gentium* derives from its complicated overlap with neighbouring categories of law, the *ius naturale* and the *ius civile*. Civilians and canonists alike traditionally located the *ius gentium* as a kind of intermediate hybrid category of law in between the other two, reflecting the fact that the *ius gentium* shared some

14 Jeremy Waldron, 'Foreign Law and the Modern *Ius Gentium*', *Harvard Law Review* 119 (2005): 132–33; cp. Jeremy Waldron, *Partly Laws Common to All Mankind: Foreign Law in American Courts* (New Haven: Yale University Press, 2012).

15 *De Republica* 47 [1.6].

16 Shuger, *Renaissance Bible* 76–82, tracing the classical roots of the idea in Cicero, *Tusculan Disputations*, trans. J.E. King, Loeb Classical Library 141 (Cambridge: Harvard University Press, 1927) 36–37 [1.30]. More generally, Straumann, *Roman Law in the State of Nature* 61–66, 79–80.

17 *Methodus* sig. ∴3_{ro}. The *ius universum* mentioned here (and at the bottom of the same page: *iuris universi formam ... in tabula*) is a reference to the *Distributio*, completed just before Bodin turned his attention to the *Methodus*.

18 *Methodus* sig. ∴3_{vo}, cp. 230. Shuger, *Renaissance Bible* 78, argues that, unlike Grotius, Bodin 'treats his historical material as rhetorical exempla rather than evidence'.

of the features of both. It bore, specifically, features of positive legislation characteristic of *ius civile*, as well as the universal scope and grounding in 'natural reason' characteristic of *ius naturale*.

Given this overlap, was there anything irreducibly distinctive or necessary about the *ius gentium*? Why not simply bypass the category altogether, as modern natural law theorists have done, so that, instead of an unruly trifurcation of law (i.e. of *ius naturale*, *ius gentium*, and *ius civile*), all law could instead be neatly organized by simple bifurcation, separating positive legislation of *ius civile* from *ius naturale*? (As we have seen earlier in Chapter 4, this was in fact Bodin's suggestion.)

Still, as tempting as that solution might have been, jurists, both canonist and civilian, retained the standard trifurcation in the *divisio iuris* because they believed the *ius gentium* was *sui generis* and ultimately irreducible to either *ius civile* or *ius naturale*.[19] There *was* something, they thought, unique about the *ius gentium* that couldn't quite fully be captured by either *iura civilia* or by *ius naturale*.

To show this, jurists typically presented two sets of contrasts (1) the *ius gentium/ius civile* contrast and (2) the *ius gentium/ius naturale* contrast. With respect to the first, the *locus classicus* was Gaius who famously, in his *Institutes*, described the *ius gentium* as 'the common law of mankind' [*commune omnium hominum ius*], binding upon, and accessible to, all of humanity. Here, what distinguished *ius gentium* from the more locally limited positive law of any *ius civile* was its universal scope. Unlike the *ius civile* which, as Gaius put it, was simply the body of 'law specific to a particular citizen-body' [*ipsius proprium civitatis ius*], *ius gentium* was, by contrast, accessible to all humans, of whatever *civitas* or *gens*.[20] Thus, Gaius was able to say that all law-governed peoples (like the Romans) 'use partly their own law and partly the law common to all mankind' [*partim suo proprio, partim communi omnium hominum iure utuntur*].[21] It is likely that Gaius was appealing to the same Stoic legal theory that shaped Cicero's philosophy of law who also appealed to the *ius gentium* prominently in *De Officiis* 3.69, in explaining the ancient Roman *mos maiorum* as originally made up of both *ius civile* and *ius gentium*.[22]

There's a practical reason why Roman jurisconsults, like Gaius, were particularly motivated to investigate and make such grand appeal to the *ius gentium*. The archaic law of the early Roman Republic, and especially the civil law of the XII Tables (Rome's first written code of legislation, promulgated by special commission of the Decemvirate), was what Romans specifically called *ius Quiritium* – a law made exclusively for 'Quirites', or full Roman citizens. The exclusive quality of early Roman

[19] D.1.1.1.3, 1.1.1.4, 1.1.6; *Decretum* Pars I, Dist. I, c.6, c.9.

[20] D.1.1.9. Gaius, thus, supplies the vocabulary for the distinction between *ius commune* and *ius proprium* that would become vital in medieval jurisprudence.

[21] Gaius' view at 1.83–91 (discussing conflicts between the Senatusconsultum Claudianum and the *ius gentium* on the personal status of a child whose free mother conceived by a slave) seems to be that, where there is a conflict between *ius civile* and *ius gentium*, the *ius gentium* rule tends to carry greater weight.

[22] *De Off.* 3.23; *De Re Publica* 3.33; *Tusculan Disputations* 1.13.30.

law as a form of *ius civile* – a body of law providing protections and advantages only for *cives* (in other words, 'civil rights') – reflected the standing of early Rome as merely one among other peoples, or *gentes*, populating ancient Italy.

Only with the expansion of Rome through commerce and its conquest and domination of foreign peoples later in its history did Roman jurists begin to really feel the practical limitations of their exclusive 'Quiritian' civil law. Rome, once a relatively insignificant city-state on the Tiber, became the most important state in classical antiquity, in effect, a heterogeneous multi-national state, made up not only of Romans, but also of non-Romans drawn from the many *gentes* and free *populi* and lands subdued under Roman *imperium*. As a matter of policy (one later to be emulated by modern imperial states), Romans did not generally impose their civil law on conquered peoples, allowing them instead the legal autonomy to continue practising their own local laws and customs, or *iura propria*, so long as they paid tribute and recognized Roman superiority, or *maiestas Romani populi* (literally, the 'greater-ness' [from *maior*] of the Roman state).[23] The inevitable result of this Roman policy was a fragmented condition of legal pluralism in the later Republic, wherein the Quiritian civil law became but one among other bodies of civil law, all coexisting alongside each other.

Practically, it was a mess. Since *peregrini*, or foreigners, could not assert any of the Quiritian civil rights reserved exclusively to Roman citizens – even for simple commercial transactions like transferring property or memorializing a contract – commerce between Romans and non-Romans was legally impossible. And even among Romans, transactions could be excessively onerous. To take an example from the law of property: simple conveyance of property such as cattle or slaves was, under the Quiritian law, an arduous process, *mancipatio*, that involved the presence of multiple witnesses (all legally qualified to act in that role) or, *cessio*, if before a judge, a ceremonial striking of scales, and recitation of a set text effecting the transfer.

Seeing the inequity (and probably also the inefficiency) of the situation in an increasingly imperial economy, Roman judges acknowledged the urgent need for legal reform so that its civil law could be 'updated' to reflect better the reality of Rome's transformation to empire. It was, as Bodin liked to say, the 'duty of the judge' (cp. Inst. 4.17, *De officio iudicis*), to act as the 'living voice of the civil law' (D.1.1.8: *viva vox iuris civilis*) to allow such change to take place.

The principal vehicle for introducing these reforms was the praetorian edict, judge-made law introduced by the Roman peregrine praetors intended, as Papinian put it, to modify deficiencies in (what was thought to be) ossified civil law by 'supplementing' [*supplendi*] or 'correcting' [*corrigendi*] it with new, more equitable rules of law, so as to update it and, consequently, better serve the 'public

[23] Ando, *Law, Language, and Empire* 74, 103–6.

good' [*propter utilitatem publicam*].[24] Taken together, these accumulated praetorian edicts introducing such legal innovations were collectively called *ius honorarium*, so called (says Papinian) to reflect the 'honour' and equity of the praetorian office.[25]

But what's especially noteworthy is the substance of these edicts which were aimed at reforming and 'modernizing' the archaic Quiritian law of the *ius civile*. Most important, in this respect, was the legal craftsmanship of the so-called peregrine praetor, a Roman magistracy created specifically to address the 'great multitude of foreigners' in Rome [*multa turba peregrinorum in civitatem*] and resolve the inevitable conflict of laws.[26] While these foreigners, due to their alien status, couldn't access the *ius civile*, they *could* access the *ius gentium* (just as any Roman could). And it was by the peregrine praetor's appeal to the equity in this shared *ius gentium* that new rules were introduced and assimilated into Roman law.

Later Roman jurists, thus, recognized the validity of both *ius civile* and *ius gentium* rules, as sources of law justiciable in Roman courts. We might return to the earlier example of property to illustrate this point. It was through the work of the praetors that conveyance needn't be restricted to the narrow archaic rules of Quiritian civil law. Thanks to the praetors, foreigners could now be party to property transactions via *ius gentium* rules such as simple delivery or prescription.

So much, then, for the *ius civile*. What about the difference between *ius gentium* and *ius naturale*? The difficulty here is that both share one key feature in common – the universality of scope: all humans, even sovereigns (as we've seen in Chapter 2), are supposedly bound by the rules of *ius gentium* and *ius naturale*.[27] Some commentators have even suggested that, at least in the classical context, there was no meaningful difference between these two categories of law. They were used interchangeably, and this equivalence of meaning was further sanctioned in Justinian's *Institutes*, where *ius naturale* was said to be simply a synonym for *ius gentium*.[28] Even in Renaissance jurisprudence, the *ius naturale* and *ius gentium* continued to

[24] D.1.1.7. Cp. W.W. Buckland, *Textbook of Roman Law: From Augustus to Justinian*, 3rd ed., rev. Peter Stein (Cambridge: Cambridge University Press, 1963) 55 [Ch. 1]: 'There is no justification for treating the Edict as originating in the *ius gentium*. Many ideas in the Praetor's Edict no doubt were due to this idea, but many had no direct connexion with it'.

[25] D.1.1.7; 1.2.2.10. Donellus observes that the word, *magistratus*, is a *verbum anceps*, or 'twofold word', meaning both the legal office [*honor*] of the magistracy and the person occupying that office. *Popular Sovereignty* 113.

[26] D.1.2.2.28. See, in general, David Daube, 'The Peregrine Praetor', *Journal of Roman Studies* 41 (1951): 66–70 and, more generally, T. Corey Brennan, *The Praetorship in the Roman Republic*, vol. 1, *Origins to 122 BC* (Oxford: Oxford University Press, 2000). Modern classical scholarship indicates some doubts on Pomponius' view at 1.2.2.28 that the peregrine praetor was introduced specifically to handle jurisdiction in cases involving foreigners. R.L. Gilbert, 'The Origin and History of the Peregrine Praetorship, 242–166 B.C.', *Res Judicatae* 2 (1939): 50–8. A more recent account can be found in Brennan, *Praetorship* 1:133–35.

[27] D.1.1.1.3 suggests that the scope of natural law is even wider. It is *quod natura omnia animalia docuit*.

[28] Inst.2.1.11. Buckland, *Textbook of Roman Law* 52–5. A classic account, prepared in response to Maine, can be found in Henry Nettleship, '*Ius Gentium*', *Journal of Philology* 13–14 (1885): 169–81.

be treated as interchangeably equivalent. Alberico Gentili, for example, opens his treatise on the law of war with the statement that 'the law of nations . . . is the law of nature'.[29]

Of the major classical jurisconsults, Gaius is perhaps most responsible for promoting this connection. In an apparent gesture to Stoic principles, Gaius defined *ius gentium* as the juridical expression of an unchanging and universally valid 'natural reason':

> The law which natural reason has established among all humans is equally observed among all and called 'the law of nations', just as if it were the law which all nations observe.[30]

The reference to *ratio naturalis* reveals an engagement with philosophical argument on the nature of law, possibly even with Cicero's Stoic-inflected view that law is *recta ratio naturae congruens*, which made it hard to see any salient difference between *ius gentium* and *ius naturale.*[31] For Gaius, anyway, it seems that both were simply two different appellations for the same thing.

But as influential as his writings were, Gaius was not the only classical source to treat the relationship between *ius gentium* and *ius naturale*. Nor was his thesis of equivalence the *opinio communis* of all Roman lawyers. We only need to turn to the Roman legacy of slavery to see how the *ius gentium* could diverge from *ius naturale* in quite dramatic ways. Florentinus' famous text on the subject, recorded in the *Digest* (which we've encountered already in Chapter 3), acknowledged the legality of slavery, but indicated that, insofar as slavery was legally permissible, it was legal *ex iure gentium*, not *ex iure naturali*. And that is because, as classical lawyers frequently observed, all humans are by nature (i.e. according to *ius naturale*) free.[32] It was, as Hermogenian famously observed, the *ius gentium* that not only introduced slavery into the world, but also the legal means by which one's slave status [*status servi*] can be nullified [*annihilatus*] – that is, manumission.[33] Slavery was, thus, described as a derogatory *constitutio iuris gentium contra naturam*, revealing

[29] Gentili, *De Iure Belli* 8 [1.1], cp. F. Iurlaro, 'The Burden of Reason: Ratio Probabilis, Consensio Omnium and the Impact of Humanitas on Alberico Gentili's Theory of Customary International Law', *History of Political Thought* 38 (2017): 409–38.

[30] Gaius 1.1; D.1.1.9: *Quod vero naturalis ratio inter omnes homines constituit, id apud omnes peraeque custoditur vocaturque 'ius gentium,' quasi quo iure omnes gentes utuntur*; cp. 41.1.1.pr., 9.2.4.pr.; cp. Cicero, *De Legibus* 1.35.

[31] *Recta ratio* was, in turn, derived from Hellenistic sources, such as the ὀρθός λόγος of the Greco-Jewish philosopher, Philo of Alexandria. Straumann, *Roman Law in the State of Nature* 47. Commentators, however, have cautioned modern readers of civil law not to read civil lawyers as though they were philosophers, or to connect Gaius' *ratio naturalis* too hastily with Stoicism, Academic Scepticism, or with any other specific philosophical school. Benedikt Forschner, 'Law's Nature: Philosophy as a Legal Argument in Cicero's Writings', in *Cicero's Law: Rethinking Roman Law of the Late Republic*, ed. Paul J. du Plessis (Edinburgh: Edinburgh University Press, 2016).

[32] D.1.1.4.

[33] D.1.1.5; Bartolus, Paul de Castro, and Giasone del Maino on D.12.6.64.

a critical point of disagreement showing that the two bodies of law can't be entirely coterminous with each other.[34]

This conflict between *ius gentium* and *ius naturale* continued to widen until, as W.W. Buckland put it, 'the distinction became a standing part of mediaeval political thought'.[35] One important piece of evidence for this is medieval canon law, which featured the same tripartite *divisio iuris* as in civil law: *Ius aut naturale est, aut civile, aut gentium.*[36] Gratian specifically designated *ius gentium* the law that 'almost all nations use' [*eo iure omnes fere gentes utuntur*], suggesting that mere desuetude was enough to invalidate or abrogate a rule of the *ius gentium*, however reasonable, natural, or equitable it may be.[37]

Yet, medieval jurists stubbornly insisted on recognizing that, even despite these differences, there remained a confusing point of overlap between *ius naturale* and *ius gentium*, prompting jurists to introduce even finer analytical distinctions for clarity. The medieval Commentators, beginning with Bartolus of Sassoferrato, all approached the issue as a commentary on D.12.6.64, in an important title of the *Digest* concerning recovery of money that was not due in the first place, *De condictione indebiti*.[38] The title dealt at length with the concept of a 'natural obligation' [*obligatio naturalis*].

As we've seen in Chapter 2, natural obligations do not arise from civil law – and therefore, are technically not actionable through a civil remedy. By what 'law', then, do natural obligations arise, if not from the positive legislation of *ius civile*? The standard answer is *ius naturale*. The problem, however, is that Ulpian, in one of his most famous texts appearing in the *Digest*, defined *ius naturale* as *quod natura omnia animalia docuit* (what nature has taught all animals), humans and non-humans alike.[39] If that's true, then even animals should, in principle, be capable of being bound by natural obligations, liable just like humans. But, of course, animals can't be bound by debt or sued for wrongdoing.[40] Ulpian, thus, clarifies that there is a subset of the *ius naturale* that is specific to humans only [*solis hominibus*] – this is what he calls *ius gentium*.

It was in this subset that Bartolus located the juridical source of natural obligations and allows him to say that natural obligations originate from the *ius gentium*.[41] But he adds that the *ius gentium* carries a subtle double-meaning [*duplex*],

[34] D.1.5.4.1. cp. Buckland, *Textbook on Roman Law* 54.

[35] Buckland, *Textbook on Roman Law* 53.

[36] *Decretum* Pars I, Dist. 1., c.6.

[37] At *Decretum* Pars I, Dist. 1., c.7, Gratian cites Isidore's description of *ius naturale* as the 'common law of all nations' [*commune omnium nationum*], held to be 'natural and equitable' [*naturale equumque*] everywhere.

[38] Fedele, 'Ius Gentium' 233, however, locates an earlier starting point in Pierre Belleperche.

[39] D.1.1.1.

[40] D.9.1.1.1.

[41] Later commentators make the same point. Baldus de Ubaldis, *In II^am^ Digesti Veteri Partem Commentaria* (Venice, 1577) fol. 75_{ro} [on D.12.6.64]; Paul de Castro, *In II^am^ Digesti Veteri Partem* fol. 59_{vo} [on D.12.6.64]: *Obligatio naturalis est de iure gentium;* Giasone del Maino, *In II^am^ Digesti Veteri Partem* (Lyon, 1583) fol. 181_{vo} [on D.12.6.64].

so it is crucial to distinguish between two different categories of *ius gentium*, what would later be called the 'primary' and the 'secondary' *ius gentium*. Whereas the primary (or *primaevum*) *ius gentium* was the law which existed at the dawn of humanity and originated simply through 'natural reason' [*naturali rationali inductum*], the secondary *ius gentium* arose from the usages of various nations and peoples [*gentes utuntur*] over time, as if it were a collective 'decree of all nations' [*constitutione earum*].[42]

What separated the secondary *ius gentium* from the primary was twofold. One *differentia* was the positivistic character of secondary *ius gentium*. Like the *ius civile*, the secondary *ius gentium* resembled positive legislation, in that it wasn't a permanently fixed system of rules based in a sempiternal reason, like *ius naturale*. Instead, secondary *ius gentium* came into existence only gradually through human history, through continued and widespread usage of common legal practices. This is precisely why later jurists felt it necessary to characterize this secondary *ius gentium* as 'voluntary', 'arbitrary', or 'positive' in nature. (This is also likely why Bodin chose to designate this body of law as *lex gentium*, rather than with the traditional form, *ius gentium*.)

The other principal *differentia* between primary and secondary *ius gentium* concerned the substance of each. The primary *ius gentium*, being a subset of the *ius naturale*, was an expression of universally valid principles of justice based on natural reason, such as the right of self-defence and the duty to perform obligations.[43] The secondary *ius gentium*, by contrast, captured everything in Hermogenian's famous description of the *ius gentium* as the law which introduced wars, captivity, slavery, and the differentiations of property.[44] While such acts may not be just or based on natural reason, many nations and peoples over time appear to have arrived at a sort of consensus that these are at least legally permissible and, thus, should be recognized as lawful.

The wide gap between the primary *ius gentium* (which was, by definition, a part of the *ius naturale*) and the secondary *ius gentium* was sufficient to persuade humanist and Protestant jurists, such as Ulrich Zasius, Johann Oldendorp, John Selden, and Richard Zouch, that the *ius gentium* (and, in particular, the secondary *ius gentium*) was *sui generis* and must be treated separately from *ius naturale*.[45]

[42] Bartolus, *Secunda Super Digesto Veteri* (1530) fol. 65_{ro} [on D.12.6.64]. Baldus de Ubaldis, *In I^am^ Digesti Veteri Partem Commentaria* (Venice, 1577) fol. 10_{vo} [on D.1.1.4]. I thank Ryan Greenwood and Jon Robinson for guiding me through the medieval juridical literature on this primary/secondary distinction.

[43] On the right of self-defence, D.1.1.3.

[44] D.1.1.5. Cp. Giasone del Maino, *In II^am^ Digesti Veteri Partem* fol. 181_{vo} [on D.12.6.64].

[45] Shuger, *Renaissance Bible* 79 cites John Selden, *De Iure Naturali Iuxta Disciplinam Ebraeorum* (London, 1640) 73–98. Johann Oldendorp, *Iuris Naturalis, Gentium et Civilis Isagoge* (Köln: Johann Gymnicus, 1539) fol. b4–b5 [Title II: *De Iure Gentium*]. David Boucher, *Appropriating Hobbes: Legacies in Political, Legal, and International Thought* (Oxford: Oxford University Press, 2018) 145–46, suggests that additional early modern criticisms of the *ius naturale* = *ius gentium* equivalence, specifically in response to Hobbes, can be found in works by the English Civilian, Richard Zouch, and the German jurist, Samuel Rachel. Brett, *Changes of State* 75–77 traces additional responses in the School of Salamanca,

War

Of the many areas of law falling under the umbrella of (secondary) *ius gentium*, war was, by far, the most important.[46] The Roman jurisconsult, Hermogenian, whose description of the *ius gentium* would become canonical, lists war first in the law, *Ex hoc iure* (D.1.1.5). He did so for a very important reason: war is what makes possible everything else that follows in his list, such as the differentiation of nations, the founding of states, and the origin of private property and commerce.[47] Later commentators (above all, Gentili and Grotius) associate war so closely with the *ius gentium* that *ius gentium* and *ius belli* are used almost interchangeably with each other.

Locating war as a provision (or, as Brian Tierney suggests, a 'permission'[48]) of the *ius gentium* implied that war was to be understood fundamentally as a law-governed (rather than as an extralegal) condition: *bellum* was, by definition, *iustum*. That's not to say that all war was necessarily morally just, as it might be understood in the Western just war tradition of Augustine, Aquinas, and Grotius – far from it.[49] Instead the idea was that war could be understood as strictly legal, in the same way we might see any law-governed transaction like sale, marriage, or conveyance of movable property as strictly legal.

Bodin displays this legal transactional understanding of war as a legal right under the *ius gentium*, immediately on the opening page of the *De Republica* where he defines the essential qualities of statehood. There, he writes that what makes a state [*respublica*] distinctive, inter alia, is its legal capacity (we might even say its legal *right* [*ius; droit*]) to declare and wage a lawful war.

Bodin's not denying, of course, the reality of organized violence (and as we'll see, such *de facto* violence is part of the problem he's trying to address). He's simply saying, in typical lawyerly fashion, that not all acts of organized violence, such as reprisals, deserve to be called 'war', and thus don't deserve the legal recognition, the advantages, and the protections that a genuinely lawful war confers.[50]

beginning with Fernando Vázquez de Menchaca, *Illustrium Controversarium* (Frankfurt: Sumptibus Joannis Baptistae Schönwetteri, 1668) 355 [2.89.24–28].

46 This is also the reason why early modern pioneers of international law focus on the *ius gentium*.

47 Paul de Castro, *In I^{am} Digesti Veteris Partem Commentaria* (Lyon, 1583) fols. 5_{ro}–5_{vo} [on D.1.1.5, §§2–6] suggests the sequence of topics in the *ius gentium* follows Gaius' tripartite division of *ius civile* into persons, things, and actions.

48 Tierney, *Liberty and Law* 240–42.

49 Clifford Ando, 'Empire and the Laws of War: A Roman Archaeology', in *The Roman Foundations of the Law of Nations: Alberico Gentili and the Justice of Empire*, ed. Benedict Kingsbury and Benjamin Straumann (Oxford: Oxford University Press, 2010).

50 *République* 2–3; *De Republica* 1–2 [1.1]. The most important legal advantage that belligerents have in a legal war is the right of *postliminium*. Bodin comments extensively on these legal rights discussed at D.49.15.5.pr and D.49.15.7.pr. Bartolus' *Tractatus represaliarum* and Giovanni da Legnano's *Tractatus de bello, de represaliis et de duello*, ed. Thomas Erskine Holland and James Leslie Brierly (Oxford: Oxford University Press, 1917) distinguish between war and reprisal. Jacob Giltaij, 'Roman Law and the *Causa Legitima* for Reprisal in Bartolus', *Fundamina* 20 (2014): 349–56.

Such illicit violence deserves another name – *latrocinium* – variously translatable as piracy, brigandage, banditry, robbery, and other acts of unlawful and unjustified force. Borrowing a line from Cicero, Bodin insists on differentiating proper states, which *do* have this exclusive legal right to wage war, from mere 'bands of robbers' or 'pirates' [*societates latronum*], which don't (and therefore aren't states).

There's a vital theoretical reason why Bodin devotes considerable attention to this distinction between the transactional character of *bellum iustum* and the illegal violence of *latrocinium*, and that concerns the legal consequences of war. Some of these legal consequences are described in standard Roman law sources, in connection with rights of postliminy and legal protections afforded to prisoners of war.[51] And while Bodin makes creative use of these classical doctrines in examining the juridical consequences of a *bellum iustum*, he has something more fundamental in mind: wars can, under the right conditions, activate new titles and new rights of sovereignty. Victorious combatants who successfully conquer their enemies in a *bellum iustum* acquire titles of sovereignty and become sovereigns over those they've vanquished.

And not just any title of sovereignty. Because it was a title acquired specifically through war and conquest, as permitted under the *ius gentium*, what conquerors acquire over their captives is the form of sovereignty most closely resembling mastership over slaves – *seigneurie* or *dominium* – that is, seigneurial sovereignty. This was what, in Bodin's analysis, William the Conqueror, for example, acquired when he invaded and conquered England: He became *seigneur du royaume*, the lord and master of that realm.[52] This was also the same seigneurial title of sovereignty Rome acquired over its provinces through its wars and conquests of neighbouring peoples throughout the Mediterranean world.[53] Even the first title of sovereignty in recorded history, as we've seen in Chapter 3, was a seigneurial title acquired as the result of war and conquest.[54]

[51] One of the first topics of discussion in the opening chapter of *République* 2; *De Republica* 1 [1.1] concerns the 'benefit of the law of arms' [*ius fetiale*] which only 'lawful enemies being taken prisoners [but not robbers and pirates, *latrones et praedones*] … enjoy'. The marginalia in the Latin *De Republica* indicate that Bodin wrote this discussion in connection with his reading of D.50.16.118 on the legal status of 'enemies'.

[52] *République* 277; *De Republica* 192 [2.2]. Though William was, by *ius gentium*, entitled to seigneurial sovereignty and ownership of his subjects and their properties, he voluntarily allowed his English subjects to retain their liberty and property over their goods [*la liberté, & la pleine proprieté de leurs biens*].

[53] Bodin uses this to stress the heterogeneous character of Roman sovereignty in the early Empire: While its sovereignty was seigneurial over conquered peoples, it asserted *droit* sovereignty over free Roman citizens. This heterogeneity would dissolve with promulgation of the Antonine Constitution extending citizenship to all free persons.

[54] The first sovereign [*la premiere Monarchie*] was Nimrod who established sovereignty over those he conquered in Assyria. *République* 273; *De Republica* 189 [2.2]. Notably, Bodin observes here that, before Nimrod, everyone was free and equal [*Nam ante Nimerodi aetam, aequa erat omnium libertas*], living only under the *ius naturale primaevum*. Nimrod, whose name in Hebrew, Bodin observes, means

Any lawyer trained in Roman law would surely have found this formulation familiar, and that is because this theory of conquest as a source of sovereignty is modelled explicitly on the law of slavery. Under the *ius gentium*, one is said to become a slave instantly when one is 'captured by enemies' [*ab hostibus ... capiuntur*] (D.1.5.5.1) in a lawful war and to be, thereafter, subject to the *dominium* of the conqueror [*in potestate ... dominorum*] holding the power of life and death [*vitae necisque potestatem*] over their newly acquired slaves (D.1.6.1.1).[55] Indeed, Bodin himself repeats this theory in the opening of his chapter on slavery in the *République*.[56]

Bodin, however, gave this analysis of slavery a twist. Traditionally, under the *ius gentium*, the victors in a war were said to acquire only a private right of *dominium* over their captives whom they are entitled to take as their slaves. Bodin took a step further in saying that the *ius gentium* allowed for something even more: the victors acquired a public right of sovereignty [*ius summi imperii*] over their captives. It is for this reason, then, that the *ius gentium* allowed, as Hermogenian was quoted in the *Digest*, for new 'kingdoms to be founded' (D.1.1.5: *regna condita*).

What's noteworthy is Bodin's view that this rule of the *ius gentium*, sanctioning the creation and acquisition of new titles of sovereignty by conquest, theoretically remained valid even in Bodin's day.[57] Of course, such a right need not be exercised for it to remain valid, and there may even be good compelling reasons, whether moral or instrumental, why one *shouldn't* exercise such a right as this, howsoever permissible it may be under the *ius gentium*. But non-exercise of a right, Bodin seems to think, does nothing to alter, or unmake, its continuing legal validity.[58] For this reason, the right to wage war remains, even in Bodin's day, a legally valid instrument of state-building (or, what is essentially the same thing in this context, 'empire-building'), just as it was for the Romans who also used war as the single most important tool to widen the scope of their *imperium*.[59]

seigneur terrible/dominus metuendus, was the first who made possible the division of humans into sovereigns and subjects as well as masters and slaves.

[55] In the *Methodus* 261, Bodin lists this *potestas vitae et necis* as one of the exclusive rights of sovereignty. And, according to Florentinus, they are called slaves [*servi*], not because their purpose is 'to serve' [*dominos servire*] their masters, but instead because they have been 'saved' [from *servare*] – saved from death by conquerors trying to profit by selling their captives into slavery (D.1.5.4.2). *Gloss Ord.* on D.1.5.4.2, s.v.: *servare*, however, challenges this etymology. This is the same etymology of *servus* that appears in Hobbes, *De Cive* 102–3 [8.1].

[56] *République* 47; *De Republica* 31 [1.5].

[57] Le Thiec, 'Le droit de conquête en guise de constitution' 355–56; Pierre Mesnard, *L'Essor de la Philosophie politique au XVIe siècle* (Paris: Vrin, 1951) 463–72.

[58] Not even prescription of time can prejudice rightholders in this respect.

[59] One crucial application of this doctrine touched upon the legality of European conquest and colonization of the Americas, such as Peru: *République* 277; *De Republica* 192 [2.2].

Legal and Illegal War: *Bellum Iustum* and *Latrocinium*

War was, thus, a transformative and creative force in human affairs, by activating new obligatory bonds of sovereignty and subjection where previously there were none. But in order for these legal consequences of war to be valid, the war *itself* must be legally valid. The *bellum* must be *iustum* – and *iustum* specifically *ex iure gentium* (i.e. the war must be 'legal' as recognized under the law of nations). What this means, in effect, is that no act of brigandage or piracy – *latrocinium* – can ever create a new valid title of sovereignty, let alone a bond of obligation owing to pirates or brigands [*latrones, praedones*].[60] This is precisely why Bodin insists that all those 'taken by brigands or pirates ... nevertheless remain free [*libres*]' – free in the Hohfeldian sense of a 'privilege' or 'liberty-right' that such captives are free of any duty owing to their captors.[61]

All this, of course, hinges on how we should understand the distinction between a legal war [*bellum iustum*] and an illegal force [*latrocinium*], a distinction central to Bodin's conceptual architecture. It's important to stress, first, that *bellum iustum*, as Bodin used the term, doesn't mean 'just war'.[62] It is, instead, a classical reference to the notion of a legally permissible war originating in the Roman *ius fetiale*, the body of law governing the activities of the Roman 'fetial' priesthood, the college of twenty priests charged with the legal formalities of foreign relations, embassies, treaties, and war.[63] These fetials functioned as a kind of 'foreign ministry' for the Roman state and performed, among other solemn duties in upholding public faith and credit, the ceremonial rites necessary to declare war [*bellum indicere*; *denunciatio*]. For this reason, the fetial law was a crucial source for early international law.

Often compared to the civil procedure of *legis actio sacramento* in early Roman law, these fetial rites (as they were recounted in Late Republican authorities) were intended to ensure piety and good faith in foreign affairs and, when necessary, required the head of the college of fetial priests, the *pater patratus populi Romani*, to make formal demands for satisfaction, a *rerum repetitio* (or *clarigatio*), of grievances.[64] The fetial rites of war, ultimately requiring the casting of a blood-stained spear into enemy territory, were documented in a number of classical authorities,

[60] *De Off.* 3.107: Oaths, or otherwise any promise or other mode of contractual obligation, can never be made with pirates or brigands.

[61] *République* 48; *De Republica* 32 [1.5]. This captive of brigandage or piracy, I'd argue, is comparable to Hobbes' discussion of the *ergastulus* in *De Cive* 103–4 [8.2–8.4], in that both remain 'free' in one fundamental respect: they are $\sim O(\varphi)$, under no obligation to their capturer, and so, do no injury if they are able to escape from their captive status.

[62] Greenwood, 'War and Sovereignty' 41. This point extends also to Grotius' usage of the term, *bellum iustum*, and it is one important reason why Grotius isn't simply a theorist of 'just war', but also a theorist of 'licit war' (that is, licit under *ius naturale* and *ius gentium*). Peter Haggenmacher, *Grotius et la doctrine de la guerre juste* (Paris: Presses Universitaires de France, 1983).

[63] Bodin translates *ius fetiale* (or rather, *ius feciale*) to translate as *droits des alliances et traictez*.

[64] Bederman, *International Law in Antiquity* 235; cp. Ando, 'Empire and the Laws of War'.

such as Plutarch, Dionysius of Halicarnassus, and Livy, all of which Bodin cited and would, in later generations, become the key raw data for early modern jurists commenting on the *ius gentium* and *ius fetiale* such as Gentili, Grotius, and Zouch.[65]

The most important source for all of them, however, was Cicero who explicitly connected the *ius fetiale* rites to his general theory of *bellum iustum*.[66] Bodin evidently took to heart Cicero's principle that, 'No war is deemed to be lawful [*iustum*] if it has not been legally declared and proclaimed [*nisi denuntiatum, nisi indictum*]', through the required fetial procedure, or some equivalent.[67] What ultimately 'authorizes' or 'legalizes' organized state violence, so that it becomes a *bellum iustum* capable of creating a new title of sovereignty, is this formal process of declaration [*indictio*].[68]

Such declarations of war, whether by fetial or some other procedure, functioned as what one philosopher once labelled 'declarative illocutionary acts', speech-acts whose illocutionary function was to introduce, by declarative fiat, a new social and juridical condition, a state of war.[69] Like other formal legal acts, such as marriage and adoption, with a transactional and ritualistic quality to them in classical law, war too featured this, what Clifford Ando has described as a 'strong nominalism'.[70] Through proper performance of legally prescribed words and actions one can produce a new social reality – in this case, from a state of peace to a state of war.

Indictio belli, accomplished in the Roman *ius fetiale* by ritualistic utterance of the required formula and the throwing of a blood-stained spear into enemy territory, effectively transformed relationships, created and assigned new roles, and distributed rights that otherwise would not exist *ante bellum*. It defined, in short, those who were to be counted legally as 'enemies' [*hostes*].

On this point, Bodin often cited, as we've seen earlier, a famous text by Pomponius in the *Digest*, supplying the legal definition of 'enemies' in a state of war:[71]

[65] Dionysius of Halicarnassus, *Roman Antiquities*, 1:520–27 [2.72]; Plutarch, *Lives: Theseus and Romulus, Lycurgus and Numa, Solon and Publicola*, vol. 1, Loeb Classical Library 46, trans. Bernadotte Perrin (Cambridge: Harvard University Press, 1914) 1:346–51 [*Numa* 12]; Livy, *Ab Urbe Condita* 1.24.3–9; 1.32.5–14. Zouch, *Juris et Judicii Fecialis* 62. Grotius, *Commentary on the Law of Prize and Booty* [*De Iure Praedae Commentarius*], ed. Martine Julia van Ittersum (Indianapolis: Liberty Fund, 2006) 148 cites Bodin, *République* I, 7 on the *rerum repetitio* and the right to declare war.

[66] Federico Santangelo, 'The Fetials and their *Ius*', *Bulletin of the Institute of Classical Studies* 51 (2008): 81. Cicero, *De Off.* 1.36; *De Re Publica* 2.31, 3.35; *De Legibus* 2.21; Livy 1.24.3–9 and 1.32.5–14.

[67] Cicero, *De Re Publica* 3.35.

[68] *République* 109; *De Republica* 70 [1.7]. Bodin elsewhere, at *République* 760; *De Republica* 563 [5.5], seems to follow Cicero in specifying that, while declaration is necessary, it is, by itself, insufficient to create a lawful state of war. The *causa belli* itself must also be just.

[69] John Searle, 'A Classification of Illocutionary Acts', *Language in Society* 5 (1976): 13–16.

[70] Ando, *Law, Language, and Empire* 53.

[71] For example, at *République* 278; *De Republica* 193 [2.2]. Bodin's first citation in the Latin *De Republica* 1 [1.1] is to D.50.16.118.

> 'Enemies' are those who declare war against us, or those against whom we publicly declare war: all others are 'brigands' or 'pirates'.[72]

Both passages, and the accumulated commentaries associated with them, are notable, not only because they highlight the distinction between lawful war among belligerents [*hostes*] and the unlawful violence of brigandage and piracy [*latrunculi vel praedones*], but also because it reveals the centrality of formal public declaration in drawing that distinction: public declaration of war [*publice bellum decrevimus*] is sufficient to create legal enemies, so long as the declaration is procedurally valid.[73]

Can just anybody declare war? Could, say, an ambitious power-hungry duke formally under the jurisdiction of a superior, or an independent republic, such as an autonomous Italian commune or city, declare war? Views varied in the major modern treatments of sovereignty. Probably the most prominent example is Grotius, who, by distinguishing himself from the principle established in D.49.15.24, allows for the legality of private wars and mixed wars.[74] Vattel, by contrast, reserves the right of war, and specifically the right of conquest, to the state and its sovereign authority, never to private parties.[75] Another noteworthy contrasting example is Rousseau who, in the *Social Contract*, stipulated explicitly against Grotius that the right of declaring war wasn't a proper right of sovereignty at all, but merely a 'particular' administrative act of government proper to government officials.[76]

Bodin, for his part, addressed this question specifically in his enumeration of the various rights of sovereignty. In all his major theoretical works on the state, Bodin explicitly identified the right to declare war and peace as cardinal among the exclusive prerogative *marques*, or *capita*, of an independent state's sovereignty, a point he says is *verifie non seulement par les loix Rommaines, ains aussi de tous les autres peuples* 'verified not only by the law of the Romans, but of all other nations [i.e. the *ius gentium*]'.[77] His most definitive statement in *République* I, 10, identified the sovereign right of declaring war and peace as the paramount right of sovereignty, second in rank only to the principal sovereign right of making and unmaking law.

[72] D.50.16.118, cp. 49.15.24: *Hostes hi sunt, qui nobis aut quibus nos publice bellum decrevimus: ceteri latrones aut praedones sunt.*

[73] Bodin rehearses a typically Machiavellian argument at *République* 760; *De Republica* 563 [5.5], concerning the usefulness of enemies in minimizing the risk of civil war and reinforcing political unity, especially in democracies.

[74] *De Iure Belli ac Pacis* 1.3.1.

[75] Vattel, *Law of Nations* 598–603 [3.13, §§201–202] specifically denounces the 'monstrous principle, that the conqueror is absolute master of his conquest ... [like a] despotic government'. It is hard to see how Vattel could not have been familiar with Bodin's original analysis of this point. Cp. *Law of Nations* 214 [1.18, §207], which restricts the original right of occupation exclusively to states.

[76] Rousseau, *Basic Political Writings* 144–45; 155 [*Social Contract* 1.4; 2.2].

[77] *Distributio* fol. A, s.v.: *Ius Publicum*; *Methodus* 261; *République* 224; *De Republica* 155 [1.10]: *decerner la guerre, ou traicter la paix, qui est l'un des plus grands points de la maiesté; bellum indicere, aut pacem inire: quo iure maiestatis nullum fere maius esse potest.*

While wars might be carried out by generals and subordinates authorized and empowered by sovereigns, the right of declaring war and peace was to be reserved exclusively to sovereigns. Thus, on this argument, no government officer or subordinate could ever declare war on their own. Seeing that they are not sovereign themselves, they have no right to do so. They could, of course, engage in violence, but without the authorization that the sovereign right of war ensures, it would be an illicit violence and thus outside the legal boundaries of what is legally permissible under the *ius gentium*.[78]

By limiting the right of declaring war and peace exclusively to genuine sovereigns, Bodin effectively limited the legal consequences of war and peace to sovereigns. The clear implication was that the *ius gentium* right of conquest, whereby the victor of a *bellum iustum* was legally entitled to acquire a new title of sovereignty over the conquered *hostis*, was a limited right accessible only to sovereign states who enjoyed the *droit souverain* of declaring war and peace.

By contrast, those *without* sovereignty and, therefore, without the sovereign right of declaring war and peace were not entitled to any of the legal advantages or protections of the *ius gentium* typically given to legal combatants of a lawful war. Earlier (in Chapter 1), we saw this in connection with the legal right of postliminy. But Bodin extended this same principle to the right of conquest in a *bellum iustum*, to argue that those without sovereignty, even if they are successful in subduing others by force, are not entitled to claim the lawful acquisition or transfer of a new title of sovereignty or to declare a legal peace.

Anybody who uses such illegal force *ipso facto* acts outside what is permissible by the *ius gentium* and has, through their illicit actions, placed themselves outside the law and the boundaries of legality. They have become, in other words, 'outlaws' [*proscripti*], stripped not only of the civil rights and protections of their native *ius civile*, but also of human rights (so to speak) of the *ius gentium*.[79] As we've seen, Bodin collectively labelled these outlaws as brigands, bandits, robbers, thieves, and pirates – in a word, *latrones*. And they presented a particular danger to genuine sovereign states. Because of their propensity to use lawless force, brigands and pirates threaten the 'destruction and ruin' [*l'éversion & ruine*; *eversionem*] of states. For this reason, Bodin observes that there can be 'neither commerce, nor alliance' [*ny commerce, ny alliance; nulla contractuum*

[78] Bodin often cited Caesar's illicit violence during the Gallic Wars as a usurpation establishing an illegitimate tyranny, a pattern that would be repeated in Rome itself, *Methodus* 266; *République* 224; *De Republica* 155–56 [1.10], citing Plutarch on Cato. Cp. Grotius, *De Iure Belli ac Pacis* 1.3.5, likely read this passage in Bodin. Grotius cited this mutual hostility between Cato and Caesar and concluded that, in conducting an illicit war, Caesar had stepped beyond the boundaries of his proconsular authority over Gaul. Turchetti 709 [1.10] identifies Bodin's sources for this principle: D.3.3.48, 2.14.28, 12.6.6, Baldus on C.4.35.15, Giasone del Maino on Inst.4.6.28, D.17.1.5, 17.1.46, 17.1.51, 29.2.25.7.

[79] *Proscriptio*, *relegatio*, and *exilii deportationis* appear in *Distributio* fol. F, s.v.: *Poenale* as other forms of punishment.

fides, nulla iuris societas] between sovereign states and such outlaws, nor can the sovereign rights of war ever be shared with, or extended to, them [*iura belli cum illis communicari nec debent*].[80]

While these *latrones* are, in a way, enemies, they must be differentiated from 'legal enemies' of state engaged in a *bellum iustum*, the *hostes*, identified earlier by Ulpian. In order to do this, Bodin, following his classical sources, distinguished between two principal types of 'enemies'. The first were the *iustos ac legitimos hostes*, the 'legal enemies' of a legal war [*bellum iustum*]. The second, however, were the outlawed brigands and pirates, the *latrones* who, lacking any right or title of sovereignty (as the jurists put it, *defectus tituli*), exercised an illegal force [*latrocinium*] upon another without any right to do so. These too are enemies, but they are not 'legal enemies'. Rather, they are enemies of a special kind, what Cicero once famously designated *hostes omnium communes*, and what Bodin following Cicero called 'the enemies of mankind' [*ennemis du genre humain*].[81]

	Legal war *Bellum iustum*	**Illegal war** *Latrocinium*
Conflict based on	*Droit; Ius* (permissible under the *ius gentium*)	*Force; Vis*
Participants in conflict	*Hostes*: Sovereign states; 'legal enemies' (D.50.16.118)	*Latrones*: Brigands, pirates; 'enemies of mankind'
Legal consequences	The lawful conqueror acquires a new title of sovereignty; postliminy; right of conquest	No new title of sovereignty; no transfer or exchange of sovereignty

These common enemies of mankind are *sui generis*, and to be distinguished from those 'legal enemies' with the sovereign right to engage in a legal war. As

[80] *République* 2; *De Republica* 1 [1.1]. Cp. Walter Reich, *Enemies of Mankind: Vattel's Theory of Collective Security* (Leiden: Martinus Nijhoff, 2013) 50–54 places Bodin's analysis in the context of Barbary warfare.

[81] *République* 3 [1.1]; Peter Schröder, 'Vitoria, Gentili, Bodin: Sovereignty and the Law of Nations', in *The Roman Foundations of the Law of Nations*, ed. Benedict Kingsbury and Benjamin Straumann (Oxford: Oxford University Press, 2010) 178–79, identifies Bodin as the source of Gentili's own analysis. Unlike Carl Schmitt's famous friend-enemy distinction in *Concept of the Political*, trans. George Schwab (Chicago: University of Chicago Press, 2007) 26, then, Bodin imagines a tripartite division, consisting of friends [*amici*], legal enemies [*hostes*], and enemies of mankind [*hostes omnium*]. Whereas friend and legal enemy are within the boundaries of the *ius gentium*, only the enemy of mankind remains outside. Cp. Hostiensis' classifications of just and unjust wars in Gregory Reichberg, *Thomas Aquinas on War and Peace* (Cambridge: Cambridge University Press, 2016) 29–30.

we've seen, because they stand outside the *ius gentium*, they enjoy no special advantages or protections of those laws, such as the right of postliminy or the right of conquest. Nor did they enjoy what Roman law regarded as *commercium*, the legal right to engage in commercial transactions based on good faith. Lacking legal standing in the law, such perfidious omnilateral enemies of all who only use force to get their way cannot be trusted to be parties to any such international relations, as are only appropriate between 'friends' [*amici*] who practise humane norms of gentle civility (see Chapter 1) and are appropriate to be legal subjects of the *ius gentium* that is meant for a civil society of friends.[82] For this reason, Bodin insists, as a general rule, that no contract or pact made with brigands and pirates should be regarded as binding.[83] Indeed, nothing is due to *latrones*, with whom no obligatory bond can be valid.

Probably the most striking consequence of all concerns what might be described as the dehumanizing effect of being branded an enemy of mankind.[84] Because of the threats they pose, by their unpredictable use of force or fraud, to the security of civic life, brigands and pirates have typically been characterized as wild savage beasts, which it is permissible for anybody, even private persons, to hunt down, attack, and kill.[85] Cicero famously depicted them as lions and foxes.[86] Locke too reduced anybody who would make war a beast, a 'tiger', a 'wolf or a lion ... not under the ties of the common law of reason ... but that of force and violence'.[87] The purpose of this dehumanization was all the same. It was a blanket authorization for 'latronicide', a universal licence to kill all enemies of mankind.

Bodin has one more to add to this list of *latrones* – the tyrant. And the reason is because, like brigands and pirates, tyrants too lack all the humane qualities of civility and law and instead use illicit force over others to seize what properly belongs to others. But tyrants are exceptional in that the target of their unlawful *latrocinia* isn't private persons or private property. Rather, it is sovereignty.

[82] *République* 593–94; *De Republica* 436 [4.4].

[83] *République* 2; *De Republica* 1–2 [1.1]: Moreover, there is 'no injury' or wrongdoing [*nulla fraus*] for breaking a pact made with a brigand. Bodin's doctrine, thus, is fundamentally at odds with the Hobbesian doctrine that covenants extracted through force and fear are nevertheless obligatory.

[84] On this theme, see Daniel Luban, 'The Enemy of All Humanity', *Netherlands Journal of Legal Philosophy* 47 (2018): 112–37; Marc de Wilde, 'Enemy of All Humanity: The Dehumanizing Effects of a Dangerous Concept', *Netherlands Journal of Legal Philosophy* 47 (2018): 158–75.

[85] Bodin's argument is based on the *ius gentium* argument on the permissibility of hunting wild animals, explored in Bodin's translation of Oppian. Note that Nimrod, who Bodin regarded as the first sovereign in Scriptural chronology, was also a hunter.

[86] *De Off.* 1.41. Machiavelli, referring to this passage, famously counsels his inexperienced new princes to do just the opposite and rely on the the beastly force and fraud of lions and foxes to maintain their states. Notably, Bodin refers to Machiavelli's advice only in the exceptional cases of changes of state, *République* 519; *De Republica* 376 [4.1].

[87] Locke, *Two Treatises of Government* 274, 279 [II, §§11, 16].

The Common Enemy of Mankind: The Tyrant

The topic of tyranny arises chiefly in Book II of the *République*, where Bodin outlines the three principal forms of state – monarchical, aristocratic, and popular.[88] The difference between these three forms ultimately hinges on the constitutional form of a state's sovereignty [*status reipublicae*]: if a state is bound together under the authority of one person, the state is a 'monarchy'. If bound under the supreme authority of a 'numerical minority' of the state, it is an 'aristocracy'. And if it is bound under the supreme authority of a 'numerical majority' or of the 'people acting as a whole' [*populus universus*], it is a 'popular state'.

In studying these three basic forms of state, however, Bodin observes that each can be further sub-divided according to the different ways in which each state is governed [*gubernatur*] by the sovereign authority.[89]

Form of Sovereignty		
Monarchical [*monarchie*; *monarchia*]	**Aristocratic** [*aristocratie*; *optimates*]	**Popular** [*estat populaire*; *populus*]
Royal, *droit monarchie* [*royal*; *regia*]	Lawful [*legitime*; *legitimum imperium*]	Lawful [*legitime*; *legitimum imperium*]
Seigneurial [*seigneurial*; *dominatio*]	Seigneurial [*seigneuriale*; *sine lege*]	Seigneurial [*seigneurial*; *sine lege*]
Tyrannical [*tyrannie*; *tyrannis*]	Factious [*factieuse*; *factioso*]	Turbulent [*turbulent*; *furentis ac turbulentae plebis impotentia*]

For example, popular states, wherein the whole people [*populo universo*] or the numerical majority thereof [*maior pars*] collectively hold the indivisible right of sovereignty, differ yet in terms of how those popular states are governed. The

[88] However, mentions of tyranny pop up in several revealing, though interpretively challenging, spots in Book I. Three examples are worth noting at this stage. One is the case of Nimrod. Two others are the Roman general, Sulla, and the Florentine ruler, Cosimo de Medici, which would be a focal point for Machiavelli.

[89] This arrangement is based on *République* 507; *De Republica* 368 [4.1], which indicates the different forms of constitutional and political change in states. Constitutional changes in the form of sovereignty (e.g. from popular sovereignty to monarchy) are called 'perfect changes' [*changements parfaicts*; *conversiones perfectae*], while political changes in the style of governing are called 'imperfect changes' [*changements imparfaicts*; *imperfectae*]. Cp. *République* 272–3; *De Republica* 189 [2.2]: *Eadem distinctio ad Aristocratiam et Democratiam adhiberi potest: nam tyrannis quoque omnium maxima a Marco Tullio appellatur, furentis ac turbulentae plebis impotentia.*

Roman Republic is a classic example. Even though it was a pure democracy in its sovereignty, Rome was nevertheless governed aristocratically, a point he demonstrated with the structure of high Republican magistrates such as consuls, praetors, and censors, which, though elected by popular voting assemblies, were in practice reserved to free citizens of patrician rank. Only when offices and functions of government are open to 'the base', those of lower social rank, can a state be described not only as a democracy, but as a democracy also being governed 'democratically'.

A similar analysis is offered in the case of monarchical states – which Bodin defines as that 'form of state [*Reipublicae genus*], in which the sovereign power of the whole state belongs to one person' [*penes unum summa totius Reipublicae potestas*].[90] This genus, however, is sub-divided into three species of monarchical rule. One is the *seigneuriale monarchie* [*rerum omnium dominus*], those states exemplified by the despotic, yet fully legal, *ex iure gentium et naturale*, rulership of the Biblical hunter-king, Nimrod and, in Bodin's time, the seigneurial rule of the sultans and the tsars. The second other major species was *droit monarchie*, states characterized by a monarch observing the rule of law.

But there was a third species of monarchical rule – tyranny. How did this species differ from the other two? And, in particular, how did tyranny differ from the despotic rule of the seigneur, which some might argue as also being 'tyrannical'? It's important to observe, as Mario Turchetti has stressed in an important study, that there is a world of difference between the 'tyrant' and the 'despot' [*seigneur, seigneurie*; *dominus, dominium*; δεσπότης, δεσποτεία] in Bodin's system of thought.[91] While modern political discourse treats both terms as functionally equivalent to each other, signifying an undifferentiated generic notion of oppressive misrule, Bodin (and arguably also some of his contemporaries) insisted on distinguishing sharply between the usurping tyrant, the seigneurial despot, and the lawful king.[92]

Bodin's first move in addressing these questions, as he has done with so many other concepts, is an observation concerning the term's semantic elasticity over time. In its classical origins, the term, 'tyrant', actually signalled a positive connotation (or at least, a value-neutral term):

[90] This is the famous passage, at *République* 272; *De Republica* 189 [2.2], where Bodin introduces the distinction between the constitutional form of a sovereign state [*l'etat*; *status reipublicae*] and the manner in which the state is governed [*gouvernement*; *administratio*; *gubernatio*]. Here, he states explicitly, *tout Monarchie est seigneuriale, ou Royale, ou Tyrannique*; *Is qui Imperium habet, rerum omnium dominus est, aut Rex, aut tyran*[n]*us*.

[91] Mario Turchetti, 'Despotism and Tyranny: Unmasking a Tenacious Confusion', *European Journal of Political Theory* 7 (2008): 159–82.

[92] Mary Nyquist investigates the strategic purposes of the three-way distinction in *Arbitrary Rule* 81–5.

> The word, *tyrannus*, was once thought to be honourable and splendid, indicating the one who had, without the citizen's consent, seized power by force or by fraud, even if he later may have governed temperately and equitably.[93]

Thus, Bodin observes, both a 'wise and just prince' [*sage & iuste Prince*] as well as a 'wicked' [*meschant*] prince could both equally be described as 'tyrants', so long as they acquired their power 'by force or by finesse' [*par forcer, ou par finesse*], rather than by lawful means (including by conquest in a lawful war).[94] The many Greek examples of populist leaders who, with popular approval and yet contrary to law and custom, seized power through coups reinforced for Bodin the complicated nature of ancient tyranny.[95]

It was only because tyrants increasingly abused their ill-gotten power that 'the most venerable and sacred [*augustissima ac sanctissima*] offices and charges [such as the 'tyrant'] have become abominable' and 'hateful' [*odiosum*] to all nations.[96] Nor was this pattern unique to tyrants. Titles such as 'king' [*rex*] and 'dictator', once honourable and even 'most holy' [*sanctissima*] among Romans, were defiled by the inexcusable actions of Tarquin and Sulla. Indeed, 'tyrant' had, by the later sixteenth century, become weaponized as something of a catch-all term designating, without differentiation, all forms of corrupt and oppressive misrule.[97]

Such abuse of language, Bodin thought, presented a positive danger: anybody could potentially be labelled a 'tyrant' and attract the odium once reserved for a Periander, a Tarquin, or a Sulla:

> He who taxes too heavily would be a tyrant ... he who gives commands that the people do not like would be a tyrant, as Aristotle defined a tyrant in the *Politics*; he who maintains guards for his security would be a tyrant; he who punishes conspirators against his rule would be a tyrant.[98]

Even a ruler or an inferior officer of state with a fully legitimate title to authority could have that title undermined in an instant by the taint of tyranny. The volatile

[93] *République* 287; *De Republica* 199 [2.4]: *Tyranni vox, olim honesta ac splendida, de eo dicebatur, qui dominationem, civibus inuitis ac nolentibus, vi aut fraude arripuisset, tametsi moderate ac iuste imperaret.*

[94] *République* 287, 288 [2.4].

[95] *République* 526; *De Republica* 381 [4.1]: Bodin observes tyrannies tend to transform into democracies. His illustrations include Pisistratus, Tarquin, Hiero of Syracuse, and Dionysius.

[96] *République* 288; *De Republica* 200 [2.4]: Bodin cites in particular the example of Periander of Corinth, Dionysius, and 'a most cruel tyranny' [*une cruelle tyrannie*; *crudelissimam tyrannidem*] of the Roman dictator, Sulla, *République* 124, 506; *De Republica* 80, 368 [1.8, 4.1]. On the significance of Sulla in Bodin's analysis, see Straumann, *Crisis and Constitutionalism* 284–86.

[97] Mario Turchetti, *Tyrannie et tyrannicide de l'Antiquité a nos jours* (Paris: Presses Universitaires de France, 2001).

[98] *République* 307; *De Republica* 213; Franklin 120 [2.5].

language of tyranny, thus, opened the way for (an entirely artificial, in Bodin's view) crisis of legitimacy.

This didn't mean, of course, that the language of 'tyrant' must be extirpated entirely – that would be unrealistic and undesirable. Bodin's goal, rather, was something like linguistic reform, to undo this abuse of language and restore a narrowly classical conception of the 'tyrant'. The thought was that, by restoring the classical notion, it would then be possible to draw the distinction between the tyrant, the seigneur, and the lawful monarch more lucidly.

Key to this tripartite distinction was the notion of legal title: what *droit* sovereigns and *seigneurial* sovereigns, whether monarchical or republican in form, all have in common is that they are legally 'entitled' to rule. Both can point to some law, legal principle, or precedent that gives them their right to rule, their *ius imperii* (Chapter 2). To be sure, it's true that a ruler with title may exercise their right in an arbitrary or corrupt manner – as seigneurial sovereigns surely do. But, as despicable as such rulership may be, *that* is not what makes one a tyrant. What makes one a tyrant is want of legal title – as the lawyers put it, a *defectus tituli*.

The principal source for Bodin's analysis was, once again, Bartolus of Sassoferrato, who authored an influential standalone tract on tyranny, *Tractatus de Tyranno*.[99] For this reason, Bartolus would become Bodin's primary target. As Bodin would put it in the opening sentence of *République* II, 5, it was Bartolus' analysis, above all others, which 'has led many astray, and has been the cause of so many inconveniences'.[100]

Bartolus' starting point was relatively uncontroversial. Like his classical antecedents, Bartolus accepted the definition that the 'tyrant of a *civitas* is he who does not rule by law [*iure*]'.[101] But what counts as not ruling by law? Classical sources, as we've seen, defined it strictly and narrowly in terms of usurpation. What makes one a tyrant is the illicit manner by which power is acquired – that is, by an illegal seizure or coup, approximating a theft or piracy, of someone else's rightful authority.

Bartolus, however, identified two problems highlighting the limitations of the usurpation theory. Suppose, first, that a tyrant used his ill-gotten power in a noble and just manner for the common benefit. Could a reformed tyrant's later good behaviour excuse and absolve the tyrant from his original misdeed and thereby erase the stain of illegitimacy? The classical view utterly denies this; no amount of good works (so to speak) can, in principle, nullify the tyrant's original sin of usurpation.

Now consider a second case, where a sovereign with a lawfully acquired title of sovereignty – say, by a lawful war [*bello iusto*] or by hereditary succession – decided

[99] Bartolus of Sassoferrato, *Politica e diritto nel Trecento italiano: Il 'De tyranno' di Bartolo da Sassoferrato con l'edizione critica dei trattati 'De guelphis et gebellinis,' 'De regimine civitatis' e 'De tyranno.' Il Pensiero Politico*, Biblioteca 11, ed. Diego Quaglioni (Florence: Leo S. Olschki Editore, 1983).

[100] *République* 297; *De Republica* 207 [2.5].

[101] Bartolus, *Politica e diritto* 184 [*De Tyranno* §5].

to exercise sovereignty in an excessively cruel, harsh, or corrupt manner. There's no question of title here: it is settled and accepted that the sovereign, in this case, is entitled to rule and is recognized legally as having the right to rule. The issue here strictly concerns maladministration or abuse of (legitimate) power. Could misrule somehow invalidate a sovereign's lawful title to sovereignty and transform a legitimate sovereign into an illegitimate 'tyrant'? Even posing the question itself was potentially seditious. Since no one is duty-bound to obey a tyrant, this line of reasoning could theoretically expose even a legitimate sovereign to tyrannicidal resistance.

What worried Bartolus, in both of these cases, was that defining tyranny strictly in terms of usurpation didn't, in his view, fully capture the whole range of what should (and shouldn't) count as 'ruling without lawful right'. Tyranny had to be more than just about determining the original legal title to authority. It also had to be about the factual exercise of power.

Bartolus, thus, makes a quintessentially 'Bartolist' move: 'Just as not ruling by law happens in many ways, so are there many species of tyrants'.[102] While some are tyrants simply on account of their lack of a lawful title [*ex defectu tituli*], others are tyrants on account of their maladministration of power [*ex parte exercitii*]; such misrule, even if lawful and based on proper title, can be enough to transform a ruler into a tyrant.[103]

Notice what Bartolus has done – all to Bodin's ultimate dismay. He took a simple category – tyranny defined as 'ruling without law' – and opened up numerous subspecies and categories of tyrannical rule, some of which seem, at first glance, to be at odds with the classical analysis of tyranny. Whereas usurpation of someone else's authority by force or fraud was traditionally thought to be the sole criterion for tyranny, Bartolus allowed a much looser interpretation of 'ruling without law' that extended far beyond usurpation and included all varieties of misrule and maladministration.

It would be easy for a reader of Bartolus' tract to conclude that our world (or at least the bloody world of medieval Italian politics) must be full of tyrants, and the flexible Bartolist analysis explains why. It was this Bartolist category of the tyrant *ex parte exercitii* that most worried Bodin, as it potentially emboldened subjects and made lawful *de iure* sovereigns fair game for tyrannicidal resistance and wars for liberty.[104] Bodin's solution was to eliminate outright the invented Bartolist category of tyranny *ex parte exercitii*, reserving *tyrannie* exclusively for those who have, in

[102] Bartolus, *Politica e diritto* 184 [*De Tyranno* §5].

[103] Bartolus, *Politica e diritto* 185 [*De Tyranno* §5]. There is another layer of complexity to Bartolus' distinction, where he distinguishes between the 'open and manifest' tyrant and the 'hidden' tyrant.

[104] The Bartolist category of *ex parte exercitii* tyrants took centre stage in Calvinist resistance theory – most notably in Theodore Beza's *De iure magistratuum* and the pseudonymous *Vindiciae contra tyrannos*.

effect, stolen their power from someone else – or, in other words, those without any legal title to the power they wield.

In Bodin's strategy, legal title, thus, becomes crucial in identifying who is and isn't a tyrant. How, then, do we determine title? Bodin's analysis tracked the degree of a regime's legal compliance. Imagine an abstract scale or continuum measuring the degree to which a state complies with the law at all levels. He is thinking not only of positive legislation (*ius civile*), but also the higher laws of the *ius gentium, naturale, et divinum*. Keeping in mind this legal pluralism, Bodin thinks it is theoretically possible to ascertain title – and therefore, classify states – by observing how far their rulers do in fact comply with legal duties, as follows:

	De Iure		De Facto
	Droit	*Seigneurie*	*Tyrannie*
Ius divinum et naturale	Compliant	Compliant	Non-compliant
Ius gentium	Compliant	Compliant	Non-compliant
Ius civile	Compliant	Non-compliant	Non-compliant

Droit sovereignty represented one extreme along this scale of compliance: it was the monarchical state whose sovereignty was fully compliant with the law, at all levels. To wit: *droit* sovereigns were compliant not only with the *ius divinum*, the *ius naturale* and the *ius gentium*, but also with its own *ius civile* (and thus, following the idealized example of the emperor that is observant of his own laws in the Roman law *Digna vox*, C.1.14.4).

Seigneurial sovereigns, by contrast, were located further down this scale with a corresponding decline in the degree of compliance. This was the species of monarchical state that was partially or minimally compliant with the *ius divinum*, the *ius naturale*, and the *ius gentium*. But because this was a regime where the sovereign ruled by arbitrary will [*arbitrio*], rather than by positive legislation [*lege*], it was typically regarded as a lawless, despotic, 'slavish' regime without the rule of law that *droit* sovereigns require. Thus, the seigneurial state scores lower on this scale of compliance, yet it formally retains a basic right of sovereignty, by the *ius gentium*.

Tyranny scores the worst along this scale and represented the other extreme on this continuum: it was the regime of complete non-compliance, *par excellence* – the state whose sovereign was compliant with no law whatsoever. As Bodin put it, this was a regime of 'one man trampling upon the divine and natural laws' [*unus homo divinis ac naturae legibus sublatis; foulant aux pieds les loix de nature*].[105]

105 *République* 287; *De Republica* 199 [2.4].

Tyranny was, thus, the quintessential lawless regime. For clarity here, it might be useful to draw a comparison between the tyrant and the *seigneur*. It's true that seigneurial despots, who governed not by laws [*legibus*], but by will [*arbitrio*], were also lawless, in the sense that they rejected the rule of law as a technique of government. But, unlike tyrants, seigneurial despots could at least claim a minimal legal right to sovereignty, on the grounds that their sovereignty was conferred upon them lawfully, as the *ius gentium* allows and recognizes, by a right of conquest in a *bellum iustum*, a right recognized *consensu omnium gentium*, just as slavery was.[106] This was, it will be recalled from Chapter 3, the legal foundation of Nimrod's claim to a just title of sovereignty in Bodin's Biblical chronology; he 'lawfully' acquired Assyria by conquering and enslaving the Assyrians in a *bellum iustum*, as the *ius gentium* allowed.[107] The argument could, thus, be made (as Bodin did) that, even though seigneurial despots don't govern according to the rule of law, they nevertheless comply with certain fundamentals of the *ius gentium* recognized by most peoples.[108]

Tyrants, however, can't even claim that because, by definition, tyranny is a regime ultimately based, not on lawful war [*bello iusto*], but simply on unlawful theft [*latrocinio*] – namely, the usurpation of someone else's title to rule. Like brigands and pirates, tyrants too seize and take goods properly belonging to someone else by force or fraud, and Bodin exploited this moralized juridical language of injury and wrong to explain the illicit origin of all tyrannical regimes [*vi aut fraude arripuisset*].

While there is a powerful rhetorical force in this language of theft, there is ultimately a strategic purpose in Bodin's appeal to this analysis. Since no theft – whether of land, of movable goods, or of sovereignty – can ever be regarded as lawful under the *ius gentium* or *ius naturale*, it follows likewise that no regime originally based on such a 'theft' of power can be regarded as lawful.[109] No prior wrong, as international lawyers say, can make a subsequent right: *ex iniuria ius non oritur*. This is true even if the usurper of that ill-gotten power exercises it thereafter in a just and noble manner. Bodin utterly rejects such a utilitarian style of political reasoning: it is still a power to which the tyrant has no right to exercise in the first place.[110] Therefore, even a ruler with a reputation for 'wisdom and virtue' (such as Cosimo de Medici who seized control of Florence) or a ruler wildly popular with

[106] *République* 300; *De Republica* 208 [2.5] identifies five principal ways in which sovereignty is lawfully conveyed from one to another as a derivative title: lawful war, hereditary succession, election, lottery, and by divine commission.

[107] Bodin models this on the *ius gentium* argument of D.1.5.4 and 1.5.5.1.

[108] And for this reason, even seigneurial states can be legal parties to international obligations, while tyrannies (like pirates and brigands) cannot.

[109] Bodin, however, allows that a tyranny can become a lawful state by prescription of time. He addresses this briefly in passing in *République* 299; *De Republica* 208 [2.5].

[110] Bodin does not seem consistent on this point: see *République* 281 [2.3]; 297–8 [2.5].

the commonalty (such as Pisistratus) still deserves to be called 'tyrant', precisely because they lack valid title.[111]

One immediate implication follows. Since a tyrant has effectively *stolen* someone else's power and can have no right to that power, it follows that there can be no correlative duty to obey that tyrant.[112] They are, like brigands and pirates, outlaws and, thus, enemies to all of humanity. And, as enemies of all, tyrants who have unlawfully seized someone else's sovereignty 'may be lawfully killed [*tué iustement*; *iure occidi possit*] without form or shape of a trial ... it is permissible to kill him [*est licite de le tuer*; *iure occidi licere statuo*], even by extralegal means [*quidem citra legis ullius actionem*]'.[113]

Suppose, as an illustration of this point, that terrorist hijackers seize an airliner and, after having forcefully removed its captain and crew, take the passengers hostage. It would be difficult (though not unheard of, as we'll see below) to argue that the passengers owe a 'duty' to obey the hijackers, in the same way that the passengers *did* take on a duty to obey their originally assigned captain and crew. Even if we were to suppose that the hijacker turned out to be a far more experienced and able pilot than the original crew, that would not excuse the originally illicit seizure. Of course, from the hostage's point of view, compliance with tyrants, even if it isn't obligatory, might nevertheless be prudential, arising from an abiding concern for one's own safety, just as compliance with hijackers threatening deadly force may *similiter* be prudential.

Bodin's point is that such prudential compliance, whether with the commands of hijackers or of tyrants, is categorically different from the sort of dutiful obedience that Bodin requires for sovereignty.[114] But in order to see this difference, what we need is a kind of legal phenomenology. We want to examine this situation, not exclusively from what H.L.A. Hart calls the 'external point of view', but from the 'internal point of view' of those hostages who, unlike the disinterested outside observer exploiting her external (Archimedean even) point of view, have to make the difficult choice of complying out of fear.[115] The first (i.e. prudential compliance)

[111] On Cosimo de Medici, *République* 294, 299; *De Republica* 204; 208 [2.4, 2.5].

[112] It can be argued that the tyrant has no 'subjects', properly speaking. This is a point that Locke makes later on: Locke, *Two Treatises of Government* 386 [II, §176]: 'he that conquers in an unjust war [*bellum non iustum*], can thereby have no title to the subjection and obedience of the conquered'.

[113] *République* 299; *De Republica* 208 [2.5]. Even more remarkable is the addition appended to the Latin text of *De Republica* 207: A tyrant 'may be killed whether collectively by the whole community, or by any individual' [*ab universis, & singulis occidi licere*]. Bodin supports this conclusion with citations to C.1.23.6 and 12.8.1. Among the examples of tyrannicides he cites were the Athenian Tyrannicides, Harmodius and Aristogeiton, who (lawfully, in Bodin's view) killed the Pisistratid tyrant, Hipparchus; Thrasybulus who killed Critias as head of the Thirty of Athens; Brutus and Cassius, who assassinated Julius Caesar.

[114] As we'll see in the next section, Hobbes elides this distinction, such that prudential compliance with a tyrant's wishes, insofar as it signals a rational choice and free act of will, can be sufficient to activate an obligation requiring obedience to that tyrant. This is a crucial point of difference between Bodin and Hobbes.

[115] Hart, *Concept of Law* 89.

is the desperate response of the hostage acting out of a primal fear of his captor. The second (i.e., dutiful obedience) is the subject making the deliberate choice to act out of a bona fide duty owed to a lawful sovereign, which requires something more than brute force. We mustn't – Bodin thinks – mistake the former for the latter. Nor should we conclude from the mere external, observable appearance of orderly compliance (a compliance that might be 'extracted' or 'extorted' by threats of violence or other inducements) that there is an underlying structure of obligation binding subjects to sovereigns.

There's a potentially radical consequence following from this analysis. If I owe no performance to the tyrant (just as I owe, Bodin thinks, no performance of surrender and obedience to the highway robber or of obedience to the hijacker), my non-compliance can't be, from a juridical point of view, seen as an injury or wrong to the tyrant (or hijacker, robber, or pirate).[116] Hijackers and robbers aren't entitled to claim they've been 'wronged' by non-compliant hostages, let alone to seek relief for the goods that *weren't* handed over as ransom.[117]

Neither are tyrants so entitled. For this reason, victims of tyrannical wrongdoing, just as much as victims of hijackers, robbers, and pirates, can never be, on this line of reasoning, guilty of disobedience or treason for their non-compliance. *Crimen laesae maiestatis* presupposes a *ius maiestatis* to be injured. But *nullum crimen sine iure*: there can be no crime or injury where there is no right to be violated in the first place. And tyrants, by definition, can have no such rights, for the same reason that robbers, pirates, or hijackers can have no rights.

What this effectively means is that victims of tyrannical usurpation (and even non-victimized external bystanding third parties) are, in principle, always within their rights to resist and depose tyrants, as much as they are entitled to resist robbers, pirates, and hijackers out of self-defence. It is always open season on the tyrant who, like the brigand and the pirate (and now the slave trader, the torturer, and the terrorist, as the United States Court of Appeals and the International Criminal Court have respectively suggested), is (as Cicero put it) 'the common enemy of mankind' [*communis hostis omnium*].[118] This is why Bodin must conclude – and notably in *limited* agreement with Monarchomach resistance theorists against whom Bodin is so often juxtaposed – that tyrannicidal resistance is always legally

[116] This is precisely what Hobbes, however, argues. He fuses together non-compliance with disobedience, so that the former is taken to be equivalent to the latter and, thus, an injury incurred by a tyrant controlling others by the use of threats. Bodin seems to have anticipated the sort of argument that Hobbes would eventually make. *République* 299: *on ne peut appeller consentement, ce que les tirans sont faire au peuple despouillé de sa puissance*; *De Republica* 208 [2.5]: *Non potest id civium consensione factum censeri, quod erepta libertate fiat*, citing sources on actions *quod metus causa* (remedies for transactions done out of fear): C.2.19.11; D.4.2.22; *Gloss. Ord.* on D.15.4.1; Giovanni D'Andrea, *Comm. In libros Decretalium* [on X.4.6.7, cap. 23, q.8].

[117] Another claim that Locke makes on conquest and usurpation. The highway robber can't sue in court that he was somehow wronged because of a non-payment of a ransom from his hostage. We may, however, ultimately trace these arguments to Cicero.

[118] *Filartiga v. Peña-Irala*, 630 F.2d 876 (2nd Cir., 1980) ¶54.

permissible.[119] Indeed, tyrannicide turns out to be a species of (what I have earlier called) latronicide.

Two stipulations need to be made in order to avoid misconstrual of this conclusion. The first is that Bodin is only talking about tyrannicide and not what we might call 'seigneuricide' (or, as Turchetti has suggested, 'despoticide').[120] Tyrannicide is permissible; seigneuricide is not. Unlike seigneuricide, tyrannicidal resistance to the rightless tyrant is always permissible because, by definition, tyrants have no right protecting their hold on power – just as hijackers, pirates, and robbers similarly have no right protecting what they've illegally seized.

That's not true, however, for the despotic *seigneur* who, unlike the tyrant, *is* entitled to the protection of legal rights under the *ius gentium* and the *ius naturale* – including the right of sovereignty over duty-bound subjects. The slave-subjects of a *seigneurial* monarch, like Nimrod, owe obedience (and not simply prudential compliance of the sort that hostages show to hijackers), by virtue of that monarch's 'master-like' *seigneurial* right which originally can be traced to conquest *in bello iusto*. Because of this *seigneurial* right [*ius dominii*], sovereigns can claim immunity from any obligation or accounting due to their duty-bound subject. This effectively eliminates any hope of lawful resistance by subjects to their sovereign, and actually places the full burden of obligation on the subject. Failure to perform (i.e. disobedience, whether active or passive) is a genuine crime – and not just any crime, but specifically *crimen laesae maiestatis* (treason).[121]

The second stipulation: it's vital to distinguish between the *permissibility* of resistance and the *cost* of resistance. While tyrannicidal resistance may be permissible, that's *not* to say that tyrannicide is costless or risk-free. Indeed, resistance may be very costly, as there are considerable risks to one's own security and well-being when engaging in an act of resistance – even if one has the *right* to resist. The same might be said of war and lawsuits. A state may have every right to engage in war, but that's different from the question of the real costs of war. And so, in balancing rights and costs, it may just be better to forego war, given the cost that would inevitably be incurred. The same with lawsuits: you may have been injured and, thus, have the right to sue – or, as the lawyers say, an *in personam* action against the offending party. That doesn't mean the lawsuit is costless; it may be very costly. Litigation just might not be worth it.

119 Indeed, 'resistance' may not even be the appropriate term.

120 Turchetti, 'Despotism and Tyranny: Unmasking a Tenacious Confusion': 160 points out that, while there is a rich discourse of tyrannicide in Western political thought since antiquity, there is no corresponding discussion of 'despoticide', precisely because the 'despot' [*dominus*; *seigneur*; *signore*; *Herr*] has title. This is, in my view, Franklin's critical error in his treatment of tyrannicide in Bodin's theory: he treats despoticide and tyrannicide as equivalent.

121 Note, however, Bodin's clarification at *République* 300; *De Republica* 208–9 [2.5] that the obligation binds only subjects. It does not bind foreigners, so technically, those outside the state are free of obligatory tie. The implication is that a foreign state may declare a *bellum iustum*, specifically for the purpose of liberating subjects from an oppressive seigneurial sovereign.

Consider again the example of the hijacker. A hostage may certainly have a right (in the Hohfeldian sense of a liberty-right that it is permissive and not formally prohibited) to resist a hijacker, but there are still considerable risks that enter into the calculation in determining whether or not to exercise that right on one's own authority. On balance, it may be more prudential and more instrumentally rational, from a self-interested perspective, simply to comply, though under duress. While it might not be *right* for me to surrender my money to the robber or obey the hijacker's orders, it can be argued that it is still prudentially rational for me to comply, so as to avoid getting shot or harmed in some other way.

But the important point that Bodin will insist upon is that such prudential, cost-minimizing compliance isn't the same as obedience, performing an obligation due to a lawful sovereign. The tyrant can maintain his new tyrannical regime by threats of violence, which effectively forces the captive population, for prudential reasons, to comply with the tyrant's rule. Like the hostages complying with their hijackers' orders, they comply, *not* because they are driven by duty, but by plain self-interest to avoid harm. That's a perfectly understandable reason why one would comply with a tyrant.

But there is, Bodin argues, a huge difference between prudential compliance and dutiful obedience. The most that tyrants can expect to have is the former, but they are never entitled to the latter. For this reason, tyranny is always to be characterized by a perpetual insecurity to conspiracies, thereby giving rise to the sort of tactics with which tyrants have traditionally been associated since at least Plato and Aristotle – the need for personal bodyguards and spies – a surveillance and security apparatus to protect their tenuous hold on power.[122]

Are Tyrants Sovereign?

Suppose a tyrant *is* successful (say, by a *coup d'état* or other act of force or fraud) in usurping – indeed, 'stealing' – someone else's power and creating a new regime. Bodin offers numerous examples of such illegal tyrannical usurpation: Pisistratus, the Thirty of Athens, Periander, Hiero, Dionysius, the Decemvirate, Sulla, Pompey, Caesar, Cosimo de Medici, among many others. We could probably think of additional examples drawn from more recent historical experience of such illegal seizures of state through *coups d'etat*, civil wars, forced annexations, and revolutions. In all of these cases, the crucial interpretive question to ask is this: is the resulting regime genuinely a 'sovereign' authority entitled to all the legal rights of sovereignty?

[122] Plato, *Republic* VIII, 567^{d-e} and Aristotle, *Politics* 5.11, $1313^{b}3$–15. *République* 288; *De Republica* 199 [2.4] continues this theme. Bodin uses the example of the many conspiracies against Medici's regime, *République* 519, 640, 972; *De Republica* 376, 472, 716 [4.1, 4.7, 6.4].

Needless to say, views will differ on this question. No doubt, there will be some who, without hesitation, will say that tyrants are indeed sovereigns, simply by virtue of the brute fact that they are able, through coercive force or fraud, to maintain an effective control and secure the compliance of their captive population. They may be, as one writer has famously put it, sovereigns 'misliked' or without a proper title, but the fact that they can maintain order under their ill-gotten command is, these critics will say, sufficient to regard them as sovereign.

But in considering this interpretive question more carefully, it is necessary first to make a more basic linguistic point about how the terms, 'sovereign' and 'sovereignty', are being used in formulating the question. While some will understand the question to be asking whether the tyrant has the formal title or legal right to rule, others will understand the question to be asking something else – whether the tyrant has effective control, regardless of right.

Ultimately, this is symptomatic of the more basic interpretive disagreement on how we ought to conceptualize sovereignty, whether as a descriptive concept of *de facto* control, or as a normative concept of *de iure* right. But the point here is that Bodin has already staked a clear position on this interpretive dispute. Sovereignty must properly be understood as a legal concept of right: Bodinian sovereignty is *de iure* sovereignty.

One place where we might locate this normative structure is in the very definition of sovereignty in the French *République*. There, Bodin declares the distinctive quality of sovereign power to be its 'absolute and perpetual' [*absolue & perpetuelle*] character.[123] One point that is worth reiterating about this definition is just how much this phrasing coincides with the then-extant French juridical definition of property ownership, a title that is *absolue et perpetuelle* (and *exclusif*) over some asset, including even slaves.[124] This, I argue, is more than mere coincidence. The *droit de propriété* and the notion of an 'absolute, exclusive, and perpetual' right of ownership was vital in Bodin's attempt to explain how genuine sovereignty entails something like a full proprietary right, and not simply a temporary leasehold, precarious tenancy, or deposit.[125] Given this, it cannot be possible for a tyrant (who, by definition, has no right to his *imperium* over others) to be considered a proper sovereign.

[123] This explicit gesture to the *droit de propriété* is missing in *De Republica* 78 where Bodin decides to emphasize the connections to the jurisprudence relating to the *princeps legibus solutus*. But even in the Latin formulation, the proprietary basis of argumentation is unmistakably clear. In fact, it is even clearer in the vocabulary of proprietary interests and obligations he is lifting straight from Roman law.

[124] On the connections between property and sovereignty, see Lesaffer, 'Argument from Roman Law in Current International Law'; Fitzmaurice, *Sovereignty, Property, and Empire*; Arthur Ripstein, 'Sovereignty and Property: How to Tell the Difference', *Theoretical Inquiries in Law* 18 (2017). See also the classic studies of Morris Cohen, 'Property and Sovereignty', *Cornell Law Review* 13 (1927) and Lauterpacht, *Private Law Sources*.

[125] This is precisely why Bodin specifies that a sovereign is comparable to one who retains both *dominium* and *possessio* over a leased or deposited good for a fixed period of time. The marginal reference in *République* 122 cites D.41.3.33 and 41.2.18.

At this point, one might object that this directly contradicts those places in Bodin's system where he does seem, at first glance, to assert that tyrants are *de iure* sovereign. Take, for example, the following passage in *République* I, 8 on the relation between sovereigns and 'sovereign magistrates':[126]

> If a sovereign magistrate [which is *not* the same thing as a proper sovereign], whose term is only annual or is for a fixed and limited time, contrives to prolong the power entrusted to him, it must either be by tacit consent [*sponte superioris*] or by force [*per vim*]. If by force, it is called a tyranny. Yet the tyrant is nonetheless a sovereign [*tyranni quoque maiestas est*], just as the violent possession of a robber is true and natural possession even if against the law, and those who had it previously are dispossessed. But if a magistrate prolongs sovereign power by tacit consent, I say that he is not a sovereign prince, since he has nothing except by sufferance, and all the less so if no time limit is set, for then he has only a precarious commission.[127]

This remarkable passage appears alongside other theoretical test cases, intended to specify the scope of sovereignty.[128] The case here highlights an all-too-familiar act of treachery documented by classical historians of ambitious subordinates, originally entrusted with the lawful exercise of an unrestricted power but for a fixed period of time (usually in response to some emergency or crisis situation), later usurping that entrusted power, by failing to relinquish and remit that power as required at the conclusion of the fixed term.

The specific case that Bodin likely has in mind here is that of first-century Roman dictators, military strongmen who, though legally authorized and entrusted at first to hold and exercise an extraordinary 'absolute power' for a fixed period of time, later extended their hold on sovereignty beyond the original term – and, in the case of Julius Caesar, to last in perpetuity. Three famous classical examples of such Roman military juntas dominate Bodin's discussion of the matter: Sulla (originally authorized by the *lex Valeria*), Pompey (originally authorized by the *lex Gabinia*), and Caesar (originally authorized by the *lex Servia*).

In all these sorts of cases, there's no question or dispute that usurping tyrants, like the terrorist hijacking the airliner, are in effective control of the hijacked state. (Rome, for example, in Bodin's constitutional history of the Roman Republic, is subjected under the effective control and absolute power of Sulla and Pompey

[126] The term, 'sovereign magistrate', can be misleading (especially for readers of Hobbes). What Bodin calls 'sovereign magistrates' are public officials who are lawfully delegated the full exercise of sovereignty for a legally defined term of office. Although they exercise sovereignty and are in effective control of government, these 'sovereign magistrates' are not truly sovereign, but mere delegates, agents, or *locum-tenentes* ('lieu-tenants'). Cp. *République* 451; *De Republica* 312 [3.6].

[127] *République* 126; *De Republica* 81; Franklin 6 [1.8].

[128] Cp. *République* 298; *De Republica* 207; Franklin 110 [2.5].

during their respective military dictatorships.) The interpretive question, then, is whether these tyrants are 'sovereign' over the state they've seized, *par force* [*per vim*].

There's no easy answer; he can't deny the reality of the tyrant's fearsome control, nor the fact of the tyrant's possession of a stolen sovereignty. But neither is it the case that the tyrant has any claim of right, accruing to the tyrant's advantage as a sort of exclusive possessory claim, let alone proprietary claim. As we've seen, tyrants by definition have no *right* and are not entitled to what they possess in fact. So, it is not quite so clear cut.

But what modern readers of Bodin seem to overlook is that Bodin treats tyranny as a kind of threshold test case to explore a conceptually ambiguous grey area. Bodin's lawyerly instinct is, once again, to begin by drawing a legal analogy to the law of property.[129] The usurping tyrant's hold on sovereignty, he thinks, is comparable to the 'violent possession of a robber', in that both involve an unlawful dispossession: someone must wrongfully lose their sovereignty in order for the tyrant wrongfully to gain it. Bodin's point is that, despite the plain illegality of the 'robbery' resulting in the dispossession, it is nevertheless true as a simple matter of descriptive fact that the stolen asset is, *post furtum*, in the robber's possession. The robber has become possessor.

What's crucial to observe here is that, following a basic axiom of Roman legal theory, Bodin treats possession [*possessio*] as distinct from ownership [*dominium*].[130] Like sovereignty, ownership is similarly an absolute and perpetual title. Mere possessory fact cannot (by itself) translate or ripen into such proprietary right and title, nor does possession, in civil law, entail ownership.[131] So, even if a robber is the factual possessor of the stolen good, he is not *ipso facto* its owner. Much less can the robber claim any right of ownership based on the mere fact of possession; no robber can sue, by an *in rem* or possessory action, to protect possession of a stolen good.[132]

The same logic applies to tyrants. By definition, tyrants have illegally usurped and forcefully seized a sovereign power belonging to someone else. Bodin doesn't deny the bare fact of the tyrant's possession of sovereignty, notwithstanding the illegality of that possession.[133] He only denies the tyrant's legal title. This is what

[129] Bodin is referring to the body of jurisprudence and commentary on D.1.21.1, 2.1.5, and 2.1.6, which he cites in connection with this discussion about possession.

[130] Bodin is deeply sensitive to this distinction: He makes sure his readers know that sovereigns are not only the owners [*domini*] of sovereignty [*summum imperium*], but 'possessors' [*possessores*]. *République* 122, 125; *De Republica* 79, 81 [1.8].

[131] James Gordley and Ugo Mattei, 'Protecting Possession', *American Journal of Comparative Law* 44 (1996): 293–334.

[132] Franklin, thus, makes a huge mistake in thinking that unjust possession is the same as robbery.

[133] The marginalia of *De Republica* at 81 (but not *République* 126) indicates that Bodin is thinking specifically of the Roman law distinction of *dominium* and possession. He cites the lengthy provision of D.41.2.3 which develops the civilian notion that possession is constituted by *corpus* and *animus*.

Bodin means to convey when he compares the tyrant's hold on sovereignty to the robber's 'violent possession' of a stolen good as a 'true and natural possession ... against the law' [*vraie possession et naturelle ... contre la loy*]. One can easily miss the irony in Bodin's tone: It may be possession, but it isn't ownership. And proprietary title of ownership is what really matters because that is what makes sovereignty solidly 'absolute and perpetual'.

The novelty of Bodin's analysis can't be stressed enough. Bodin has, in these passages, managed to distinguish *de iure* sovereignty (like ownership) from the tyrant's *de facto* sovereignty (like possession). Failure to distinguish has been especially problematic in the scholarship on Bodin which inevitably, though perhaps inadvertently, transforms Bodinian sovereignty from a *de iure* concept to a *de facto* concept.

If I may be permitted to speculate on why this tends to happen, I'd point to two principal causes. One concerns the gap between the treatment of possession in civil law and common law traditions. The common law of the English-speaking world connects possession (even the doctrine of 'adverse possession') to title, so that there is no discernible conceptual gap between ownership and possession: possession, in the common law mind, *is* a normative value-laden, right-laden concept.

No such connection exists in Roman law, which separates possession as a matter of fact and ownership as a matter of right. This is due, in no small measure, to the modern transformation of the concept of sovereignty in modern academic political science, and especially in the 'realist' school of international relations theory, wherein 'sovereignty' has undergone a seismic semantic shift toward a *de facto* concept. What was once a concept of *de iure* right has instead become a concept of *de facto* control, so that it is now possible to interpret the question of sovereignty ultimately as a measurable empirical question.

To be sure, there may be compelling methodological reasons for this *de facto* turn in how the concept of sovereignty is operationalized and deployed in the modern social sciences. But what is often overlooked and unacknowledged is the retrospective 'spillover' of this modern *de facto* concept onto theoretical and historical scholarship aimed at reconstructing the intellectual history of sovereignty, before the advent of the modern social sciences. This spillover is particularly problematic in the modern interpretation of Bodin's theory of sovereignty which has created the (false) expectation that Bodinian sovereignty must have been a concept of *de facto* control, when it is reasonably clear that Bodin, following conventional practice, intended to frame sovereignty as a concept of *de iure* right and title. This interpretive gap between *de iure* and *de facto* sovereignty potentially forces Bodinian sovereignty to become something it is not.

Who, if anybody, can be ultimately responsible for the *de facto* interpretation of Bodinian sovereignty? One name stands out above all others: Thomas Hobbes. More than anyone else, Hobbes has transformed sovereignty into a *de facto* concept, and that has become, especially in the English-speaking world of the social sciences, our inherited legacy.[134]

Bodin, for his part, adamantly refuses to walk down this line of *de facto* reasoning that Hobbes seems so cheerfully willing to do, because it would allow, even require, tyrants to be regarded as fully and lawfully sovereign. *Ex factis ius oritur*: that's the implication of the Hobbesian worldview. Tyrants who usurp and seize someone else's right are just as legitimate and deserving of obedience as a sovereign created and authorized by the terms of a covenant – *ex pacto*, as Hobbes describes it in *De Cive*. Hobbes fails, wilfully, to see the difference between a *de iure* and *de facto* sovereignty; the *de facto* control is what activates the *de iure* right of sovereignty, as the prudential compliance of those subject to a tyrant indicates a sign of valid will and obligation-creating consent.

Bodin treks down an altogether different path, which requires a differentiated treatment of the tyrant's power. He refuses to recognize the tyrant with defective title as a legitimate *de iure* sovereign. But neither can he ignore the reality of that tyrant's real power. Think of the hijacker example. We can refuse to recognize the hijacker as the legitimate captain of the seized airliner and the rights attached to such title and authority, but we can't ignore the reality of the hijacker's control over the airliner and its passengers. The challenge for Bodin is how to treat such tyrants.

Tyrannicide and Seigneuricide

So, what to do about despotic seigneurs, the so-called (misleadingly, in Bodin's view) 'tyrants by exercise?' This is, Bodin admits, 'the principal difficulty',[135] because, unlike genuine tyrants – the true 'enemies of mankind' – *seigneurs* are legally entitled to rule their subjects. That is because of the lawful way in which a *seigneur* 'come[s] into possession of the state by way of election, or lot, or right of succession, or just war [*ex iure gentium*], or by a special calling from God'.[136] Because these methods of acquiring title are lawful, it is never licit for subjects to resist them, nor is it lawful for a subject to assassinate a seigneur in an act of 'seigneuricide'.[137]

In addressing the question whether seigneuricidal resistance is permissible, Bodin introduces two sets of distinctions for clarity: 'We need to distinguish

[134] This is why I believe it is a mistake to 'read back' Hobbes into Bodin's text; even though they are both conceptualizing the sovereignty of the state in a systematic way, they are each tacitly committed to two different concepts of sovereignty, whether as *de iure* or *de facto*. One immediate consequence of this *de facto* turn has been the wholesale elimination of the category of 'tyrant by title': Kinch Hoekstra, 'Tyrannus Rex vs. Leviathan', *Pacific Philosophical Quarterly* 82 (2001): 437.

[135] *République* 300; *De Republica* 208 [2.5].

[136] *République* 300; *De Republica* 208 [2.5].

[137] It should be noted that Franklin develops his argument that Bodin prohibited tyrannicidal resistance based on these statements specifically focusing on seigneuricidal resistance. He overlooks the distinction that Bodin himself requires us to see – the distinctions between tyrant and *seigneur*, and between permissible tyrannicide and impermissible seigneuricide.

between (1) the absolutely sovereign prince and the one who is not, and (2) between subjects and foreigners'.[138]

The difficulty with the first distinction (1) is trying to imagine what a 'non-sovereign prince' would be like. Fortunately, Bodin has already given us numerous examples, perhaps the most famous of which is the ante-Vespasian Roman Principate. Because the early Roman *princeps* was not technically sovereign over the Roman Empire, it is theoretically permissible to remove that *princeps*: Bodin gives the example of Nero. The same point might be made about, say, the Holy Roman Emperor who was but a high officer appointed by the true sovereign of the Empire, the assembled *Reichstag*.

The 'non-sovereign prince' case thus turns out really just to be a high-ranking official in a democratic or aristocratic state. Such officers, even those who carry the bare title of 'prince', are not sovereign, but rather agents, mandataries, or delegates of sovereigns. But they do not carry the right of sovereignty and, thus, are not entitled to unconditional obedience from subjects, solely on their own authority. This puts such princes in a vulnerable position: what if such a prince starts to use the powers of office in a 'seigneurial' manner, as a kind of petty despot while legally in office or with some other public charge?

Bodin responds: 'There is no doubt that it is permissible to proceed against [this sort of] tyrant either by way of law [*par voye de iustice*] if one can prevail against him, or else by way of fact and open force [*par voye de faict & force ouverte*], if one cannot otherwise have justice'.[139] The first is, by far, the more preferable remedy for Bodin: you sue. But the judicial remedy, proceeding 'by way of law' through litigation, is only available if there's a forum with a competent judge to begin with. What does one do where there is no such remedy?

Some of Bodin's examples on this point help illustrate how these remedies work. One, drawn from the Venetian experience, is especially revealing. Venice, according to Bodin, was constitutionally an aristocratic state, with sovereignty located in the Great Council – this was despite the fact that Venice had a nominal princely *doge* as its non-sovereign head of state. Bodin cites the extrajudicial condemnation of the *doge*, Marin Faliero, the subject of a Donizetti opera, who was summarily executed in 1355 for plotting a plebeian conspiracy to overthrow the Venetian nobility that controlled the Great Council. In Bodin's view, the nobles on the Council were fully within their sovereign rights to depose their *doge* as an instance of permissible tyrannicide.

[138] *République* 300; *De Republica* 208 [2.5]: *il est besoin de distinguer le Prince absoluement souverain, de celuy qui ne l'est pas, & les subiects d'avec les estrangers.*

[139] *République* 301; *De Republica* 209 [2.5]. The first is exemplified by senatorial action against Nero, while the second by assassination of Maximinus. Both examples offered by Bodin are unusual, but especially, Maximinus who was a lawful emperor. He does not seem to fit the category being identified, the 'non-sovereign prince'. Bodin also cites Solon's law, which forbids tyrannicide and requires instead a court trial, and the *lex Valeria*, which permits tyrannicide.

Observe, moreover, *who* is lawfully entitled to act as tyrannicide in the Venetian case. No private Venetian citizen can on his own authority resist the *doge*. Instead, tyrannicide is open only to the Great Council, by virtue of its sovereignty. But because such tyrannicide is technically an act of sovereignty, it's not even accurate to describe it as an act of 'resistance', as it is often described in the contemporaneous Calvinist literature defending 'ephoral resistance'.[140] No one, Bodin thinks, would describe a sovereign prince dismissing and forcefully removing an insubordinate minister from a public charge as 'resistance'. For the same reason, no one should see the Council's extrajudicial killing of the *doge* as anything but a lawful exercise of the Council's right of sovereignty.

This all however only applies to the case of 'non-sovereign' princes like *doges* (and the argument could, in principle, be extended to cover any subordinate holder of public authority).[141] What about the bona fide 'absolutely sovereign prince' who *does* have title and, yet, exercises that sovereignty in a despotic manner? Here, and only in these cases, is Bodin forced to conclude that:

> It is not the part of any subject individually, or all of them in general, to make an attempt on the honour or the life of the monarch, either by way of force [*par voye de faict*] or by way of law [*par voye de iustice*], even if he has committed all the misdeeds, impieties, and cruelties that one could mention.[142]

Observe the explicitly normative and juridical character of this statement, which Bodin emphasizes: 'The question here is not to discover who is the strongest [*qui est le plus fort*], but only whether it is permissible in law [*licite de droit*], and whether a subject has the power to condemn his sovereign prince'.[143]

His unequivocal answer to that question is no: it is never permissible. Sovereign immunity eliminates the one option of resistance by way of law. Subjects can't sue or prosecute sovereigns in their own courts without sovereign consent: 'The subject has no right of jurisdiction over his prince, on whom all power and authority to command [including the authority of courts] depends'. Nor can, *a fortiori*, subjects licitly engage in any extrajudicial act of resistance by way of force against their sovereign, at least not in the same way that the Venetian nobles *could* carry out licitly an extrajudicial killing of Faliero. As Bodin asks, 'If it is not permissible to proceed against one's king by way of law, how could it be licit to do so by way of force?'

Of course, Bodin's no fool. He acknowledges the reality that subjects do and will, as a matter of fact, resist their lawful sovereigns. Prudence or self-interest may

140 *République* 306; *De Republica* 212, n.2 [2.5]; cp. *Popular Sovereignty* 159.

141 Bodin provides several other examples beyond the Venetian case: The ante-Vespasian Roman Principate (Nero); the Holy Roman Emperor (Wenceslas); the kings of Sparta (Agis and Pausanias); the *regulos* [ancient kings] of Gaul.

142 *République* 302; *De Republica* 210; Franklin 115 [2.5].

143 *République* 303; *De Republica* 210 [2.5].

demand it. But when they do so, they do so without right. That is why such acts aren't simply treasonous; they're treacherous. And sovereigns would be, Bodin affirms, in their right to punish such treachery, 'by a special rule of sentencing' calling for extraordinary penalties, even beyond the ordinary penalties of criminal law.[144]

It seems, then, that the subjects of an 'absolutely sovereign' prince, including the seigneurial sovereign, are stuck with no recourse or remedy. But at this point, it's vital to remember the earlier distinction (2), between subjects and foreigners, that Bodin highlighted, a distinction we treated at length in Chapter 3. It's true that it is impermissible and contrary to duty for a subject to resist one's sovereign, whether by way of law or by way of force. But the duty of non-resistance is limited and applies *only* to subjects: foreigners are not likewise bound by such duty of non-resistance, for the simple reason that foreigners, by definition, owe no obligation to any sovereign other than their own.

Since the foreigner is not so bound by such duty of non-resistance, recourse is to be found abroad. The foreigner – and specifically, the foreign sovereign – plays the role of liberator from oppressive rulers. This is why Bodin 'would not say that it is illicit for other princes to proceed against tyrants by force of arms ... but it is not for subjects'.[145]

> It makes a great difference whether we say that a tyrant can be lawfully killed by a foreign prince or by a subject. For just as it is glorious and becoming ... for someone, whoever he may be [Bodin cites the example of Moses], to use force in defence of the goods, honour, and life of those who have been unjustly oppressed ... so is it a most beautiful and magnificent thing for a prince to take up arms in order to avenge an entire people unjustly oppressed by a tyrant's cruelty [Bodin cites the example of Hercules]. [Moreover] it makes no difference whether this virtuous prince proceeds against a tyrant by force, deception, or judicial means.[146]

Taken together, what Bodin seems to be piecing together is the foundation of a theory of intervention, precisely what a modern Westphalian theory of sovereignty could not allow. As much as Bodinian sovereignty is a bundle of rights, so too is it accurate to say that it is a bundle of duties, including what we might, using a more familiar contemporary language, describe as a sovereign duty of aid, to protect and liberate those who are oppressed.[147]

144 *République* 303; *De Republica* 210 [2.5], referencing D. 48.4.11 and Inst. 4.6.12. Bodin's principal source in this discussion of treason is the *lex Iulia maiestatis* governing crimes of lese-majesty.

145 *République* 307; *De Republica* 213; Franklin 120 [2.5].

146 *République* 300; *De Republica* 208–9; Franklin 112–13 [2.5]. The examples he has in mind are Hercules, Dion, Timoleon, Aratus. Bodin's use of the term, 'tyrant', here merely follows conventional usage, seigneurial sovereigns with title who govern in a 'cruel, oppressive, or excessively wicked' manner. 'For that is the meaning [ordinarily] given to the word tyrant'.

147 Given the context of the Wars of Religion, Bodin must certainly have been thinking of religious minorities and Protestant refugees fleeing Catholic oppression. Bodin's reply in the *Apologie de René*

This duty of aid is universal to all sovereigns: it is *constitutive* of sovereignty, because it is written into the *ius naturale* and *ius gentium* that define and give content to sovereignty in the first place. Moreover, because it is a shared – and potentially collectively actionable – obligation, Bodin's treatment of seigneuricidal intervention opens the possibility of imagining what we might characterize as a 'society of states', an international community of sovereigns.

Herpin, a pseudonymous reply to critics, suggests that this point was one of the immediately controversial points of the *République*, attracting an especially vitriolic attack by Bodin's critic de la Serre who seems to think that Bodin requires sovereigns to take arms on behalf of exiles and intervene by force into the affairs of others states. Bodin's reply is ambiguous but seems (in my view) to reinforce the basic point that sovereigns have a *ius-naturale* obligation to fight injustices of oppressive regimes.

Conclusion

The Duties of Sovereignty

Since the end of the Cold War, academic commentators in law and across various fields in the social sciences have struggled to justify the value of sovereignty in an increasingly globalizing world, where allegiances to sovereign states and the boundaries enclosing their territorial holdings stand as harmful and morally arbitrary obstacles to the achievement of arguably more urgent priorities such as the protection of human rights, global justice, climate change, and global health. Sovereignty, they declared, was rapidly eroding – so rapidly, indeed, that some felt obliged even to herald the oncoming 'end of sovereignty'.[1] Emboldened cosmopolitans gladly took up the task of imagining what a 'politics without sovereignty' might look like.[2]

Not everybody, however, has been so willing to give up on sovereignty altogether. In the recent academic literature examining the moral legitimacy of territorial boundaries and national allegiances, for example, theorists manoeuvring skilfully to avoid cosmopolitanism have, by default, had to acknowledge and even embrace the merits of sovereignty.[3] So too have specialists in international relations likewise seen sovereignty as a vital source of international security.[4]

But there is a fundamental problem in the way this debate has typically been framed. Partisans on both sides proceed from a largely uncontested, and mythically Westphalian, picture of sovereignty, what commentators have variously described

[1] As did Joseph Camilleri and Jim Falk in *The End of Sovereignty? The Politics of a Shrinking and Fragmenting World* (Cheltenham: Edward Elgar, 1992). This is an old utopian fantasy, one of the luxuries of so-called 'ideal political theory'.

[2] Thomas Pogge, 'Cosmopolitanism and Sovereignty', *Ethics* 103 (1992): 48–75; David Held, *Democracy and the Global Order: From the Modern State to Cosmopolitan Governance* (Stanford, California: Stanford University Press, 1995); James Bohman, 'Cosmopolitan Republicanism', *The Monist* 84 (2001): 3–22; Kok-Chor Tan, *Justice Without Borders: Cosmopolitanism, Nationalism, and Patriotism* (Cambridge: Cambridge University Press, 2004); Charles Beitz, 'Cosmopolitanism and Global Justice', *Journal of Ethics* 9 (2005): 11–27; Kwame Anthony Appiah, *Cosmopolitanism: Ethics in a World of Strangers* (New York: W.W. Norton, 2006); Christopher Bickerton, *et al.*, eds., *Politics Without Sovereignty: A Critique of Contemporary International Relations* (London: UCL Press, 2007).

[3] For example, David Miller, *On Nationality* (Oxford: Oxford University Press, 1995); Andrew Mason, 'Special Obligations to Compatriots', *Ethics* 107 (1997): 427–47.

[4] For example, Friedrich Kratochwil, 'Leaving Sovereignty Behind? An Inquiry in the Politics of Post-Modernity', in *Legality and Legitimacy in Global Affairs*, ed. Richard Falk, Mark Juergensmeyer, and Vesselin Popovski (Oxford: Oxford University Press, 2012); Lake, 'The Sovereignty in International Relations'.

The Right of Sovereignty. Daniel Lee, Oxford University Press. © Daniel Lee 2021.
DOI: 10.1093/oso/9780198755531.003.0007

as a 'traditional' or 'classical' notion of sovereignty.[5] Francis Deng, a former Special Adviser to the United Nations Secretary-General for the Prevention of Genocide and a principal advocate of the Responsibility to Protect (or 'R2P') doctrine, typifies this 'traditional' notion of sovereignty when he defined it as a 'supreme, independent, original authority' expressing the 'inviolability of the state ... the right to be undisturbed from without'.[6] This debate on sovereignty essentially boiled down, then, to a binary interpretive choice – a future with (traditional) sovereignty and a future without (traditional) sovereignty.

Is there a third way? Some theorists, unwilling to give up on sovereignty so quickly, have proposed reimagining the principal function of sovereignty in terms of responsibility, wherein sovereignty is to be understood, not so much or exclusively in terms of absolute or discretionary rights, guaranteeing political independence and shielding states from foreign interference, but rather in terms of fiduciary duties that all sovereigns are called upon, and expected, to perform.[7] Instead of discarding sovereignty altogether, it was suggested that it might be more appropriate to repurpose sovereignty in terms of these fiduciary responsibilities of states.

The origin of this recent turn in the interpretive debate on sovereignty might be traced to the 1990s when the notion of 'sovereignty-as-responsibility' was first developed in connection with the larger policy debates on the permissibility of humanitarian intervention in the major crises of that period such as Kosovo, Rwanda, Somalia, and East Timor. Not only did this principle of sovereign responsibility feed directly into the formal promulgation of the R2P doctrine at the 2005 World Summit by Member States of the United Nations as the core normative principle governing the function of sovereignty in international law, it breathed new life into a stale anachronism that many viewed as an artefact of a bygone era.[8] Sovereignty-as-responsibility made sovereignty respectable again and specifically allowed theorists of sovereignty to reimagine and repurpose the concept as an instrument of protection, rather than as a marker of preterlegal power.

[5] Andreas Osiander, 'Sovereignty, International Relations, and the Westphalian Myth', *International Organization* 55 (2001): 251–87; Luke Glanville, 'The Myth of Traditional Sovereignty', *International Studies Quarterly* 57 (2013): 79–90. To be fair, this has started to shift in the most recent theoretical literature. For example, Stilz, *Territorial Sovereignty*.

[6] Francis Deng, *et al.*, *Sovereignty as Responsibility: Conflict Management in Africa* (Washington, D.C.: Brookings Institution Press, 1996), Preface, xviii; 17. Deng, like many jurists and specialists in international relations searching for a theory of sovereign responsibility, rely on a convenient, though misleading, history of sovereignty tracing the origins of sovereignty to the 1648 Peace of Westphalia. Francis Deng, 'From Sovereignty as Responsibility to the Responsibility to Protect', in *Global Responsibility to Protect* 2 (2010): 355–57. Cp. Georg Nolte, 'Sovereignty as Responsibility?' *Proceedings of the Annual Meeting (American Society of International Law)* 99 (2005): 389–92.

[7] Eyal Benvenisti, 'Sovereigns as Trustees of Humanity: On the Accountability of States to Foreign Stakeholders', *American Journal of International Law* 107 (2013): 295–333.

[8] 'Each individual State has the responsibility to protect its populations from genocide, war crimes, ethnic cleansing and crimes against humanity'. (§138). R2P was frequently invoked in 2011 as the justification for UN Security Council Resolution 1973 in connection with the violence in Syria. Adom Getachew, 'The Limits of Sovereignty as Responsibility', *Constellations* 26 (2019): 225.

Introducing sovereignty-as-responsibility also fundamentally changed the contours of this sovereignty debate; what was once seen as a binary interpretive choice became instead a tertiary choice. Recognizing the perceived faults of 'traditional' sovereignty needn't entail cosmopolitanism. 'Traditional' sovereignty could simply be revamped as a 'new-and-improved' sovereignty – or, as one commentator put it, 'sovereignty-modern'.[9] That is, in fact, precisely what Kofi Annan, a former Secretary-General of the United Nations, once argued in a famous 1999 article in *The Economist* – to jettison 'traditional notions of sovereignty', in favour of one that directly acknowledges sovereign states as 'instruments at the service of their peoples, and not vice versa'.[10]

There is one point in this debate, however, that deserves closer scrutiny in this Conclusion. The fiduciary theory of sovereignty-as-responsibility, it is often said, represents a radical reinvention, even a tacit rejection, of an old idea. But where did that old idea really come from? Almost without exception, this 'classical' or 'traditional' theory of sovereignty is attributed to Jean Bodin who, as the representative canonical theorist of sovereignty, becomes by default one of the targets – if not the principal target – of this critical literature.[11] Bodin becomes the villain in this intellectual history of sovereignty, not unlike a Fritz Haber or an Edward Teller whose intellectual achievements translate into disastrous consequences for international peace.

Does Bodin really deserve this ignominy? In closing this study, I wish to end on two points. The first is that there's nothing new about envisioning sovereignty as responsibility or postulating a putative sovereign responsibility to protect. Since its theoretical inception in the formal treatises of Bodin, Gentili, and Grotius, sovereignty was always understood to be, at some fundamental level, as much a concept of duty, emerging from the juridical requirements of the *ius naturale* and *ius gentium*, just as much as it was also a concept of right.[12]

While international lawyers and specialists in international relations cannot help but see the emerging fiduciary theory as a *departure* from the Westphalian

[9] John H. Jackson, 'Sovereignty-Modern: A New Approach to an Outdated Concept', *American Journal of International Law* 97 (2003): 782–802.

[10] Kofi Annan, 'Two Concepts of Sovereignty', *The Economist* (18 September 1999) 81. Fox-Decent, *Sovereignty's Promise*.

[11] Evan Criddle and Evan Fox-Decent, *Fiduciaries of Humanity: How International Law Constitutes Authority* (Oxford: Oxford University Press, 2016) 5, for example, credits Bodin as the originator of the 'classical model of sovereignty'. One notable exception is Luke Glanville, who specifically names Bodin as a theorist belonging to this sovereignty as responsibility tradition in 'The Antecedents of Sovereignty as Responsibility', *European Journal of International Relations* 17 (2011): 237–38.

[12] This is a point that recent theorists of ethics and international politics have recognized: 'Where there are rights, there are duty-imposing rules'. Henry Shue, 'Limiting Sovereignty', in *Humanitarian Intervention and International Relations*, ed. Jennifer Walsh (Oxford: Oxford University Press, 2004) 15. Shue's footnote on this statement, denying the converse 'that where there are duty-imposing rules, there are rights', would likely be contested by the jurists of the *ius commune*, for reasons explored in Chapter 2. Non-performance of a legal duty (as required by some law, whether *ius civile*, *ius gentium*, or *ius naturale*) gives rise to a claim, a *ius*, for an action to remedy the injury.

principle of non-interference, this study suggests a different conclusion. To wit: the fiduciary theory of sovereign responsibility isn't so much a *departure* from some imagined 'classical' theory of sovereignty, as it is a *return* to, and potentially the vital restoration of, a pre-Westphalian (and pre-territorial) theory of sovereignty.

The second and perhaps more surprising point, then, concerns Bodin himself, the unnamed arch-rival and foil of this emerging fiduciary theory of sovereignty-as-responsibility. Bodin not only belongs to this intellectual tradition of interpreting sovereignty in terms of the responsibilities attached to fiduciary obligations, he really deserves to be considered its originator. When I started writing this book, I did not expect to arrive at this conclusion. But as I now complete this study and reflect on Bodin's legacy in the modern intellectual history and theory of sovereignty, I cannot avoid it. In this concluding essay, I'll explain why.

The Mutual Obligations of Sovereigns and Subjects

To begin, let us return to Bodin's key conceptual thesis about sovereignty, which is that sovereignty is a special kind of obligatory relationship tying subjects and sovereigns together, like duty-bound obligors and right-holding obligees.[13] The structure of sovereignty, as Bodin understood it, took the transactional shape of a bilateral (or, as he put it, 'synallagmatic': from συνάλλαγμα = transaction, exchange) obligation, constituted by mutual duties flowing in both directions. Just as subjects owe performance of certain duties to their sovereigns, so too do sovereigns owe performance of certain duties to their subjects.[14]

Subjects are, of course, bound by a general duty to obey sovereign commands.[15] And since commands of sovereigns are, by definition, laws, this translates to a general duty to obey sovereign-authored positive legislation. Such a duty to obey the

[13] *De Republica* 45–6 [1.6]: *Est autem civis nihil aliud quam liber homo qui summae alterius potestati obligatur* ('The citizen is nothing other than the free person who is bound to someone else's sovereign power'.) It is important to stress that Bodin was indifferent with respect to the constitutional form of sovereignty. It could take the form of a monarchy, where sovereignty is a *princeps*. But it could just as well take the form of a republic, where sovereignty is vested in the *populus*, or the citizen-body of the people. Bodin, thus, is the first major theorist of popular sovereignty, a thesis I argue in *Popular Sovereignty*.

[14] *De Republica* 99 [1.8]: *princeps mutuae fidei inter privatos*. Cp. *De Republica* 87, citing D.2.14.58 (which is the same passage Bodin cites at *Distributio* fol. B, s.v.: *Conventio: Contractu cui synallagma*) and 50.16.19 and 50.17.35. To recall from Chapter 2, the legal humanist, François Connan, most controversially among the major French humanists, argued that συνάλλαγμα was the essence of all valid and actionable contracts in *Commentariorum de Iure Civili*. Bodin was applying Connan's theory of synallagmatic contracts in explaining contractual obligations between sovereigns and subjects.

[15] *République* 85 [1.6]: *l'obligation mutuelle du souverain au subiect, auquel, pour la foy & obeisance qu'il reçoit, il doit iustice, conseil, confort, aide, & protection*. This language is missing in the corresponding passage of the Latin *De Republica* 56.

law, moreover, is correlative in a Hohfeldian sense: it corresponds to the sovereign's correlative right to command and issue such laws. We have seen the architecture of this theory already in Chapter 2.

What too often gets overlooked in this Bodinian analysis, however, is that sovereigns too are duty-bound. But the substance of their duties requires differentiated treatment. Unlike subjects whose duties arise primarily from positive legislation [*droit civil*; *ius civile*], sovereigns are, by definition, *legibus soluti* (from D.1.3.31 of Roman law: they are 'exempt' or 'immune' from the obligation to comply with positive laws of their own making). Sovereign duties, therefore, must be traced to some other non-positive legal source – namely, the *ius naturale* and the *ius gentium*, the anterior legal rules that confer rights of sovereignty in the first place. Bodin states this point explicitly at several places, reminding his readers that all sovereigns with legally valid title have duties to provide *iustice, garde, & protection* to their subjects, a duty that is *mutuelle* and *reciproque* to the subject's duty of showing *obeisance, aide & cognoissance.*[16] These might be understood as duties to provide public goods such as justice (by which he means a legal system with courts capable of enforcing first-order legal obligations) and protection (by which he means a system of security).[17]

What is perhaps most remarkable is that Bodin interpreted such sovereign duties as 'special obligations' (using the lexicon of contemporary moral philosophy) due only to citizens (or 'subjects' or 'nationals'), but 'not due to foreigners' [*n'est point deu aux estrangers*].[18] They were meant, it seems, only to benefit one's fellow citizens.

Consider, for example, the sovereign's duty to provide justice [*officium ius dicentis*; cp. 'juris-diction'] for their subjects, by empowering them with the right to seek actionable remedies in court for legal injustices. Bodin, as we've seen in the preceding chapters, thought extensively about this problem in the context of Roman legal history. The original Roman civil law – encoded in the early Republican XII Tables and reserved exclusively for 'Quirites' (an antiquated term for full Roman citizens: hence, *ius Quiritium* 'law of the Quirites') – was intended only to benefit

[16] *République* 85 [1.6], 610–11 [4.6]; cp. the corresponding passage in the Latin *De Republica* 450 which is much less specific about the duties owed. This is the famous chapter where Bodin discusses whether sovereigns should exercise jurisdiction [*officium ius dicentis*] over subjects directly, or through subordinate judges.

[17] Bodin apparently didn't think of these as nonexcludable public goods.

[18] *République* 85 [1.6]. Bodin's discussion of patron-client relations of protection in *République* I, 7 indicates that subjection and protection are not equivalent. One need not be a subject to enjoy the benefits of protection. Protection (which defines the patron-client relation) is categorically different from subjection (which defines the sovereign-subject relation), so that one can, for example, purchase or enter into a foreign power's protection while remaining a subject of another sovereign. On 'special obligations', see Mason, 'Special Obligations to Compatriots', and, more generally, Samuel Scheffler, *Boundaries and Allegiances* (Oxford: Oxford University Press, 2001).

Romans. Roman courts – and by implication, Roman remedies – were, thus, inaccessible to 'peregrines' (say, a Carthaginian), except by special permission.[19]

Did that mean, then, that foreigners were out of luck? This became a real problem in Rome, as military expansion and conquest of foreign nations transformed Rome into a multinational empire, a pluralistic and heterogeneous collection of different peoples, intermingling through commerce and intermarriage among Romans and non-Romans. Rome's increasing heterogeneity, especially after the Punic Wars, forced lawyers to confront the question whether foreigners, who flooded every aspect of Roman society, now should have legal standing in Roman courts. Technically, they couldn't, since Roman civil law [*ius civile*] was intended only for the advantage of Roman citizens [*cives*].[20]

Recognizing the rapidly changing social realities of imperial Rome, the lawyers' creative solution instead was gradually to introduce a supplemental body of law, the so-called 'praetorian law' [*ius honorarium*], as an equitable corrective to the strict rigidities of the *ius civile*, which reserved Roman justice only for Roman citizens.[21] What ultimately gave Roman jurists the confidence to open Roman courts to peregrines in this way was the Stoic-inflected concept of the *ius gentium*, most famously memorialized in Gaius' *Institutes* of Roman law:

> All nations who are ruled by laws and customs [like the Romans] use, in part, their own law, as well as that law which is common to all men. The law which every nation establishes for itself is specific to that state and is called its 'civil law' [*ius civile*] because it is the law particular [*ius proprium*] to that *civitas*. By con trast, the law which natural reason has established among all humans is equally observed among all and called 'the law of nations', just as if it were the law which all nations [*omnes gentes*] observe.[22]

Gaius' statement reveals, then, that the legal remedies applied by Roman courts actually derive from two distinct sources – the *ius civile*, which was exclusive to

[19] That special permission was established typically in treaties, and a special procedure, *recuperatio*, introduced to settle suits involving peregrines. David Daube, 'The Peregrine Praetor', *Journal of Roman Studies* 41 (1951): 67.

[20] Bodin classified the Roman Republic (roughly from the time of the Decemvirate to Vespasian) as a democracy, where sovereignty of the Roman state belonged entirely to the Roman people, when assembled in one of its formal legislative *comitia* or assemblies. Roman citizens were 'subjects' not of a king, but of the people.

[21] The praetorian law was so called because of the chief instrument used for its creation – the praetorian edict issued by the peregrine praetors, a formal public office [D.1.1.7.1: *honor praetorum*]. praetorian legislation was thought to be an exercise of the praetor's equitable jurisdiction, which appealed to the equity of the *ius gentium*, rather than the formal strict requirements of the *ius civile*. See Alan Watson, 'The Development of the Praetor's Edict', *Journal of Roman Studies* 60 (1970): 105–19. D.1.1.7.1, 1.1.8, 1.2.2.28. Bodin often speaks of the equitable function of courts as a corrective to the strict justice of the civil law [*supplendi vel corrigenda iuris civilis*], and it is clear that he is thinking of the praetorian law. *République* 412, 438; *De Republica* 288, 304 [3.4, 3.5].

[22] D.1.1.9.

Roman citizens, and the *ius gentium*, which was open to all humans.[23] Only by appealing to the 'natural equity' of the latter, the *ius gentium*, could Roman jurists finally recognize the legal standing of foreigners to obtain justice in their courts – not as Romans, but as fellow humans entitled to justice.

The point that Bodin apparently wanted to make with this overview of Roman legal history was to underline how sovereign duties needn't always be 'special duties'. Rome may certainly and rightly have had a 'special duty' to provide justice to Romans. But that 'special duty' didn't then preclude Rome from being additionally burdened by more general duties owed to foreigners as well – and indeed to all of humanity, as a show of comity. While a sovereign state may try, in vain, to restrict its courts only for its own citizens and exclude foreigners, the *ius gentium* – or, as Gaius put it, the 'law common to all men' [*ius omnium hominum commune*] – requires that foreigners should have their day in court as well, on the principle that the 'legal rights of foreigners [*ius peregrinis*] are held to be equal [*aeque*] to the rights of citizens'.[24]

The Duties of Humanity

Bodin called these general duties, due to all humans, the 'duties of humanity' [*officia humanitatis*].[25] In describing the substance of this duty, it might be useful, first, to clarify what 'humanity' [*humanitas*] signifies.[26] Bodin fundamentally imagined humanity in explicitly Stoic terms as a kind of grand association, or *societas* – as Cicero once put it, a *societas humani generis*.[27] It was an association made up of different nations and peoples, joined together as partners [*socii*] and as friends [*amici*]. What tied this association together, however, wasn't so much that bond of political allegiance which subjects owe to a common sovereign, as it was the inbuilt desire for the fellowship and company of others – in a (Greek) word, οἰκείωσις (sociability). What bound a 'human together with another human in fellowship' [*homini cum homine rationis societatem*] was one and the same reason

[23] Hence, in Roman private law, there were *ius civile* methods (exclusive to Romans) of acquiring and conveying property, manumission, marriage, writing a will, contracting an obligation as well as *ius gentium* methods (open to Romans and non-Romans alike) of doing the same.

[24] *Methodus* 247.

[25] Bodin introduces this term at *De Republica* 66 [1.7]. Cp. Grotius, *De Iure Belli ac Pacis* 2.12.9, 3.13.4 [*regula caritatis*]; 2.17.9 [*norma caritatis*]; 3.13.4 [*regula humanitatis*]; Pufendorf, *De Iure Naturae et Gentium* 3.3 [*De promiscuis officiis humanitatis*].

[26] Diego Panizza, 'The Freedom of the Sea and the Modern Cosmopolis in Alberico Gentili's *De Iure Belli*', *Grotiana* 30 (2009): 92–6.

[27] *De Off.* 1.53, 3.21–22, 3.28. *Societas* is a technical term from the Roman law of obligations, signifying a 'contract of partnership' whereby prospective partners [*socii*] set out the terms of their collective efforts.

[*sub unam eandemque rationis*].[28] Bodin's 'humanity' wasn't, then, a cosmopolitan picture of deracinated unencumbered selves. Instead, it was one that embraced the full diversity – linguistic, religious, cultural – of all peoples and nations.

But there was a limit to this ever-widening circle of humanity. Modern humanitarianism imagines 'humanity' as an all-inclusive blanket idea, encompassing every human being. For Bodin, however, 'humanity' functioned as an *exclusive* term. It included only those who valued and shared a commitment to cultivating those humane values such as civility, comity, courtesy, and hospitality necessary for a common life. While that likely encompassed a great many people featuring these qualities of sociability, it nevertheless excluded many others who repudiated such shared commitments, through the use of force or fraud. These 'enemies of humanity' [*hostes humani generis*] which, as we've seen in Chapter 5, were exemplified by the Ciceronian trope of pirates and brigands and other such outlaws (tyrants), fell outside the protective scope of the *ius gentium* and were, therefore, not entitled to enjoy advantages of humanity.[29]

Humanity was, thus, a closed *societas* with a closed membership. What worried Bodin, however, was that the bond of sociability tying humanity together was thoroughly weak, ultimately contingent on the continuing good faith, the amity, and courtesy of its members.[30] It only takes the violence of one pirate or the perfidy of one liar to crush that 'humane' bond and undermine the trust necessary to maintain humanity.

The general duty of humanity, thus, might be understood as a general duty intended to fortify and preserve the bonds tying humanity together. They might even be understood as moral requirements, binding on all members of humanity, to act in ways that build mutual trust and reinforce one's 'credit' so as to improve the future likelihood of cooperation and friendship. Humanist courtesy books of the period, ultimately inspired by the civilizing mission of Cicero's ethical thought, typically treated such humane duties ultimately at the individual level. Hospitality, aid, courtesy, and other such courtly conduct, were the sort of decorous acts that virtuous individuals were expected to perform in their relations with others.

These duties of humanity, however, placed the heaviest burdens of all on sovereigns. But why? In short, Bodin seems to have accepted the principle that, with great power comes great responsibility. While sovereignty was conceptualized an

[28] *Methodus* 247, 254. Bodin observes the limitations of a humanity-wide law of nations based only on reason: *Imperium rationis cogit neminem*. He clarifies at 247, *Nullum talem est imperium illos* [that is, *peregrinos*] *nisi scelere pactove se obligarint*.

[29] On the trope of the pirate as outlaw, see Daniel Heller-Roazen, *The Enemy of All* (Princeton: Princeton University Press, 2009).

[30] *République* 476–77; *De Republica* 329–30 [3.7]; cp. Jean Bodin, *Response to the Paradoxes of Malestroit*, trans. and ed. Henry Tudor and R.W. Dyson (Bristol: Thoemmes Press, 1997) 85, 87. On the theme of good faith in this context, see P.-L. Vaillancourt, 'La notion de "foi jurée" dans l'ordre politique', in *Aequitas, Aequalitas, Auctoritas: Raison théorique et legitimation de l'autorité dans le XVI*[e] *siècle européen*, ed. D. Letocha (Paris: Vrin, 1992) 199.

'absolute power', it nevertheless entailed positive, if imperfect, duties with respect to the exercise of such power. The reason why sovereigns have their sovereignty is to promote humanity.

Several duties oblige all sovereigns for the sake of humanity. One notable way that Bodin develops this point is in terms of '*commerce & traffique*'.[31] Commerce among nations, Bodin postulated, was one of the surest means to reinforce the naturally weak bonds of humanity. He, thus, saw it as a positive duty of all lawful sovereigns to take whatever steps necessary to promote international commerce.[32]

Bodin expressed this commitment to international commerce in his defence of the free seas. Anticipating Grotius' own canonical treatment of the topic in *Mare Liberum*, Bodin acknowledged the general principle that *aequor ac mare ipsum privatorum proprium esse non potest* (the sea cannot belong as property to private owners).[33] He did so for a simple reason: privatizing the high seas, by claiming *dominium* over them in the same way that a sovereign might claim *dominium* over territory, would irreparably injure humanity by closing off and eliminating the ability of peoples to engage in free commerce with each other.[34] Sovereigns were generally bound, therefore, by duties owing to humanity – that is, to fellow members of the *societas humani generis* – to keep the seas open to all.[35]

Yet, while maintaining the freedom of the seas and guaranteeing safe conduct were vital for commerce, they weren't the only ways by which sovereigns could promote commerce and preserve the bonds of humanity. International commerce, as

[31] *République* 108 [1.7].

[32] Cp. *République* 106 [1.7]; *De Republica* 579 [5.6]. Bodin discusses the class of treaties known as *aequo foedere* treaties, one type of treaty used by Romans in their relations with foreign powers, to establish commercial relations [*amitié, commerce, & hospitalité; amicitia, ius hospitii, commerciorum*] and even to eliminate tariffs [*sine vectigalis ullius solutione*]. Economic historians have, for this reason, sometimes characterized Bodin as an exceptional early modern theorist of free trade in a world that was already moving inexorably in a mercantilist direction. But if that is so, Bodin is the accidental free trade theorist, since for him, the goal wasn't profit, but friendly relations. He is one of the first of the *doux commerce* theorists. I thank Stefan Eich for this observation.

[33] Turchetti 751 [1.10]. Bodin continues, *iure quodammodo Principum omnium maris accolarum communi receptum est.* Bodin did, however, allow the customary allowance of maritime sovereignty over the thirty leagues [*XXX lieuës loing de sa terre; sexaginta miliaribus a littore*] of coastal waters, citing Baldus on D.1.8 and C.4.33.4.

[34] The seas thus fall outside any sovereign state's territorial jurisdiction. Pirates (as enemies of humanity) exceptionally remain the universal jurisdiction of everyone.

[35] So too were sovereigns duty-bound, for similar 'reasons of humanity', to provide guarantees and letters of safe conduct [*guidagium; brevia salvi conductus*] to foreigners. On the *guidagium*, Bodin cites the *Gloss. Ord.* on X.5.40.26, and the related commentaries of Panormitanus, Antonio da Butrio, Hostiensis, as well as Pierre Antiboul [Petrus Antibolus Allobrogis], *Tractatus de Muneribus*, which can be found in the massive early modern collection, *Tractatus Illustrium in Utraque Tum Pontificii, Tum Caesarei*, vol. 12 (Venice, 1584) fols. 41_{vo}–42_{ro} [§42]. Antiboul treats *pedagium* and *guidagium* together: *Pedagium dicitur quod datur a transeuntibus in locis a principe constitutis. Guidagium vero quod datur pro ducatu per terram alicuius, ut securus vadat.*

Bodin worries here that sovereigns who now claim a so-called 'right of wreckage' [*Warech*, citing Const. Navigia on C.6.2.18] – that is, the right to seize goods by forfeiture from a shipwreck on one's shore – or a right to levy fees on a foreign ship dropping an anchor in one's territorial waters (L.F. 2.56) contravenes the more permissive liberty of the *ius gentium* which is intended to promote commercial activity. Such alleged sovereign rights, Bodin claims, are based on 'error', *De Republica* 171.

Bodin observed, cannot be possible without reliable monetary instruments which are, ultimately, creations of sovereignty. He concluded, therefore, that sovereigns have other related duties as well, such as the duty to maintain the value of their money, as trustworthy instruments of commerce in which citizens and foreigners can confidently have faith.

It will be recalled that all sovereigns have, as one of their principal rights of sovereignty, the exclusive right of coinage [*droit de moneage*; *ius cudendae monetae*; *nummi percutiendi ius*] within their state.[36] Indeed, he sees the right of coinage simply as one particular instance of the more general sovereign legislative right of command [*ius summi imperii*].[37] But his treatment of this right of coinage is particularly useful in explaining one of the principal themes of this study, how Bodinian sovereignty can have a double-aspect, through its juridical expression, not only as a *right*, but also as a *duty* – a duty, even, towards humanity.

Bodin is, of course, writing before the innovation of modern independent central banking and issuance of banknotes. (Indeed, Bodin's death predates the founding of the French Banque Générale by over a century, yet he was evidently already aware of the introduction of Italianate innovations and usurious banking practices in the Banque de Lyon, the principal credit market in sixteenth century Europe which, Bodin declared, was largely responsible for the growing epidemic of sovereign debt.)[38] Without a system of independent bankers appointed to determine monetary policy, Bodin operated on the assumption that sovereigns may directly set, as well as alter, the value of their coins, just as they may make and alter their laws.

Did this mean, then, that a sovereign could devalue its own national currency at will, as a discretionary assertion of its sovereign right? Poor fiscal choices, or simply weak state institutions, might require it. Consider the case of the French monarch, François I, whose government borrowed at extortionate interest rates from the Banque de Lyon, partly as a strategic manoeuvre to cut off access by other foreign

[36] *République* 242; *De Republica* 167 [1.10]. Bodin does, however, acknowledge that the right of coinage can, by special permission, be granted or conceded to subordinates as a limited and revocable privilege. He cites the French examples of the viscount of Touraine, the bishoprics of Meaux, Cahors, Agde, and Ambrun, and the counts of Saint Paul, la Marche, Nevers, and Blois, who all had limited rights of coinage, *alieno beneficio*.

[37] Citing a commonplace etymology at *République* 242; *De Republica* 167, he observes the linguistic connection in the Latin *nummus* (coin), the Greek νομός (law or convention), and the French *loy* (law, which Bodin connects to *aloy*, a term indicating 'the statutory degree of purity in gold and silver', according to Franklin 78). Money, Bodin writes, 'is of the same nature as the law, and so, only the one who has the power to make law [*puissance de faire la loy*; *leges iubere*] can legally determine the value, the weight, the form of money [*donner loy aux monnoyes*; *nummorum pretium, pondus, figuram praescribere*]'. The etymology already appears in Bodin, *Response to the Paradoxes* 126. On the Aristotelian origin of this connection, see Stefan Eich, 'Between Justice and Accumulation: Aristotle on Currency and Reciprocity', *Political Theory* 47 (2019): 363–90.

[38] *République* 893; *De Republica* 667 [6.2]. See also Nadia Matringe, 'The Fair Deposit: Credit Reallocation and Trade Finance in the Early Modern Period', *Annales HSS* 72 (2017): 275–315; Christine Desan, *Making Money: Coin, Currency, and the Coming of Capitalism* (Oxford: Oxford University Press, 2014).

powers, especially the Emperor Charles V, to much-needed credit to finance on-going wars. By the time Bodin entered the service of the Royal Household, France was, as a result of the disastrous Valois fiscal policy, saddled with exorbitant debt obligations payable to foreign creditors (Bodin quoted interest rates of up to 20 per cent).[39] The French monarchy itself was rated a 'notoriously poor credit risk'.[40]

During the time Bodin articulated his theory of sovereignty, France desperately needed to raise revenue to meet its debt obligations, and partly for this reason, the monarchy convened, after many years of dormancy, the medieval body of the Estates-General of France in the latter half of the sixteenth century specifically to explore possible solutions. One solution suggested by Henri III (François I's grandson) to address the debt crisis was the sale of lands and other liquid assets in the royal domain, a proposal debated at length in the Estates-General of 1576 at Blois.

For Bodin, this was not an abstract academic question.[41] He attended the Estates-General as an elected deputy for Vermandois and advocated policies, especially on matters of royal finance, that alienated himself from the king's favour by stubbornly insisting on the inalienability of the royal domain: kings can't simply sell the palace silverware to pay for sovereign debts. Why? It's not his to sell; such assets belong to the state [*république*; *respublica*].[42] Bodin's own published notes of the proceedings of the Third Estate reveal his firm conviction that the monarch was not the owner of the royal domain and, thus, had no right to alienate royal assets – let alone the sale of public offices and honours.[43] The king was, rather, the 'simple usufructuary of an estate' [*simple usaiger du domaine*] 'belonging to the people' [*proprieté dudit domaine, qu'il appartenoyt au peuple*].[44] It was a principle he already articulated in the *République*, where he clarified the principle, drawing from the Roman law of property, that 'sovereign princes, properly speaking, are merely

[39] Bodin, *Response to the Paradoxes* 66.

[40] Philip Hoffman, 'Early Modern France, 1450–1700', in *Fiscal Crises, Liberty, and Representative Government, 1450–1789*, ed. Philip Hoffman and Kathryn Norberg (Stanford, CA: Stanford University Press, 1994) 232.

[41] Bodin, at *République* 381; *De Republica* 264–65 [3.2], recalls an incident during his tenure as the royal commissioner for general reform of the forests in Normandy in 1570, requiring him to sue the *tout corps de la ville de Rouën* to prevent an illegal alienation of crown lands. Lloyd, *Jean Bodin* 94.

[42] In developing this point, Bodin, at *République* 158, 859; *De Republica* 104, 640 [1.8; 6.2], relied on a commonplace of medieval legal science, a legal analogy drawn from the Roman law of guardianship, especially C.2.53(54).4, concerning the legal status of pupils and minors *in tutela* – that is, in the care of tutors, curators, and guardians: 'The state itself is a minor', the implication being that sovereign princes serve the function of a legal guardian over the minor's estate. See my 'The State Is a Minor: Fiduciary Concepts of Government and the Roman Law of Guardianship from Azo to Hobbes', in *Fiduciary Government*, ed. Evan Criddle, *et al.* (Cambridge: Cambridge University Press, 2018).

[43] Cp. *République* 874; *De Republica* 651. On the venality of office in Bodin's thought, see my 'Office Is a Thing Borrowed': 409–40.

[44] Bodin kept a journal of the proceedings of the Third Estate, the *Recueil de tout ce qui s'est negotié en la compagnie du Tiers Estat de France, en l'assemblée géneralle des trois Estats, assignez par le Roy en la ville de Bloys, au XV Novembre 1576* (1577) 97–8. See, in general, Owen Ulph, 'Jean Bodin and the Estates-General of 1576', *Journal of Modern History* 19 (1947): 289–96.

usufructuaries [*usufruictiers*; *usumfructum*], or to put it better, users [*usagers*] of the public domain.'[45] Assets attached to the domain belong to the whole kingdom and its people. Thus, Bodin reasoned, decisions about alienation ultimately can only be made by deputies (like himself) given 'express power of attorney for that purpose' [*baillé procuration expresse à ceste fin, & non autrement*] by the provinces, as agents to principals, not by the king.[46]

Since alienation of royal assets isn't a viable option, the only other immediate option to relieve France of its sovereign debt burden was currency devaluation. While Bodin acknowledged, in general, the right of coinage included the sovereign ability to alter the value of its currency, he nevertheless insisted firmly that sovereigns are strictly prohibited by the *ius gentium* from arbitrarily devaluing or debasing its currency (for example, by coin clipping).[47] His principal reason pointed to the devastating 'loss and damage' [*perte & dommage incroyable*] that devaluation would invariably cause on a societal and systemwide scale, beyond simply the fiscal politics of royal finance. It would be nothing short of a catastrophic breakdown of society:

> If money, which must regulate the price of all things, is mutable and uncertain, then no one can make a true accounting of what one holds. Contracts and agreements will similarly be uncertain, as well as related charges, taxes, wages, pensions, annuities, interests, and exemptions. So too would all pecuniary penalties and fines set by custom and ordinances be mutable and uncertain.[48]

For these reasons, Bodin thought debasement practices were fundamentally unfair and prejudicial to all those who relied on monetary and price stability, especially 'foreigners who deal with the sovereign and with its people' [*des estrangers,*

[45] *République* 182; *De Republica* 124 [1.9]; cp. *République* 860; *De Republica* 641 [6.2]. Bodin is most explicit in the Latin text, insisting that *reges enim ac summi principes non modo praediorum publicorum dominium aut proprietatem non habent* (by no means do kings and sovereign princes have ownership or property over public lands).

[46] *Recueil* 98; cp. *République* 388; *De Republica* 269; *Stato* 2:101 [3.2], citing D.2.14.28.10, 2.15.8, 3.3.60–63, 12.2.2, 46.4.3, to show that even with a *mandemant general* conferring power of attorney, the agent may not alienate or transfer property without securing first an additional *charge speciale* from the principal. Most striking about Bodin's claim here is that this doctrine is most often associated with radical Monarchomach lawyers, most notably François Hotman and Stephanus Junius Brutus, the pseudonymous author of the *Vindiciae Contra Tyrannos*. Bodin's analysis of the inalienability aligns him with the very radical Huguenots that so many commentators of this period have often juxtaposed him against. See my 'Private Law Models for Public Law Concepts: The Roman Law Theory of *Dominium* in the Monarchomach Doctrine of Popular Sovereignty', *Review of Politics* 70 (2008): 370–99.

[47] *République* 914; *De Republica* 681 [6.3] cp. Bodin, *Response to the Paradoxes* 126–27.

[48] *République* 914 [6.3]. The corresponding passage in the Latin *De Republica* 680 specifies what types of contractual obligations would be thrown into obscurity as a result of currency devaluation. What follows is a list of various contracts in Roman private law: *pacta conventa quae versantur in societatibus* (partnerships), *tutelis* (guardianships), *fiduciis* (trusts), *mandatis* (mandates), *rebus emptis, venditis* (contracts of purchase-sale), *conductis, locatis* (contracts of let-hire).

qui traictent avec luy et traffiquent avec les siens].[49] Sovereigns have a positive duty, as a legal requirement of the *ius gentium*, to maintain the value of their monies.

As venal as it may sound, Bodin seems to have believed that, through commercial activity, money could actually bring people together and build lasting amicable relations of trust necessary for an international *societas humani generis*: money preserves humanity. Declining confidence in the stability of currency could only frustrate such efforts. It was, thus, critical that sovereigns forbear devaluation as a matter of policy, even if that meant sacrificing short-term advantages, like paying off debts incurred by predecessors. Otherwise, sovereigns risk loss of faith and credit by incurring 'the infamy of being a counterfeiter' [*l'infamie de faux monnoyeur; falsae monetae fabricator*].[50]

'To Protect the Good and To Repel the Evil'

Promoting commerce, however, wasn't the only way that sovereigns could satisfy their duty to promote and preserve humanity. The more important service to humanity consisted in the sovereign's role to ensure that obligations, including even obligations of other sovereigns, were performed.

Bodin was the consummate 'non-ideal' political theorist.[51] Despite his theoretical analysis of sovereignty as an ideal abstraction of legal science, he was through and through a realist, in that he well knew and even expected that sovereigns, despite their many obligations under the *ius naturale* and *ius gentium*, would nevertheless routinely fall short and even defiantly skirt them. Sovereigns (like their non-ideal subjects) will fail to observe and perform the duties of justice and protection they owe to their own subjects.

From Bodin's non-ideal point of view, however, this places sovereigns in a real quandary. Recall that one of the principal reasons why sovereigns have their 'absolute power' to begin with is to ensure that private persons under their sovereignty perform *their* obligations – so that, for example, debts are repaid, purchased goods delivered, deposits returned, and so on. Just as sovereigns are burdened by natural and *ius gentium* obligations, they are also enforcers of natural and *ius gentium* obligations.[52]

[49] *République* 914; *De Republica* 680 [6.3].

[50] *République* 914; *De Republica* 680 [6.3]. See also Jotham Parsons, 'Governing Sixteenth-Century France: The Monetary Reforms of 1577', *French Historical Studies* 26 (2003): 1–30; 'Money and Sovereignty in Early Modern France', *Journal of the History of Ideas* 62 (2001): 59–79; Martti Koskenniemi, *To the Uttermost Parts of the Earth: Legal Imagination and International Power, 1300–1870* (Cambridge: Cambridge University Press, 2021) 372.

[51] The distinction between 'ideal' and 'non-ideal' political theory originates in John Rawls' *A Theory of Justice*. A statement of the interpretive problems associated with the distinction is found in A. John Simmons, 'Ideal and Nonideal Theory', *Philosophy and Public Affairs* 38 (2010): 5–36.

[52] Cp. Grotius, *De Iure Belli ac Pacis* 2.20.40.

Sovereigns accomplish this, as we've seen, chiefly through the exercise of jurisdiction and provision of actionable remedies to injured litigants – by creating a court system, appointing judges to staff those courts and 'declare the law' [*ius dicere*], and, when necessary, by sitting personally in judgment as a supreme court of final jurisdiction. As Bodin put it, the sovereign of a state acts, in these ways, as a kind of 'surety' [*vindex*] or 'guarantor' [*garant*] to assure satisfactory performance of first-order duties owed by subjects.[53]

Needless to say, acting as a surety or guarantor to ensure that someone *else's* duty is duly performed is a demanding obligation, perhaps too demanding for most self-interested sovereigns, motivated instead by prudential calculation, to undertake realistically. It will not be too surprising, therefore, to witness sovereigns strategically choosing to shirk their duties, effectively abandoning their suretyship role and leaving their neglected subjects, who depend on their sovereign's protection and assurance, vulnerable to the harms of injustice in a corrupt system.

While injurious, that is, at most, a sin of omission. But it wasn't what Bodin most feared. In the worst cases, sovereigns will be guilty of something more, not only of such sins of omission, but additionally guilty of sins of commission in direct contravention of those duties – by *doing* harm as well as *allowing* harm to their subjects.

How does Bodin propose to ensure that sovereigns do perform their duties, as they're supposed to? Two ways: one was to insert reputational costs as a salient variable in a sovereign's calculation, so that shirking duties is seen to be costlier than simply honouring and performing them. Because sovereigns must function as the *garand* [sic] *formel a tous ses subjects de la foy qu'ils ont entr'eux*, they are additionally bound by supererogatory duties, even beyond what 'natural equity' (D.2.14.1) requires, to act in ways that may even require sacrificing one's short-term advantage and incurring loss [*dommage*; *sui detrimento*], all for the sake of maintaining the sovereign's good faith and name, honour, and credit in the eyes of others [*la foy du Prince*; *principis dignitatem*].[54] Loss of this public confidence, Bodin reasoned, was far more damaging and simply not worth the trouble.

The other strategy, however, sought to exploit the international *societas* of which all sovereigns are members. All sovereigns are fiduciaries entrusted to enforce obligations of the *ius naturale* and the *ius gentium*. In this respect, sovereigns are sort of like co-equal partners of a self-governing club of sovereigns. Membership in this exclusive club operates on a principle of mutual aid: if one fails or is otherwise incapacitated, for whatever reason, in carrying out their functions to enforce natural and *ius gentium* obligations (the obligations arising from the *ius naturale* and the

[53] *République* 152; *De Republica* 99 [1.8]. Lloyd, *Jean Bodin* 133 speculates that Bodin's positioning of the sovereign as a 'guarantor' of the obligations contracted by private persons is a feature of feudal law. But Bodin's repeated use of the term, *vindex*, in corresponding Latin texts suggests instead that his source was more likely the guarantor in the Roman law of suretyship.

[54] *République* 153; *De Republica* 100 [1.8].

ius gentium), then it is incumbent on the others, as co-equal partners with the same enforcement function, to step into their place to ensure that those obligations are being enforced.

Consider, for example, the sovereign's duty of protection. It is taken, as given, that all sovereigns have a positive duty to protect their own subjects. But even this is a duty that sovereigns will often fail to perform, a point that is at the heart of Bodin's treatment of tyranny and the lawfulness of tyrannicide. The bloody state-sanctioned violence of St. Bartholomew in 1572, which would become among Huguenots one of the most terrifying and traumatic illustrations of a sovereign's failure to protect, earned for Charles IX (and his Florentine mother, the Queen Catherine de Medici) the label of tyrant *par excellence*.

Radicalized by this religious violence, Huguenot resistance theorists – later known as Monarchomachs, or 'king-killers' – developed elaborate theories justifying the legal permissibility of regicide, variously in terms of lawful self-defence, ephoral resistance, and as assertions of an ordinarily dormant popular sovereignty. It is well known that Bodin distanced himself from these radical Monarchomach theories, which he denounced as 'frivolous' [*frivoles*] and even 'mutinous' [*mutins*]: subjects may never, even in such cases of oppression, lawfully and actively resist their lawful sovereign.[55] Consistency to his own theory of political obligation forced him to reject the Monarchomachs' radical conclusions. There is no such right of resistance, whether individual or collective, to depose or even assassinate their sovereigns.[56]

What subjects *can* lawfully do, however, is flee their oppressors and seek refuge in the protection of another sovereign state.[57] All sovereigns must, as an extension of the duty of mutual aid, be prepared to receive refugees from foreign states whose sovereigns have failed in their duties to provide protection. And Bodin provides numerous (though questionable) illustrations of such dutiful shows of sovereign responsibility: Louis XII taking the Bentivoglio Family of Bologna and the Houses of Ferrara and of Mirandola into protection from Pope Julius II during the Italian Wars (at the time of Machiavelli); Henri II taking the princes of the Empire into his protection from the Emperor Charles V.[58]

But Bodin goes further: not only must sovereigns receive refugees, they are additionally bound, once they have admitted refugees, by the duty of

55 *République* 305, 306 [2.5].

56 Note, however, that he is only talking about subjects. The appropriate remedy to such oppression, apparently, is to look outside the state, to foreigners who are under no obligation to obey the offending sovereign.

57 Bodin was likely thinking of Protestant exiles fleeing Catholic persecution, and vice-versa, as refugees and asylum and refuge in other states. Cp. Richard Tuck, 'Grotius, Hobbes, and Pufendorf on Humanitarian Intervention', in *Just and Unjust Military Intervention: European Thinkers from Vitoria to Mill*, ed. Stefano Recchia and Jennifer Welsh (Cambridge: Cambridge University Press, 2013) 105.

58 *République* 822. These are, it should be noted, terrible examples. Giovanni Bentivoglio was a prisoner of Louis XII and died in prison, so it is a real stretch to call it 'protection'.

non-refoulement – that is, the negative duty prohibiting sovereigns from repatriating refugees to their country of origin where they would likely be in danger of suffering persecution and some other harm.[59]

For Bodin, this duty of protecting refugees was one of the most important duties that sovereigns owe to humanity. But he takes it one step further:

> If a sovereign prince, surpassing other sovereigns in power or in dignity, is duly informed that subjects in another state are being oppressed [*tirannizé*; *tyrannidis*] and seeking refuge [*confugisse*], not only must the more powerful sovereign dutifully receive the refugees seeking his protection, the sovereign must free [*l'exempter*] them and humanely [*humaniter tueri*] protect them from their oppressor. Although the [Roman] law [D.1.6.2] protects slaves from the power of their cruel masters, it is better to free [*vindicari*] the subject altogether from the subjection of others, and to restore them to full liberty [*remettre en pleine liberté*], rather than subjecting those refugees to oneself.[60]

What Bodin seems to have in mind here are offensive wars of liberation, aimed at disabling and even toppling oppressive *seigneurial* sovereigns – sovereigns who, despite their lawful title to rule, nevertheless abuse that lawful authority.[61] All sovereign states must be prepared to wage such offensive wars, precisely because they are all, as Eyal Benvenisti suggested, 'trustees of humanity', entrusted with the solemn enforcement of the *ius naturale* and *ius gentium* governing all of humanity.[62] It is the job of all sovereigns 'to protect [*bouclier*] the good and to repel [*rembarrer*] the evil', if those offenders may be sovereigns.[63]

[59] *République* 471, 473; *De Republica* 325, 327; *Stato* 2:240–41 [3.6]. Bodin stresses that the duty of *non-refoulement* is exceptional and applicable only in those cases where a foreigner is seeking refuge specifically to escape oppression. The duty does not, however, extend to fugitives who, having been lawfully tried and condemned, are escaping punishment. In those sorts of cases involving fugitives, sovereigns, Bodin argues, are required under the *ius naturale* and *ius gentium* to repatriate foreigners to their home countries without retrial or reexamination, a position in conflict with the growing *opinio communis* of medieval legal science which interpreted *non-refoulement* obligations broadly and extending even to fugitives. The consensus view, represented chiefly by Baldus on C.6.1.2, Odofredus on C.3.15.2, Jacobus de Belviso on VI.2.2.1, Angelus de Ubaldi on D.5.1.19, Felino Sandeo on X.2.2.20, among others, was that even fugitives were entitled to a *de novo* trial in a foreign state before repatriation.

[60] *République* 824; *De Republica* 611 [5.6].

[61] Bodin comments at length in the *République* on the different strategies and purposes of defensive and offensive wars. By no means was Bodin a pacifist. In a world constituted of independent sovereigns, the right to wage war, even offensive war, is one of the most essential legal rights of sovereignty. But war, in Bodin's view, could be an instrument of justice, a theme that would influence Gentili and Grotius. Like Bodin, Gentili saw nations of the world as forming a worldwide *societas humana* and acknowledged the legality of interventionist wars undertaken for support of humanity and liberty in this society, as well as remedies for violations under the *ius gentium* [*honesta belli inferendi causa*]. Panizza, 'The Freedom of the Sea and the Modern Cosmopolis in Alberico Gentili's *De Iure Belli*' 94. On defensive and offensive wars in Bodin, see Miglietti, 'Sovereignty, Territory, and Population in Jean Bodin's *République*': 17–34.

[62] The *République/De Republica* is unique in that he also includes the divine law alongside natural law and the law of nations.

[63] *République* 760 [5.5]

'Truly no cause is more just', Bodin proclaims, 'than the protection of innocent lives [*pro innocentium vita tuenda*]', especially where those innocent lives are threatened and oppressed by cruel despots who ruled their subjects as if they were their slaves.[64] Indeed, 'of all the most illustrious deeds [*de pulcherissimis omnibus factis*], none is more distinguished than for one to defend the lives, the reputations, and the fortunes of the weak and the innocent from the injustices of those more powerful'.[65] Moses, whom Bodin calls the *Israelitarum Imperator*, epitomized the virtue of the liberator who 'freed [*liberavit*] the oppressed Israelites from the harshest slavery [*crudelissima servitute*]' of their Egyptian masters.[66] So too were the heroic intercessions of Hercules, Dion, Timoleon, Aratus (Plutarch), and Tamarlane (Prince of the Tartars) who championed the cause of the weak in other states who couldn't fight back against the brutality of their oppressors.[67]

Bodin's articulation of a sovereign responsibility to protect didn't escape the notice of his earliest readers. Alberico Gentili, one of the first to deploy Bodin's theory of sovereignty in the analysis of the law of war and international law more generally, specifically credited Bodin with the principle that, 'if subjects [in another state] are treated cruelly and unjustly', it is not only permissible, but obligatory, to intercede in the domestic affairs of that other sovereign state.[68]

Note the one point that must be underlined: Bodin, the supposed prophet of an unconditionally absolute Westphalian sovereignty, actually turns out to endorse the direct violation of that very principle, in the most urgent cases where the sovereign's fiduciary duty to protect and preserve humanity outweighs and overrides any other sovereign's right to non-interference.

[64] *République* 760; *De Republica* 562–63: *Iustior vero causa nulla est quam pro sua deinde pro innocentium vita tuenda.* This cause, by itself, is sufficient to wage a lawful war on behalf of another oppressed party. Bodin makes this point as a reply to Cicero's theory of *bellum iustum* and the fetial procedure (that is, the rites of the Roman college of fetial priests – ancient Rome's foreign ministry) of the *rerum repetitio* and denunciation.

[65] *De Republica* 208 [2.5]; cp. 66 [1.7], where he uses the same language [*pulcherissima*] to describe 'protection'.

[66] *De Republica* 209 [2.5]. Note that the Moses example doesn't fully demonstrate his point, since Moses, in Exodus 2:11–12, defends the Hebrew from the abuses of the Egyptian slave-driver.

[67] Bodin cites Hercules again in *République* 822 [5.6] who took in *la protection des peoples affligés, contre la violence & cruauté des titans.* This is an interesting passage because he uses Hercules as an illustration of international arbitration between the sovereign and subjects of a foreign state: *le sage Prince* [like Hercules] *peut & doit intervenir pour accorder le subiect d'autruy avecson Prince. Et s'il congnoist l'outrageux traictement d'un tyran envers ses subjects estre irreconciliable, il doit en padre la protection d'un coeur haut et genereux.*

[68] Gentili, *The Three Books on the Law of War* 2:75 [*De Iure Belli Libri Tres* 1.16]. Gentili uses Bodin's example of Hercules, 'the subduer of tyrants and monsters', and adds the analogy in support of the principle that 'we defend sons against fathers who are unjust'. In addition to Bodin (at *République* 2.5 and 5.4), Gentili cites Covarruvias, Cicero, *De Off.* 3.25; Baldus on C.6.25.4.

Applied Principle of Collegiality

What is the theory that led Bodin to this surprising conclusion? We might start by returning to Bodin's idea, ultimately of Stoic origin, that all sovereigns of humanity are like co-equal partners [*socii*] or fellows [*foederati*] of an international club of sovereigns.[69] Humanity, in Bodin's view, might best be understood as a kind of club [*consociatio*], an international *societas* made up of 'all nations' [*omnes populi*], all governed by a common code based on an overlapping 'consensus of all nations' [*consensus omnium populorum*].[70]

Why a club? What seems to have caught Bodin's attention was the principle of equality that characterized the self-government of such autonomous bodies. Bodin commented on this point at length, especially in his discourse in *République* III on colleges and corporations where he observed the equality among members of such bodies.[71]

Like self-governing colleges and corporate bodies, Bodin's vision of the international society of states operated on a similar principle of equality. Despite whatever differences in geography, population, or wealth there may be between sovereign states, they are all nevertheless equals in the international society of humanity. In this way, Bodin actually originated the fundamentals of the doctrine of sovereign equality, an idea often attributed to Emer de Vattel.[72] So wrote Bodin: 'Just as in the enumeration of houses, where a small household is to be counted for one family, as much as the largest and the richest manor in the city, so too is a small king [*un petit Roy*] as much a sovereign [*autant souverain*] as the greatest monarch on earth [*le plus grand Monarque de la terre*]'.[73]

But what made Bodin's approach truly original and different from Vattel's wasn't simply the principle of equality. It consisted specifically in what I might describe as an applied principle of collegiality. Bodin points out that, because members

[69] Note that they are not always equal. Bodin cited the Roman difference between treaties *aequo foedere* and treatise *iniquo* at *De Republica* 579 [5.6] (or *traités d'alliance inegale* at *République* 105 [1.7]). Pufendorf cites this specific passage in Bodin as an authority in *De Iure Naturae et Gentium* 8.9.4, particularly in the category of the treaty *inaequus*: if the superior in a treaty is far more powerful than the other, he gradually comes to exercise the sovereignty.

[70] Bodin uses the phrase frequently as a synonym for the *ius gentium* – for example, at *De Republica* 47 [1.6].

[71] The example that Bodin returned to frequently were collegial courts staffed by judges of equal rank, as well as colleges of priests, such as the Roman fetial college.

[72] For examples in recent scholarship, Benedict Kingsbury, 'Sovereignty and Inequality', *European Journal of International Law* 9 (1998): 603; Jennifer Pitts, 'Intervention and Sovereign Equality: Legacies of Vattel', in *Just and Unjust Military Intervention: European Thinkers from Vitoria to Mill*, ed. Stefano Recchia and Jennifer Welsh (Cambridge: Cambridge University Press, 2013).

[73] *République* 13; *De Republica* 10 [1.2]; cp. *Methodus* 238: *Enim elephas non magis animal dici debet, quam formica*. This passage may very well have been the inspiration for Vattel's statement in *The Law of Nations* 75 [Preliminaries, §18]: 'A dwarf is as much a man as a giant; a small republic is no less a sovereign state than the most powerful kingdom'.

of colleges and corporations are generally held to be equal (and thus, 'peers'), no individual member has any authority, or *imperium*, over any other. One cannot, therefore, command [*imperare*; *iubere*] another within that body of equals, as in the doctrine, *par in parem non habet imperium*.[74]

But it's one thing to say that a member cannot *command* another, like a sovereign commanding a subject. It's another thing, however, to ask whether it is permissible for one to *intercede* or even *hinder* the actions of another. From Bodin's point of view, the two weren't the same thing: whereas a sovereign's legislative command [*commandement*; *imperium*] alters the structure of obligations binding others, either by creating or eliminating legal duties, intercession [*empeschement*, *opposition*; *intercessio*], by contrast, simply delays or temporarily suspends the carrying out of an existing obligation (without altering that obligation). It was, thus, no contradiction to say, that:

> Even if one has no authority [*puissance*; *nullum imperium*] over a colleague, one may nevertheless hinder [*prohibere*; *empescher*] that colleague through interceding public actions.[75]

Bodin developed this argument partly through observations of Roman Republican institutional design which consistently deployed this principle of collegiality by which one magistrate, such as praetor or a consul, could hinder or prevent the decision of a colleague, equal in rank and power, from being carried out.[76] Perhaps the most notable example of all was tribunician intercession on behalf of a pleb against magisterial authority, illustrating how even one without *imperium* (the tribune) could nevertheless act in a way to hinder another with *imperium* (the magistrate).

Bodin readily applied these principles of collegiality in explicating the collegial relations of co-equal sovereigns in the international society of humanity. As equals, one sovereign state can have no authority, no *imperium*, over another state. Like consuls who both have an 'equal power' [*par potestas*], states too have an equal right of sovereignty. Yet, they have no right to assert that sovereignty over an equal; nor, by the same token, is one under any duty to obey an equal. This is, of course, perfectly consistent with what we would expect to find in a strictly Westphalian world.

But Bodin's wasn't a Westphalian world. At least, Bodin didn't see it as such.

[74] D.4.8.4, 36.1.13.4, X.1.6.20; *Gloss. Ord.* on Nov. 6. Cp. *De Republica* 316. Kantorowicz, *King's Two Bodies* 452, suggests additional sources in Dante Alighieri, *Monarchy*, ed. and trans. Prue Shaw (Cambridge: Cambridge University Press, 1996) 14 [1.10.2], citing *Gloss. Ord.* on D.36.1.13.4 s.v. *imperium*; C.1.14.4. s.v., *indicamus*.

[75] *De Republica* 316; *République* 457 [3.6].

[76] Provincial governors such as the various *praesides provinciarum* and prefectures (perhaps the most famous prefect: Pontius Pilate), by contrast, had no colleague in their province. Provincial governments in the Roman Empire were, thus, a collection of miniature despotisms of governors, subject only to the Roman emperor. For this reason, an argument might be made that provincial governors, and their mutual relations to each other, formed an important model for Bodin's theory of international relations.

Membership Duties

Since at least the time of Thomas Hobbes, it has become customary to visualize sovereign states as disconnected, autonomous islands of political activity separated by a lawless sea of anarchy. Whatever 'international relations' do emerge between such inward-looking states amidst these fragile conditions of anarchy will ultimately be shaped by their mutual distrust and self-interest. It is, therefore, not surprising that modern international law and politics have been characterized as always being one precarious step away from war.

Bodin, for his part, did not begin from this Hobbesian axiom of anarchy.[77] He postulated, instead, that all states, by virtue of their sovereignty, belong, as co-equal members and partners (variously *socii* and *foederati*), to an international club, a *consociatio*, of states together comprising the whole of humanity.[78] Each retaining their independence and sovereignty, member states remain foreigners with respect to each other. Yet, because they are all members of a common human society built ultimately on friendship [*amitié*; *amicitia*] and the natural human desire for society, all sovereign states are understood to be burdened by 'membership duties' in their relations with fellow states, in the same way that members of a private club are likewise understood to be burdened by reciprocal membership duties in their conduct with fellow club members.[79]

Perhaps for this reason Bodin arrived at a very different portrait depicting the international order among sovereign states. While Bodin might have agreed, in principle, that the world lacks a common 'global' sovereign, he nevertheless refused to define and identify such absence of a 'global' sovereign authority as a lawless and duty-free anarchy.[80] There can, he thought, still be a robust international

[77] Bodin used the term *anarchie* or ἀναρχία on several occasions to describe that lawless condition where 'no one commands and no one obeys'. *République* 75, 937; *De Republica* 49, 692 [1.6, 6.4] He illustrates this anarchy by the examples of Israel after the death of Jephthah, Syracuse after the death of the tyrant Dion, Florence after the expulsion of the *ottimatti*. But remarkably, Bodin acknowledges that, even in anarchy, it is possible for the amicable bonds of human society to thrive in families and in collegial and corporate bodies. *République* 508; *De Republica* 369 [4.1]. There can be some degree of harmonious social order even in Bodin's version of anarchy. On these themes in Bodin, see also Ioannis Evrigenis, *Images of Anarchy: The Rhetoric and Science in Hobbes's State of Nature* (Cambridge: Cambridge University Press, 2014); David Grewal, 'The Domestic Analogy Revisited: Hobbes on International Order', *Yale Law Journal* 125 (2016): 618–80.

[78] *Consociatio*: Cp. D.50.16.85.

[79] A useful analogy might be self-governing professional associations such as a bar or medical association, a learned society, or a guild, whose members are, in the practice of their profession, duty-bound to observe standard professional ethics and are expected to show professional courtesies. Violation of such 'membership duties' associated with a profession may result in sanctions such as the rescission of professional privileges and expulsion from the profession (for example, disbarment for moral turpitude or revocation of academic tenure for plagiarism).

[80] Bodin might, therefore, be regarded one of the antecedents of the so-called 'English School' of international relations associated with Martin Wight and Hedley Bull. I thank Julian Arato for suggesting another modern connection in Judge Bruno Simma, 'From Bilateralism to Community Interest in International Law', *Recueil des Cours de l'Académie de Droit International* 250 (1994): 217.

order, an 'anarchical society' (as Hedley Bull famously put it), constituted of rules and duties of membership, even without a global sovereignty.

Some of these duties, of course, derive from multilateral conventions and treaties contracted by, and between, sovereigns. Sovereigns may, as we've seen earlier, voluntarily enter into an *aequo foedere* treaty with other *foederati* to establish relations of friendship, commerce, and hospitality [*traité d'amitié, commerce, & hospitalité*] through trade in all types of goods [*traffiquer ensemble de toutes marchandises*].[81] Indeed, what Bodin seems to have envisioned here was a customs union, a *Zollverein*. His point, however, was that membership of such unions, as sovereign trading partners, entails collective observance of positive duties explicitly specified in treaties. For example, treaties establishing commercial relations among states might introduce a positive duty limiting any member state's sovereign right to introduce or raise tariffs and other customs duties [*la charge de certains imposts accordés par les traités*].[82]

So too might states enter treaties establishing leagues and alliances for collective security, such as the Amphyctionic, Achaean, Aetolian, Hanseatic, and Schmalkaldic Leagues of ancient and medieval history, imposing duties on member states of those alliances. Not only did such treaties bind their members by the negative duty to forswear their sovereign right to declare and wage war on a fellow member state, it further bound members by the positive duty to assist any member state under armed attack, including the duty to provide military assistance.

All of these 'membership' duties – such as the duties to regulate and limit tariffs in a customs union, to forswear the use of war and to assist other states in distress in a security alliance – are obligatory. Yet they do not require a global sovereignty for their validity or (to use a term of art in modern international law) their *effectivité*.[83] What matters is an instrument in the form of a treaty memorializing the show of the good faith and the agreement between sovereigns creating such international obligations in the first place.

Does that, then, mean all such duties ultimately must originate in a treaty, pact, or convention of some kind? If there's one crucial finding emerging from this study, it is that Bodin rejected such a simplistic legal-positivism with respect to the origin of duties: even in the absence of positive legislation, humans, including even those empowered with sovereignty, are always bound by duties arising from the unlegislated *ius naturale* and *ius gentium* (duties from which even the absolute power of popes cannot release sovereigns).

[81] *République* 106 [1.7]. Turchetti 405, n.25 observes that the corresponding Latin passage appears in the Latin *De Republica* 5.6.

[82] *République* 106 [1.7].

[83] On 'effectivity', see Jean d'Aspremont, 'Effectivity in International Law: Self-Empowerment Against Epistemological Claustrophobia', *AJIL Unbound* 108 (2017): 103–5.

That same point now can be extended to include formal instruments such as treaties and conventions: Even in the absence of formal treaties and conventions, in a world where (as Pomponius put it in the *Digest*) there is 'neither friendship, hospitality, nor any pact of friendship' [*neque amicitiam neque hospitium neque foedus amicitiae*], sovereigns still are bound by 'membership duties' originating from the *ius naturale* and *ius gentium* in their mutual relations with each other.[84]

Sovereignty and Protection

Some of these *officia humanitatis* may appear at first glance to be purely supererogatory – honourable or noble, but not required. And in one sense, Bodin was right: no positive legislation, nor any formal pact or treaty, can truly *require* sovereigns to show hospitality, benevolence, comity, and kindness to others. These humane obligations, Bodin posited, derive instead from higher sources of law, so that, while they may not be strictly obligatory *ex iure civile*, they are always obligatory *ex iure gentium* and *ex iure naturale*, as well as by divine law. Nor must such duties be observed simply for duty's sake. Observing these duties of humanity serve a useful purpose, by fortifying amicable bonds of trust and good faith, between sovereign and sovereign, as much as between human and human.

Probably the most dramatic illustration of this point – and the point most relevant for defenders of a putative sovereign responsibility to protect – is captured in Bodin's explicit recognition of a sovereign duty of protection in the *République*. Here's what Bodin observes about the term, 'protection':

> The word, *protection* [*advocatiam aut protectionem*] in general is extended to all subjects who are duty-bound to obey a prince or seigneurial sovereign. And as we have already said, a sovereign prince is obliged to maintain [*le prince est oblige de maintenir*] his subjects in the security of their persons, properties, and families by force of arms and by laws [*par le force des armes et des lois*].[85]

Sovereigns, of course, aren't the only ones duty-bound to protect. Reflecting on the whole range of possible obligatory relations of authority, Bodin carefully observes

[84] D.49.15.5.2, which Bodin cites at *De Republica* 70 [1.7]. They are bound *propter eam quae homini cum homine intercedit humanitatis rationem*.

[85] *République* 101 [1.7]. The corresponding passage in *De Republica* 65–66 allows a much looser translation into Latin, translating 'protection' by *clientela*, *advocatia*, and *protectio*. These words capture *omne genus subditorum, seu servi, seu liberti, seu vasalli, seu cives fuerint, qui summae cuiusdam potestatis imperio tenentur. Nam ut principes suae potestati subditos armis ac legibus ab iniuria vindicare, ita subditi principes obsequio, amore, cura & officiis omnibus colere ac prosequi debent.* Bodin's classical etymology derives 'protection' from the Latin verb, *protegere*, a conjugation of which [*protexit*] features in the penultimate book of the *Digest*, D.49.16.6.8, discussing the inferior's duty to protect the superior when attacked.

that protection is an essential duty that shapes the relations of masters towards their slaves [*la protection des maistres envers leurs esclaves; heri ac servi*], of patrons towards their freedmen [*des patrons envers leurs affranchis; patroni & liberti*], and of feudal lords towards their vassals [*des seigneurs envers leurs vassaux; domini ac vassalli*].[86] And so likewise are sovereigns bound to protect their own subjects. As Bodin put it, *le droit de protection est plus beau, plus honorable, & plus magnifique que tous les autres.*

For sovereigns, however, their duty of protection isn't limited or reserved only to their own subjects. In Bodin's analysis, it is a duty extending, in principle, to all of humanity. Even foreigners, who are otherwise outside the moral boundaries of one's state are nevertheless potential beneficiaries of the protection only sovereigns, in virtue of their absolute power, can provide. One might reasonably ask and worry that perhaps this goes too far, that the sovereign duty of protection could easily slip into a regime of colonial protectorates, whereby what begins as a well-intentioned protection mutates over time into an imperial quasi-sovereignty, or suzerainty, over others.

Bodin, ever the careful student of Roman techniques of empire-building, anticipated this worry and specifically the colonial tendencies of protection.[87] His reply, perhaps not entirely satisfactory, nevertheless reaffirmed a basic conceptual distinction: protection isn't the same as sovereignty.[88] One may, in principle, serve as a protector for another, without also, at the same time, being sovereign over that other. Indeed, he clarifies, one who serves as a *protecteur* only takes up 'the defence and protection' of another, but does not acquire a single mark of power [*sur lesquels le protecteur n'a point de puissance*] over the other, nor does protection diminish in any way the other's sovereignty [*sans autre diminution de la maiesté*].[89] We know this, Bodin insists, because of the way sovereign states carefully tailor their foreign relations with others, as documented in treaties and pacts which both affirm duties of protection to others while, at the same time, 'observe with affection the respect due to each other's sovereignty' [*comiter maiestatem conservare*].[90]

[86] *République* 101; *De Republica* 66 [1.7].

[87] These passages are developed in connection with the principle expressed in D.49.15.7.1, the accuracy of which text Bodin claims he has verified from the *Littera Florentina* of the Roman law and which he quoted directly, with some minor modifications, in *De Republica* 68–69. *Stato* 1:323, n.13, suggests an alternate source in Guillaume Budé, *Annotationes reliquae in Pandectas* (Paris, 1542) 86.

[88] *République* 105; *De Republica* 69 [1.7]. *La protection n'emporte point de subjection, mais bien superiorité, & prerogative d'honneur.*

[89] *République* 101 [1.7]. This is why, as I pointed out earlier, Bodin distinguishes *intercessio* from *imperium*. A protector may 'intercede' [*intercedere*] in the affairs of another, without 'commanding' [*imperare; iubere*] as a sovereign. *Intercessio* is, thus, consistent with the principle, *pari in parem non habet imperium*. The tribune who intercedes upon the decision of a magistrate, exercising *imperium*, on behalf of a pleb doesn't derogate from or diminish the magistrate's *imperium*.

[90] *République* 105. Isnardi Parente, *Stato* 1: 323 and Turchetti 403–4, n.23 both attribute this clause to Cicero, *Pro Balbo* 8.20. Carlo Sigonio, *De Antiquo Iure Italiae* (Frankfurt, 1574) 124 [1.1] is also cited as an authority on this point. Cp. *République* 822, in which Bodin observes that Louis XII's terms of protection of Bentivoglio, Ferrara, and Mirandola were specifically crafted 'without prejudice to the legal rights of the Roman Church'.

Unlike genuine subjects, then, who owe obedience as a duty, those who benefit from the protection of sovereigns owe nothing beyond the simple courtesy of showing 'honour and reverence to the protector' [*honneur et reverence des adherans envers le protecteur*]. That is, in fact, the most that a protector can justly demand and expect for protecting and interceding on behalf of others.[91] That is also why protection is so heroic and noble, even (as Bodin seems to think) Herculean. One protects another out of a sense of duty and honour, not for potential gain.

Observe the many ways, then, these duties of humanity burden the right of sovereignty. Sovereigns are duty-bound to protect the vulnerable; to intercede on behalf of foreigners oppressed by their sovereigns; to maintain the value and credit of their money for international commerce; to provide foreigners with a forum to obtain justice; to offer safe conduct; to ensure the performance of valid obligations; to honour treaties and pacts, even when it is to their prejudice. Bodin, of course, was theorizing about sovereignty in a very different world. But his fundamental theoretical insight here, integrating sovereign duties into sovereign rights, resonates even into our times with profound consequences.

One of the more forceful criticisms of sovereignty in the recent academic literature highlights its supposedly 'hypocritical' quality. Sovereignty, it is said, establishes certain rules of conduct, norms such as the absolute immunity of sovereignty and the right of non-interference. And yet, as a point of fact, those very rules are knowingly and routinely flouted, so much so that an unavoidable contradiction erupts between norm and fact.

One might reasonably ask whether Bodin's own theory, the supposed archetype of the classical theory of sovereignty, is vulnerable to this criticism of hypocrisy. And, at first glance, it appears so. After all, enjoining sovereigns to intercede into the affairs of other states or to ensure that others perform their obligations, as the duties of humanity require, seems to contravene directly the very principle of sovereignty, by chipping away from its supposedly 'absolute' and inviolable character.

Such revelations of hypocrisy have only emboldened today's critics to revise, repurpose, and reimagine sovereignty, as a way to repair this hypocrisy and to secure for it a viable future in a far more interdependent world – legally, politically, socially, economically, culturally, even digitally – than the one Bodin had experienced. In practice, this has translated into a resounding rejection of the classical

[91] *République* 101 [1.7]. Anything more – say, in the form of a fee or other monetary tribute – reduces protection to mercenary profiteers, not unlike what Robert Nozick once described as 'protective associations', quasi-state entities in which one might, for a fee, enjoy the benefits of membership in a collective security alliance with others. Robert Nozick, *Anarchy, State, and Utopia* (New York: Basic Books, 1974) 12–17. Nozick's analysis is apposite in this context, since his purpose is just the same as Bodin's – to show that membership of a 'protective association' isn't quite the same as membership of a sovereign state.

theory exemplified by Bodin. And so, the search for a better, more responsible, vision of sovereignty begins, it seems, with a purging – by eliminating the source of those hypocrisies we have supposedly inherited from Bodin and continue to endure.

What I hope we can now see is that, instead of distancing ourselves from Bodin's theory and looking elsewhere in history for inspiration, what we really should have been doing is returning to his ideas in earnest. But we should do so, *not* because the classical theory which Bodin supposedly represented deserves to be defended. We should do so, instead, because Bodin offers us a worthy alternative to the classical theory, one that prioritizes the responsibilities entailed by sovereignty as essential cornerstones to building an international legal order for an uncertain future.

Bibliography

Works by Jean Bodin

Bodin, Jean. *Apologie de René Herpin pour La République de I. Bodin*. Paris: Jacques Du Puys, 1581.

— *The Colloquium of the Seven about Secrets of the Sublime* [*Colloquium Heptaplomeres*]. Trans. Marion Leathers Kuntz. University Park, Pennsylvania: Pennsylvania State University Press, 1975.

— *De Republica Libri VI*. Paris: Jacques Du Puys, 1586.

—*Exposé du Droit Universel*. Ed. Lucien Jerphagnon, Simone Goyard-Fabre, René-Marie Rampelberg. Paris: Presses Universitaires de France, 1985.

— *Iuris Universi Distributio*. Paris: Jacques Du Puys, 1578.

— *Juris Universi Distributio*. Cologne: Ioannes Gymnicus, 1580.

— *La méthode de l'histoire: Traduite pour la première fois et presentèe*. Paris: Société d'édition 'Les Belles lettres', 1941.

— *Methodus ad Facilem Historiarum Cognitionem*. Paris: Apud Martinum Iuvenem, 1572.

— *Methodus ad facilem historiarum cognitionem*. Ed. Sara Miglietti. Pisa: Edizioni della Normale, 2013.

— *Oppiani de Venatione*. Paris: Apud Michaëlum Vascosanum, 1555.

— *I Sei Libri dello Stato di Jean Bodin*. Ed. Margherita Isnardi Parente and Diego Quaglioni. 3 Vols. Turin: Unione Tipografico-Editrice Torinese, 1964.

— *Les Six Livres de la République*. Paris: Jacques Du Puys, 1583.

— *Les Six Livres de la République. De Republica Libri Sex*. Vol. 1. Ed. Mario Turchetti. Paris: Classiques Garnier, 2013.

— *On Sovereignty: Four Chapters on Sovereignty*. Ed. Julian Franklin. Cambridge: Cambridge University Press, 1992.

— *La Response de Maistre Iean Bodin Advocat en la Cour, au Paradoxe de Monsieur de Malestroit*. Paris: Chez Martin le Ieune, 1568.

— *Response to the Paradoxes of Malestroit*. Trans. and ed. Henry Tudor and R.W. Dyson. Bristol: Thoemmes Press, 1997.

— *Recueil de tout ce qui s'est negotié en la compagnie du Tiers Estat de France, en l'assemblée géneralle des trois Estats, assignez par le Roy en la ville de Bloys, au XV Novembre 1576*. 1577.

— *Universae Naturae Theatrum*. Lyon: Apud Iacobum Roussin, 1596.

Knolles, Richard [Jean Bodin]. *The Six Bookes of a Commonweale*. London, 1606. [Facsimile reprint edited by Kenneth McRae. Cambridge: Harvard University Press, 1962].

Kocin, Jan [Jean Bodin]. *Nova Distributio Iuris Universi*. Prague: George Nigrinus, 1581.

Legal Authorities: *Corpus Iuris Civilis*

Lyon

Codicis Iustiniani. Lyon: Apud Hugonem à Porta, 1560.

Pandectarum Iuris Civilis. 3 Vols. Lyon: Apud Hugonem à Porta [Hugues de la Porte], 1560. *Volumen*. Lyon: Apud Hugonem à Porta, 1558.

Venice

Codicis Dn. Iustiniani. Editio Postrema. Venice: Apud Nicolaum Bevilaqua, 1574.
Institutiones Divi Caesaris Iustiniani. Editio Postrema. Venice: Apud Nicolaum Bevilaqua, 1569.
Novellae Constitutiones Divi Caesaris Iustiniani, Quae Authentica Vulgo Appellant. Editio Postrema. Venice: Apud Nicolaum Bevilaqua, 1569.
Pandectarum, seu Digestorum Iuris Civilis. 3 Vols. Editio Postrema. Venice: Apud Nicolaum Bevilaqua, 1569.

Legal Authorities: *Corpus Iuris Canonici*

Gregory IX. *Decretales [sive Liber Extra] D. Gregorii Papae IX*. Rome: In Aedibus Populi Romani, 1582.
Gratian. *Decretum Gratiani: Emendatum et notationibus illustratum una cum glossis, Gregorii XIII Pont. Max. iussu editum*. Rome: In Aedibus Populi Romani, 1582.
Boniface VIII. *Liber Sextus Decretalium*. Rome: In Aedibus Populi Romani, 1582.

Legal Authorities: *Responsa Prudentum atque Commentaria*

Alciato, Andrea. *Opera Omnia*. Vol. 4. Basel: Thomas Guarinus, 1582.
Angelus de Ubaldis. *Super Prima Parte Digesti Veteris*. 1534.
Antiboul, Pierre [Petrus Antibolus Allobrogis]. *Tractatus de Muneribus*. In *Tractatus Illustrium in Utraque Tum Pontificii, Tum Caesarei*. Vol. 12. Venice, 1584.
Baisio, Guido da [Archidiaconus]. *Super Sexto Decretalium*. Lyon: Apud Haeredes Iacobi Guintae, 1547.
Baldus de Ubaldis. *Ad Tres Priores Libros Decretalium Commentaria*. Turin: Apud Haeredes Nicolai Bevilaquae, 1578.
— *Consiliorum sive Responsorum*. Vol. 3. Venice: 1575.
— *In I^{am} Digesti Veteri Partem Commentaria*. Venice, 1577.
— *In II^{am} Digesti Veteri Partem Commentaria*. Venice, 1577.
— *In Usus Feudorum Commentaria*. Lyon, 1550.
— *Super Primo, II, et III Codicis*. Lyon, 1539.
Bartolus de Sassoferrato. *Commentaria in I^{am} Digesti Novi Partem*. Lyon: Excudebat Petrus Fradin, 1555.
— *Commentaria in I^{am} Infortiati Partem*. Lyon, 1552.
— *In I^{am} Codicis Partem Commentaria*. Turin: Apud Haeredes Nicolai Bevilaquae, 1577.
— *In I^{am} Partem Digesti Novi Commentaria*. Basel: Ex Officina Episcopiana, 1588.
— *Secunda Super Digesto Veteri*. 1530.
Budé, Guillaume. *Annotationes Reliquae in Pandectas*. Paris: Michel de Vascosan, Robert Estienne & Jean de Roigny, 1542.
Butrio, Antonio da. *Super Secunda Secundi Decretalium Commentarii*. Venice: Apud Iuntas, 1578.
Castro, Paul de. *In I^{am} Digesti Veteris Partem Commentaria*. Lyon, 1583.
— *In II^{am} Digesti Veteri Partem Commentaria*. Lyon, 1583.

Connan, François. *Commentariorum Iuris Civilis*. Paris: Jacques Kerver, 1553.
— *Commentariorum Iuris Civilis Libri X*. Lyon: Apud Haeredes Iacobi Iunctae, 1566.
Cujas, Jacques. *Observationes et Emendationes*. Vol. 2. Köln: Apud Ioanem Gymnicum, 1587.
Doneau, Hugues [Donellus]. *Opera Omnia: Commentariorum de Iure Civili*. Vol. 3. Lucca: Typis Joannis Riccomini, 1763.
Faure, Jean de Roussines. [Faber]. *In Iustiniani Imperatoris Codicem* Lyon, 1550.
Freigius, Johann Thomas. *Partitiones Iuris Utriusque*. Basel, 1571.
Gaius. *Institutes of Gaius*. Ed. Francis de Zulueta. Oxford: Clarendon Press, 1953.
Hostiensis [Henry of Segusio]. *Summa Aurea*. Venice: Ad candentis Salamandrae insigne, 1570.
Hotman, François. *Partitiones Iuris Civilis Elementariae*. Basel: Apud N. Episcopium Iuniorem, 1571.
Innocent IV [Sinibaldo Fieschi]. *Commentaria Super Libros Quinque Decretalium*. Frankfurt am Main, 1570.
Maino, Giasone del [Jason de Mayno]. *De Actionibus Titulus Institutionum Iustiniani*. Venice: Excudebatur apud Franciscum & Gasparem Bindonum & fratres, 1574.
— *In I^am^ Digesti Veteris Partem Commentaria*. Turin: Apud Nicolaum Bevilaquam, 1573.
— *In II^am^ Digesti Veteri Partem*. Lyon, 1583.
Pistoia, Cino da. [Cynus]. *Super Codice & Digesto Veteri Lectura*. Lyon: Thomas Bertheau, 1547.
Recueil général des anciennes lois Françaises. Vol. 14, Part 1. Ed. Isambert, Decrusy, Taillandier. Paris: Belin-Leprieur, 1829.
Sandeo, Felino [Felinus Sandeus]. *Commentariorum ad Quinque Libros Decretalium, Pars Secunda*. Venice, 1601.
Soccini, Marianus and Bartolommeo [Socinus]. *Consiliorum seu Potius Responsorum*. Venice: Apud Franciscum Zilettum, 1579.
Spiegel, Jakob. *Lexicon Iuris Civilis*. Basel: Apud Ioan. Heruagium, 1554.
Tartagni da Imola, Alessandro [Alexander Tartagnus Imolesnsis]. *Consiliorum Alexandri Tartagni Imolensis*. Venice: Ex Officina Damiani Zenari, 1578.
Tudeschi, Nicolas de [Panormitanus]. *Commentaria in Secundam Secundi Decretalium Libri Partem*. Venice, 1571.
— *Commentaria in Tertium Decretalium Librum*. Venice, 1571.
Zabarella, Francesco. *Consilia*. Venice: Apud Ioannem Baptistam a Porta, 1581.

Table of Authorities

Cases

Alden et al. v. Maine. 527 *U.S.* 706 (1999).
Customs Regime between Germany and Austria. Advisory Opinion. 1931 *P.C.I.J.* (ser. A/B) No. 41 (5 September).
Filartiga v. Peña-Irala. 630 F.2d 876 (1980).
Island of Palmas. United States v. Netherlands. Award. The Hague, April 1928. 2 *Reports of International Arbitrial Awards* 829.
Jurisdictional Immunities of the State (Germany v. Italy: Greece intervening). Judgment. *I.C.J. Reports* 2012 (3 February) 99.
Lighthouses in Crete and Samos (France v. Greece). Judgment. 1937 *P.C.I.J.* (ser. A/B) No. 62 (8 October).
Seminole Tribe of Florida v. Florida. 517 *U.S.* 44 (1996).

S.S. Wimbledon (United Kingdom, France, Italy, Japan v. Germany). 1923 *P.C.I.J.* (ser. A) No. 1 (August 17).

Statutes

Civil Code of the Netherlands. Trans. Hans Warendorf, Richard Thomas, and Ian Curry-Sumner. Alphen aan den Rijn: Kluwer Law International, 2009.
Civil Code of the State of California. Vol. 1. 1st Ed. Annotated by Creed Haymond and John Burch. San Francisco: A.L. Bancroft & Company; Sumner Whitney & Co., 1874.
Code Napoleon, or The French Civil Code. London: William Benning, 1827.

Works Cited

Abizadeh, Arash. 'Democratic Theory and Border Coercion: No Right to Unilaterally Control Your Own Borders'. *Political Theory* 36 (2008): 37–65.
Achinstein, Sharon. 'Hugo Grotius and Marriage's Global Past: Conjugal Thinking in Early Modern Political Thought'. *Journal of the History of Ideas* 81 (2020): 195–215.
Acton, John Emerich Edward Dalberg [Lord Acton]. 'Letter of Lord Acton to Bishop Creighton, 5 April 1887'. In *Historical Essays & Studies*. Ed. John Neville Figgis and Reginald Vere Laurence. London: Macmillan and Co., 1907.
Administration of Donald Trump/White House. 'Remarks Announcing United States Withdrawal from the United Nations Framework Convention on Climate Change Paris Agreement'. Daily Comp. Pres. Docs., 2017 DCPD No.: DCPD201700373. 1 June 2017.
Althusius, Johannes. *Politica Methodice Digesta*. Ed. Carl Friedrich. Cambridge: Harvard University Press, 1932.
Ando, Clifford. Ed. *The Antonine Constitution after 1800 Years: Citizenship and Empire in Europe, 200–1900*. Stuttgart: Franz Steiner Verlag, 2016.
— 'Empire and the Laws of War: A Roman Archaeology'. In *The Roman Foundations of the Law of Nations: Alberico Gentili and the Justice of Empire*. Ed. Benedict Kingsbury and Benjamin Straumann. Oxford: Oxford University Press, 2010.
— *Law, Language, and Empire in the Roman Tradition*. Philadelphia: University of Pennsylvania Press, 2011.
— 'The Origins and Import of Republican Constitutionalism'. *Cardozo Law Review* 34 (2013): 917–35.
Annan, Kofi. 'Two Concepts of Sovereignty'. *The Economist* 18 September 1999.
Appiah, Kwame Anthony. *Cosmopolitanism: Ethics in a World of Strangers*. New York: W.W. Norton, 2006.
Arendt, Hannah. *The Origins of Totalitarianism*. New Edition. New York: Harcourt, 1976.
Aristotle. *Nicomachean Ethics*. Loeb Classical Library 73. Trans. Harris Rackham. Cambridge: Harvard University Press, 1926.
— *Politics*. Loeb Classical Library 264. Trans. Harris Rackham. Cambridge: Harvard University Press, 1932.
— *Posterior Analytics, Topica*. Loeb Classical Library 391. Trans. Hugh Tredennick and E.S. Forster. Cambridge: Harvard University Press, 1960.
Arnisaeus, Henning. *De Jure Majestatis Libri Tres*. Frankfurt: Typis Andreae Eichorn, 1610.
Augustine. *City of God*. Vol. 2. Loeb Classical Library 412. Trans. William Green. Cambridge: Harvard University Press, 1963.
— *City of God*. Vol. 5. Loeb Classical Library 415. Trans. Eva Sanford and William Green. Cambridge: Harvard University Press, 1965.

Austin, John. *Province of Jurisprudence Determined*. Ed. Wilfrid Rumble. Cambridge: Cambridge University Press, 1995.

Bartelson, Jens. *War in International Thought*. Cambridge: Cambridge University Press, 2018.

Bartolus of Sassoferrato. *Politica e diritto nel Trecento italiano: Il 'De tyranno' di Bartolo da Sassoferrato con l'edizione critica dei trattati 'De guelphis et gebellinis,' 'De regimine civitatis' e 'De tyranno'. Il Pensiero Politico*. Biblioteca 11. Ed. Diego Quaglioni. Florence: Leo S. Olschki Editore, 1983.

Baudrillart, Henri. *J. Bodin et son temps: Tableau des theories politiques et des idées économiques au XVIe siècle*. Paris: Librairie de Guillamin, 1853.

Bauman, R.A. 'Maiestatem Populi Romani Comiter Conservanto'. *Acta Juridica* 19 (1976): 19–36.

Bayle, Pierre. 'Jean Bodin'. In *Dictionnaire historique et critique*. 5th ed. Amsterdam, 1734.

Bazzoli, Maurizio. 'Il diritto naturale nella *République* di Jean Bodin'. *Critica Storica* 7 (1968): 586–93.

Beaulac, Stéphane. *The Power of Language in the Making of International Law: The Word Sovereignty in Bodin and Vattel and the Myth of Westphalia*. Leiden: Martinus Nijhoff, 2004.

— 'The Social Power of Bodin's "Sovereignty" and International Law'. *Melbourne Journal of International Law* 4 (2003): 1–28.

Becker, Anna. *Gendering the Renaissance Commonwealth*. Cambridge: Cambridge University Press, 2020.

Bederman, David. *International Law in Antiquity*. Cambridge: Cambridge University Press, 2001.

Beever, Allan. 'Aristotle on Equity, Law, and Justice'. *Legal Theory* 10 (2004): 33–50.

Beitz, Charles. 'Cosmopolitanism and Global Justice'. *Journal of Ethics* 9 (2005): 11–27.

Bellomo, Manlio. *The Common Legal Past of Europe, 1000–1800*. Trans. Lydia Cochrane. Washington, D.C.: The Catholic University of America Press, 1995.

Belluga, Pierre. *Speculum Principum*. Paris, 1530.

Bentham, Jeremy. 'Power and Right'. [Bentham Mss., UCL, Box 88a: 120–32, 'Exposition']. In *Bentham's Political Thought*. Ed. Bhikhu Parekh. London: Croom Helm, 1973.

— 'Preface'. In *The Collected Works of Jeremy Bentham: An Introduction to the Principles of Morals and Legislation*. Ed. J.H. Burns and H.L.A. Hart. Oxford: Oxford University Press, 1970.

— 'Source of a Law'. [Bentham Mss., UCL, Box 88b: 229–37]. In *Bentham's Political Thought*. Ed. Bhikhu Parekh. London: Croom Helm, 1973.

Benton, Lauren. *A Search for Sovereignty: Law and Geography in European Empires, 1400-1900*. Cambridge: Cambridge University Press, 2009.

Benvenisti, Eyal. 'Sovereigns as Trustees of Humanity: On the Accountability of States to Foreign Stakeholders'. *American Journal of International Law* 107 (2013): 295–333.

Berns, Thomas. 'Bodin: La Souveraineté Saisie Par Ses Marques'. *Bibliotheque d'Humanisme et Renaissance* 62 (2000): 611–23.

Bickerton, Christopher, *et al*. Eds. *Politics Without Sovereignty: A Critique of Contemporary International Relations*. London: UCL Press, 2007.

Bierling, Ernst Rudolf. *Zur Kritik der juristischen Grundbegriffe*. Gotha: Friedrich Andreas Perthes, 1883.

Birks, Peter. *The Roman Law of Obligations*. Ed. Eric Descheemaeker. Oxford: Oxford University Press, 2014.

Black, Jane. *Absolutism in Renaissance Milan: Plenitude of Power under the Visconti and the Sforza, 1329–1535*. Oxford: Oxford University Press, 2009.

Blair, Ann. 'Authorial Strategies in Jean Bodin'. In *The Reception of Bodin*. Ed. Howell Lloyd. Leiden: Brill, 2013.

— *The Theater of Nature: Jean Bodin and Renaissance Science*. Princeton: Princeton University Press, 1997.

— *Too Much to Know: Managing Scholarly Information before the Modern Age*. New Haven, Connecticut: Yale University Press, 2010.

Bohman, James. 'Cosmopolitan Republicanism'. *The Monist* 84 (2001): 3–22.

Bonney, Richard. 'Bodin and the Development of the French Monarchy'. *Transactions of the Royal Historical Society* 40 (1990): 43–61.

Boucher, David. *Appropriating Hobbes: Legacies in Political, Legal, and International Thought*. Oxford: Oxford University Press, 2018.

Branch, Jordan. *The Cartographic State: Maps, Territory, and the Origins of Sovereignty*. Cambridge: Cambridge University Press, 2013.

Brennan, T. Corey. *The Praetorship in the Roman Republic*. Vol. 1. *Origins to 122 BC*. Oxford: Oxford University Press, 2000.

Brett, Annabel. *Changes of State: Nature and the Limits of the City in Early Modern Natural Law*. Princeton: Princeton University Press, 2011.

Brinz, Alois von. *Lehrbuch der Pandekten*, Vol. 1 Erlangen: Andreus Deichert, 1873.

Brundage, James. *Medieval Canon Law*. London: Longman, 1995.

Brunner, Otto. *Land and Lordship*. Trans. Howard Kaminsky and James Van Horn Melton. Philadelphia: University of Pennsylvania Press, 1992.

Bryson, William Hamilton. *Dictionary of Sigla and Abbreviations to and in Law Books before 1607*. 2nd printing with corrections. Buffalo: William S. Hein & Co., Inc., 1996.

Buckland, W.W. *The Roman Law of Slavery*. Cambridge: Cambridge University Press, 1973.

— *Textbook of Roman Law: From Augustus to Justinian*. 3rd Ed. Rev. Peter Stein. Cambridge: Cambridge University Press, 1963.

Burgess, Glenn. *Absolute Monarchy and the Stuart Constitution*. New Haven: Yale University Press, 1996.

Burns, J.H. *Lordship, Kingship, and Empire 1400–1525*. Oxford: Clarendon Press, 1992.

— 'Sovereignty and Constitutional Law in Bodin'. *Political Studies* 7 (1959): 174–77.

Calasso, Francesco. *I glossatori e le teoria della sovranità: Studio di diritto commune pubblico*. Milan: Giuffré, 1951.

— '*Iurisdictio* nel diritto comune classico'. *Annali di Storia del Diritto* 9 (1965): 89–110.

Camilleri, Joseph and Jim Falk. *The End of Sovereignty? The Politics of a Shrinking and Fragmenting World*. Cheltenham: Edward Elgar, 1992.

Canning, Joseph. *Ideas of Power in the Late Middle Ages, 1296–1417*. Cambridge: Cambridge University Press, 2011.

— *The Political Thought of Baldus de Ubaldis*. Cambridge: Cambridge University Press, 1987.

Carens, Joseph. *Culture, Citizenship, and Community*. Oxford: Oxford University Press, 2000.

Carl, Noah, James Dennison, and Geoffrey Evans. 'European But Not European Enough: An Explanation for Brexit'. *European Union Politics* 20 (2019): 282–304.

Chanteur, Janine. 'L'idee de loi naturelle dans le *République* de Jean Bodin'. In *Verhandlungen der Internationalen Bodin Tagung in München*. Ed. Horst Denzer. München: Beck, 1973.

Charron, Pierre. *De la Sagesse Trois Livres*. Paris: Robert Fuge, 1632.

Chauviré, Roger. *Jean Bodin, auteur de la République*. Paris: É. Champion, 1914.

Church, William Farr. *Constitutional Thought in Sixteenth-Century France: A Study in the Evolution of Ideas.* Cambridge: Harvard University Press, 1941.
Cicero. *De Legibus.* Trans. Clinton Walker Keyes. Loeb Classical Library 213. Cambridge: Harvard University Press, 1928.
— *De Officiis.* Trans. Walter Miller. Loeb Classical Library 30. Cambridge: Harvard University Press, 1913.
— *De Re Publica.* Trans. Clinton Walker Keyes. Loeb Classical Library 213. Cambridge: Harvard University Press, 1928.
— *Letters to Atticus.* Vol. 1. Loeb Classical Library 7. Ed. and Trans. D.R. Shackleton Bailey. Cambridge: Harvard University Press, 1999.
— *On Invention, The Best Kind of Orator, Topics.* Loeb Classical Library 386. Trans. H.M. Hubbell. Cambridge: Harvard University Press, 1949.
— *Philippics 1–6.* Ed. and Trans. D.R. Shackleton Bailey. Rev. John Ramsey and Gesine Manuwald. Loeb Classical Library 189. Cambridge: Harvard University Press, 2010.
— *Pro Balbo.* In *Pro Caelio, De Provinciis Consularibus, Pro Balbo.* Trans. R. Gardner. Loeb Classical Library 447. Cambridge: Harvard University Press, 1958.
— *Pro Caecina.* Trans. G. Grose Hodge. Loeb Classical Library 198. Cambridge: Harvard University Press, 1927.
— *Pro Sestio.* In *Cicero Orations: Pro Sestio and In Vatinium.* Trans. R. Gardner. Loeb Classical Library 309. Cambridge: Harvard University Press, 1958.
— *Tusculan Disputations.* Trans. J.E. King. Loeb Classical Library 141. Cambridge: Harvard University Press, 1927.
Cocks, Joan. *On Sovereignty and Other Political Delusions.* London: Bloomsbury, 2014.
Cohen, Morris. 'Property and Sovereignty'. *Cornell Law Review* 13 (1927): 8–30.
Coing, Helmut. 'Zur Geschichte des Begriffs 'subjektives Recht''. In *Gesammelte Aufsätze zu Rechtsgeschichte, Rechtsphilosophie, und Zivilrecht, 1947–1975.* Vol. 1. Frankfurt am Main: Klostermann, 1982.
Comparato, Vittor Ivo. 'Mediazione politica e teoria dello Stato: Note su Bodin e Hobbes'. *Archivio Storico Italiano* 1 (1986): 17–33.
— 'Note su Bodin e Aristotele, sovranità e proprietà nella definizione di Stato'. *Materiali di storia: Annali della Facoltà di Scienze politiche di Perugia* 18 (1982): 7–13.
— 'Sulla teoria della funzione pubblica nella *République* di Jean Bodin'. *Il Pensiero Politico* 14 (1981): 93–112.
— 'La teoria del *magistratus* nella *Methodus* di Jean Bodin'. *Annali della Facolta di Scienze Politiche: Materiali di Storia* 17 (1980): 197–209.
Contarini, Gasparo. *De Magistratibus et Republica Venetorum Libri V.* Basel, 1547.
Cortese, Ennio. *La norma giuridica: Spunti teorici nel diritto comune classico.* 2 Vols. Milan: Giuffrè, 1962–64.
— *Il problema della sovranità nel pensiero giuridico medioevale.* Rome: Bulzoni, 1982.
Costa, Pietro. 'La celebrazione della sovranità: Jean Bodin'. In *Civitas, storia della cittadinanza in Europa, I: dalla civiltà comunale al settecento.* Ed. Pietro Costa. Rome/Bari: Laterza, 1999.
Couzinet, Marie-Dominique. *Histoire et Methode a la Renaissance.* Paris: J. Vrin, 1996.
Crawford, James. *Brownlie's Principles of Public International Law.* 8th ed. Oxford: Oxford University Press, 2012.
— *The Creation of States in International Law.* 2nd ed. Oxford: Oxford University Press, 2007.
Cremer, Albert. 'Le genèse du droit des gens modern et la conscience européenne: Francisco de Vitoria et Jean Bodin'. In *La conscience européenne aux XVe et XVIe siècles: Actes du*

Colloque international organisé à l'ENSJF, 30 septembre–3 octobre 1980. Paris: École Normale Supérieure des Jeunes Filles, 1982.

Criddle, Evan and Evan Fox-Decent. *Fiduciaries of Humanity: How International Law Constitutes Authority*. Oxford: Oxford University Press, 2016.

Croce, Benedetto. *Politics and Morals*. Trans. Salvatore J. Castiglione. New York: Philosophical Library, 1945.

D'Aguesseau, Henri François. 'Essai d'une institution au droit public'. In *Discours et oeuvres mêlées de M. le Chancellier D'Aguesseau*. Nouvelle Édition. Vol 2. Paris: Chez les Libraires Associés, 1786.

D'Aspremont, Jean. 'Effectivity in International Law: Self-Empowerment Against Epistemological Claustrophobia'. *AJIL Unbound* 108 (2017): 103–5.

Daly, James. 'The Idea of Absolute Monarchy in Seventeenth-Century England'. *Historical Journal* 21 (1978): 227–50.

Dante Alighieri. *Monarchy*. Ed. and Trans. Prue Shaw. Cambridge: Cambridge University Press, 1996.

Darjes, Joachim Georg. *Institutiones Iurisprudentiae Universalis*. Editio Nova. Frankfurt: Sumptibus Societatis, 1754.

Daube, David. 'The Peregrine Praetor'. *Journal of Roman Studies* 41 (1951): 66–70.

David, Marcel. *La souveraineté et les limites juridiques du pouvoir monarchique du IXe au XVe siècle*. Paris: Dalloz 1954.

De Smet, Ingrid A.R. 'Philosophy for Princes: Aristotle's Politics and Its Readers During the French Wars of Religion'. *Journal of the Warburg and Courtauld Institutes* 76 (2013): 23–47.

De Wilde, Marc. 'Enemy of All Humanity: The Dehumanizing Effects of a Dangerous Concept'. *Netherlands Journal of Legal Philosophy* 47 (2018): 158–75.

Decock, Wim. *Theologians and Contract Law: The Moral Transformation of the Ius Commune, c.1500–1650*. Leiden: Brill-Nijhoff, 2012.

Dedek, Helge. 'From Norms to Facts: The Realization of Rights in Common and Civil Private Law'. *McGill Law Journal* 56.1 (2010): 77–114.

Deng, Francis, *et al*. 'From Sovereignty as Responsibility to the Responsibility to Protect'. *Global Responsibility to Protect* 2 (2010): 353–70.

— *Sovereignty as Responsibility: Conflict Management in Africa*. Washington, D.C.: Brookings Institution Press, 1996.

Dennert, Jürgen. *Ursprung und Begriff der Souveränität*. Stuttgart: Gustav Fischer, 1964.

Desan, Christine. *Making Money: Coin, Currency, and the Coming of Capitalism*. Oxford: Oxford University Press, 2014.

Di Bello, Anna. *Stato e sovranità nel De Republica libri sex di Jean Bodin*. Naples: Liguori Editore, 2014.

Dionysius of Halicarnassus. *Roman Antiquities*. Vol. 1. Loeb Classical Library 319. Ed. Earnest Cary. Cambridge: Harvard University Press, 1937.

Domingo, Rafael. *The New Global Law*. Cambridge: Cambridge University Press, 2010.

Donahue, Charles. '*Ius* in the Subjective Sense'. In *A Ennio Cortese*. Ed. Domenico Maffei. Vol. 1. Rome: Il Cigno, 2001.

Drogula, Fred. 'Imperium, Potestas, and the Pomerium in the Roman Republic'. *Historia: Zeitschrift für Alte Geschichte* 56 (2007): 419–52.

Duarte d'Almedia, Luis. *Allowing for Exceptions: A Theory of Defences and Defeasibility in Law*. Oxford: Oxford University Press, 2015.

Duguit, Léon. *Law in the Modern State*. Ed. Frida Laski and Harold Laski. London: Allen & Unwin, 1921.

Duns Scotus, John. *Quaestiones in Lib. III Sententiarum*. Lyon: Sumptibus Laurentii Durand, 1639.

Edelstein, Dan. 'Rousseau, Bodin, and the Medieval Corporatist Origins of Popular Sovereignty'. *Political Theory* January 2021: doi: 10.1177/0090591720985452

— *The Terror of Natural Right: Republicanism, the Cult of Nature, and the French Revolution*. Chicago: University of Chicago Press, 2009.

Eden, Kathy. 'Between Friends All Is Common: The Erasmian Adage and Tradition'. *Journal of the History of Ideas* 59 (1998): 405–19.

Elden, Stuart. *The Birth of Territory*. Chicago: University of Chicago Press, 2013.

Eleftheriadis, Pavlos. 'Law and Sovereignty'. *Law and Philosophy* 29 (2010): 535–69.

Ellis, Harold. *Boulainvilliers and the French Monarch: Aristocratic Politics in Early Eighteenth-Century France*. Ithaca: Cornell University Press, 1988.

Esmein, Adhemar. 'La maxime *princeps legibus solutus est* dans l'ancien droit public français'. In *Essays in Legal History*. Ed. Paul Vinogradoff. Oxford: Oxford University Press, 1913.

Evrigenis, Ioannis. *Images of Anarchy: The Rhetoric and Science in Hobbes's State of Nature*. Cambridge: Cambridge University Press, 2014.

— 'Sovereignty, Mercy, and Natural Law: King James VI/I and Jean Bodin'. *History of European Ideas* 45 (2019): 1073–88.

Fasolt, Constantin. *The Limits of History*. Chicago: University of Chicago Press, 2004.

Fedele, Dante. 'Ius Gentium: The Metamorphoses of a Legal Concept'. In *Empire and Legal Thought: Ideas and Institutions from Antiquity to Modernity*. Ed. Edward Cavanaugh. Leiden: Brill, 2020.

Feenstra, Robert. '*Dominium* and *Ius in Re Aliena*: Origins of a Civil Law Distinction'. In *New Perspectives in the Roman Law of Property: Essays for Barry Nicholas*. Ed. Peter Birks. Oxford: Clarendon Press, 1989.

Feinberg, Joel. 'The Nature and Value of Rights'. *Journal of Value Inquiry* 4 (1970): 243–60.

Fell, A. London. *Origins of Legislative Sovereignty and the Legislative State*. 5 Vols. Cambridge: Oelgeschlager, Gunn and Hain, 1983.

Ferrière, Georges. 'Sujets et citoyens selon Bodin'. In *Sujet et Citoyen: Actes du Colloque de Lyon, 11–12 Septembre 2003*. Ed. J.-L. Harouel. Aix-en-Provence: Presses Universitaires d'Aix-Marseille, 2003.

Fitzmaurice, Andrew. *Sovereignty, Property and Empire, 1500–2000*. Cambridge: Cambridge University Press, 2014.

Forschner, Benedikt. 'Law's Nature: Philosophy as a Legal Argument in Cicero's Writings'. In *Cicero's Law: Rethinking Roman Law of the Late Republic*. Ed. Paul J. du Plessis. Edinburgh: Edinburgh University Press, 2016.

Fowler, Michael Ross and Julie Marie Bunck. 'What Constitutes the Sovereign State?' *Review of International Studies* 22 (1996): 381–404.

Fox-Decent, Evan. *Sovereignty's Promise: The State as Fiduciary*. Oxford: Oxford University Press, 2011.

Franklin, Julian. *Jean Bodin and the Rise of Absolutist Theory*. Cambridge: Cambridge University Press, 1973.

— *Jean Bodin and the Sixteenth-Century Revolution in the Methodology of Law and History*. New York: Columbia University Press, 1963.

Freegard, William. *Roman Law and Resistance Right: A Study of Question Three of the Vindiciae Contra Tyrannos*. Ph.D. Dissertation. Iowa City: University of Iowa, 1971.

Frier, Bruce. *The Rise of the Roman Jurists*. Princeton: Princeton University Press, 1985.

Fukuyama, Francis. *The End of History and the Last Man*. New York: Free Press, 1992.

Fuller, Lon. *The Morality of Law*. Rev. Ed. New Haven: Yale University Press, 1969.

Gallie, W.B. 'Essentially Contested Concepts'. *Proceedings of the Aristotelian Society* 56 (1956): 167–98.

Garimberto, Girolamo. *De Regimenti Publici de la Citta*. Venice, 1544.

Garnsey, Peter. 'The Criminal Jurisdiction of Governors'. *Journal of Roman Studies* 58 (1968): 51–59.

— *Thinking about Property: From Antiquity to the Age of Revolution*. Cambridge: Cambridge University Press, 2007.

Gentili, Alberico. *De Iure Belli Libri Tres*. Vol. 2. *The Translation of the Edition of 1612*. Trans. John Rolfe. Oxford: Clarendon Press, 1933.

Getachew, Adom. 'The Limits of Sovereignty as Responsibility'. *Constellations* 26 (2019): 225–40.

Giesey, Ralph. *If Not, Not: The Oath of the Aragonese and the Legendary Laws of Sobrarbe*. Princeton: Princeton University Press, 1968.

— *The Juristic Basis of Dynastic Right to the French Throne*. Transactions of the American Philosophical Society No. 51. Philadelphia: American Philosophical Society, 1961.

— 'Medieval Jurisprudence in Bodin's Concept of Sovereignty'. In *Verhandlungen der Internationalen Bodin Tagung in München*. Ed. Horst Denzer. München: Beck, 1973.

— 'When and Why Hotman Wrote the *Francogallia*'. *Bibliothèque d'Humanisme et Renaissance* 29 (1967): 581–611.

Gilbert, Margaret. *Rights and Demands: A Foundational Inquiry*. Oxford: Oxford University Press, 2018.

Gilbert, R.L. 'The Origin and History of the Peregrine Praetorship, 242–166 B.C.'. *Res Judicatae* 2 (1939): 50–8.

Gilles, Henri. 'La Faculté de droit de Toulouse au temps de Jean Bodin'. *Annales d'histoire de facultés de droit* (1986): 23–36.

Gilmore, Myron Piper. *Argument from Roman Law in Political Thought, 1200–1600*. Cambridge: Harvard University Press, 1941.

Giltaij, Jacob. 'Roman Law and the *Causa Legitima* for Reprisal in Bartolus'. *Fundamina* 20 (2014): 349–56.

Glanville, Luke. 'The Antecedents of Sovereignty as Responsibility'. *European Journal of International Relations* 17 (2011): 233–55.

— 'The Myth of Traditional Sovereignty'. *International Studies Quarterly* 57 (2013): 79–90.

— *Sovereignty and the Responsibility to Protect: A New History*. Chicago: University of Chicago Press, 2013.

Gordley, James and Ugo Mattei. 'Protecting Possession'. *American Journal of Comparative Law* 44 (1996): 293–334.

Goyard-Fabre, Simone. 'Commentaire Philosophique de L'Exposé du Droit Universel'. In *Jean Bodin: Exposé du Droit Universel*. [*Iuris Universi Distributio*]. Paris: Presses Universitaires de France, 1985.

— *Jean Bodin et le droit de la république*. Paris: Presses Universitaires de France, 1989.

— 'Jean Bodin et les trois justices'. In *Aequitas, Aequalitas, Auctoritas: Raison théoretique et légitimation de l'autorité dans le XVIe siècle*. Ed. D. Letocha. Paris: Vrin, 1992.

Green, Leslie. *The Authority of the State*. Oxford: Clarendon Press, 1990.

Greenleaf, W.H. 'Jean Bodin and the Idea of Order'. In *Jean Bodin: Verhandlungen der internationalen Bodin Tagung in München*. Ed. Horst Denzer. München: Beck, 1973.

Greenwood, Ryan. *Law and War in Late Medieval Italy: The Jus Commune on War and Its Application in Florence, c.1150–1450*. Ph.D. Dissertation. University of Toronto. Toronto, 2011.

— 'War and Sovereignty in Medieval Roman Law'. *Law and History Review* 32 (2014): 31–63.

Grewal, David. 'The Domestic Analogy Revisited: Hobbes on International Order'. *Yale Law Journal* 125 (2016): 618–80.
Grimm, Dieter. *Sovereignty: The Origin and Future of a Political and Legal Concept.* Trans. Belinda Cooper. New York: Columbia University Press, 2015.
Grotius, Hugo. *Commentarius in Theses XI: An Early Treatise on Sovereignty, the Just War, and the Legitimacy of the Dutch Revolt.* Ed. Peter Borschberg. Bern: Peter Lang, 1994.
— *Commentary on the Law of Prize and Booty* [*De Iure Praedae Commentarius*]. Ed. Martine Julia van Ittersum. Indianapolis: Liberty Fund, 2006.
— *De Iure Belli ac Pacis Libri Tres.* Editio Nova. Amsterdam: Iohannes Blaeu, 1646.
— *Defensio Fidei Catholicae de Satisfactione Christi adversus Faustum Socinum.* Leiden: Ioannes Patius, 1617.
Grosso, E. 'Dal suddito del signore al suddito dello stato'. In *Le Vie della Cittadinanza.* Padua: CEDAM, 1997.
Guizot, François. *History of the Origins of Representative Government in Europe.* Trans. Andrew Scoble. Indianapolis: Liberty Fund, 2002.
Guzmán, Alejandro. 'Historia de la Denominación del Derecho-Facultad Como Subjectivo'. *Revista de Estudios Histórico-Jurídicos* 25 (2003): 407–43.
Haggenmacher, Peter. 'Droits subjectifs et système juridique chez Grotius'. In *Politique, droit et théologie chez Bodin, Grotius et Hobbes.* Ed. Luc Foisneau. Paris: Kimé, 1997.
— *Grotius et la doctrine de la guerre juste.* Paris: Presses Universitaires de France, 1983.
Hankins, James. 'Exclusivist Republicanism and the Non-Monarchical Republic'. *Political Theory* 38 (2010): 452–82.
Hardin, Russell. 'Sanction and Obligation'. *The Monist* 68 (1985): 403–18.
Hardt, Michael and Antonio Negri. *Empire.* Cambridge: Harvard University Press, 2001.
Hart, H.L.A. *Concept of Law.* 2nd Edition. Oxford: Clarendon Press, 1994.
Havercroft, Jonathan. *Captives of Sovereignty.* Cambridge: Cambridge University Press, 2011.
Hegel, Georg Wilhelm Friedrich. *Elements of the Philosophy of Right.* [*Grundlinien der Philosophie des Rechts*]. Ed. Allen Wood. Trans. H.B. Nisbet. Cambridge: Cambridge University Press, 1991.
Held, David. *Democracy and the Global Order: From the Modern State to Cosmopolitan Governance.* Stanford, California: Stanford University Press, 1995.
Heller, Henry. 'Bodin on Slavery and Primitive Accumulation'. *Sixteenth Century Journal* 25 (1994): 53–65.
Heller-Roazen, Daniel. *The Enemy of All: Piracy and the Law of Nations.* New York: Zone Books, 2009.
Henkin, Louis. 'That "S" Word: Sovereignty, and Globalization and Human Rights, et Cetera'. *Fordham Law Review* 68 (1999): 1–14.
Herzog, Don. *Sovereignty, RIP.* New Haven: Yale University Press, 2020.
Hinsley, F.H. *Sovereignty.* Cambridge: Cambridge University Press, 1986.
Hobbes, Thomas. *Elements of Law Natural and Politic.* Ed. J.C.A. Gaskin. Oxford: Oxford University Press, 1994.
— *Leviathan.* Ed. Richard Tuck. Cambridge: Cambridge University Press, 1996.
— *Leviathan.* [English and Latin texts]. Ed. Noel Malcolm. Oxford: Clarendon Press, 2012.
— *On the Citizen* [*De Cive*]. Ed. Richard Tuck and Michael Silverthorne. Cambridge: Cambridge University Press, 1998.
Hoekstra, Kinch. 'Tyrannus Rex vs. Leviathan'. *Pacific Philosophical Quarterly* 82 (2001): 420–46.

Hoffman, Philip. 'Early Modern France, 1450–1700'. In *Fiscal Crises, Liberty, and Representative Government, 1450–1789*. Ed. Philip Hoffman and Kathryn Norberg. Stanford, CA: Stanford University Press, 1994.

Hogg, Martin. *Obligations: Law and Language*. Cambridge: Cambridge University Press, 2003.

Hohfeld, Wesley Newcomb. 'Fundamental Legal Conceptions as Applied in Judicial Reasoning'. *Yale Law Journal* 26 (1917): 710–70.

— 'Some Fundamental Legal Conceptions as Applied in Judicial Reasoning'. *Yale Law Journal* 23 (1913): 16–59.

Hont, István. 'The Permanent Crisis of a Divided Mankind: Nation-State and Nationalism in Historical Perspective'. In *Jealousy of Trade: International Competition and the Nation-State in Historical Perspective*. Cambridge: Harvard University Press, 2010.

Iurlaro, F. 'The Burden of Reason: Ratio Probabilis, Consensio Omnium and the Impact of Humanitas on Alberico Gentili's Theory of Customary International Law'. *History of Political Thought* 38 (2017): 409–38.

Jackson, John H. 'Sovereignty-Modern: A New Approach to an Outdated Concept'. *American Journal of International Law* 97 (2003): 782–802.

Jacobsen, Mogens Chrom. *Jean Bodin et le dilemme de la philosophie politique modern*. Copenhagen: Museum Tusculanum Press, University of Copenhagen, 2000.

Janis, Mark Weston. 'Jeremy Bentham and the Fashioning of International Law'. *American Journal of International Law* 78 (1984): 405–18.

Jolowicz, H.F. *Roman Foundations of Modern Law*. Oxford: Clarendon Press, 1957.

Kahn, Paul. 'The Question of Sovereignty'. *Stanford Journal of International Law* 40 (2004): 259–282.

Kalinowski, Georges. *La Logique des norms*. Paris: Presses Universitaires de France, 1972.

Kanger, Stig. 'Rättighetsbegreppet'. In *Sju filosofiska studier tillägnade Anders Wedberg den 30 mars 1963*. Philosophical Studies No 9. Stockholm: Department of Philosophy, University of Stockholm, 1963.

Kantorowicz, Ernst. *The King's Two Bodies: A Study in Medieval Political Theology*. Princeton: Princeton University Press, 1957.

Kaser, Max. *Das Römisches Zivilprozessrecht*. München: C.H. Beck, 1966.

— 'Zum *Ius*-Begriff der Römer'. In *Essays in Honour of Ben Beinart*. Vol. 2. *Acta Juridica* 1977.

Kelley, Donald. 'Civil Science in the Renaissance: Jurisprudence Italian Style'. *Historical Journal* 22 (1979): 777–94.

— 'Development and Context of Bodin's *Method*'. In *Verhandlungen der Internationalen Bodin Tagung in München*. Ed. Horst Denzer. München: Beck, 1973.

— *Francois Hotman: A Revolutionary's Ordeal*. Princeton: Princeton University Press, 1973.

— 'The Rise of Legal History in the Renaissance'. *History and* Theory 9 (1970): 174–94.

Kelsen, Hans. *Das Problem der Souveränität und die Theorie des Völkerrechts*. Tübingen: Mohr, 1920.

— *General Theory of Law and State*. Trans. Anders Wedberg. Cambridge: Harvard University Press, 1945.

— *General Theory of Norms*. Trans. Michael Hartney. Oxford: Clarendon Press, 1991.

— *Pure Theory of Law*. Trans. Max Knight. Berkeley: University of California Press, 1967.

— 'What Is a Legal Act?' *American Journal of Jurisprudence* 29 (1984): 199–212.

Keohane, Nannerl. *Philosophy and the State in France: The Renaissance to the Enlightenment*. Princeton: Princeton University Press, 1980.

Keohane, Oisín. 'Bodin on Sovereignty: Taking Exception to Translation?' *Paragraph* 38 (2015): 245–60.

Kepler, Johannes. 'Political Treatise'. In *The Harmony of the World*, Trans. E.J. Aiton, A.M. Duncan, and J.V. Field. Philadelphia: American Philosophical Society, 1997.

Kim, Keechang. *Aliens in Medieval Law: The Origins of Modern Citizenship*. Cambridge: Cambridge University Press, 2000.

— 'L'étranger chez Jean Bodin'. *Revue historique de droit français et étranger* 76 (1998): 75–92.

King, Preston. *The Ideology of Order: A Comparative Analysis of Jean Bodin and Thomas Hobbes*. New York: Barnes and Noble, 1974.

Kingsbury, Benedict. 'Sovereignty and Inequality'. *European Journal of International Law* 9 (1998): 599–625.

Kirshner, Julius. '*Ars Imitatur Naturam*: A Consilium of Baldus on Naturalization in Florence'. *Viator* 5 (1974): 289–332.

— '*Civitas sibi faciat civem*: Bartolus of Sassoferrato's Doctrine on the Making of a Citizen'. *Speculum* 48 (1973): 694–713.

Koebner, R. 'Despot and Despotism: Vicissitudes of a Political Term'. *Journal of the Warburg and Courtauld Institutes* 14 (1951): 275–302.

Koskenniemi, Martti. *From Apology to Utopia: The Structure of International Legal Argument*. Cambridge: Cambridge University Press, 2009.

— *The Gentle Civilizer of Nations: The Rise and Fall of International Law, 1870–1960*. Cambridge: Cambridge University Press, 2001.

— *To the Uttermost Parts of the Earth: Legal Imagination and International Power, 1300–1870*. Cambridge: Cambridge University Press, 2021.

Krasner, Stephen. *Sovereignty: Organized Hypocrisy*. Princeton: Princeton University Press, 1999.

Kratochwil, Friedrich. 'Leaving Sovereignty Behind? An Inquiry in the Politics of Post-Modernity'. In *Legality and Legitimacy in Global Affairs*. Ed. Richard Falk, Mark Juergensmeyer, and Vesselin Popovski. Oxford: Oxford University Press, 2012.

Kymlicka, Will. *Multicultural Citizenship*. Oxford: Oxford University Press, 1995.

Lake, David. 'The New Sovereignty in International Relations'. *International Studies Review* 5 (2003): 303–23.

Lane, Melissa. 'The Idea of Accountable Office in Ancient Greece and Beyond'. *Philosophy* 95 (2020): 19–40.

Lauterpacht, Hersch. *Private Law Sources and Analogies of International Law*. London: Longmans, Green and Co., 1927.

Lavie, Jean Charles de. *Abrégé de la République de Bodin*. Vol. 1. London: Chez Jean Nourse, 1755.

Lazzarino Del Grosso, Anna Maria. 'Le Magistrature in Bodin'. *Il Pensiero Politico* 40 (2007): 395–409.

Le Roy, Louis [Aristotle]. *Les Politiques d'Aristote*. Paris: Michel de Vascosan, 1576.

Le Thiec, Guy. 'Le droit de conquête en guise de constitution: Jean Bodin et les penseurs protestants face au régime politique ottoman'. *Il Pensiero Politico* 39 (2007): 353–68.

Legnano, Giovanni da. *Tractatus de bello, de represaliis et de duello*. Ed. Thomas Erskine Holland and James Lesley Brierly. Oxford: Oxford University Press, 1917.

Lee, Daniel. 'Citizenship, Subjection, and the Civil Law: Jean Bodin on Roman Citizenship and the Theory of Consensual Subjection'. In *Citizenship and Empire in Europe, 200–1900: The Antonine Constitution after 1800 Years*. Ed. Clifford Ando. Stuggart: Franz Steiner Verlag, 2016.

— 'Office Is a Thing Borrowed: Jean Bodin on Offices and Seigneurial Government'. *Political Theory* 41 (2013): 409–40.

— *Popular Sovereignty in Early Modern Constitutional Thought*. Oxford: Oxford University Press, 2016.

— 'Private Law Models for Public Law Concepts: The Roman Law Theory of *Dominium* in the Monarchomach Doctrine of Popular Sovereignty'. *Review of Politics* 70 (2008): 370–99.

— 'Sources of Sovereignty: Roman *Imperium* and *Dominium* in Civilian Theories of Sovereignty'. *Politica Antica* 2 (2012): 79–94.

— 'Sovereignty and *Dominium*: The Foundations of Hobbesian Statehood'. In *Hobbes's On the Citizen: A Critical Guide*. Ed. Robin Douglass and Johan Olsthoorn. Cambridge: Cambridge University Press, 2020.

— 'The State Is a Minor: Fiduciary Concepts of Government and the Roman Law of Guardianship from Azo to Hobbes'. In *Fiduciary Government*. Ed. Evan Criddle, *et al.* Cambridge: Cambridge University Press, 2018.

— 'Unmaking Law: Jean Bodin on Law, Equity and Legal Change'. *History of Political Thought* 39 (2018): 269–96.

Leibniz, Gottfried Wilhelm, Freiherr von. 'Codex Iuris Gentium' [Praefatio]. In *Leibniz: Political Writings*. Ed. Patrick Riley. 2nd Ed. Cambridge: Cambridge University Press, 1988.

Lesaffer, Randall. 'Argument from Roman Law in Current International Law: Occupation and Acquisitive Prescription'. *European Journal of International Law* 16 (2005): 25–58.

— *European Legal History: A Cultural and Political Perspective*. Cambridge: Cambridge University Press, 2009.

Levy, Jacob. *Rationalism, Pluralism, and Freedom*. Oxford: Oxford University Press, 2015.

Lijphart, Arend. 'Consociational Democracy'. *World Politics* 21 (1969): 207–25.

Lindahl, Lars. *Position and Change: A Study in Law and Logic*. Dordrecht: D. Reidel Publishing Company, 1977.

Livy. *History of Rome*. Vol. 4. Loeb Classical Library 191. Trans. B.O. Foster. Cambridge: Harvard University Press, 1926.

— *History of Rome*. Vol. 7. Loeb Classical Library 367. Trans. Frank Gardner Moore. Cambridge: Harvard University Press, 1943.

— *History of Rome*. Vol. 9. Loeb Classical Library 295. Ed. Trans. J.C. Yardley. Cambridge: Harvard University Press 2017.

— *History of Rome*. Vol. 11. Loeb Classical Library 313. Ed. Trans. J.C. Yardley. Cambridge: Harvard University Press, 2018.

Lloyd, Howell. *Jean Bodin, 'This Pre-eminent Man of France': An Intellectual Biography*. Oxford: Oxford University Press, 2017.

— Ed. *The Reception of Bodin*. Leiden: Brill, 2013.

Locke, John. *Two Treatises of Government*. Ed. Peter Laslett. Cambridge: Cambridge University Press, 1988.

Lorentzen, Ernest. 'Huber's De Conflictu Legum'. *Illinois Law Review* 13 (1918–19): 375–418.

Loughlin, Martin. *The Idea of Public Law*. Oxford: Oxford University Press, 2004.

— 'Why Sovereignty?' In *Sovereignty and the Law*. Ed. Peter Rawlings, *et al.* Oxford: Oxford University Press, 2013.

Loyseau, Charles. *Cinq livres du droit du offices*. In *Les oeuvres de Maistre Charles Loyseau*. Lyon, 1701.

Luban, Daniel. 'The Enemy of All Humanity'. *Netherlands Journal of Legal Philosophy* 47 (2018): 112–37.

MacCormick, Neil. 'Beyond the Sovereign State'. *Modern Law Review* 56 (1993): 1–18.

Machiavelli, Niccolo. *The Prince*. Ed. Quentin Skinner and Russell Price. Cambridge: Cambridge University Press, 1988.

Mackie, J.L. 'Evil and Omnipotence'. *Mind* 64, No. 254 (1955): 200–12.
Maine, Henry Sumner. *Ancient Law*. 4th Ed. London: John Murray, 1870.
Maissen, Thomas. *Die Geburt der Republik: Staatsverständnis und Repräsentation in der frühneuzeitlichen Eidgenossenschaft*. Göttingen: Vandenhoeck & Ruprecht, 2006.
Mannori, Luca. 'Per una preistoria della funzione amministrativa'. In *Quaderni Fiorentini per la storia del pensiero giuridico moderno* 19(1) (1990): 323–504.
March, James and Johan Olsen. 'The Logic of Appropriateness'. In *The Oxford Handbook of Political Science*. Ed. Robert Goodin. Oxford: Oxford University Press, 2011.
Maritain, Jacques. 'The Concept of Sovereignty'. *American Political Science Review* 44 (1950): 343–57.
Marsilius of Padua. *The Defender of Peace*. Trans. Alan Gewirth. New York: Columbia University Press, 1956.
Mason, Andrew. 'Special Obligations to Compatriots'. *Ethics* 107 (1997): 427–47.
Mastellone, Salvo. 'Bodin e la scienza politica dei gens de loi'. In *Diritto e potere nella Storia Europea*. Florence: Olschki, 1982.
Matringe, Nadia. 'The Fair Deposit: Credit Reallocation and Trade Finance in the Early Modern Period'. *Annales Histoire Sciences Sociales* 72 (2017): 275–315.
Mautner, Thomas. 'How Rights Became Subjective'. *Ratio Juris* 26 (2013): 111–32.
McCormick, John. *Machiavellian Democracy*. Cambridge: Cambridge University Press, 2011.
McGuinn, T.A.J. 'The Expressive Function of Law and the *Lex Imperfecta*'. *Roman Legal Tradition* 11 (2015): 1–41.
McIlwain, Charles Howard. 'Sovereignty Again'. *Economica* 18 (1926): 253–56.
McRae, Kenneth. 'Ramist Tendencies in the Thought of Jean Bodin'. *Journal of the History of Ideas* 16 (1955): 306–23.
Mesnard, Pierre. *L'Essor de la Philosophie politique au XVIe siècle*. Paris: Vrin, 1951.
— 'Jean Bodin à Toulouse'. *Bibliothèque d'Humanisme et Renaissance* 12 (1950): 31–59.
— Ed. *Oeuvres Philosophiques de Jean Bodin: Auteurs Modernes Tome V, 3*. Paris: Presses Universitaires de France, 1951.
Metzger, Ernest. 'Outline of Roman Civil Procedure'. *Roman Legal Tradition* 9 (2013): 1–30.
Meynial, Edouard. 'Notes sur la Formation de la Théorie du Domaine Divise'. In *Mélanges Fitting*. Ed. Herman Fitting. Montpellier: Impr. Générale du Midi, 1907.
Miglietti, Sara. 'Amitié, Harmonie et Paix Politique chez Aristote et Jean Bodin'. *Astérion: Philosophie, Histoire des Idées, Pensée Politique* 7 (2010).
— 'Sovereignty, Territory, and Population in Jean Bodin's République'. *French Studies: A Quarterly Review* 72 (2018): 17–34.
Miller, David. *On Nationality*. Oxford: Oxford University Press, 1995.
Mitchell, Ryan Martinez. 'Jean Bodin's Law of Nations'. *Political Theology* 21 (2020): 550–69.
Mommsen, Theodor. *Römisches Staatsrecht*. Vol. 3(1). Leipzig: Verlag von S. Hirzel, 1887.
Montaigne, Michel de. *Essays*. Trans. J.M. Cohen. New York: Penguin, 1958.
Montesquieu, Charles-Louis de Secondat, Baron de. *Spirit of the Laws*. Ed. Anne Cohler, Basia Miller, and Harold Stone. Cambridge: Cambridge University Press, 1989.
Moreau-Reibel, Jean. *Jean Bodin et le droit public compare dans ses rapports avec la philosophie de l'histoire*. Paris: Vrin, 1933.
Mousnier, Roland. *The Institutions of France Under the Absolute Monarchy, 1598–1789*. 2 Vols. Trans. Arthur Goldhammer. Chicago: University of Chicago Press, 1984.
Muniz-Fraticelli, Victor. *The Structure of Pluralism*. Oxford: Oxford University Press, 2014.
Nanz, Klaus-Peter. *Die Entstehung des allgemeinen Vertragsbegriff im 16 bis 18 Jahrhundert*. München: J. Schweitzer, 1985.

Nettelbladt, David. *Systema Elementare Universae Iurisprudentiae Naturalis*. Editio Tertia. Halle: In Officina Libraria Rengeriana,1767.

Nettleship, Henry. '*Ius Gentium*'. *Journal of Philology* 13–14 (1885): 169–81.

Nicholas, Barry. *Introduction to Roman Law*. Oxford: Clarendon Press, 1962.

Nicholls, Sophie. 'Sovereignty and Government in Jean Bodin's Six Livres de la République (1576)'. *Journal of the History of Ideas* 80 (2019): 47–66.

Nolte, Georg. 'Sovereignty as Responsibility?' *Proceedings of the Annual Meeting (American Society of International Law)* 99 (2005): 389–92.

Nye, Joseph. *Soft Power: The Means to Success in World Politics*. New York: Public Affairs, 2009.

Nyquist, Mary. *Arbitrary Rule: Slavery, Tyranny, and the Power of Life and Death*. Chicago: University of Chicago Press, 2013.

Oakeshott, Michael. *On Human Conduct*. Oxford: Clarendon Press, 1975.

Oakley, Francis. 'Jacobean Political Theology: The Absolute and Ordinary Powers of the King'. *Journal of the History of Ideas* 29 (1968): 323–46.

Ober, Josiah. *Mass and Elite in Democratic Athens*. Princeton: Princeton University Press, 1989.

Odorisio, Ginevra Conti. *La famille et l'état dans la République de Jean Bodin*. Paris: L'Harmattan, 2007.

Oldendorp, Johann. *Iuris Naturalis, Gentium et Civilis Isagoge*. Köln: Johann Gymnicus, 1539.

Osiander, Andreas. 'Sovereignty, International Relations, and the Westphalian Myth'. *International Organization* 55 (2001): 251–87.

Ostwald, Martin. *From Popular Sovereignty to the Sovereignty of Law: Law, Society, and Politics in Fifth-Century Athens*. Berkeley: University of California Press, 1986.

Panizza, Diego. 'The Freedom of the Sea and the Modern Cosmopolis in Alberico Gentili's De Iure Belli'. *Grotiana* 30 (2009): 88–106.

Parsons, Jotham. 'Governing Sixteenth-Century France: The Monetary Reforms of 1577'. *French Historical Studies* 26 (2003): 1–30.

— 'Money and Sovereignty in Early Modern France'. *Journal of the History of Ideas* 62 (2001): 59–79.

Parsons, Talcott. *The Structure of Social Action*. New York: McGraw-Hill, 1937.

Patrick, Stewart. *The Sovereignty Wars: Reconciling America with the World*. Washington: Brookings, 2019.

Pennington, Kenneth. *The Prince and the Law, 1200–1600*. Berkeley: University of California Press, 1993.

Pettit, Philip. *Republicanism: A Theory of Freedom and Government*. Oxford: Oxford University Press, 1997.

Philpott, Daniel. *Revolutions in Sovereignty: How Ideas Shaped Modern International Relations*. Princeton: Princeton University Press, 2001.

Piffanelli, Luciano. 'Crossing Boundaries: A Problem of Territoriality in Renaissance Italy'. *Viator: Medieval and Renaissance Studies* 49 (2018): 245–75.

Pitts, Jennifer. *Boundaries of the International: Law and Empire*. Cambridge: Harvard University Press, 2018.

— 'Intervention and Sovereign Equality: Legacies of Vattel'. In *Just and Unjust Military Intervention: European Thinkers from Vitoria to Mill*. Ed. Stefano Recchia and Jennifer Welsh. Cambridge: Cambridge University Press, 2013.

Plato. *Complete Works*. Ed. John Cooper, D.S. Hutchinson. Indianapolis: Hackett, 1997.

Plutarch. *Caesar.* In *Lives: Demosthenes and Cicero, Alexander and Caesar.* Vol. 7. Loeb Classical Library 99. Trans. Bernadotte Perrin. Cambridge: Harvard University Press, 1919.

— *Cato the Younger.* In *Lives: Sertorius and Eumenes, Phocion and Cato the Younger.* Vol. 8. Loeb Classical Library 100. Trans. Bernadotte Perrin. Cambridge: Harvard University Press, 1919.

— *Numa.* In *Lives: Theseus and Romulus, Lycurgus and Numa, Solon and Publicola.* Vol. 1. Loeb Classical Library 46. Trans. Bernadotte Perrin. Cambridge: Harvard University Press, 1914.

— *Pericles.* In *Lives: Pericles and Fabius Maximus, Nicias and Crassus.* Vol. 3. Loeb Classical Library 65. Trans. Bernadotte Perrin. Cambridge: Harvard University Press, 1916.

— *Pompey.* In *Lives: Agesilaus and Pompey, Pelopidas and Marcellus.* Vol. 5. Loeb Classical Library 87. Trans. Bernadotte Perrin. Cambridge: Harvard University Press, 1917.

Pogge, Thomas. 'Cosmopolitanism and Sovereignty'. *Ethics* 103 (1992): 48–75.

Polybius. *Histories.* Vol. 3. Loeb Classical Library 138. Trans. W.R. Paton. Cambridge: Harvard University Press, 1923.

Poole, Thomas. 'The Idea of the Federative'. In *The Double-Facing Constitution.* Ed. Jacco Bomhoff, David Dyzenhaus, and Thomas Poole. Cambridge: Cambridge University Press, 2020.

Post, Gaines. 'Bracton as Jurist and Theologian on Kingship'. In *Proceedings of the Third International Conference of Medieval Canon Law, Strasbourg, 1968.* Ed. Stephan Kuttner. Rome: Biblioteca Apostolica Vaticana, 1971.

Pufendorf, Samuel. *De Iure Naturae et Gentium Libri Octo.* Amsterdam: Apud Joannem Wolters, 1698.

— *Elementorum Jurisprudentiae Universalis Libri II.* Jena: Sumptibus Johannis Meyeri, Typis Johannis Wertheri, 1669.

— *On the Duty of Man and Citizen.* Ed. James Tully. Trans. Michael Silverthorne. Cambridge: Cambridge University Press, 1991.

Pugliese, Giovanni. '*Res corporales, res incorporales* e il problema del diritto soggetivo'. In *Studi in onore di Vincenzo Arangio-Ruiz.* Vol. 3. Naples: Jovene, 1953.

Putnam, Robert. *Making Democracy Work: Civic Traditions in Modern Italy.* Princeton: Princeton University Press, 1993.

Quaglioni, Diego. 'Les citoyens envers l'État: The Individual as a Citizen from Bodin's *République* to Rousseau's *Contract Social*'. In *The Individual in Political Theory and Practice.* Ed. Janet Coleman. Oxford: Clarendon Press, 1996.

— *I limiti della sovranità: Il pensiero di Jean Bodin nella cultura politica e giuridica dell'età moderna.* Padova, CEDAM, 1992.

— 'Sovranità e autolimitazione: Rileggendo la *Dotttrina Generale del Diritto dello Stato* di Georg Jellinek'. In *Crisi e metamorfosi della sovranità.* Ed. Maurizio Basciu. Milan: Giuffré, 1996.

— 'Una fonte del Bodin: André Tiraqueau, giureconsulto: appunti su *De Republica*, III.8'. In *La République di Jean Bodin: Actes du Colloque de Pérouse, 14–15 Novembre 1980.* Florence: Olschki, 1981; *Il Pensiero Politico* 14: 113–27.

Quaritsch, Helmut. *Souveränität: Entstehung und Entwicklung des Begriff in Frankreich und Deutschland vom 13. Jahrhundert bis 1806.* Frankfurt: Duncker & Humblot, 1986.

Radin, Max. 'Secare Partis: The Early Roman Law of Execution against a Debtor,' *American Journal of Philology* 43 (1922): 32–48.

Rainbolt, George. 'Perfect and Imperfect Obligations'. *Philosophical Studies* 98 (2000): 233–56.

Rawls, John. *A Theory of Justice*. Rev. Ed. Cambridge: Belknap Press of Harvard University Press, 1999.

Raz, Joseph. *The Authority of Law*. Oxford: Clarendon Press, 1979.

Rehm, Hermann. Ed. *Handbuch des Öffentlichen Rechts*. Freiburg: Mohr, 1896.

Reich, Walter. *Enemies of Mankind: Vattel's Theory of Collective Security*. Leiden: Martinus Nijhoff, 2013.

Reichberg, Gregory. *Thomas Aquinas on War and Peace*. Cambridge: Cambridge University Press, 2016.

Reulos, Michel. 'Les Sources juridiques de Bodin: Textes, auteurs, pratique'. In *Jean Bodin: Verhandlungen der Internationalen Bodin Tagung in München*. Ed. H. Denzer. München: C.H. Beck, 1973.

Ribeiro de Barros, Albert. 'Bodin et le projet d'une science du droit: *La Juris universi distributio* (1578)'. *Nouvelle revue du XVIe siècle* 21 (2003): 57–70.

Riesenberg, Peter. 'Citizenship at Law in Late Medieval Italy'. *Viator* 5 (1974): 333–46.

— *Citizenship in the Western Tradition: Plato to Rousseau*. Chapel Hill, North Carolina: University of North Carolina Press, 1992.

Rigaux, François. 'Hans Kelsen on International Law'. *European Journal of International Law* 9 (1998): 325–43.

Ripstein, Arthur. 'Sovereignty and Property: How to Tell the Difference'. *Theoretical Inquiries in Law* 18 (2017): 243–68.

Rose, Paul Lawrence. *Bodin and the Great God of Nature: The Moral and Religious Universe of a Judaiser*. Geneva: Librairie Droz, 1980.

Ross, Alf. *Directives and Norms*. London: Routledge & K. Paul, 1968.

Rousseau, C. 'L'indépendence de l'État dans l'Ordre International'. *Hague Recueil des Cours* 73 (1948): 171–253.

Rousseau, Jean-Jacques. *The Basic Political Writings* [*Social Contract*]. Trans. Donald Cress. Indianapolis, Indiana: Hackett, 1987.

Runciman, David. *Pluralism and the Personality of the State*. Cambridge: Cambridge University Press, 1997.

Sahlins, Peter. *Unnaturally French: Citizens in the Old Regime and After*. Ithaca: Cornell University Press, 2018.

Saint-Bonnet, François. 'La notion d'exécution chez Bodin'. *Revue Français d'Histoire des Idées Politiques* 34 (2011): 231–44.

Salmon, J.H.M. *The French Religious Wars in English Political Thought*. Oxford: Clarendon Press, 1959.

— 'The Legacy of Jean Bodin: Absolutism, Populism or Constitutionalism?' *History of Political Thought* 17 (1996): 500–22.

Samuel, Geoffrey. 'Le Droit Subjectif and English Law'. *Cambridge Law Journal* 46 (1987): 264–86.

Santangelo, Federico. 'The Fetials and their *Ius*'. *Bulletin of the Institute of Classical Studies* 51 (2008): 63–93.

Sarooshi, Dan. 'The Essentially Contested Nature of the Concept of Sovereignty: Implications for the Exercise by International Organizations of Delegated Powers of Government'. *Michigan Journal of International Law* 25 (2004): 1107–39.

Scattola, Merio. 'Jean Bodin on International Law'. In *System, Order, and International Law*. Ed. Stefan Kadelbach, Thomas Kleinlein, and David Roth-Isigkeit. Oxford: Oxford University Press, 2017.

Schall, James. 'Friendship and Political Philosophy'. *Review of Metaphysics* 50 (1996): 121–41.

Scheffler, Samuel. *Boundaries and Allegiances*. Oxford: Oxford University Press, 2001.

— *Equality and Tradition: Questions of Value in Moral and Political Theory*. Oxford: Oxford University Press, 2012.
Schiller, A. Arthur. *Roman Law: Mechanism and Development*. The Hague: Mouton Publishers, 1978.
Schmitt, Carl. *Concept of the Political*. Trans. George Schwab. Chicago: University of Chicago Press, 2007.
— *Dictatorship: From the Origin of the Modern Concept of Sovereignty to Proletarian Class Struggle*. Trans. Michael Hoelzl and Graham Ward. Cambridge: Polity, 2014.
— *Political Theology: Four Chapters on Sovereignty*. Trans. George Schwab. Chicago: University of Chicago Press, 2005.
Schröder, Peter. 'Vitoria, Gentili, Bodin: Sovereignty and the Law of Nations'. In *The Roman Foundations of the Law of Nations*. Ed. Benedict Kingsbury and Benjamin Straumann. Oxford: Oxford University Press, 2010.
Schwartzberg, Melissa. 'Was the *Graphe Paranomon* a Form of Judicial Review?' *Cardozo Law Review* 34 (2013): 1049–62.
Schwarzenbach, Sibyl. 'On Civic Friendship'. *Ethics* 107 (1996): 97–128.
Scott, Johnathan. *England's Troubles: Seventeenth Century English Political Instability in European Context*. Cambridge: Cambridge University Press, 2000.
Searle, John. 'A Classification of Illocutionary Acts'. *Language in Society* 5 (1976): 1–23.
Selden, John. *De Iure Naturali Iuxta Disciplinam Ebraeorum*. London, 1640.
Seuffert, Lothar. *Zur Geschichte der obligatorischen Verträge*. Nördlingen: C.H. Beck, 1881.
Seyssel, Claude de. *Speculum Feudorum*. Basel: Thomas Guarinus, 1566.
Shapiro, Ian. *Democratic Justice*. New Haven, Connecticut: Yale University Press, 1999.
Shklar, Judith. 'The Liberalism of Fear'. In *Liberalism and the Moral Life*. Ed. Nancy Rosenblum. Cambridge: Harvard University Press, 1989.
Shue, Henry. 'Limiting Sovereignty'. In *Humanitarian Intervention and International Relations*. Ed. Jennifer Walsh. Oxford: Oxford University Press, 2004.
Shuger, Debora. *The Renaissance Bible: Scholarship, Sacrifice, and Subjectivity*. Berkeley: University of California Press, 1994.
Sigonio, Carlo. *De Antiquo Iure Italiae*. Frankfurt, 1574.
— *De Republica Atheniensium Libri IV*. Bologna, 1564.
Simler, Josias. *De Republica Helvetiorum Libri Duo*. Zurich: Christopher Froschauer, 1576.
Simma, Bruno. 'From Bilateralism to Community Interest in International Law'. *Recueil des Cours de l'Académie de Droit International* 250 (1994): 217.
Simmons, A. John. 'Ideal and Nonideal Theory'. *Philosophy and Public Affairs* 38 (2010): 5–36.
— *Moral Principles and Political Obligations*. Princeton: Princeton University Press, 1979.
— 'On the Territorial Rights of States'. *Philosophical Issues* 11 (2001): 303–14.
Skinner, Quentin. 'A Genealogy of the Modern State'. *Proceedings of the British Academy* 162 (2009): 325–70.
— *Liberty Before Liberalism*. Cambridge: Cambridge University Press, 1998.
Smith, Constance. 'Filmer, and the Knolles Translation of Bodin'. *Philosophical Quarterly* 13 (1963): 248–52.
Smith, Holly. 'Subjective Rightness'. *Social Philosophy and Policy* 27 (2010): 64–110.
Smith, M.B.E. 'Is There a Prima Facie Obligation to Obey the Law?' *Yale Law Journal* 82 (1973): 950–76.
Sommerville, Johann. 'English and European Political Ideas in the Early Seventeenth Century: Revisionism and the Case of Absolutism'. *Journal of British Studies* 35 (1996): 168–94.

Song, Sarah. 'The Boundary Problem in Democratic Theory: Why the Demos Should Be Bounded by the State'. *International Theory* 4 (2012): 39–68.

Spruyt, Hendrik. *The State and Its Competitors: An Analysis of Systems Change*. Princeton: Princeton University Press, 1994.

Stacey, Peter. 'Free and Unfree States in Machiavelli's Political Thought'. In *Freedom and the Construction of Europe*. Vol. 1. *Religious Freedom and Civil Liberty*. Ed. Quentin Skinner and Martin Van Gelderen. Cambridge: Cambridge University Press, 2013.

Stern, Philip. *The Company-State: Corporate Sovereignty and the Early Modern Foundations of the British Empire in India*. Oxford: Oxford University Press, 2011.

Stern, W.B. 'Kelsen's Theory of International Law'. *American Political Science Review* 30 (1936): 736–41.

Stilz, Anna. *Territorial Sovereignty: A Philosophical Exploration*. Oxford: Oxford University Press, 2019.

— 'Why Do States Have Territorial Rights?' *International Theory* 1 (2009): 185–213.

Stolpe, Audun. 'A Theory of Permission Based on the Notion of Derogation'. *Journal of Applied Logic* 8 (2010): 97–113.

Story, Joseph. *Commentaries on the Conflict of Laws*. 3rd Ed. Boston: Charles Little and James Brown, 1846.

Straumann, Benjamin. *Crisis and Constitutionalism: Roman Political Thought from the Fall of the Republic to the Age of Revolution*. Oxford: Oxford University Press, 2016.

— *Roman Law in the State of Nature*. Cambridge: Cambridge University Press, 2015.

Tan, Kok-Chor. *Justice Without Borders: Cosmopolitanism, Nationalism, and Patriotism*. Cambridge: Cambridge University Press, 2004.

Terrel, Jean. *Les théories du pacte social: Droit naturel, souveraineté et contrat de Bodin à Rousseau*. Paris: Editions du Seuil, 2001.

Theocarakis, Nicholas. '*Nicomachean Ethics* in Political Economy: The Trajectory of the Problem of Value'. *History of Economic Ideas* 14 (2006): 9–53.

Thomson, Judith Jarvis. *The Realm of Rights*. Cambridge: Harvard University Press, 1990.

Thucydides. *History of the Peloponnesian War*. 4 Vols. Loeb Classical Library 108–11, 169. Trans. C.F. Smith. Cambridge: Harvard University Press, 1919–1923.

Tierney, Brian. *The Idea of Natural Rights: Studies on Natural Rights, Natural Law, and Church Law, 1150–1625*. Atlanta: Scholars Press, 1997.

— *Liberty and Law: The Idea of Permissive Natural Law*. Washington: The Catholic University of America Press, 2014.

— *The Origins of Papal Infallibility, 1150–1350*. Leiden: Brill, 1972.

— 'The Prince Is Not Bound by the Laws: Accursius and the Origins of the Modern State'. *Comparative Studies in Society and History* 5 (1963): 378–400.

Tiraqueau, André. *Commentarii de Nobilitate et Iure Primigeniorum*. Basel: Hieronymus Froben and Nicolaus Episcopius, 1561.

Tocqueville, Alexis de. *Democracy in America*. Trans. Ed. Harvey Mansfield and Delba Winthrop. Chicago: University of Chicago Press, 2000.

— *The Old Regime and the French Revolution*. Trans. Stuart Gilbert. New York: Anchor Books, 1955.

Todd, Anne Marie. 'Environmental Sovereignty Discourse of the Brazilian Amazon: National Politics and the Globalization of Indigenous Resistance'. *Journal of Communication Inquiry* 27 (2003): 354–70.

Traversino Di Cristo, Massimiliano. 'The Classic Age of the Distinction between God's Absolute and Ordered Power: In, Around, and After the Pontificate of John XXII'. *Franciscan Studies* 76 (2018): 207–66.

— 'The Mediaeval Distinction of God's *Potentia Absoluta/Ordinata* as an Archaeology of the Early Modern Investigation of Power'. In *The Theology of Potentia Dei and the History of European Normativity. Divus Thomas* 115. Bologna: Studio Domenicano, 2012: 35–82.

Tuck, Richard. 'Grotius, Hobbes, and Pufendorf on Humanitarian Intervention'. In *Just and Unjust Military Intervention: European Thinkers from Vitoria to Mill*. Ed. Stefano Recchia and Jennifer Welsh. Cambridge: Cambridge University Press, 2013.

— *Natural Rights Theories*. Cambridge: Cambridge University Press, 1979.

— *The Sleeping Sovereign: The Invention of Modern Democracy*. Cambridge: Cambridge University Press, 2016.

Turchetti, Mario. 'Despotism and Tyranny: Unmasking a Tenacious Confusion'. *European Journal of Political Theory* 7 (2008): 159–82.

— 'Nota su Bodin e la tirannide: il diritto di revoca e gli editti irrevocabili'. *Il Pensiero Politico* 30 (1997): 325–338.

— *Tyrannie et tyrannicide de l'Antiquité a nos jours*. Paris: Presses Universitaires de France, 2001.

— 'Une question mal posée: la qualification de perpétuel et irrévocable, appliquée à l'Édit de Nantes de 1598'. In *Bulletin de la Société d'Histoire du Protestantisme Français* 139 (1993): 41–78.

Uehlinger, Christoph. 'Nimrod'. In *Neues Bibel-Lexikon*. Ed. Manfred Görg and Bernhard Lang. Vol. 2. Zurich: Benziger, 1995.

Ullmann, Walter. 'Juristic Obstacles to the Emergence of the Concept of the State in the Middle Ages'. *Annali di Storia del Diritto* 12/13 (Milan: Guiffré, 1968/69): 43–65.

Ulph, Owen. 'Jean Bodin and the Estates-General of 1576'. *Journal of Modern History* 19 (1947): 289–96.

Vaillancourt, P.-L. 'La notion de 'foi jurée' dans l'ordre politique'. In *Aequitas, Aequalitas, Auctoritas: Raison théorique et legitimation de l'autorité dans le XVIe siècle européen*. Ed. D. Letocha. Paris: Vrin, 1992.

Valla, Lorenzo. *On the Donation of Constantine*. I Tatti Renaissance Library. Trans. G.W. Bowersock. Cambridge: Harvard University Press, 2008.

Van Gelderen, Martin. Ed. *The Dutch Revolt*. Cambridge: Cambridge University Press, 1993.

Vander Waerdt, Paul. 'Philosophical Influence on Roman Jurisprudence? The Case of Stoicism and Natural Law'. In *Aufstieg und Niedergang der römischen Welt*. Vol. 2. Ed. Wolfgang Haase. Berlin: De Gruyter, 1994.

Varro, Marcus Tarentius. *On Agriculture* [*De Re Rustica*]. Trans. William Davis Hooper and Harrison Boyd Ash. Loeb Classical Library 283. Cambridge: Harvard University Press, 1934.

Vasoli, Cesare. *Armonia e giustizia: Studi sulle idee filosofiche di Jean Bodin*. Florence: Olschki, 2008.

— 'Il tema dell'assoluta potenza divina nell'*Universae naturae theatrum* di Jean Bodin'. In *Potentia Dei: l'omnipotenza nel pensiero dei secolo XVI e XVII*. Ed. G. Canziani, M.A. Granada, and Yves Charles Zarka. Milan: Franco Angeli, 2000.

Vattel, Emer de. *On the Law of Nations*. [*Le Droit des Gens*]. Trans. Thomas Nugent. Ed. Béla Kapossy and Richard Whatmore. Indianapolis: Liberty Fund, 2008.

Vázquez de Menchaca, Fernando. *Illustrium Controversarium*. Frankfurt: Sumptibus Joannis Baptistae Schönwetteri, 1668.

Villey, Michel. *La Formation de la Pensée Juridique Moderne*. Paris: Montchrestien, 1968.

— 'Le genèse du droit subjectif chez Guillaume d'Occam'. *Archives de philosophie du droit* 9 (1964): 97–127.

— 'L'idée du droit subjectif et les systems juridiques romains'. *Revue historique de droit*. Series 4v, 24–5 (1946): 201–28.
— 'Le *jus in re* du droit romain Classique au droit modern'. *Publications de l'Institut de droit romain de l'université de Paris* 6 (1950): 187–225.
— 'La justice harmonique selon Bodin'. *Archives de philosophie du droit* 15 (1970): 301–15.
— *Leçons d'Histoire de la Philosophie du Droit*. Paris: Dalloz, 1957.
Vitoria, Francisco de. *De Indis et De Iure Belli Relectiones*. Ed. Ernest Nys. Trans. John Pawley Bate. Washington: Carnegie Institution of Washington, 1917.
Waldron, Jeremy. 'Foreign Law and the Modern *Ius Gentium*'. *Harvard Law Review* 119 (2005): 129–47.
— *Partly Laws Common to All Mankind: Foreign Law in American Courts*. New Haven: Yale University Press, 2012.
Watson, Alan. 'The Development of the Praetor's Edict'. *Journal of Roman Studies* 60 (1970): 105–19.
— *Joseph Story and the Comity of Errors*. Athens, Georgia: University of Georgia Press, 2012.
Wauters, Bart. '*Ius Commune* and Contract Law'. In *Uniform Rules for European Contract Law?: A Critical Assessment*. Ed. Francisco de Elizalde. Oxford: Hart Publishing, 2018.
Wells, Charlotte. *Law and Citizenship in Early Modern France*. Baltimore, Maryland: Johns Hopkins University Press, 1995.
Wenar, Leif. 'The Nature of Rights'. *Philosophy and Public Affairs* 33 (2005): 223–52.
Whelan, Frederick. 'Democratic Theory and the Boundary Problem'. In *Nomos 25: Liberal Democracy*. Ed. J.R. Pennock and J.W. Chapman. New York: New York University Press, 1983: 13–47.
Winkel, Laurens. 'Die stoische *oikeiosis*-Lehre und Ulpians Definition der Gerechtigkeit'. *Zeitschrift der Savigny-Stiftung für Rechtsgeschichte, Romanistische Abteilung* 105 (1988): 669–79.
Wolff, Robert Paul. *In Defense of Anarchism*. New York: Harper and Row, 1970.
Wolin, Sheldon. *Politics and Vision: Continuity and Innovation in Western Political Thought*. Princeton: Princeton University Press, 2004.
Wright, G.H. von. 'Deontic Logic'. *Mind* 60 (1951): 1–15.
Wyduckel, Dieter. *Princeps Legibus Solutus: Eine Untersuchung zur frühmodernen Rechts- und Staatslehre*. Schriften zur Verfassungsgeschichte 30. Berlin: Duncker & Humblot, 1979.
Young, Iris Marion. 'Polity and Group Difference'. *Ethics* 99 (1989): 250–74.
Ypi, Lea. 'A Permissive Theory of Territorial Rights'. *European Journal of Philosophy* 22 (2014): 288–312.
Zarka, Yves Charles. *Jean Bodin: Nature, Histoire, Droit et Politique*. Paris: Presses Universitaires de France, 1996.
Zimmermann, Reinhard. *The Law of Obligations: Roman Foundations of the Civilian Tradition*. Oxford: Clarendon Press, 1990.
Zollschan, Linda. *Rome and Judaea: International Law Relations, 162–100 BCE*. London: Routledge, 2017.
Zouch, Richard. *Elementa Jurisprudentiae*. Leiden: Elzevir, 1652.
— *Juris et Judicii Fecialis Sive Iuris Inter Gentes*. The Hague: Johannes Verhoeve, 1659.

Index

For the benefit of digital users, indexed terms that span two pages (e.g., 52–53) may, on occasion, appear on only one of those pages.

The manufacturer's authorised representative in the EU for product safety is Oxford University Press España S.A. of el Parque Empresarial San Fernando de Henares, Avenida de Castilla, 2 – 28830 Madrid (www.oup.es/en or product.safety@oup.com). OUP España S.A. also acts as importer into Spain of products made by the manufacturer.

www.ingramcontent.com/pod-product-compliance
Lightning Source LLC
LaVergne TN
LVHW011915200926
848484LV00002B/633

* 9 7 8 0 1 9 8 7 5 5 5 3 1 *